The Autobiography

The Autobiography

JOHNNIE WALKER

MICHAEL JOSEPH
an imprint of
PENGUIN BOOKS

MICHAEL JOSEPH

Published by the Penguin Group

Penguin Books Ltd, 80 Strand, London WC2R ORL, England

Penguin Group (USA) Inc., 375 Hudson Street, New York, New York 10014, USA

Penguin Group (Canada), 90 Eglinton Avenue East, Suite 700, Toronto, Ontario, Canada M4P 2Y3
(a division of Pearson Penguin Canada Inc.)

Penguin Ireland, 25 St Stephen's Green, Dublin 2, Ireland
(a division of Penguin Books Ltd)

Penguin Group (Australia), 250 Camberwell Road, Camberwell, Victoria 3124, Australia
(a division of Pearson Australia Group Pty Ltd)

Penguin Books India Pvt Ltd, 11 Community Centre, Panchsheel Park, New Delhi – 110 017, India

Penguin Group (NZ), 67 Apollo Drive, Rosedale, North Shore 0632, New Zealand
(a division of Pearson New Zealand Ltd)

Penguin Books (South Africa) (Pty) Ltd, 24 Sturdee Avenue, Rosebank, Johannesburg 2196, South Africa

Penguin Books Ltd, Registered Offices: 80 Strand, London WC2R ORL, England

www.penguin.com

First published 2007

4

Copyright © Johnnie Walker, 2007

Photograph of 'Hedge' Heritage Softail Classic by Kevin Wilson;
photograph of Johnnie and Tiggy's wedding taken by Kate Caldicott;
all other photographs taken from Johnnie Walker's private collection.

The moral right of the author has been asserted

Set in 12/14.75 pt Monotype Bembo
Typeset by Rowland Phototypesetting Ltd, Bury St Edmunds, Suffolk
Printed in Great Britain by Clays Ltd, St Ives plc

A CIP catalogue record for this book is available from the British Library

ISBN: 978-0-718-14853-9

www.greenpenguin.co.uk

To the Great Spirit, Trevor, Mary, Tiggy, Sam and Beth

Contents

Prologue

1965

It had all started so well. It was amazing that I'd managed to wangle myself an audition to be a DJ for Radio Luxembourg in the first place, considering that I had no experience apart from talking to the friendly silence of my bedroom while I cued up tapes of the hit parade pirated from the BBC. But the producer I'd telephoned didn't know that. After all, it took some front for a young nobody to call an experienced producer like Eggy Lay and ask for a chance to present one of the shows; he'd scheduled an audition for me at the London office, telling me to bring four records with me, and three copies of my script. Easy.

This was my great opportunity. Boasting to all my friends and family that I was about to become a famous DJ, I'd managed to get the day off from work, dressed myself in my best suit, taken the train to Paddington, stepped into a taxi and given the driver the address. It was my first trip to London and I stared out of the window of the taxi, overwhelmed by the size of the city and the sheer number of people. I was dropped off in a narrow street next to the Park Lane Hilton. The highly polished brass plate on the door proclaimed 36 Hertford Street, home of Europe's biggest and most powerful radio station and, for music fans, essential night-time listening.

Now I was seriously scared. Walking into the enormous studio was the most daunting experience of my life so far and I was suddenly aware that I might have taken on a bit more than I could handle. Radio Luxembourg had been broadcasting since 1933 and had reached the peak of its popularity in the fifties, particularly among the young, who were able to listen to the kind of music they craved. Now, in the early sixties, it was still a powerful force, answering a need in the youthful listening public that the BBC had not yet begun to address beyond its once-weekly pop programme. Radio Luxembourg boasted DJs such as David Jacobs, Alan Freeman, Pete Murray and Tony Hall – the big names, who fronted the radio shows sponsored by record companies – as well as the lesser-known presenters like Barry Aldiss, who lived and worked in Luxembourg. It was a job as one of these minor DJs that I was hoping to get from my audition.

Eggy Lay, the producer, was businesslike, and not at all friendly. He wasn't there to be my chum but to give me the ten minutes necessary to see if I was any use to him.

'Where's your script, then?' he asked.

I handed over what I had brought with me, and then glanced nervously around the studio. It wasn't at all as I'd imagined it. When I'd listened to Radio Luxembourg, I'd always pictured the DJ talking to me from somewhere small and intimate, but this was a vast room, big enough to contain an entire orchestra. In the middle was a round table with a huge, black microphone suspended above it, but there was no sign of a turntable for me to play my records on. I clutched them even more tightly.

'I'll take those,' said Eggy Lay. 'You sit here, read your script and cue us in when you want the track to begin.'

'How?' I asked.

'Like this.' He made a gesture with his hand. 'We'll be in there.' He indicated a room separated from the studio by a glass wall. Behind it, I could see two other men sitting in front of a desk. 'Right, let's get going.'

He walked off with my scripts and records, leaving me with my own copy and that big black microphone. I sat down, absolutely terrified. Putting my script out on the table in front of me, I tried to concentrate on the words I had spent so long carefully crafting. When Eggy Lay had told me I'd need a script, I'd been taken aback. My favourite DJs didn't sound like they read from scripts, and I'd certainly never used one when broadcasting to my imaginary audience in my bedroom. I reacted spontaneously to the music I heard and tried to convey my own emotions as I felt them. But a script was obviously the required thing, so I'd done my best. The first one I wrote was probably the best, but it seemed pretty rubbish to me, so I rewrote it and rewrote it, until I ended up with something that sounded like the kind of thing I'd heard on the BBC: careful, prepared and completely unnatural.

Clearing my throat, I glanced at the three intimidating men sitting behind the glass wall, and saw them give me the signal to start. So off I went.

As the large ten-inch metal reels of Radio Luxembourg's professional tape recorders came to a stop, I looked at the three faces behind the glass window in the studio wall. I could see from their expressions that it didn't look good.

I knew in my heart that I'd been truly dreadful. I didn't know what I sounded like, but it had felt stilted and forced, and simultaneously under- and overrehearsed. I wasn't going to get another chance, not even a second read-through. My audition had lasted about four minutes and I had failed it spectacularly. Eggy Lay came back into the studio with my records, a look of annoyance on his face, as though I had wasted his valuable time with my pathetic ramblings and utter lack of experience.

I attempted a friendly smile.

'Tell me honestly what you thought,' I said. 'Don't try to be kind or spare my feelings.'

So he didn't.

'You'll never be a DJ as long as you live. You just haven't got the personality for it. I'll show you out.'

It was devastating to hear. My dreams instantly collapsed and I followed him down a corridor in a daze of disappointment and rejection. He couldn't get me out of the building quickly enough. Instead of the smart front door I'd come in by, I was shown out of a fire-escape door and into a mews behind the main building. With a curt goodbye, Eggy Lay slammed the door shut after me.

I stood there, forlorn and lost. I had walked boldly through the front door with such high expectations: my talent was about to be recognized; soon I would have my own radio show. Now I had been shown out of the back door, my hopes destroyed and with no idea of where I was. I wandered about the streets of Mayfair until eventually I found my way back to Park Lane. I decided to walk back to Paddington Station. There was no point now in hailing a taxi and wasting more money on this foolish dream.

Well, at least I tried, I told myself as I walked through Hyde Park. At least I won't spend a lifetime saying 'if only'. Now I know the answer – I'll never be a DJ.

It was back to my quiet, respectable life as a car salesman in Solihull – a career in radio had been a stupid pipe dream and I resolved to forget it for good.

PART ONE
Early Days

Chapter One

There were seven of us in the Dingley family: Trevor and Mary and five kids, all crammed into a semi-detached in Heaton Road, Solihull. We were taught to pronounce the name Soley-hull *not* Solly-hull. It's a leafy, somewhat posh and pretentious suburb of Birmingham, though we didn't ever mention that city when saying where we were from. Oh no, we lived in Warwickshire.

My mother's maiden name was Waters and hers broke on Good Friday, 30th March 1945. I don't know the exact time I began my tortuous journey but the cord was cut and the first cries were heard in that nursing home in Olton, Birmingham at 'about teatime', my mum said vaguely. But I was her fourth child, so it was probably getting a little difficult to remember exactly who was born when. The eldest was my sister Maureen, then brothers John and Michael, and then me. I was to be called Peter and my middle name paid homage to my mum's family. So Peter Waters Dingley it was, and stayed, until 1966. I was followed by Christine, the fifth and last of the Dingley children.

My father was a salesman for W. Canning & Co. Ltd, a company that made electroplating equipment for chromium-plating car parts. Dad travelled about in his company car, selling the machinery to car factories. He was very good at it, earning enough to provide a living for his large family, and later, with the help of some family money from my mother's side, we were able to move to a grander, detached house in Broad Oaks Road. My mother devoted herself to bringing up her large and often boisterous family.

Although our home was always noisy and full of activity, it was not a place where we talked much about our feelings. Both of my parents had the kind of upbringing where adults didn't show all that much affection to their children. Mum, in particular, was raised in a strict Victorian household dominated by a fearsome father, who she only saw at the evening meal when talking was not allowed. There was no touching or any expression of love in that home so it's no wonder that as a parent herself she found it so difficult to express the love she felt for her children. As we grew up our parents became progressively more distant; hugging and touching were out of the question.

There is no doubt that my parents cared about us a great deal but, because they found it difficult to tell us or to show their affection, all five of us were desperately clamouring for attention and praise that never seemed to be forthcoming. This led to tensions, strains and arguments, and an atmosphere where any sign of weakness was mocked and derided. Pretty soon I realized that survival meant all feelings must be buried deep down. There's a certain kind of loneliness you can only feel in a big family where love – or any emotion, come to that – isn't something that is expressed.

By all accounts I started well: I was a very good little chap and Mum said I was a pleasure to have around the house. It was only later I became a rebel and a disappointment. I remember how, as a little lad, I used to love getting into my parents' cosy warm bed in the morning for hugs and a cup of tea brewed automatically by a thing called a Teasmade that sat on Dad's side of the bed. I don't think I got many hugs, but it was nice and warm in the middle and it was still my early-morning ritual when my younger sister, Christine, arrived and duly claimed her place in the bed.

'Oh, for God's sake, Peter,' Dad complained grumpily one morning as he clung on to what little space he had at the edge of the bed. 'There isn't room for the two of you in here. And anyway, you're too old to be coming in our bed every morning.'

After that, I was not allowed in the bed any more, and it felt to me as though I'd been banished from my place of warmth, love and security. It obviously had a profound effect on me – Dad had no idea just how rejected I felt. Back then there were no self-help books on parenting, and hardly anyone took courses on psychology, so I can't really blame my old man. Nevertheless, it was my first big lesson in quashing my feelings and learning to get on alone.

My brother John and I were different from the others. Like most older sisters, Maureen could be a bit bossy, Michael was the goody-goody, and we all considered Christine, who was the baby of the family, a bit spoilt. But John and I were kindred spirits in the art of rebellion, and we stuck together despite the four years in age between us.

It was John who got me into rock 'n' roll and pop. But, before that, my first introduction to music was in 1955, when I was ten. Dad came striding into the front room with a big cardboard box and an excited grin on his face.

'Have I got a surprise for you!' he declared.

The five of us gathered round the table, fascinated. Inside the cardboard box was another box, cream-coloured with daisies all over and two clasps on one side.

Dad opened the lid, proclaiming, 'It's a gramophone. You wait. Watch this.'

He took out a bent handle, put it in a hole in the side and started winding the thing up. From a smaller case he removed a large, flat disc in a brown cover and placed it on the circular pad. He slid open the cover of a small compartment in the corner and removed a needle, which he put carefully in the lever at the side. None of us five kids had any idea what on earth this contraption was.

'What's it do, Dad?'

'Wait, just wait.'

He moved a lever, the disc revolved and he placed the pick-up arm on to the black disc. There were crackles and pops and scratching noises, and then, and then . . .

'If you go down to the woods today, you're sure of a big surprise . . .'

A voice began singing 'Teddy Bears' Picnic'. It sounded terribly tinny and the music choice was not great, but it was a very special moment for a ten-year-old. I was completely hooked by the way this funny box could conjure noise out of thin air.

Then, when I was about twelve years old, John introduced me

to the magical sound of rock 'n' roll courtesy of his collection of 78rpm gramophone records, as they were quaintly called back in the fifties. The records were large, brittle black discs, heavily grooved, that came in flimsy paper covers. John played them in the living room on the precious gramophone. The sound was metallic and not very loud, and we had to sit almost on top of the gramophone player to hear anything, but that didn't matter. I was still entranced by the fabulous sounds of Elvis Presley, Chuck Berry, Little Richard and Jerry Lee Lewis. We listened as often as we could, in the face of our parents' disapproval.

John only allowed me to listen when I was with him. He banned me from playing his records after I inadvertently sat on Tommy Steele's 'Singin' The Blues' and broke it. But every time he went out, I still played them – even though I risked getting into big trouble if I was found out. They were full of such energy and raw excitement. They opened the door to another world so very different from the boring predictable one the BBC portrayed on its Light Programme, the kind of music that my parents liked.

On Sundays the radio played while Mum and Dad cooked the roast. We listened to *Two-Way Family Favourites*, and the theme tune 'With A Song In My Heart' accompanied the smell of roasting beef and potatoes, a steaming kitchen and Dad stirring the gravy. It was hosted by Cliff Michelmore and Jean Metcalfe and played the music that appealed to my parents' generation: Perry Como, Matt Monro, Vera Lynn and Alma Cogan. It had big bands and polished singing that was neat and tidy and a million miles away from the kind of stuff that got me excited.

The only time I liked to listen to the BBC was at the weekend. On Saturday mornings there was Brian Matthew's *Saturday Club*, which had a mixture of records and bands that played in front of a live studio audience. It was a huge hit with listeners, particularly young people hungry for pop music, because there was almost nothing else like it on the airwaves. As a result, it attracted the biggest stars of the day, who performed on the show. On Sunday afternoons there was *Pick of the Pops*, which played down the hit parade to the Number One record. It was hosted by a variety of presenters including David Jacobs and, of course, Alan Freeman. I loved the show and was glued to the radio for the two hours it was on.

Apart from those music shows, the radio didn't hold much appeal for me. It just didn't seem to be aimed at kids like me, who were under the spell of American music and couldn't get enough of it. Our big radiogram in the living room was only ever tuned to the BBC. But it was a different story when I was able to listen to the radio in the privacy of my own room. There, I could tune in to Radio Luxembourg. At seven o'clock in the evening, we'd be able to pick up the signal and then I'd listen in to my favourite shows, the ones that played pop music and all the hits.

There was great excitement when our family gramophone was replaced by an electric record player. Now records came in a cool seven-inch format and went round at 45 rpm – the 'single' had arrived. The discs were unbreakable now, the sound reproduction was much better, with more bass and volume, and there was a stacking system on the record player, which allowed half a dozen records to be placed on the centre spindle, and they'd play one after the other. That was the theory, anyway. In practice, they slipped and skidded on each other. I found that it was much better to put them on one at a time, and, if I left the top arm off, the record would play over and over again automatically. I loved that – my current favourite record on endless repeat. My parents hated it, of course. And the more they hated it, the better it became.

As I got older, I didn't have to listen to John's records or get his permission to play music. I had started my own collection and did as many odd jobs as I could to earn the money to pay for them. On Saturdays I washed cars at Brunton's Garage and spent everything I earned on records. The very first one I bought was 'Let There Be Drums' by Sandy Nelson. It got to Number Three in the charts and was unusual for being an instrumental piece, which wasn't typical for the pop parade. In general, I loved the classic American rock 'n' roll artists: Elvis Presley, Chuck Berry, Buddy Holly and Fats Domino, just for starters. The British artists didn't seem able to compete – they didn't have the magic of the US stars. Most British groups and singers just covered successful American songs, and their versions were never as good. Cliff Richard managed one good record with 'Move It' but otherwise he seemed tame and appealed too much to grown-ups for my taste.

That music was the one thing that added spice to my otherwise dull life as I grew up in my secure but predictable home, a boy in the middle of a pack of brothers and sisters, going about my daily round of school and home, bound in by rules and regulations and a stifling pressure to conform.

Chapter Two

1957

Things were different when Bob Wilson and the boys came into town. Invading the respectable leafy suburbs of Solihull every May came a gang of scruffy roughnecks. Their convoy consisted of huge trucks, backed up by a fleet of vans and caravans. You could feel the buzz that went around as they trundled through town heading for the local park where, over the next two days, they'd build their temporary city of glamour, noise, lights, thrills, excitement and danger. Bob Wilson's funfair was one of the highlights of the year.

I loved it. I'd break the strict 'go straight home after school' rule. Stuffing my cap and tie in my pockets, I'd ride my bike through the park and stop to watch the feverish activity. The waltzers, dodgems, helter-skelter, ghost train, big wheel and wall of death all took shape at amazing speed along with dozens of small stalls and tents. Back home, I'd change out of my school stuff, have the usual fight around the table for tea and toast and maybe some cake, and then plead with my mum to let me go down the fair.

As I got nearer, I could hear the music. The sound systems of the various attractions battled with each other as Eddie Cochran, Elvis Presley, Gene Vincent and Jerry Lee Lewis strove to be heard above the cacophony of laughter and screams, the whirling and grinding of the rides, and the roar of the generators. In the air was the smell of diesel, toffee apples, nougat, popcorn and candy floss. Soon the families with young kids would head for home and darkness would fall, the coloured lights becoming brighter and ever more garish, the music even louder and more raucous.

On the waltzers, the funfair guys would nonchalantly ride the undulating wooden decks, eyeing up which car had the prettiest girls. Then, with a casual flick, they'd spin the car around even faster, eliciting piercing screams from the girls. Sexual energy charged the atmosphere and everything was to the soundtrack of the finest American rock 'n' roll. And it was the volume that made the difference. Some of the sound gear was wound up and past the point of distortion, but it didn't seem to matter; maybe it was a bonus. I'd never heard great pop records played so loud, and it gave them such power.

I'd been taught that young people should be seen and not heard, but this music represented another way. The fantastic noise pumping out into the night air seemed to show me a way to break free from conformity. It almost hypnotized me with its promises of freedom and self-expression. And I wasn't the only one. The seeds of the sixties' revolution were being sown right here, through the eager ears and into the minds of young people, with music as the driving force. No wonder it was frightening the hell out of parents, teachers and the government – all the people whose authority would be rocked by the liberation of the young.

I longed for the life my music promised, so different from the life my parents wanted for me: education, knuckling down, obeying the rules and getting a safe job for life. I envied the workers who travelled with the funfair: a few days in town, liven up the place, turn on the local girls, and then take off for a new adventure. That seemed more like living to me.

Then there was Sheringham. The annual Dingley holiday for years and years was spent at this little seaside town on the Norfolk coast, a couple of hundred miles due east of Birmingham. It was a major effort for my parents to get five kids and two weeks' worth of their stuff packed and to get the journey under way. It was a two-vehicle expedition: Dad had his car from work, a Vauxhall Cresta, a classy motor with fins on the back and lots of chrome; Mum drove the family Morris 8, registration DAD 300.

It took the whole day to get to Sheringham and it was a long, boring journey. We went every year for most of my childhood and teens and yet still Mum or Dad would take a wrong turn and get lost. We children seemed to be in a permanent state of war with each other, squabbling and fighting in the back seat. It must have been pure hell for our parents.

Going across East Anglia took forever but eventually I'd see walls and houses built of seaside stones and get the first hint of that salty tang in the air. Soon the contest would be on for who would be the first to see the sea, and then Sheringham itself and our base for the next two weeks, the Bijou Hotel. I would hang out of the car window as we made our way through the narrow streets, breathing in deeply and getting high on that intoxicating, fresh, salty sea air. It never smelt so good as on that first day in Sheringham. As soon as we parked, I ran down to gaze at the sea and absorb the whole wonderful atmosphere, savouring the fact that I had two whole weeks there. I'll always be grateful to my folks for their hard work and effort to make that annual pilgrimage.

In the short-trouser years on holiday I was a model son, helping carry my mum's portable Bush radio (which weighed an absolute ton) and other stuff down to the beach every day. There we would play on the sand, dig holes, build castles and swim in the sea. When it was raining we'd sit in the beach hut, listen to *Mrs Dale's Diary* and whinge a lot. As I got older, it was on those days I would sneak off when no one was looking and walk back up the promenade to the amusement arcade that we always called the 'penny in the slots'. It was a great place, crammed with all sorts of machines. There was a driving game I mastered, where the object was to negotiate a big ball bearing through a series of 'streets' by means of a large steering wheel. It called for a really delicate touch; if you did have the skill and patience to get the ball all the way home, you'd get your penny back and so could start all over again. I must have set the house record for the number of winning journeys home, and so could entertain myself for hours all for the price of a penny piece.

I loved gadgets, so the machines fascinated me. The other great attraction was the arcade's jukebox. Set right at the back, it was enormous, with a fantastic bass sound and a stock of the latest and best rock 'n' roll and pop records, like Fats Domino's 'Blueberry

Hill', Johnny Burnette's 'Dreamin'' or Eddie Cochran's 'Summer-time Blues'. After a day playing the machines and listening to my beloved rock 'n' roll, I'd wander back to the hotel at around the time I figured the rest of the mob would be returning from the beach. They'd be cross with me for disappearing and Dad would give me a bollocking.

'We pay all this money, bring you all this way for some fresh air and what d'you do? Spend all your time in the amusement arcade, listening to the same stuff you hear at home.'

He and Mum would then be getting ready for their favourite time, a leisurely dinner on their own in the hotel's cosy dining room. For us children a waitress would bring over a tray of corn-flakes into the big bedroom we three boys shared. When I was younger I had to be in pyjamas and dressing gown before they arrived. They were the best-tasting cornflakes ever, eaten to the sound of the waves breaking on and then sucking at the stones just the other side of the promenade outside our window. I'd fall asleep to that sound, blissfully happy and dreaming of another day of excitement tomorrow.

As I got older, a bowl of cornflakes and an early night were no longer my idea of the perfect evening. By the time I was thirteen, I'd be getting restless as my parents began preparing for their long and boring dinner routine, and the minute they'd gone, I'd be back out again. They didn't mind if I headed off, as long as I was back at a decent time. Sometimes I'd head for the slots to see what was going on in there, or perhaps down the steps to the lower promenade and Fisherman's Corner, where there was another amusement arcade and a bingo place run by a husband-and-wife team from Yorkshire. The 'missus', as her husband called her, would be bustling around the four sides of their stall, making sure all the squares were uncovered on the illuminated plastic cards, while her old man kept up this constant patter with the microphone, trying to tempt more punters to come and join in the game.

It was amazing the power that microphone gave him. He could reach out and grab people's attention and create a real atmosphere. But bingo is bingo, and I didn't linger all that long. I always hoped

I'd find a bit more action back up the slots. On those late-summer evenings, the dusk would be beginning to fall and the coloured lights along the seafront glowed brightly against the dark blue sky, illuminating the promenade. In the distance, the jukebox would be playing, with all its promise of excitement and adventure.

In the back of the slots, leaning up against the counter of the rifle range, would be Mick the Keys, who kept the machines running, and my brother John, who was usually with a great-looking girl. I loved being out with John, but at times like these the four years between us was a lifetime. No seventeen-year-old wants to be bothered by his little brother hanging around him, especially when there are girls to impress. If I showed up, he'd come up with some quip to put me down, so I'd bugger off and leave him free to turn the charm on the new bird he'd pulled. God, I was so jealous of John. Why couldn't I be a few years older than I was?

But by the time I was fifteen, life seemed even more cruel. I was growing up and now I was plagued with awful spots. Who was going to fancy a gangly jerk with a serious acne problem? Then, one summer, there was one girl who did. Her name was Laura; she was nineteen with shoulder-length auburn hair and the most kissable mouth I'd ever seen. For some reason she had a serious crush on me. She was the first girl that ever did, and I can remember her saying, 'Oh, Peter. If only you were a few years older, I could really fall in love with you.'

She sparked all sorts of feelings in me. I was frightened, overawed and sexually turned on by her, but I knew I couldn't do anything about it. I often wondered if she was just playing a game and humouring me. Maybe she thought my brother was being a bit cruel and she wanted to boost my confidence, but I think the attraction was genuine. She certainly made a vulnerable, mixed-up and insecure teenager feel more of a man, and I'll always be grateful to her for that.

Those holidays were the best. It's no wonder there are so many great pop songs about summer. Somehow one can do more growing up in those two weeks of summer holiday than in a whole year back home. But all too soon it was time to return to normal life – and bloody school. How I hated the torment of getting an education: for a teenager, life was so bloody cruel.

It gave me a taste of something so good and then, just as I was really getting into it, grabbed it back off me again, stuffing me back into my boring, humdrum existence.

Chapter Three

'You may think you're being really clever by not working hard. But let me tell you, you're being stupid.' Geography master Harry Fisher was in full flow. 'If you boys don't put the effort in now, you'll end up sweeping the factory floor.'

We'd heard it all so many times before. Not only did it make me switch off, it actually encouraged my rebellion. I wondered: Surely there's much more to a person than the ability to soak up and remember information about stuff that doesn't really seem to have any relevance to the world beyond the school walls? Perhaps I only reacted this way because I wasn't very good at the academic stuff. I'd always thought Tudor Grange Comprehensive down the road was a much cooler place. They had girls there and a better uniform. But my dad had got into debt to send his three sons to Solihull School and provide them with the best possible start in life. To him, money spent on our education was better than money left in a will, which could be wasted and frittered away. It was a very noble sacrifice, and I will always be grateful to him, but unfortunately, I didn't make the most of it.

Solihull School was an unusual mix of boarding and day school. Of the 750 pupils, about 250 were boarders and the rest attended on a normal daily basis, except that it was a six-day week with sports on a Saturday afternoon. I'm sure it's a very different place now, but back in the late fifties and early sixties the regime was brutalizing. It treated all boys exactly the same, no matter what kind of character or temperament they had; it prized academic and sporting achievement and nothing else; and if a boy became known as difficult, or rebellious, he was written off as a hopeless case and, as a result, he became one.

I started quite well. I liked rugby and was fairly popular, and I was good at reading and English. In fact, my reading was considered so good that I was asked to read the lesson in morning assembly when I was only about nine years old. I was so small that I couldn't be seen over the top of the lectern – despite being very nervous, I think I did quite well. Later, at home, Mum asked how it had gone. My brother John laughed and said, 'He was crap.' It crushed me. No doubt, with hindsight, John was a bit jealous of my star turn, but at the time I felt put down by the boy I considered my hero. It diminished my enjoyment in the things I was actually any good at, and further encouraged me to reject everything about school, even those things I quite liked.

There are always boys like me in a school: a little bit sensitive, and lonely, looking for a way to be understood. The luckier ones are helped by a special mentor or teacher, who spots their potential and helps them develop it. That didn't happen to me. I never met the kind of teacher who could inspire me to be interested in school or take it seriously. As time went by, I became regarded more and more as one of the hopeless cases.

It wasn't helped by the fact that the school was dominated by corporal punishment. The assistant headmaster, Mr McKenzie, spent most of his time roaming around the school hoping to find a pupil who, for some minor misdemeanour, had been told to stand outside the classroom. McKenzie would knock on the door and inquire of the master taking the class if he had any objection to his taking the errant pupil away for a beating. On one occasion, McKenzie found me standing outside the classroom, where I'd been sent to ponder the error of my ways after making some kind of inappropriate joke in class.

'Ah, Dingley,' said McKenzie, with evident relish. 'You can come with me.'

Having obtained his usual permission, McKenzie led me to his office and, with military precision, took me through the whole process of a beating in such a way as to cause maximum pain and humiliation.

First, he made me touch my toes while he slowly folded up my jacket and stepped back to admire the young schoolboy posterior clad in taut, stretched trousers. Then, taking his time, he whacked down the cane with maximum force: this wasn't a beating, this was a thrashing. He paused between each stroke to allow the pain to begin to subside before the sound of the cane swishing through the air signalled the next blow was about to land. After the fifth there was a longer pause and just as I started to straighten up, thinking it was all over, he barked out the command, 'Stay down, boy, I've not finished with you yet!'

The sixth and final stroke landed with even more force than the previous ones and then, to my great relief, it was all over. The challenge, of course, was to hold back the tears that were stinging the back of the eyes and never, ever to let him know just how much he'd hurt me. I hobbled out of his study, cursing him, the school and the whole bloody system that gave this miserable example of a human being the right to attack me and totally rob me of my dignity.

The head boy also had the 'privilege' of administering the cane. His team of prefects, or 'benchers' as we called them, would patrol the village of Solihull after school and the names would be noted of any boys who were seen talking to the girls from the nearby Malvern High School or, even worse, were found to be in one of the local coffee bars. At the next day's morning assembly the announcement would be made: 'Would the following boys please report to the head boy's study at eleven o'clock . . .'

There, as the unfortunate victim was held down by benchers, the head boy would wield his cane. His beating may have been without the McKenzie venom but it was painful and humiliating all the same.

The regular masters at the school weren't allowed to administer corporal punishment, so some of them would do it on the sly, knowing that we'd be too frightened to report them. The worst culprit was Mr Page, the music master. Over the years he'd per-fected his own special brand of punishment involving the use of an old violin bow. If you gave anything less than full attention in his class, he would pick someone out at random to make an example of them.

One day it was my turn and I was called up to the front. Page's technique was to make you hold out your left hand, which he would then hit with full force using his bow. While that hand was stinging, you would then hold out your right hand for the same treatment. Then he'd go back to the left, and so on until he'd administered three strokes on each hand. I think he thought that the pain would last longer this way. Part of the public school ethos is about being a 'real man' and not showing pain or hurt, or telling parents about the tough stuff at school, so I kept my punishment to myself. But Mum couldn't fail to notice the welts and dark bruises all over my hands.

'What on earth has happened to you?' she asked, horrified, holding my hands to examine them.

'Mr Page thought I wasn't paying enough attention in music class.'

Both Mum, and Dad, when he later came home and saw the wounds, were incensed. It was a punishment that could have injured my hands for life. The next day they made a complaint to the headmaster, and Mr Page left to seek employment elsewhere. I hope that his future pupils were spared the violin-bow treatment.

I just longed for the day when I could walk out of the place for the last time.

In the summer of 1960, when I was fifteen years old, something else happened that compounded my rejection of school and exams – I got my first job.

I'd set my heart on something really special and extremely expensive: a Philips reel-to-reel tape machine that I'd seen in the shop in the high street. I'd stared at it hundreds of times through the window, dreaming about how it could revolutionize my life. With a tape machine, I'd be able to record pop programmes off the radio and have all the music I wanted for free. But it cost serious money – about ninety pounds – and I needed to earn more than mere pocket money to afford it.

After much nagging from me, my dad got in touch with one of his cousins, who ran a small factory in Birmingham and, yes, they did have some work for a few weeks during the summer. Harris

& Sons Brass Founders was in the heart of Birmingham's industrial area and if you wanted anything in brass, you'd found the right place. My job was in the polishing shop where, after a morning's training, I was in charge of a centre-less automatic polishing machine. It was a massive thing with a spinning polishing wheel and a rest where I laid various cylindrical tubes that would start off dull and grey and emerge at the other side gleaming and highly polished with that lovely deep brassy shine. Part of the skill was to know just how much 'compo' to apply to the polishing brush. The compound came in brick-size blocks and the air was full of mucky particles of the stuff. I soon learnt why all the others covered their cups of tea with little bits of cardboard.

The hours were eight a.m. to six p.m. with just half an hour for lunch. It was hard, dirty work in a noisy, smelly environment but I loved it. At one o'clock I rushed down to the greasy spoon at the corner of the street for eggs, beans and chips, buttered slice and a mug of tea, all for one and ninepence. All spare sixpences went into the huge Bel Ami jukebox that dominated the corner of the tiny café. Massive speakers on each side boomed out my favourites like Fats Domino's 'Blueberry Hill' and The Shirelles' 'Will You Still Love Me Tomorrow?'.

Every Friday I collected my pay packet in its small brown envelope. I joined in with my workmates examining the little white slip, moaning and muttering about how much tax and insurance we'd been stopped, but by the end of the summer I had earned enough to buy the Philips tape machine. I went into the shop with my wadge of cash and left, elated, with a huge box containing the gadget of my dreams. When I got it home, the whole family came to stand around and look at it, impressed by this latest piece of technology. It looked just the thing, with big clunky buttons and an illuminated tube on the front with its glowing green bars that would bounce back and forth to indicate the recording level.

The small plastic microphone attached to the machine meant I'd be able to record myself talking and act out my private dream of having my own radio show. Now my bedroom became my

studio and a whole new world opened up to me. Sunday afternoon's *Pick of the Pops* was the best for my purposes: the whole of
the Top Twenty hit records were played one after the other.
God bless DJ Alan Freeman, who never talked over the record's
introduction. With good anticipation and skilful use of the pause
button, I could cut off Alan coming back in at the end of the
record. It was an early example of home taping – highly illegal,
but loads of people did it.

With plenty of tapes of hit records in stock, I could now do my
own radio shows, telling the imaginary listeners why I liked a
particular record and introducing the artist and the song. My vast,
unseen audience was occasionally supplemented by one of my
brothers or sisters, who would craftily listen at the door and then
burst in with guffaws of mocking laughter. Flushed with embarrassment, I pretended not to care and silently apologized to my listeners
for the abrupt end to my show, then switched off the tape machine
until next time. I loved my tapes and got enormous pleasure out
of my private radio broadcasts.

Then, about six months later, there was a huge family row, the
kind that happened periodically. I was so upset by the violent
argument that I rushed upstairs, picked up my tape machine and
hurled it out of the window, completely destroying it in some
kind of mad, grand gesture. There it lay – in pieces – the product
of a whole summer's work and the source of real enjoyment in
my life. I'd wrecked it. When the anger had passed, I bitterly
regretted what I'd done.

It was an early example of my stupid tendency to self-destruct
and to trash something I loved for no good reason.

Chapter Four

1960

It was time to go back to Solihull School: now, after my taste of freedom in the brass foundry, it was worse than ever. I had proved I could hold down a job, earn money, be independent and be treated as an adult. So what was I doing back in this awful place?

This was the big year: the all-important O levels. I absolutely had to get lots of those or it would be a lifetime with a broom, as Mr Fisher had threatened. I still had a letter from my brass-foundry boss praising my dedication to the job and hoping that he would have the opportunity to employ me again as I was an excellent worker. I was pretty sure that I didn't want to be a centre-less polishing machine operator for the rest of my life but I was also certain that, if I wanted, I could work my way up the ladder there. My brother John had left school and, like me, he wasn't academic. He'd signed up for a six-year apprenticeship in a factory that made heating and ventilation units, and he would no doubt end up in management. Surely I could do something like that, couldn't I?

The more the teachers whinged on about how hard I had to study and how vital the exams were, the more rebellious I became and the less work I did. I was going through a Teddy boy phase – everyone seemed to want to be one, and at school all the boys were taking in their trousers so that they tapered down into a narrow fit at the ankle. I had a whole Teddy boy outfit that I loved: tight striped jeans in spearmint green, a bootlace tie and a long drape jacket. I wore this lot with those heavy, crêpe-soled shoes called brothel creepers. My skin was still a source of agony to me as I was tormented by spots, but I drew attention away from my complexion by greasing my hair up into a Brylcreemed quiff.

When I appeared in the full get-up, my parents were absolutely appalled. They couldn't understand why anyone would want to make themselves look so outlandish – and they weren't the only ones. When I walked up and down Solihull High Street in my gear, I would outrage passers-by, getting the most extraordinary looks from them. One day I came home to find my mum had been in my room, gathered up my beloved Teddy boy clothes and thrown the whole lot out with the rubbish.

On a Saturday, there was only one place to be and that was Frestons coffee bar. Everyone went there to hang out, talk to girls and find out where that night's party would be. If we weren't in Frestons, we would go down to the park and watch the older guys on their motorbikes. They rode Nortons, BSAs and Triumphs – these were the last glory days of the British motorbike industry – and they got all the attention from the girls, who loved to go for rides with them. The girls climbed on the back in their big skirts with all the petticoats underneath, put scarves over their back-combed, beehived hair, and then screamed with delight as the lads took them racing around the car park.

We younger ones watched with badly concealed envy. I yearned for a motorbike of my own, but my dad had made it quite clear that this would never happen. Without a motorbike or a car, I didn't see how I would ever attract a girl. Cars were a major status symbol back then and any guy who could persuade his father to lend him the car had a major advantage with the opposite sex, both in pulling ability and in having somewhere comfortable and private for a good snog.

I went along to the parties that I heard about in Frestons, but nothing much happened when I got to them. I was too shy and insecure to talk much to the girls, so I moped around a bit, drank pints with my friends, smoked Woodbines and tried to pretend that I was older and cooler than I felt inside.

Inexorably, the summer arrived and with it came the dreaded examinations. Well, I decided, if I was going to fail them I was going to fail in style. For some, I didn't turn up at all. For others,

I was late. If I did turn up on time, I just wrote my name at the top of the page and sat back and waited for the interminable hour and a half or so until the time was up. I wasn't going to play their game by putting even an ounce of effort into my exams. I knew that as soon as I had my freedom, I would be successful at something that had nothing to do with school or bits of paper proclaiming what exam results I had. I would show them all.

Finally the exams were all over and the end of term approached. When the holidays got under way, I hung around the house and spent most of the mornings in bed. I knew the axe was about to fall as soon as those results came out, so there didn't seem any point in getting a job, making plans or going out.

And then it came. One day, I heard the sound of heavy footsteps on the stairs and my bedroom door burst open. In came my very angry father.

'What the hell is the meaning of this?' he shouted, waving a postcard at me.

'The meaning of what? I dunno what you're on about,' I said, with fake bravado.

'It's your exam results. Look at this, you've failed them all!' he shouted.

I sleepily sat up in bed and took the card off him. Beside each exam subject was a small cross. There was only one way to deal with it and that was to joke my way out of it.

'Hey, look at that, Dad. Eight kisses, they must really love me.'

He was close to exploding with rage.

'I go into debt to get you a good education and look what you've done – thrown it all away!'

He was on the verge of belting me one so I slid back under the blankets. I'd never seen him this angry.

'It doesn't matter, Dad, it'll be okay,' I mumbled.

'I've got to go to work now, I'll deal with you later,' were his ominous last words.

Oh shit, what am I going to do now? I thought. I was quaking inside. I had known that facing the consequences of my lack of application was going to be bad but now that the exam results were actually here, I wasn't quite prepared for the feelings that were churning around inside me. I felt really sorry for my old man. He was clearly very angry but also deeply disappointed. All his dreams and ambitions for his youngest son were in tatters. He must have gone off to work with a heavy heart that day.

I wanted my father to respect me and I hated to disappoint him and let him down. But he just couldn't see that the supposedly privileged education he'd bought for me was all wrong. It wasn't going to take me where I wanted to go, and that was all there was to it. I knew I could still make a success of my life, without those exam passes everyone seemed to think would guarantee my happiness.

Not long after the fateful postcard with those eight crosses of failure, my father received a letter from the headmaster. He wrote to suggest that my father might consider it unwise to send me back to school and incur further fees. I was an unacademic boy and he thought it unlikely I would be any more successful if I were to retake my O level exams. He ended his letter by saying he hoped I had gained something from the school in terms of character development and that my time there had not been totally wasted.

Following the results, Dad had told me I'd have to go back, work hard this time and retake the exams all over again. It was an idea that filled me with total dread. I had already decided that I was going to fight for my freedom as hard as I could. Now I didn't have to. The good old headmaster had done something right at last. Had I been expelled? Not really. I'd been given a way out instead, with a polite suggestion that I should retire from school. I was delighted: how absolutely bloody fantastic – freedom at last! No more school. The only downside was that I'd left Solihull School for ever without knowing that I'd left. I had missed the chance of any last-day mayhem and the pleasure of hurling desks into the swimming pool.

Dad was not so pleased.

'What the hell are we going to do with you now? I'm certainly not having you hanging around the house all day, sponging money off your mother. You can leave home. You've thrown away the chances I've given you so now you'll have to make your own way in the world.'

It was a measure of my father's deep disappointment that he said this. My older brothers and sister all still lived at home even though they were out working. For my father to suggest that his son of barely sixteen should move out and get a job showed how much I'd wounded him with my failure to make anything of my education.

I was secretly pleased. Even if leaving home was a terrifying prospect, it was still an exciting one.

'What do you want to do?' Dad asked.

There was only one thing I could think of that fulfilled all my desires: I wanted to be close to engines, to drive and to experience the kind of freedom my father enjoyed as he went about the country in his company car.

'I want to be a lorry driver, Dad.'

'Oh, don't be ridiculous. Is that all you want to do? Is that all the ambition you have, to be a lorry driver? God, you disappoint me, son.'

'Well, I'll be a racing driver, then.'

That didn't impress him either. He obviously considered all my dreams to be just that: ludicrous, childish castles in the air that gave me no hope of earning a living or realizing my potential.

I kept out of the way for a few days, taking off on my bicycle during the day and hanging out in my bedroom in the evening, listening to music. Eventually a plan was formed. Dad's network of far-off cousins came through for me again. Apparently there was some distant relative named Roy Coup, who was a big cheese in a company that owned three garages in the West Country. He persuaded them to take me on as an apprentice on a six-year course. I would start as a trainee and work in all the various garage departments, go to college once a week to study City and Guilds motor mechanics and, after three years, graduate into the showroom as a salesman.

My father was very pleased with this: it was a respectable thing to do and it was quite obvious that I was mad about cars, so it had every chance of providing me with a fulfilling career and a good way of earning my living. Dad announced that I'd be moving to Gloucester and starting work in a few weeks' time. It sounded okay to me – as long as it had something to do with cars, I was happy. So, at the age of sixteen, I left home. I had always said you didn't need bits of paper to get on in life.

Now I had to prove it.

Chapter Five

1961

From a public schoolboy in uniform, I became a grease monkey in overalls at St Aldgate Garage, Westgate Street, Gloucester. It wasn't such a big transition for me. I was familiar with the garage environment from a Saturday job I'd had washing cars, and I was used to work from my time at the brass foundry in Birmingham. I liked taking responsibility for turning up on time, clocking in, working hard and getting along with my workmates.

I turned up for my first day bright-eyed and eager but it took a while before I was accepted. For one thing, I was the youngest in the garage and for another, I talked differently from everyone else. My accent was a public schoolboy Brummie, and all the other mechanics – there was a staff of about twenty – had broad West Country accents. To add to my troubles, word had got around, as it always does, that this new apprentice was somehow connected to the boss. As a result, I wasn't given the warmest welcome in the world but, as time went on and everyone got used to me, they began to accept me and we all got along.

St Aldgate Garage was enormous, located in the centre of the town. It had a very narrow frontage with split showrooms either side of the narrow entrance, which was just large enough to accommodate a car or small truck. At the end of the passageway, the space opened out into a vast workshop, with an electric turntable in it. There were a couple of petrol pumps out the front, and when a car had been filled up, it would drive down to the turntable and be turned round, ready to go back out on to the street.

I enjoyed the work from the start. I already knew a lot about cars just from looking under the bonnet of my dad's car and fiddling about with the engine. I'd always been fascinated by how an engine works, and now I had the chance to work on the real thing. I earned £6 a week, but found it really hard to get through the week on my wages. My lodgings cost me £3 and that left me only £3 for all my other expenses. Dad and I had found my digs together just before I started at St Aldgate, and it had seemed like a safe, respectable kind of place, with my breakfast and evening meal thrown in as part of the deal.

I was the only lodger in the little house on the Tuffley Road, a couple of miles from the city centre. Willy and Hilda were my landlord and landlady: he was a sweet little chap, a milkman who somehow had the misfortune to marry a woman who was built like a Russian wrestler and ruled the household with a rod of iron and took no nonsense from anyone.

My room was a typical, tiny third bedroom with just enough room for a narrow bed, a wardrobe and a small chest of drawers. After the uninspiring evening meal that Hilda cooked (everything came with chips, night after night) I could either lie on my bed and read, or sit with Willy and Hilda watching boring TV programmes, which I hated. I had no music system, there was nothing worth listening to on the radio and, once winter had arrived, it was freezing cold.

I had signed up to spend six years in Gloucester learning my trade, and perhaps longer if I got taken on once I'd qualified. I didn't know how I was going to stand it. Within six months, I was miserable and desperately homesick. Being hard up was the toughest part: often I was so broke I had to make the decision to buy either a cheese roll for lunch or five Woodbines.

The other problem was that there was so little to do in the evening. Here I was, young, free and independent at last, earning my own money, and there was no way to take advantage of it. Most of Gloucester's cinemas had been turned into bingo halls, and the only one left played one film for an entire week. The one bright spot was the coffee bar; it was a good place to hang out and they had a jukebox. The trick was to try and make one cup of weak, milky cappuccino last the whole evening. I watched all the other kids hanging out there but it was hard making friends. Everybody knew each other, they'd all been born there and gone to school together. A spotty bloke with a Brummie accent wasn't very welcome and they kept together in their own little groups, leaving me hunched over my coffee, smoking a Woodbine and keeping myself to myself.

The music was good, though. A big favourite of mine at the time was Joe Brown's 'A Picture Of You'. It always gave me a bit of a lift and was an example of a new style of British pop music that was beginning to emerge, challenging the dominance of American music.

I lived for the days, really. It was a good feeling to do something useful. I graduated from the grease bay to general mechanics, learnt how to change plugs and points, clean a carburettor, change brake shoes and then on to major stuff like removing a gearbox and engine. Then I moved to the electrical shop, working for a placid guy named Don. He had a neat little place to himself tucked into a corner of the main workshop. The walls were made of thick wire with strategically placed girlie calendars and posters to ensure privacy – and a couple of spy slots so we could see who was coming. I had my own bench in there and Don showed me how to recondition starters and dynamos.

Once a week, I'd do a day release from the garage to attend Gloucester Technical College to study City and Guilds motor mechanics. Very different from Solihull School: discipline didn't exist and no one could be bothered to pay the slightest attention. We all went to the pub for lunch, so afternoons were totally chaotic. It was ironic, as this time I was interested and keen to learn.

Most weekends, I would go back home to Solihull, heading back on a Friday afternoon to see my family and my friends. On Friday, 30th March 1962, I turned seventeen, and it was a milestone I'd been looking forward to for ages because it meant I would finally get to taste the thrill of getting behind a steering wheel. I'd already applied for a provisional licence and was raring to start driving for real. Even so, I wasn't prepared for what happened when Dad got home from work.

Dumping his briefcase in the hall, Dad walked into the kitchen and said, 'Come on, son, put the L plates on the Morris. You're going to take me for a drive.'

I couldn't believe it. With trembling fingers, I tied the L plates on the front and back bumpers and, with the rest of the family watching, Dad got in the passenger seat and I climbed in behind the wheel. I started her up. With my heart racing, I pressed the clutch and selected first gear. Carefully and slowly I drove out of the drive and paused. I looked both ways; the road was clear.

'Are you okay, Dad?' I asked.

'Yeah, I'm fine. You can do it, off you go.'

I think he had more confidence in me than I did in myself, but away we went. I drove a couple of miles to Solihull and back again, without any drama. Learning to drive made me feel as though I was approaching adulthood for real, even if I was still just seventeen. But then something else happened that completed my rite of passage. I got my first girlfriend.

Her name was Ingrid Parker and I met her at the regular Solihull Civic Hall dance on a Saturday night. She was small and petite with a lovely pixie face and the most beautiful sparkling blue eyes. I never expected her to return the kind of admiration I felt for her and I knew she'd been going out with a good-looking guy, who drove a Ford Capri or something flash like that, so I never thought I stood a chance with her. But then I heard they'd broken up, so one night I gathered up all my courage and asked her to dance. We got on really well and, to my surprise, she seemed to like me quite a lot.

Before long, we became a regular item. Every Saturday night, we'd meet at the Civic Hall for the regular dance and, when we could, we'd indulge in a bit of kissing, though we never got much further than that – there was no question of anything more than a bit of snogging. It gave me lots of confidence that Ingrid found me attractive and wanted to be seen with me. I was infatuated with her, and seeing her was the highlight of my week. Saturday night was what I looked forward to most.

★

I'd been at St Aldgate for almost eighteen months and I was beginning to feel that it wasn't the place for me. I wanted to quit the whole scene in Gloucester. I was tired of having no friends, no car and being continually broke, and the prospect of being there for at least another four and a half years was not in the least bit attractive. The thing that was stopping me was that I needed to get another job, one that would allow me to come back home to live, which was what I really wanted.

I couldn't get much closer to my roots than opposite the nursing home where I was born. Right there was a garage called Patrick Motors Ltd. One Saturday morning when I was spending my weekend in Solihull, I called in and asked to speak to the manager. A few minutes later, I was explaining my situation to Mr Martin. He listened and, to my surprise and delight, offered me a job. I would be a mechanic for six months and then I could move to the sales department. It was more than I could possibly have hoped for. Now I could fast-track out of my dirty overalls, get myself a nice sales job with a company car, and I'd be back home with my mates and my girl. What could be better?

Back in Gloucester, I handed in my notice at the garage and told Hilda and Willy that I was going to leave my lodgings. Then I had a lot of fun telling my dad that I'd walked out of the job in Gloucester. The great thing was to tease him a bit and get a reaction before coming clean.

'Hey, Dad, guess what! I've quit my job at St Aldgate.'

'You've done *what*?'

'Yeah – I just wasn't enjoying it much any more, you know?'

My dad launched into his usual speech.

'What do you think you're doing, wasting all your opportunities like this? I'm not having you scrounging money off me and your mother . . . why would you spoil the chance to make a perfectly good living . . . ?'

And so on.

'Dad,' I said, 'it's all right – I've got another job.'

I told him all about the plan at Patrick Motors; I think he was quite impressed. He and Mum were glad to have me back home again. My older brothers and sister were still living there, paying board and lodging out of their wages, so I would do the same. I would also be able to make more use of my share of the car we'd all bought together. Now I'd be able to use it as much as the others did.

All in all, it was a very good move.

Chapter Six

1963

It was my first week back in Solihull and, the day before I was due to start my new job, there was the regular gig at the Civic Hall. The Honeycombs, a local band, were playing along with a couple of other groups. I knew all my friends would be there, including Ingrid. I was eager to see her, and to break the happy news that I was back for good, so we'd be able to see a lot more of each other.

As I had only just come back home, I persuaded the others to let me use the car that night. Putting my best suit on, with nice white shirt, slim tie and a good splash of aftershave, I went off to reintroduce myself to the local scene. I walked into the Civic Hall, thinking to myself that it was funny to have a pop music gig in such formal surroundings. The Civic was the poshest of the places I liked to hang out. There was a great deal of florid carpeting, the staff were dressed in proper uniforms, and everyone was dressed up and on their best behaviour.

It wasn't long before I spotted Ingrid. I hurried up to her with a big smile on my face.

'Hi, Ingrid. I've got some great news for you. I've come back to live in Solihull, and we can see each other a lot more from now on.'

'That's nice, Peter,' she said coolly, looking over my shoulder.

I guessed that there had to be a new man on the scene, and sure enough, a little later I saw Ingrid with a really good-looking guy, who had the use of his father's very cool Ford Zephyr anytime he wanted it. He had no spots, and the car was spearmint green with fins and lots of chrome – very impressive. Ingrid and I were no more. My heart was broken, but I put a brave face on it, wished her well and headed for the bar.

I'd already had a couple of pints but I decided what I needed was some whisky. I was not a great drinker and I'd never touched whisky before in my life, but for some reason I decided that this was the drink for a man with a broken heart. The smell was hateful but I chucked it back. Every time I was about to leave the bar, I'd meet another old friend and say to them, 'Come and have a drink! I'm celebrating coming back home.'

By the end of the night I was still at the bar, and swaying.

I said to my friends, 'Come on, fellas, I'll give you a lift home.'

One of my mates said, 'Are you sure you're all right to drive?'

'Yes, of course I am,' I slurred.

So five of us piled into the little A35, and off we went.

I managed to make all the right stops and dropped off my last friend, who begged me to leave the car and stay the night at his place. All I could think was that I had to be home to start my new job in the morning. I swung the car into the drive, stopped in front of the garage and promptly fell asleep.

My parents, worried about me being out so late, were still awake and waiting for the sound of my return. They heard the car come into the drive and were wondering why they hadn't heard me enter the house. I was vaguely aware that the back door had opened and there were Mum and Dad in their dressing gowns, looking concerned. Dad opened the car door and, as I was leaning on it at the time, I promptly fell out in a drunken heap on the drive. They had to go in and wake up John and Michael to help carry me upstairs.

I woke the next day at four o'clock – in the afternoon. They had tried to rouse me in time to get to my first day at work, but I was completely gone. When I did wake up, I felt absolutely dreadful. I had never been so ill before in my life. It was impossible to get out of bed, let alone go to work. I'd just have to start the following day instead, while I nursed the biggest hangover I could possibly imagine. I eventually appeared at Patrick Motors a day late, apologizing profusely for my non-appearance the previous day.

Once that was behind me, I settled down very quickly and enjoyed my life back home in Solihull and my new job. The mechanics were a really nice bunch of guys, and I knuckled down and worked very hard.

When I wasn't at work, it was so nice to be with my friends again, and to enjoy nights out in the pub or going to gigs. One of my favourite haunts was at the Shirley Annexe on the Stratford Road, which was in complete contrast to Solihull Civic Hall. It was a funny, run-down sort of a place but it had a really good atmosphere, and they booked in some great groups every Thursday night. Birmingham was really beginning to buzz on the music side; there was definitely a new energy in the air as more and more groups were forming and playing gigs. And there were rumblings of major things happening around Liverpool.

One day, posters went up announcing that Screaming Lord Sutch was coming to play at the Shirley Annexe. There was a lot of excited anticipation in the hall that night. As usual, all the girls gathered in front of the stage while the boys hung round at the back, propping up the bar and eyeing up the talent. The lights dimmed, and the band kicked off playing an instrumental. We all tried to figure out why there was a coffin on the stage. The music sounded like a horror movie soundtrack when suddenly the coffin lid burst open, and rising out of it came a gruesome hooded figure in a long cloak with long hair, evil make-up and brandishing a long knife, like the one Norman Bates used in *Psycho*. The girls at the front had already jumped back but when Sutch let out a blood-curdling scream and leapt towards them, they screamed in horror, and ran away from the stage.

'This is good,' we all thought.

We guys always had a streak of jealousy towards members of a group as girls gazed adoringly up at them. The fact that the girls were now running towards us for protection made a refreshing change. Two of them even ran into the safety of the Ladies, only to be pursued by Screaming Lord Sutch brandishing his knife. As he was still holding his microphone, we could hear their screams, which, combined with his and within the echoing confines of the toilet, sounded incredible. Even us boys started to get a bit frightened. What the hell was this guy doing?

Eventually Sutch came back out of the loo and on to the stage. As the two girls emerged from the Ladies, I approached the pretty brunette one and asked her if she was okay. She obviously appreciated my concern and we got chatting and went to the bar for a drink. Her name was Jenny. I'd seen her there before, being very friendly with Denny Laine, lead singer of Denny Laine and The Diplomats. We got on really well together that night and I ended up giving her a lift home in my old car. As I headed back home, I felt I had just met someone really special.

Jenny was very important to me; she was my first real love. I was eighteen when we met, and she was sixteen, just out of school and in her first job. She was very sweet, about five feet five, brunette, quite slim, and with a lovely voice. From the minute I met her, she charmed me with her personality and her impish sense of humour. It was more than just a lustful thing – there was a deep connection between us and she became the first person I could say that I was really, really in love with. And it was mutual.

We would see each other every week at the Shirley Annexe dances. I would try and get the car on a Sunday afternoon and we would go out and drive in the country and park up somewhere and listen to *Pick of the Pops* together. We both loved music, particularly the Beatles, who had been really big in Liverpool for a while now and whose fame was beginning to spread. When we heard that they were coming to play in Birmingham, Jenny and I were really excited and decided we had to go and see them.

On the night of the concert, we made our way to the Plaza Ballroom and joined the enormous queues outside. Once we were all inside, the excitement kept mounting, especially as the group weren't going to come on until late. There was an incredible atmosphere building up through the evening and when, at ten fifteen, the band finally came on, the place went absolutely nuts. Everyone surged forwards, the girls screamed and the Beatles opened with 'I Saw Her Standing There'. They looked and sounded so much better in the flesh than anything we'd seen on TV shows. It was so amazing that the actual Beatles were there in Birmingham, playing live. The Plaza was a small ballroom and the stage was just a few feet above the floor, so it was almost as though we could all reach out and touch them. In fact, security was a real problem for them that night, as the dressing room was just off to one side and you could practically step inside from the dance floor.

As they played, the music suddenly stopped and there was a moment of silence before George Harrison said laconically in his Liverpudlian drawl, 'John has bust a string.' They passed his guitar over to a guy standing at the dressing-room door, and as the instrument reached him, everyone surged forwards, trying to grab hold of him or the guitar, I'm not sure which. As another guitar was passed back, it looked like the crowd was going to get out of hand but as soon as the music resumed, the spell was recast and everybody just concentrated on the fabulous music that was driving all of us wild.

The band played for forty-five minutes but it was so intense, it seemed to go by in a flash. They ended on 'Twist And Shout'. When it became obvious they'd played their last song and that it was all over, the girls' screaming reached an even greater pitch and they all dashed forwards, pushing and shoving to get to the stage, desperate to get near their idols. The level of sexual excitement in the room was intense and extraordinary.

Jenny pushed forwards along with all the rest. I grabbed her as she went and managed to stay with her as we all rushed to get our last glimpse of the Beatles as they left the stage. It had been a fabulous, exhilarating experience.

As our feelings for each other deepened, Jenny and I would see each other virtually every night. She lived three or four miles from Solihull and I would drive over there as often as I could in the Mini that Patrick Motors provided for me when I was promoted to salesman. Jenny's parents thought the world of me. They knew that I'd been promoted very quickly and they saw me as a good catch for their daughter. We went out with each other for two years, as I made the transition from mechanic to salesman at Patrick Motors and began to feel I was really growing up.

One night I was driving her home after we'd been out for the evening and when we stopped in front of her house, she was very quiet for a moment. Then she said suddenly, 'Peter, it's all over.'

'Why?' I asked, feeling sick. 'Why is it over?'

'I'm too young to settle down,' she said simply. 'My mum keeps on at me. She keeps hinting that we should get married. She says that I'll never find a better man than you and that you've got such great prospects. But I'm too young and I'm not ready. So I think we should break up.'

I was completely devastated. Even when I managed to start sleeping, eating and working again, I was profoundly affected by the split. There would be some evenings when I would just drive to Shirley, where Jenny lived, because I'd done it nearly every night for two years, and park outside her house. I didn't know what else to do with myself. One evening I saw her walking home with a boy and they stopped at a gatepost, put their arms round each other and kissed. My stomach knotted up inside; I had hoped that we might get back together but I knew now that it would never happen. I didn't go to Jenny's house again.

It took me at least six months to get over Jenny and I simply wasn't interested in anyone else. Then, gradually, life started to get back to normal, with work occupying me in the daytime, and discos and dances taking up my evening hours and providing the escape from the everyday grind that we were all looking for.

It was at one of the dances at the Locarno that I met Pat. She was blonde, vivacious and very different from Jenny. If Jenny and I had had a connection of souls, Pat and I had a very different sort of thing going. This was a relationship based on lust and, to my delight, Pat turned out to be mad about sex. Jenny and I had never consummated our relationship but Pat was keen to go much further and she became my first lover. We were still short on privacy and room but at least I now had a car of my own, which provided just about the only opportunity to be alone for a while. We would drive out and park up somewhere and do what came naturally. It turns out that you can do quite a lot in the front seat of a Mini if the girl's on top.

Pat was a very sexy girl and enormous fun to be with. She was about eighteen and I was twenty; we both loved music and dancing, particularly the Monday-night discos at the Locarno. One Monday night was particularly exciting because Don Wardell from Radio Luxembourg was the guest DJ. I was a big fan of his radio show and was hoping to buttonhole him as he left the stage. When his set was over, he came down and signed autographs for the fans. I grasped my opportunity and started talking to him.

'Hey, Don, I'd like to do something like that myself.' I nagged him to tell me how I could get on Radio Luxembourg.

'I tell you what,' said Don Wardell. 'You should telephone Radio Luxembourg and ask to speak to Eggy Lay. He's a producer. He'll tell you what to do. He might even offer you an audition.' 'The only thing is . . .' Don Wardell passed back his autograph to an eager fan and gave me a wink. 'Don't tell him it was me who gave you his name. Okay?'

'Okay,' I said. 'Thanks, Don.'

I went home, resolving to call Radio Luxembourg the very next day, pretend to be an experienced DJ and see what happened.

Chapter Seven

1965

As the train slowly pulled out of Paddington Station after my disastrous audition at Radio Luxembourg, I thought that I would probably never see London again. It was back to my regular life in Solihull as a car salesman. Eggy Lay had told me unequivocally that I would never be a professional DJ. My dreams of making it big had crumbled into nothing.

And then, slowly, a new thought came into my mind: what the hell does *he* know? It was obvious to me that Eggy Lay and the rest of the crew were desperately old-fashioned and that their kind of radio was nothing like the stuff that was getting me excited. I had sat there reading from a pre-written script like something on the BBC news. Even with my lack of experience, I could grasp that reading from a script stultified most of the emotion and blotted out any genuine reaction to a great record. One of the most exciting shows on Radio Luxembourg was presented by Tony Hall, a radio hero of mine. As I listened to him, I pictured him standing up, fizzing with energy as he played all the great American soul and R&B records on the London-American record label owned by Decca. I knew that there was no way he used a script.

By the time I got to Birmingham, I'd overcome the setback of my failed audition. I was more determined than ever that I was going to be a DJ. I would just have to start somewhere other than Radio Luxembourg, that was all.

The following week, Pat and I went to the Monday-night disco at the Locarno as usual. I'd accepted by now that it was a bit overambitious to try and get on the radio. Playing records to a crowd on the dance floor would certainly be the next-best thing.

The place was packed as usual, with the regular crowd of young people keen to get up and dance. The latest hits boomed out of the speakers, sounding great, but the guy on the stage playing the records had about as much charisma and passion as an ironing board. He said very little in between the record changes, but mostly just stood there, formally dressed in his dinner jacket and black tie, grinning into the crowd as he lined up the discs on his double turntable.

I could do better than this, I thought. I'll go and find the manager and ask for a job. Full of confidence, I decided to act on impulse. I asked at the bar for directions to the manager's office. Once I'd found it, I knocked on the door without giving myself time to feel nervous or shy. The manager was sitting behind his desk and looked up as I came in.

'Yes?' he said.

'Hello, my name is Peter Dee. I've come to see if you've got any jobs for a DJ.'

The manager looked at me quizzically.

'Have you got any experience?' he asked.

'Oh yes – I've been DJing around little pubs and clubs for over a year now,' I lied.

I was surprised at how glib and confident I sounded, considering it was all a fib.

'Well, I've got no openings at the moment, and I'm very busy, so if you don't mind . . .'

The manager nodded at the door. My interview was obviously over and I'd got the brush-off. I rejoined Pat on the dance floor.

'How did you get on?' she asked.

'Not very well. There's nothing doing at the moment, but I'm not giving up.'

The next Monday I went to see the manager again and got an even quicker brush-off. The next Monday I knocked on his door again, and the Monday after that, and the Monday after that. It became a bit of a challenging game – he was never in his office. He'd be anywhere other than where he knew I'd find him. I had to go round the whole ballroom asking every member of staff if they'd seen the manager and knew where he was. This went on for over two months until one night I managed to get hold of him and asked again if there was an opening for an experienced DJ like myself.

To my astonishment, he said, 'Oh, all right. You can do Fridays in the Bali Hai Bar. You can start this week.'

The Bali Hai Bar wasn't exactly the main ballroom. It was a small, Hawaiian-themed bar off the main dance floor which got the overspill from the ballroom. On Fridays there would be a live band in the ballroom doing covers of the chart hits. Usually people went into the bar to have a drink and to sit down between dances. I didn't mind that, though.

'Great,' I stammered. 'Thanks very much. I'll see you on Friday, then.'

The manager walked off, leaving me in a daze. I couldn't believe it. My persistence had finally paid off. Now I had to try and match the confidence that I'd shown him.

As the week wore on, I got more and more nervous, and as I arrived at the Locarno on Friday, I was actually shaking with fear. I was smartly dressed in my best suit and I'd brought a big box of my own records and put them on the floor behind the little DJ desk, tucked away at the corner of the small dance floor. I was astonished to see there was only one turntable and a big, heavy old-fashioned microphone. It wasn't like the double-turntable set-up in the ballroom. This was going to be even harder than I'd thought. I put a record on at low volume to get some atmosphere going as I waited for the bar to start filling up.

I smiled and nodded as people came in, and as each record ended, I put the next one on as quickly as I could. But between each track, there was still an embarrassing gap of complete silence while I carefully cued up the needle. I was painfully aware that I was supposed to say something – anything – to cover it up. But I was too frightened to speak. I'll just wait for a few more people to come in before I start the chat, I thought. Gradually more and more people were coming in to sit at the tables or buy drinks at the bar. Just a few more people, I thought, and then I'll start. But the time never seemed quite right and my tongue remained resolutely frozen. Suddenly I saw the manager standing at the doorway, taking in what was going on. He was obviously expecting a bit of polished patter from the bloke who'd claimed to be an experienced DJ. Now I had no choice – I knew I had to take the big, brave, bold step. I switched the microphone on and said my first words.

'A very good evening and a warm welcome to the Bali Hai Bar,' I stammered. 'My name is Peter Dee, and I'm playing the records for you tonight.'

I dropped the arm on to the next record. It was The Four Tops, 'I Can't Help Myself'. A flood of people came on to the dance floor and I saw the manager leaving the bar. Thank God that's over, I thought, I've broken the ice. The record ended and I started chatting again, getting used to the curious experience of hearing my voice amplified over the PA system. I lifted the needle off the record, put the next one on and dropped the stylus as near as possible to the start of the grooves where the song begins. It was really difficult working with one turntable, and having no way of cueing up a record so that it started when I wanted it to, but I began to get the hang of it.

As the evening wore on, I started to enjoy it more and more and managed to keep the dance floor pretty much full. It was really satisfying to watch couples enjoying themselves. What a lovely way to earn a living! I thought.

Finally, at midnight, it was all over. I finished with the obligatory slow, smoochy ballad and wished everybody a good night and a safe journey home. The lights came up and the crowd headed out while I switched off the mike and gathered up my records. It had been a long night, from seven o'clock to midnight without a break, and afterwards I had to help collect the glasses and tidy the place up. I was exhausted but, boy, did I feel good. My dream had come true. I was a DJ.

The next day I was shattered. I hadn't got home until past one thirty a.m. and I had to be up a few hours later for my daytime job. Saturday was one of the most important days for a car salesman and I needed to take advantage of the opportunity to earn some decent commission. Still feeling exhausted, I managed to make it to the showroom on time and get through a day's work. This is going to be tough, I thought. But then, it was only one night a week. I should be able to handle that. After all, I was young and fit and, more than anything, I wanted to play records.

I went back eagerly to the Locarno the following week, and the one after that, my confidence growing with each session. I didn't get paid much – about thirty shillings a night – and I never got any feedback about how I was doing but I figured that if I hadn't been sacked, I must be doing all right. After I'd been DJing for a few weeks, I got chatting in the office of Patrick Motors to a girl called Linda about my new job at the Locarno.

'You should talk to my boyfriend, Graham,' she said. 'He's just started a new business, supplying and installing disco equipment for clubs and pubs. He might know of some more openings, places where they need a DJ. You two should meet up.'

It sounded like a good idea to me. I was already hungry for more opportunities and beginning to feel dissatisfied with the small Bali Hai Bar with its one turntable and the way I had to dress up to the nines. It was all very well enjoying the special feeling you get with lights, a ballroom and that glamorous plushness but I wanted to be somewhere much less formal, with a funkier atmosphere and those all-important twin decks.

Linda arranged for me to come round to her house and meet Graham. We hit it off immediately. His was a one-man operation and he proudly showed me the company vehicle. It was a grey Austin Mini van. He'd had it sign-painted so that underneath the company name it said 'Professionally Installed Discotheque Equipment. 24-hour radio-controlled service.'

'Wow! That's really impressive,' I said.

'Oh, it's just for show,' said Graham. 'That aerial on the roof isn't connected to anything.' He laughed. 'Linda usually knows where I am and can get hold of me if a customer has a problem.'

I loved his bravado. Little white lies maybe, but it was another expression of the new energy young people possessed in the early sixties. If you could find the confidence and the courage, there were no limits. The grey, depressing days of austerity and gloom that our parents had lived through were well and truly over. A new world was beginning and we were a part of it.

Like me, Graham was thinking big. He had installed equipment in only one club, but he was not going to be held back. With bright-eyed excitement, he explained how we could help each other.

'Listen, you're a DJ at the Locarno. That's the biggest Mecca ballroom in the country, and the name has a lot of prestige. You could get work in other clubs, and if their equipment is a bit naff, you can tip me off and I'll go in there and sell them some of my gear. Likewise, if I fit a system, I'll recommend you. This could be really good for both of us.'

'Brilliant idea,' I said. 'Let's do it.'

It worked beautifully, and soon I had a regular job at the Carlton Ballroom in Erdington and, to my delight, I also got Saturday and Sunday spots at the Navigation Inn, Wootton Wowen, on the road between Birmingham and Stratford-upon-Avon. At the Carlton, I did nights with Carl Wayne and The Vikings, the group that went on to become The Move. The band was on one stage and I was on another with my turntable, playing records between the sets. At the Navigation Inn, I played records to a packed crowd that buzzed with energy and excitement.

I absolutely loved it, but my double life was getting to be really difficult. I was DJing four nights a week and I started being late for work. When I did get there, bleary-eyed and half asleep, I was in no state to be an effective car salesman. I was also putting huge amounts of extra mileage on my Austin Mini company car. Another casualty was my relationship with Pat, which couldn't really withstand all the time I was spending at work, so we broke up without too much heartbreak on either side.

It was late one Friday afternoon when the imposing figure of my boss, Ben Martin, filled the doorway of my little glass-fronted office at the back of the showroom.

'This disc-jockey business can't go on, you know,' he said abruptly. 'I'm not happy with your timekeeping and a salesman has to be available to go and visit customers at any time, including evenings.' Then he came out with the classic phrase that will always stay with me. 'One man cannot serve two masters.'

Oh, is that so, I thought.

'You are going to have to make a decision. Do you want a good secure future in the motor trade, or are you going to waste your life messing around with this disc-jockey business?' There was complete disdain in his voice as he spoke the words 'disc jockey'.

'I'll give you two weeks to think about it,' said Mr Martin.

'I don't need two weeks,' I said. 'I can give you the answer right now.'

'Oh yes? And what is it?'

'I'm going to be a DJ, thank you very much.'

'Don't be such a bloody fool. You have a very bright future in the motor trade and you could end up managing a Patrick Motors garage one day.'

I could see that despite his gruff exterior, Ben Martin had a genuine fondness for me and was concerned about my future. But it was April 1966 and I had just reached the age of twenty-one. The day after my birthday I had sat gazing out of the showroom window, thinking once more that there must be more to life than this. I'd looked at my sales colleagues and thought: I don't want to end up like you. It wasn't the future I wanted for myself. So Ben Martin's ultimatum had come at a time when I knew something had to change.

'My mind's made up,' I told him. 'Would you like me to work a week's notice?'

'There's no need,' he snapped. 'You can go right now. Clear your desk and give me the keys to your car.'

Oh shit, I thought. I wasn't expecting this. I've really done it now. My dad is going to go ballistic and I'm not going to have a car to get to my gigs over the weekend.

And more to the point, how the fuck am I going to get home?

Chapter Eight

1966

The next day was Saturday and for the first time in ages I didn't have to be in the showroom, selling cars to customers, so after the unaccustomed luxury of a lie in, I wandered up to the newsagent's, and – unusually – bought a copy of the *Daily Mirror*. Reading through it at home, I was fascinated by a piece about a new pirate radio station. According to the article, an American team was going to come over to the UK and set up a brand-new station called Radio England, staffed by top-flight American Top Forty jocks. They claimed that they were going to show other stations like Radio Caroline and Radio London just how Top Forty radio should be done.

'We're going to blast them out of the water!' they boasted.

Radio Caroline had started broadcasting from a ship moored off the Essex coast two years earlier, in 1964. It had been founded by Irish businessman Ronan O'Rahilly and named after the daughter of President Kennedy. O'Rahilly had been returning from the US one day and he happened to see a picture in the *New York Times* of President Kennedy in the Oval Office, surrounded by his staff. Also in the picture was his little daughter, Caroline, playing on the floor, grinning and obviously disrupting things. O'Rahilly decided that was the image he wanted for his radio station. The appeal of Radio Caroline lay in the amount of pop music it was able to broadcast at a time when there was no other radio station – and certainly no legal station – offering what the music-loving public wanted, and it had become very popular.

The first ship from which Radio Caroline broadcast didn't have a powerful enough transmitter to cover the British Isles, and the station merged with a competitor. The original vessel moved to the Isle of Man and became Radio Caroline North, while the second ship, the *Mi Amigo*, remained anchored off the Essex coast and became Radio Caroline South.

Radio Caroline coming on the air was front-page news. The press and the politicians were absolutely outraged – how did anyone dare broadcast illegally over the British Isles? Tony Benn was postmaster general at the time and led the campaign against the pirate radio stations. But young people loved it because, for the first time ever, we could hear music all day. I hung a long piece of wire out of my bedroom window so that I could pick up the new station, but I still found it hard to get Radio Caroline. Birmingham was just about the worst place in England to listen to pirate radio, as it was bang in the middle of the country and as far away as you could get from the signal. I mostly listened to Radio London during the day and sometimes got Radio Caroline at night; I was a huge fan of the pirate radio stations right from the start.

Radio London had also started in 1964 and was also broadcast from off the south-eastern coast of England, but this time from a US minesweeper. It was created by American Don Pierson, who saw a huge opportunity in the small number of radio stations serving the British population, especially when compared to the number of successful stations broadcasting just to the state of Texas, where he lived. So he founded Radio London, a commercial radio station that broadcast music shows all day, and it proved a huge hit with the listeners.

Now it looked as though a brand-new station was about to hit the airwaves. Interesting timing, I thought. Here was I, without gainful employment and looking to make good my declaration that I was going to be a pirate radio disc jockey. And here was a pirate radio station, getting ready to go. The only problem was that all the DJs were going to be American.

That evening I had my usual Saturday-night gig at the Navigation Inn. It was a really brilliant place. People travelled miles to those weekend gigs, which attracted a great crowd. The people who ran it were honest and friendly, the sound system was good, and it had a reputation as being the place to hear the very latest American soul and R&B records that you couldn't hear anywhere else. There was a wonderful little record shop in Shirley where I used to buy import records like Otis Redding's 'Respect', Wilson Pickett's 'In The Midnight Hour', and Willie Mitchell's 'That Driving Beat'.

My friend Graham had installed some great equipment and the DJ desk was tucked away in the corner up on its own little stage. The place would be packed with a couple of hundred people, all squashed together in one heaving mass as this fantastic music pounded out of the sound system. I'd never known an atmosphere like it. Another bonus was the constant stream of girls coming up to ask for their favourite record – the best-looking girls went to the Navigation. One of my favourites was Lesley. I used to dance with her during the breaks, when another DJ did his set. She was juicy and curvy with a lovely open face and a broad smile. It wasn't long before we were out in the car park, having one of those knee-trembler moments. The atmosphere at the Navigation somehow created a sense of liberation.

Towards the end of my gig that evening, as things started to wind down a bit, a guy I'd never seen before came up to the DJ desk and asked if he could have a few words.

'Did you read that article in the *Daily Mirror* today about the new pirate radio station?' he asked. 'You should apply for a job on that station because I think you're a really good DJ, too good to stay here.'

'Thank you very much. But they said they were going to be all American jocks.'

'No, don't pay any attention to that. They're bound to want one or two English guys.'

And with that he disappeared into the crowd.

Back at home, I reread the *Mirror* article a number of times, and wondered how I could find out more about this new station. There were direct quotes in the article so someone at the *Mirror* was going to know how to contact the station owners. First thing on Monday morning, I rang directory enquiries, got the *Mirror*'s number and eventually was put through to the journalist who had written the feature.

'Do you know how I can get in touch with somebody involved with this new station, Radio England?' I asked.

'There's an advance party over here setting it up, and they're staying at the Hilton Hotel,' said the journalist. 'Hold on a minute, I think I've got their room number in my notes . . .' There was a pause and then he came back on the line. 'They're staying in Suite 1017.'

'Thanks very much.'

I hung up. That was pretty easy, I thought. Now for the big call. Back to directory enquiries for the Hilton's number. I dialled it and asked for Suite 1017. An American voice answered.

'Hi, this is Larry Dean. Who's this?'

'My name's Peter Dee. I'm a top DJ in Birmingham, and I've read about your new radio station. I know you're going to have American DJs but I was just wondering if you might be looking for an English jock.'

'Funnily enough, we've just been talking about that and we *are* thinking of hiring a couple. Why don't you send us a tape, and we'll give it a listen?'

'Okay, I'll send one in.'

Then I thought . . . If I send my tape through the post, maybe it'll end up in the bin. But, I reminded myself, I don't have a day job any more. Why don't I just get on the train and deliver the tape personally?

I didn't have twin decks or a good-enough tape machine at home. Maybe my old mate Graham could help. I needed to get hold of him quickly – it was a shame that his radio-controlled van wasn't for real. I called his girlfriend, Linda, at Patrick Motors.

'I've got to reach Graham quickly. I'm hoping he can help me make up a tape. Have you any idea where he is?'

She did, and a couple of hours later he called and was willing to help. That night I went round to Graham's with a collection of my favourite records and we put a ten-minute tape together. He had the good sense to realize they wouldn't want to waste time listening to the records all the way through, so he did a good editing job and cut out the middle section of each track. By the end of the night we had a great tape and I went to bed with a heady sense of anticipation for what might happen the next day.

As the train pulled in to Paddington, the sight of those tightly packed apartment blocks alongside the track reminded me of the way I had felt on my way home from the disastrous Radio Luxembourg audition. Here we are again, I thought. I never guessed I'd be back here. Maybe this time it's going to be different. I certainly felt different – now I was experienced and had a good idea of what it meant to be a DJ for real. Nevertheless, I could feel some of my confidence evaporate as I walked into the swish Hilton reception. The man behind the desk looked up as I approached.

'My name is Peter Dee. I've come to see Larry Dean in Suite 1017.'

'Go on up,' said the receptionist. 'The lifts are over there.'

I stepped out of the lift to be faced with three long identical corridors. This swanky hotel on Park Lane was a whole new world to me and it was very intimidating. Eventually I found the right suite and, gathering together all the confidence I could muster, pressed the doorbell.

A man answered and invited me into a huge sitting room with three guys sitting around, talking and smoking. The guy who'd answered the door introduced himself as Larry and the other two as Don and Gerry. They were very open and friendly. Then they looked at me expectantly.

'I didn't want to post my tape in case it got lost,' I explained. 'So I thought I'd bring it down.'

'Wow,' said one of them. 'Where have you come from?'

'Birmingham.'

'How far away is Burr-ming-ham?' The emphasis was on 'ham'.

'About three hundred and fifty miles,' I lied, banking on their knowledge of the UK not being too good.

'Tell us what experience you've got.'

I told them all about the various clubs I'd worked in, and then Larry asked, 'Can you read nuze?'

I hadn't been expecting this. It seemed that jocks in America often read the news whereas ours always came from strait-laced BBC announcers. I decided to be honest but confident.

'Well, I never have. But I'm sure I could.'

'Listen,' said Larry, 'take this newspaper into the bathroom and record on our cassette recorder.'

So I did. It was so bizarre. There I was, sitting on the lid of the loo in a luxurious Hilton suite, reading out a few paragraphs from a front-page news story into a cassette recorder.

When I took my tape back into the main room, they said, 'Why don't you go outside while we have a listen?'

I stood in the corridor for about ten minutes, and then Larry Dean opened the door and asked me back in.

'Have a seat,' he said pleasantly.

I looked around at their faces, trying to gauge what was going to happen next.

'Well, Peter Dee,' said Larry with a smile. 'We'd like to offer you a job on our new radio station. Welcome to Radio England.'

We stood up and, smiling broadly, they all shook my hand and said, 'Congratulations!'

Larry showed me to the door and said, 'We're going on air in May and we'll be in touch.'

Unbelievable. I walked along the corridor back to the lift at least twelve inches above the ground.

'I've done it! I've done it! I'm going to be a pirate radio disc jockey,' I said to myself.

It was the most amazing piece of good fortune. After quitting Patrick Motors I had told my dad I was going to be a pirate radio DJ and now, three days later, I was.

I strode back into the house feeling about ten feet tall. My mum asked how I got on.

'Not too bad, actually,' I replied.

'Well, come on. What happened?'

'They offered me a job, Mum. I'm going to be a DJ on Radio England and I'll be going out to the ship in May.'

'Oh, my God!' shrieked my mother, horrified. 'What on earth's going to become of you?'

Who cared? My dream had come true.

PART TWO
A Pirate's Life

Chapter Nine

Two Texans, Bill Vick and Don Pierson, knew there was a fortune to be made in pirate radio and they wanted to get a station on air in double-quick time, no matter what the cost. Although Don Pierson had been instrumental in setting up Radio London, it quickly took a different direction to the one he wanted and he was no longer associated with it. The idea behind this new station was that it would copy even more faithfully than Radio London the successful US formats, with short, sharp news bulletins every hour, the hits of the day on high rotation and American disc jockeys. It was going to be very new and very different and no one knew how a British audience would respond to it.

They bought an old freighter, the *Olga Patricia*, registered it in Panama and sailed it to Miami. They hired the best brains from Continental Electronics and told them they wanted to put two radio stations on the ship with a combined power of 100,000 watts. One was to be called Swingin' Radio England with the latest Top Forty format to attract the young people and the other, Britain Radio, was to be an easy-listening, middle-of-the-road station for an older audience.

They built the studios and transmitters into prefabricated structures and then lowered them into the forward hold of the ship. They hired a number of American DJs, telling them that they were going to make a fortune in England and that they would live in complete luxury on board as the ship was like a floating Hilton Hotel. Some of the jocks even went as far as selling their houses and putting their furniture on the ship ready for their new life of wealth and luxury. After all, England was making quite an impression stateside. The Beatles and all the other English bands that followed were conquering America. Roger Miller had a hit single with 'England Swings' and there was no doubt that England was the place to be.

Ever since the pirate radio stations had started up, there'd been a lot of negative press about them and the government was still proclaiming its intention to drive them off the air. Everybody in power was against them, even the record industry. Sir Joseph Lockwood, head of EMI, was convinced that playing records constantly on the radio would damage sales, and was determined to help get rid of the stations. It was not exactly the best form of job security in the world.

My parents didn't know quite what to think when I explained to them what I'd be doing. My mum had become a Conservative councillor and was aware of the government's attitude to the pirate stations. Now I had got myself a job on one of them and she was shocked that her son was about to become so anti-establishment. Neither of my parents had ever listened to pirate radio. Nevertheless, despite their shock, I think my parents were impressed at what I'd managed to pull off and secretly admired my cheek.

While I waited impatiently for May and my new life to begin, I carried on doing my usual gigs at the Carlton Ballroom and the Navigation Inn. As May approached, I called up the Radio England HQ to get the latest news and they suggested I come down to London to meet up with the rest of the team.

Their plush offices were on the ground floor of an impressive Regency building at 32 Curzon Street, Mayfair. That seemed to be the home for pirate radio: the offices of Radio London were across the road and Radio Caroline was just round the corner in Chesterfield Gardens. It was obviously important to have an impressive set-up to woo potential advertisers, the music business and the media, and clearly no expense had been spared. As a naive 21-year-old from Birmingham, I found this whole new world incredibly exciting. I remember having a hamburger at the Wimpy Bar on Park Lane, just between the Playboy Club and the Hilton, thinking I had really made the big time.

At the offices I met up with the smiling Bill and Don, the

founders of the station, and was introduced to all the staff and two other English DJs, Roger Day and Brian Tylney, who had been hired just before I was. Bill and Don told us there'd been a slight problem with the ship, repairs were being done and soon it would be anchoring in the North Sea. We'd be going on air in just a few weeks' time. In the meantime, they'd set up a small makeshift studio, and head DJ and programme director Ron O'Quinn excitedly invited us to, 'Come and have a listen to this!'

Ron was the first American I really got to know. He was slim and fit with a short crew cut, great eyes and was so full of energy his knee was constantly bouncing up and down. He smoked king-sized Pall Malls from a soft pack, wore a silver ID bracelet and had the most fantastic American accent. I was completely in awe of him. He put a spool of tape on the machine and I heard a Liverpudlian voice say, 'Hi, this is John Lennon and you're listening to Swingin' Radio England.'

'I've got the other Beatles as well,' said Ron, 'and we got them to do IDs for all you guys. I'll play them to you when we get on the ship.'

Ron also played us some of the Radio England jingles, which were so much better than the ones on Radio Caroline or London. They sounded incredibly professional and like nothing I'd ever heard before. We were all very impressed and really began to feel that this station was going to be something special, and perhaps that we were even going to become famous.

Some of our terms of employment were explained to us. We would work two weeks on board ship and then have one week off. Our pay was £25 a week, including the week we weren't working. I thought that was a good deal – for one thing, there would be nothing to spend money on when we were on board and all our meals were included. There was nothing to sign and it was all agreed by word of mouth, but that was fine with me. I'd never had a job contract anyway and, after all, this was pirate radio.

We went out afterwards to the Red Lion pub in a mews just off Curzon Street and I got to know the other English DJs. Brian Tylney was a bingo caller from Southend and I never found out how he got a job on Radio England. Roger Day had been, like me, a part-time evening DJ, balancing that with his day job as an accountant. He'd been told that a new radio station run by some Americans was recruiting, so he'd got himself along to the Hilton even before I'd got there, and bagged himself a job.

In contrast to this Mayfair excess, I was staying at a hotel I'd been recommended called the Madison in Sussex Gardens, Bayswater. I'd been told it was the rock 'n' roll hotel, and all the groups stayed there. Actually it was mostly full of people who, like me, weren't earning much money, and it was just about the cheapest place in London. The rooms were very basic and someone had nicked the plugs to my washbasin and bath. But it was fun staying there as there was a great atmosphere and there were loads of cheap places to eat near Paddington station, which was just around the corner.

Over the next few weeks, I divided my time between Birmingham and London. Whenever I contacted the office to find out when we were going to be joining the ship and beginning our broadcasts, it was always 'everything's fine' or 'any day now'. It was my first experience of Americans' great talent for optimistic bullshit. They'd much rather tell you a good-news lie than a bad-news truth. One day, I called Radio England again and spoke to Ron O'Quinn.

He gave me the usual assurances and then said, 'By the way, we want you to use a different name. We've got Roger *Day* and to have a Peter *Dee* on the station could be confusing to the listeners. Besides which, we've got some great jingles already made up that you'll be able to use. There's a terrific one for a DJ called Johnnie Walker, so we think you should call yourself that.'

I was shocked into silence.

Then I heard Ron say, 'It's quite the usual thing in America for the radio station to give the DJ their name.'

I mumbled, 'Okay, Ron.'

'Good. Johnnie Walker it is.'

'Fine by me. See you soon.'

It was as simple as that – I was now Johnnie Walker. It never occurred to me to say no, that I didn't want to change my name. The high-energy American attitude with its unshakeable faith in itself was impossible to resist. It was going to be the way Ron said, and that was that.

I felt mixed emotions. For one thing, how would my friends know it was me? They were expecting to hear the Peter Dee show, not the Johnnie Walker show. Although they would recognize my voice, it felt as though someone else was going to be on the radio intead of me. It took some of the gloss off the excitement and made the whole thing even more unreal.

I found out later that Larry Dean had brought a selection of jingles from his New York radio station; they were slick and impressive and nothing like anything heard in the UK. For the Americans, the jingles were an important part of the station sound and it was more professional for DJs to have their own jingles. It was lucky for me that Ron chose the one he did. I could have been Boom Boom Brannigan.

All things considered, Johnnie Walker seemed to be a pretty good name.

Chapter Ten

1966

Finally the great day arrived: the call came for me to go down to the ship.

I packed my bag, feeling huge excitement and anticipation, and went down to the London office, where I met up with the other DJs. Brian and Roger were there, along with the American DJs Larry Dean and Ron O'Quinn. There were also two Australians, Colin Nicol and Graham Gill. Two more American DJs, Rick Randall and Jerry Smethwick, were waiting for us on board, having crossed over on the ship from Miami. We Brits were the only ones without any broadcasting experience. We all travelled to Felixstowe and booked into a hotel overlooking the sea. It was a grey, gloomy, damp day and, as I looked out of the rain-soaked windows, the reality of working on a pirate station was looking decidedly less glamorous than I'd imagined.

While the organization in London had appeared energetic, brash and full of confidence, it seemed that the detailed planning was given scant regard. Colin Nicol was a DJ who'd worked on board ship in the early days of Radio Caroline, and he had now joined Radio England as an adviser and to bring a little of the Caroline magic with him. But all the valuable advice he offered was ignored. He asked our bosses what they'd done about fenders alongside the ship – both Caroline and London had a string of enormous tractor tyres running down each side of the ship. Colin said that without those, the *Olga Patricia* would bash the hell out of the small supply boat, known as the tender, that made daily journeys with crew and supplies. But it appeared that no one in charge thought that mattered very much and the *Olga Patricia* remained fenderless.

It was with a real sense of trepidation that Roger Day, Brian Tylney, Colin Nicol, Graham Gill and myself, along with the American DJs, climbed on board the tender for our first trip out to Swingin' Radio England. The sea was really rough, and most of us were feeling very seasick by the time we approached the ship an hour and a half later. Gradually, out of the mist, I could see three radio ships, spaced about half a mile apart, where the *Mi Amigo*, *Galaxy* and *Olga Patricia*, the homes of Radios Caroline, London and England, were moored. I'd listened all those miles away in Birmingham and now here were the actual stations, right in front of me. It was an amazing feeling.

The tender came alongside the *Olga Patricia*, bouncing its way through the stormy waters and, sure enough, there were no rubber tyres to provide protection for our vessel. The sea was still very rough and the captain of the tender said it was too dangerous to come alongside so that we were close enough to board. He was persuaded to give it a try but every time he got close to *Olga*, the huge swell crashed the tender into her sides with a sickening, wrenching scream of metal against metal. On the deck of the tender, we clung on for dear life, our faces, white with seasickness, showing genuine fear.

By now the bows of the tender were badly dented and Colin Nicol was muttering, 'I told them, I told them but they wouldn't listen.'

'I try once more,' said the Dutch captain, 'but only for two minutes.'

As the waves lifted the tender up to its highest point, our bags were hurled on to the *Olga*'s flat deck. Now it was our turn to leap on board. I looked down at the chasm between the two bows and the sea between, swirling and boiling with rage. One slip and it would be all over; what a horrible way to die. This was a huge test of our courage and commitment to pirate radio – we weren't even wearing life jackets. I stood on the narrow edge that topped the side of the tender's deck and hung on to one of the metal hawsers that supported the mast. The swell rose to its peak and, concentrating on the *Olga*'s deck, I leapt as far as I could, arms outstretched to grab the hands of the crew. The tender crashed down into the trough of the wave fifteen feet below me and I was yanked on board. I'd made it. My God, that was the most frightening experience I'd ever had.

One by one, the rest of us successfully got on board and gradually the colour returned to our faces as we sipped hot coffee in the ship's mess room. None of us had expected anything quite so terrifying but we all grinned and joked as if it was nothing and we hadn't just risked our lives getting on board – the usual bullshit male bravado. We were all keen to explore the ship, especially the studios. We were introduced to Rick Randall, one of the American DJs who'd crossed the Atlantic on board and already knew the ship well. He led the way as we clambered down a metal ladder into the vast engine room. A narrow walkway took us past the engine and we stepped through a hatch, across a smaller space housing generators and other equipment, through another water-tight hatch and into a vast, cavernous hold. It was dank, smelly and gloomy, not at all as I had imagined.

In front of us was a white prefabricated room sitting on wooden blocks. Rick led the way up small wooden steps and opened the door. Inside were two gleaming 50,000 watt transmitters manufac-tured by Continental Electronics.

'These babies are the best there is. They're gonna give us a fantastic signal.'

He led us through another bulkhead and watertight door into a second hold up in the bows, which housed the two studios. He swung open the door and ushered us in. On the right-hand side was a rack of various pieces of equipment and on the left a small DJ desk with a very professional-looking mixer with lots of knobs and buttons. This was all very new to us English DJs.

Lifting up what looked like an old-fashioned eight-track music cartridge, Rick said, 'These are what we call carts. They'll have all our jingles and commercials on. I'd play them to you now but I haven't quite finished wiring it all up. I've been working on this stuff all the way from Miami.'

Winding our way back through the hatches and engine room,

we climbed back up to deck level, to a small, dark and completely empty windowless hold.

'This is where you guys are going to sleep.'

But there're no beds! I thought.

'We've got a load of really tough sleeping bags we're gonna sling on the floor. It's only temporary. We're gonna fix up something better as soon as we can,' said Ron, seeing our expressions.

One of the others nudged me and said quietly, 'Hey, have you heard the rumour? Apparently this ship was used by the US navy for bringing back dead GIs from the Korean War. And this is where they stored the body bags.'

It gave me the chills just to think of it. But this was only the first and biggest of many shocks those first few days had in store for me. Half the original Miami crew had jumped ship in Lisbon, so the management had recruited (or maybe press-ganged) some of the roughest-looking guys I'd ever seen. None of them spoke any English, they didn't really want to be there, and they looked at us DJs with complete disdain.

There were almost twenty of us on board, ten on the radio side including the engineers. The rest were the crew and captain. The living quarters were about as far from the Hilton as it was possible to imagine. Apart from our empty, bedless sleeping hold, there was a big washroom which we all shared, and that was about it as far as the facilities went. The food was terrible – our dinner, prepared by a terrifying-looking cook, was greasy and full of fatty chunks of questionable meat and foul-tasting cabbage.

Once the seasickness had subsided (and thank goodness we were only affected by that when on the tender), I began to feel a deep sense of disappointment. As we settled down for that first unpleasant night in our chilly sleeping bags, I couldn't help feeling cheated; the vision of a warm, comfortable ship filled with every luxury had been completely dashed. The obvious hardship that lay ahead suddenly seemed a big price to pay for being a DJ.

When I woke up the next morning, things didn't seem a great deal brighter. For one thing, it became clear that we had come out too early. The equipment wasn't ready and no one had any idea when we'd start broadcasting. Until then, we'd have to endure boredom along with all the other misery. I couldn't believe that the DJs on the other ships had to live like this, but it was obvious that we were paying the price for the impatient rush to get the ship ready as soon as possible. For a start, the vessel itself wasn't really suited to its new role and the whole thing had been put together in about four months. Now the management were talking about hiring carpenters to come out and build bunks for us. They'd also realized that they had to get huge tyres for the side of the ship, all of which was so much more difficult once it was out at sea.

There were sizable technical problems, too. Every time the engineers tried to get the transmitters anywhere near full power, there'd be a mini thunderstorm at the top of the mast. With a deafeningly loud crack and a massive arcing flash of electricity, one of the main hawsers holding up the mast would crash to the deck. An engineer from the States was flown out to try and fix it. He was as hard as nails, lived on Budweisers and Marlboros, and would stand in front of the transmitter cranking up the power as the other engineers ran for cover.

I just couldn't understand why we'd been brought out to the ship when it patently wasn't anywhere near ready to go on air. But then, the delay did give Roger, Brian and me time to learn how to use the equipment and to rehearse dummy radio shows over and over again. We had the most professionally produced jingle package of all the pirate stations, better than anything I'd heard before. They'd been produced by the famous PAMS production company in Dallas. My jingle was originally recorded using a sono vox voice distorter and it gave a unique sound unlike anything DJs on other stations had, producing a deep, reverberating voice that half sang my name: '*John-nie Waaalk-aah.*' It was to become a famous signature ident.

Ron O'Quinn had worked for W-FUN in Miami and their 'fun radio' format was combined with the 'boss radio' style from K-HJ in Los Angeles. We were to be known as the 'boss jocks', had to have a permanent smile on our faces and shout in a real high-energy style. The term 'boss radio' would mean nothing to English listeners but in America it was another way of saying: 'We're the best.' Which was a pretty outrageous claim, seeing as how we hadn't even got on the air yet. I wasn't sure if the high-octane 'boss' style was going to be a hit with the British listeners. They were all used to a much quieter, subtle style, with DJs talking rather than shouting. When I heard Larry doing his thing, it was quite overwhelming: he talked at enormous speed and volume, breaking up his patter with jingles and noises and changing subject constantly. But it was exhilarating and certainly different.

One by one the various problems were solved and, after two weeks on board, we were ready to do a test transmission. The idea was for each DJ to do twenty minutes so that we would all get a turn. We'd be talking live, each one taking over from the next as their turn came. Ron O'Quinn's was going to be the first voice ever broadcast from our new station.

On 16th May 1966, we all gathered round the small radio in the tiny mess room and at two p.m., Swingin' Radio England finally came on air for its test transmission. Downstairs in the studio, Ron was giving it his all with his upbeat, American style.

'This is a brand-new station for the British Isles! Swingin' Radio England – where we play much more music.'

After every sentence he played another one of our great jingles: *'You Get A Positive Charge, Here On Swingin' Radio England.'*

Then Ron said: 'Swingin' Radio England – this is a brand-new sound for the British Isles.'

'The Boss Jocks, Bop, Bop, Play More Music – Pow!'

'Hi, this is Ron on the radio. If you're hearing this test transmission, please send us a reception report to Swingin' Radio England, 32 Curzon Street, London W1, England.'

'Swingin' Radio England, Bop, Bop, Where The Action Is!'

It sounded great, just like a real radio station. After Ron came Larry Dean, Rick Randall and Jerry Smethwick. Then it was the turn of us Brits. I was absolutely quaking in my boots. I was to go on the radio for the very first time. Unlike my first night at the

Locarno Ballroom, this audience was invisible, but Ron and the others would, of course, be listening to every word, and we were all desperate to impress them.

I went down, took my seat in front of the desk – and then I was off, talking live over the airwaves for the first time in my life. It was a fantastic feeling to play some of my favourite records and then switch on the microphone, knowing that my voice was being broadcast all over the south-east of England, France, Belgium and Holland. I think I did pretty well for my first time on air. I didn't sound as nervous as I felt, though I was a bit stiff and didn't say a great deal between the records. My one bloomer was a slight confusion in giving out the address for reception reports. I asked listeners to send a letter or postcard to Radio London, 32 Curzon Street, England, instead of Radio England, 32 Curzon Street, London. I was mortified with embarrassment at being the only one of the Brits to make such a mistake.

After we'd all done our twenty minutes the test transmission came to an end and after the long weeks of waiting and the bitter disappointment about the state of the ship, we all shared feelings of elation and great excitement. The engineers seemed pleased that no more guy lines had come crashing down from the antennae, but they did have to rope off sections of the deck around the base of the mast, which glowed hot from the huge amount of radiated power. We used to joke that our hair would fall out, we'd be rendered sterile and probably get cancer one day.

The next morning over breakfast we tuned the mess radio in to Caroline and London to see if either of them would acknowledge their brash new rival. Neither of them gave us a mention, but we were totally astonished to hear all our new jingles being played. They had been recorded, spliced and edited to fit the names of Caroline and London.

Ron was apoplectic with rage: 'Those fucking bastards, they've ripped off our entire jingle package!'

This was true radio piracy, and there was absolutely nothing we could do about it. When we eventually started regular broadcasting a few days later we were inundated with hate mail accusing us of being brash, cocky and being low enough to steal Radio London's and Radio Caroline's brand-new jingles. The listeners would never know that they were actually ours in the first place.

The DJ rota scheduled the professional American jocks from six a.m. to six p.m., and then Roger and Brian did three hours each. My shift was from midnight right the way through to six a.m. Then I had a three-hour news shift reading bulletins on the hour and half-hour on Radio England and Britain Radio.

By this time, carpenters had been working to build bunks in the bow of the ship just in front of the studios. There was no ventilation or light and the air was dank and foul-smelling. There weren't enough bunks for all of us so we had to hot swap: as one DJ got up, another one got into the same bed. I would try and grab two or three hours' sleep after my news shift, then get up to have some food at lunchtime, and then try and get a little more rest in the afternoon. Sleep was very difficult as members of the crew would pass their time banging and chipping away at rust spots on the deck above my head.

Although two radio stations were working around the clock, the crew worked a normal day, and there was no back-up at all for those who worked through the night. During my shift I was usually the only one awake – apart from maybe one of the engineers, who'd be up late drinking coffee. It took about three minutes to dash from the studio through the generator and engine rooms and up the ladder to where the mess deck and galley were. The only way to get a cup of tea or coffee was to find a long record such as Bob Dylan's 'Like A Rolling Stone'.

Before long, I was totally knackered by this huge workload, and at about three o'clock one morning listeners heard Roy Orbison's 'In Dreams' come to an end followed by a few seconds' silence, and then the ker-chunk, ker-chunk sound of the turntable stylus up against the end of the groove. Roy's wonderful dreamy love song had sent me off into a deep sleep. I was absolutely dead to the world.

After two weeks' broadcasting, it was time for my week's leave.

By now the rubber tyres had been hung on massive chains alongside the ship, the seas were much calmer and the leap on to the tender was a lot less scary and dangerous than when I'd first come on board. We used the same Dutch company that supplied Caroline and London and on the way back to Felixstowe we stopped off alongside Radio London.

All their DJs were lined up on the deck to see what these Radio England blokes looked like and I heard Kenny Everett shout out, 'Thank Johnnie Walker for the plug!'

He'd remembered how I'd mixed up Radio London and Radio England, and I had to relive the embarrassment of my first on-air mistake all over again.

Chapter Eleven

After all the problems of getting on air and coming to terms with the dreadful living conditions, we soon settled down to life as pirate radio DJs. With a rota of two weeks on and one week off, and our £25 per week, things were not bad at all. Once we were off the ship, we could have a pretty good time in London with £75 to spend. The Red Lion pub, tucked away in a little mews behind Curzon Street, where I'd first gone with Brian and Roger after we'd met, became the regular pirate pub. Despite the rivalry on air, there was mutual respect and camaraderie with the other pirate jocks and the riotous late-night drinking sessions at the Lion became legendary. I got to know DJs such as Duncan Johnson, Dave Cash, Mike Lennox and Tony Windsor from Radio London and Mike Ahern, Dave Lee Travis and Tony Prince from Radio Caroline. I liked them all and appreciated the sense of our being comrades, but they were still the big and famous guys and we Radio England jocks were just small fry in comparison. There was no way our station was competing with the big boys yet.

My week's leave would flash by and then it was time to return to the ship, now renamed the *Laissez Faire*. I had mixed feelings about going back: life on board was physically hard but I loved my job. I learnt so much about radio in those early days. You can rehearse till you're blue in the face in an off-air studio but it's the actual live on-air situation that builds skill and experience. Making mistakes and learning how to recover and get out of them without embarrassing myself or my listener was something I could only glean by actually doing it for real.

Besides that, working six hours a day on air was an opportunity I couldn't get on land. It was virtually impossible to get a show on the BBC or Radio Luxembourg – and if you did, you'd be lucky to get more than an hour or two a week, and even then it would probably be recorded. It would take years to get the experience and radio education I was getting in a matter of weeks. Ron O'Quinn was my hero and I watched and listened to everything he did. It was Ron who taught me one of the most important lessons of the American style of radio: never use plurals.

'Talk to one person,' said Ron. 'Make them feel you're doing the show just for them. Never start a show with words like "ladies and gentlemen" or "boys and girls" – that just reminds them they're one of thousands. Just come on and say, "Hi, how are you?"'

I worked really hard on perfecting that technique and was rewarded with letters that read: 'It feels like you're talking just to me.' I still had to use the house style of presenting, though, and that meant a strong, fast patter with a big smile in my voice that was never allowed to falter. We had to use American DJ-speak: big, brash and non-stop. It didn't quite feel right to me, but I did my best. It seemed to appeal to quite a lot of people because, almost at once, letters started to arrive from listeners. It was great receiving letters. It was confirmation that someone, somewhere was actually listening to us. Shut up in a ship and miles offshore, we often felt very isolated. There was no way of having contact with anyone except through the written word and the letters gave me a really important sense that what I was doing was worthwhile. They were friendly – some had requests for records to be played, and others were fan letters. Our audience might still be small, but it definitely seemed to be fond of us.

It was a very strange experience reading letters from complete strangers who wrote as though they knew me. Not only that, but they were addressed to 'Johnnie', my new alter ego. But I was beginning to get accustomed to my new persona; right from the start, everyone connected with Radio England and on board had called me Johnnie and not Peter. I was starting to feel at home with my new name, and there was something quite fitting about it. After all, Peter was that shy, shut-off, acne-ridden teenager who lived in Birmingham, whereas Johnnie was a pirate radio DJ, with endless, smooth patter and complete confidence. I knew who I would rather be.

Only my letters from home reminded me of my other life. My mum still wrote to me as Peter, and my family would never call me Johnnie, partly because my brother's name was John. It was good to hear how things were going back in Solihull and I wrote back occasionally, but my focus now was completely on my new life and the excitement of being on the radio. Besides, I didn't want to tell everyone back home about the harsh reality of living on board ship. They thought I was aboard the equivalent of the Hilton Hotel, after all, and I had no desire to shatter their illusions.

Roger 'Twiggy' Day, as he called himself on air, was also learning fast, and gradually he and I started to generate more mail than the American jocks, which was extremely gratifying. The third member of the original raw British contingent, Brian Tylney, wasn't faring so well, however. He was getting more and more morose and depressed. He saw how Roger and I were learning fast, improving with each show, and feeling keen and excited before going on air. Brian still felt physically sick before every show. As hard as he tried, he just couldn't overcome his nerves or get to feel at home on the radio. For Brian, the misery of North Sea life was compounded by his dread of having to face that microphone every day. Eventually he couldn't take it any more and decided to go. Having made his decision, Brian was much happier that it was all over and he went back to calling out the numbers at a bingo hall in Southend.

It wasn't working out for the owners of Radio England, Pier Vick Ltd, either. Don Pierson and Bill Vick's bold adventure to come to the UK and make a fortune in pirate radio was failing badly. It had all looked so good and so simple on paper: buy a cheap, used US navy freighter; fit it out in double-quick time to save expenses and put two stations on board to double the advertising revenue; get some glamorous offices in Mayfair to impress clients and hire top advertising agents Pearl & Dean to sell out the air time that would bring the cash rolling in. After all, we didn't pay any performance or copyright fees for the records we broadcast. It should be easy to make money.

In practice it was all very different. Radios Caroline, London and others around the coast of the UK had already established their audience and it seemed that listeners weren't taking to our style as much as the management had hoped they would. We had our fans but the majority of listeners weren't keen on the brash, confident, hard-sell DJs, and somehow Radio England just wasn't striking a chord with the British audience.

That's if they could hear the station at all. Swingin' Radio England was at the clearer part of the dial on 355 metres and Britain Radio was down at the crowded end on 227 metres. Neither station had a good, clear reception and at night-time, when the ionosphere lowers and medium-wave signals bounce great distances, Radio England was affected by the Pope's massive station, Vatican Radio. As Britain Radio's easy-listening format only had one main rival in Radio 390, it was decided that Britain Radio should swap frequencies with Radio England. Britain Radio was now on 355 metres, near its easy-listening rival, so that the casual listener might stumble upon Britain Radio while trying to find Radio 390.

You'd think it would be easy to change the frequencies over by simply re-routing the audio output of each station to the opposite transmitter – but no. Pier Vick's high-tech solution was to swap studios. The problem now was that all the dedicated equipment to enable Britain Radio to operate on auto-pilot through the night was in the Radio England studio. And Radio England was now on 227 metres, which was a crappy frequency with other stations all over it, especially during the hours of darkness. This was typical of the way the organization was run and led to huge frustration and very low morale for us on the ship.

Our small audience was now under threat and listening figures dropped further. This was another set-back for the fledgling station. Swingin' Radio England's lack of good audience ratings meant very few commercials were sold. Pearl & Dean, who had a world-wide reputation as being the market leaders in cinema advertising, had very little experience of commercial radio selling. Although we didn't realize it at the time, Radio England was being kept alive financially by God. The religious programme, *The World Tomorrow*, presented by Garner Ted Armstrong, ran every evening at six p.m. and we hated it. If anything was guaranteed to lose what little audience we had, it was Garner Ted. We would put the tape on to one of our vertical Scully broadcast-quality tape machines and then go up to the mess deck and leave him to it. None of us would bother to listen in so we didn't know that most nights he never finished his half-hour show. *The World Tomorrow* organization in the States was a huge operation and tapes were sent to hundreds of stations all over the world. To save money, they were sent out on small seven-inch spools using cheap Mylar recording tape. It was thin tape that would constantly stick as it wound off the spool; the sensitive Scully tape machine would sense the loss of tension and simply stop. That would be the end of Garner Ted for the evening and we'd be broadcasting silence until the end of the half-hour, when one of us DJs would pick up again.

Furious memos from London arrived on board informing us that if it happened again, Garner Ted would cancel the deal and that could mean the end of Swingin' Radio England. That night, after fast-forwarding and rewinding the tape a number of times to get rid of the stickiness, Rick Randall reverentially placed the spool on the machine. At 5.59 p.m. we knelt before the Scully as Rick led us in prayer.

'Please, God, bless this tape machine. Keep Garner Ted going to the end and don't let him stick.'

Whether it was the preparation of the tape or divine intervention, *The World Tomorrow* ran its full half-hour with the all-important plugs for books at the end of the programme.

Many times, one or other or both stations would be off the air due to yet another technical problem. We all hated being on ship when we weren't broadcasting. The whole atmosphere changed to one of gloom and despondency. When the mast was radiating our signals, the ship had power and vibrancy. It was alive with energy and purpose and it was easy to tolerate the hardships of life on board. Off air, the ship became a rusty, claustrophobic old hulk and all I ever wanted during those times was to be far away from it and back on land.

Once, a generator problem caused us to be off the air for three days. Late in the evening on day two, I went down to England's studio to while away the time practising on the Collins DJ board, which was the console we used. I climbed down the steps, pulled open the door and was blasted by music at full volume. It was dark apart from the illuminated buttons and dials of the equipment.

Ron was sitting in the broadcast chair, his face lit by the glow of the twin VU meters on the console. He was playing The Righteous Brothers at maximum volume. I could sense Ron's disappointment and regret that this pirate radio adventure hadn't fulfilled its promise. He'd been a top jock in the major radio market of Miami, Florida. Come to England, they had said, home of the Beatles, the grooviest and hippest place on the planet. You'll be living in luxury on a floating Hilton, the radio audience will love you, there'll be exciting weeks off in London where you'll be fêted and adored. None of it was happening. Americans love success; they don't do failure very well.

With his melancholy lifting, but still thinking of home, Ron made a suggestion.

'Johnnie, when we go back to the States, why don't you come with us? You've learnt fast and developed your on-air talent really well. With a bit of training and experience in a small town, you could really make it as a Top Forty jock in a major market.'

'You really think so?' I was surprised and, of course, flattered. After all the criticism and put-downs at home and school, I found the praise difficult to accept but enjoyed the warm feeling all the same. 'I'm not all that good.'

'You should give it some thought, Johnnie. With your accent, they'd love you in America.'

A seed was planted.

Chapter Twelve

My life took on a regular pattern: two weeks on board ship and then one week off on shore leave. I spent most of my time off in London. Occasionally I went back home to see my family and friends, but it was a strange experience. I felt as though I had left the world of Solihull and the Monday-night discos and Friday-night dances far behind me now and there was little calling me back. Instead, London was where everything seemed to be happening and where the pirate radio scene was buzzing.

When I was on shore, I stayed at the Madison, drank at the Red Lion with my new family of pirate radio DJs, and started finding my way around the place. I was introduced to some wonderful clubs, like the Speakeasy, the Cromwellian, the Bag of Nails and Revolution, places with fantastic musicians and even better music. I was partying and living it up, enjoying some of my new-found confidence by chatting up girls and spending my wages. The last night of our leave was always the one we partied hardest. From the incredibly vibrant London scene, I'd find myself back on the boat, with only crew, engineers and fellow DJs for company, cut off from the world again, except for the magic of my microphone, which took me into thousands of homes and cars every night.

By September 1966 Swingin' Radio England had been on the air, most of the time, for four months and hadn't made any significant dent in the audience figures for Radios Caroline and London, who were still the market leaders in the South of England. Radio Caroline was the original pirate station and, despite Radio London's more powerful transmitter and professional approach, for me, Caroline was still the best. It was a bit like the Beatles and Rolling Stones. London was the Beatles, slick and neat and the radio station you could take home to your mother for tea. Caroline was definitely the Rolling Stones, scruffy, anarchic, non-conformist and rebellious. Radio Caroline had soul. It was there to give freedom and expression to the creative artistic explosion that was the sixties. To me, Radio London was a radio station that just happened to be on a ship in the North Sea.

Imagine my delight when, going on shore leave one day, as the tender drew alongside the Caroline ship on its way back to Harwich, I heard DJ Mike Ahern shout, 'Tell that Johnnie Walker we love his show. He should come and work for us!'

The daily visit by the tender was one of the high spots of our day. It would arrive around lunchtime with supplies of food and water, new records and stuff from the office in London, letters from home and the day's newspapers. It was one blustery October day just after the tender had arrived when, quite by chance, I picked up a copy of the *East Anglian Times*, scanned the front page and turned it over to the back page. A tiny news item at the bottom of the page caught my eye. The small headline read: PIRATE SHIP TO BROADCAST TO HOLLAND. The story was only one paragraph long and the pivotal sentence read: 'One of the two stations on board the *Laissez Faire* is to change formats and broadcast to Holland in a bid to attract Dutch advertising revenue.'

I was instantly alert. One of our stations was changing formats. I started thinking fast. It was unlikely to be Britain Radio – its easy-listening, middle-of-the-road style had little competition on the airwaves. So that meant it had to be Radio England. And if Radio England was now going to be broadcasting to Holland, that would mean Dutch DJs and no further requirement for any of the English jocks.

I saw immediately that if we were all about to be sacked, there was going to be one hell of a queue for jobs outside Radio Caroline and Radio London. I rushed back to the tender, which was still making its delivery, and asked the captain how much longer he was going to be alongside.

'I go in about ten minutes,' was the reply.

I rushed down to the bunk area in the bow of the ship and packed my stuff into my bag, including a tape of a recent air-check of my show. Just before I left, I glanced around the hot, cramped cabin where I'd been spending my nights for the last five months.

This is it, I thought. I'm never going to see this place again.

Before I could think more about it, I rushed back up on deck. Once there, I hid behind the mast but still had a view of the tender. As they were preparing to cast off, I went over to the side of the ship.

'Hang on, wait for me, I'm coming on board.'

As I climbed down to the tender, Roger Day spotted me.

'Where the hell are you off to?' he demanded in surprise. 'You're not scheduled for leave yet.'

'Just a little unplanned excursion,' I replied. 'See you soon. Take care.'

I disappeared into the tender. A few minutes later, we were off, making our way back to shore and leaving the *Laissez Faire* behind. I had mixed emotions about going. I was sorry to leave Roger and my other pals behind but I also knew that if I told them what I'd discovered, I'd lose any advantage. If I was lucky, and my plan worked out, I'd be able to keep my career going. If I told the others, the chances were that none of us would get anything. But, other than my sadness at leaving my friends, I didn't have any regrets.

After a couple of hours we docked in Harwich harbour. The customs guys, who often kept us waiting for hours just to be awkward, were in a good mood that day and within half an hour I was officially back in the UK and in a taxi heading for Ipswich station. It was a Tuesday and Radio Caroline had one of their regular gigs at Wimbledon Palais that night. It was one of three venues where Radio Caroline hosted an evening with their DJs playing the music. From Liverpool Street Station I took the underground to Wimbledon and walked to the Palais. Going round the back, I found the stage-door entrance and managed to blag my way in.

The DJ appearing that night was Tom Lodge. Perfect. He was Radio Caroline's chief DJ and therefore had to be quite influential. Perhaps I would even be able to get a job off him there and then.

I'd never met him, but he'd been with Radio Caroline right from the start and was now one of the best-known names on board. I knocked on the door of Tom's dressing room where he was preparing for the gig. I introduced myself and explained the situation as quickly as I could.

'I've left Radio England, and I would really like to work on Caroline. It's always been my dream to join you guys. Is there any chance you could help me?'

Tom looked sympathetic but he said, 'It's not up to me any more. There's a couple of Canadian whizz-kids taking over things there now. I can't say yes or no, you'll have to go and see a guy called Terry Bate.'

The following morning, I went straight round to Caroline House, an imposing Gothic-style four-storey building located at 6 Chesterfield Gardens, a cul-de-sac off Curzon Street, almost opposite the Radio England office. This could be tricky. Collar well turned up, I managed to get there without being spotted. Feeling pretty nervous, I plucked up as much courage as I could muster and boldly walked through their rather grand front entrance.

'Hello, how are you?' I asked the young attractive receptionist, trying to lay on the charm. 'I've called to see Terry Bate.'

'Do you have an appointment?'

'No.'

'Who shall I say is asking for him?'

'Johnnie Walker.'

'Take a seat.' She made a call. 'Mr Bate says for you to wait, he'll be with you shortly.'

So far so good.

After about five minutes a very fit-looking guy in a suit, shirt and tie came bounding down the stairs, exuding confidence and energy. He stretched out a hand and gave me a firm, honest handshake.

'Hi ya, Johnnie, it's good to meet you. I'm Terry Bate. Follow me.'

We went into a boardroom with an imposing high ceiling and enormous table with about twenty chairs around it. We sat down at one end.

'How's things at Radio England?' asked Terry.

'They're going great, thanks,' I said, radiating what I hoped was confidence and poise.

'I hear they're switching to a Dutch format soon – so you're gonna be out of a job.'

'First I've heard of it,' I lied. I'd learnt it's much easier to get a job when you've already got one, far harder when you're out of work.

'I suppose you'd like to come and work for us. Got a tape?'

I handed over the air-check, relieved I'd had the presence of mind to bring it off the ship.

'Stay here, I'll go and have a word with Ronan.'

Ronan was Ronan O'Rahilly, the founder of Radio Caroline, and this time the wait was longer. Was this a good or a bad sign? I wondered nervously, as the minutes ticked slowly by. After half an hour Terry came back into the room.

'We want you to go out to the ship tomorrow. Any problem with that?'

'Absolutely not.'

'Welcome to Radio Caroline,' said Terry with a huge grin. 'You'll be filling in for other jocks for a while, but who knows what the future will bring?'

'Thanks very much,' I said, trying to absorb what he'd just said as we shook hands.

I couldn't believe it. Wow. I'm a Radio Caroline DJ! I thought, amazed. I had just got my dream job simply by turning up and asking for it. I remembered those years of stringing up a wire in my bedroom, trying to get a signal so I could listen to what seemed like the most exciting radio station in the world. I'd been a fan right from the start, and now I was going to become part of it.

My new life looked bright and exciting. I wondered what the ship was like. One thing was for sure – it couldn't be any worse than the *Laissez Faire*.

Chapter Thirteen

The *Mi Amigo* – the ship from which Radio Caroline was broadcast – was even better than a floating Hilton Hotel. I approached her on board *Offshore I*, a bigger and more comfortable tender than *Offshore II* used by Radio England. It was a beautiful day, crisp and clear. Under a blue sky streaked with thin white clouds, the sun sparkled off the tops of the waves. There was a gentle, rolling swell that lessened as we got near to the home of Radio Caroline. Ronan, on his rare visits to the ship, used to tell visitors and journalists that it was the calming effect of The Lady, as he referred to Caroline. His was a more romantic and mystical explanation than the fact that the ship was moored over the Knock Deep sandbank and the seas were always calmer there.

The *Mi Amigo* was much smaller than either the *Laissez Faire* or Radio London's *Galaxy* but she was beautifully fitted out for a radio station. The bridge and cabins for the captain, first mate and crew were at the aft end of the ship. The 100-foot-plus mast was well up towards the bow and in between was a single-storey structure painted in white with rectangular portholes and the words 'Radio Caroline' in blue with a ship's bell painted on each side.

Riding lower in the water, the *Mi Amigo* was much easier to board from the tender than the *Laissez Faire*. DJs Mike Ahern and Robbie Dale along with members of the Dutch crew were there to welcome me on board and take me on a tour of the ship. It was great to be on her at last, and everybody seemed delighted to see me. Mike and Robbie volunteered to show me around.

'Welcome to Caroline,' said Mike. 'Just in time, by the sound of it.'

Rumour had obviously spread quickly that Radio England was in trouble, and everyone seemed to know that its days were numbered. It made me all the more certain that I'd done the right thing.

Stepping from the narrow deck through the metal hatch-door, I was in a kind of hallway. On one side a wooden staircase led down below; to the right of that was a narrow corridor with washrooms and toilets off to the right and the galley kitchen at the end. The door to the left off the hallway led into a huge mess room which took up the entire width and most of the length of the on-deck structure. In the left-hand corner was a TV on a shelf with an electric aerial control and several easy chairs grouped round it.

In the middle of the room, there was the ship's equivalent of a sideboard with a toaster, kettle and coffee maker on the top. The cupboards and drawers housed cutlery, crockery, bread, cereals, jams, marmalade and so on. At the bow end of the room was a small door in the corner and, against the wall, a built-in bench seat that ran round two sides of a table to give a cosy dining area. With chairs on the other side, there was room enough for about ten people to sit down for meals.

The most exciting discovery for me was what lay behind that small corner door. It opened into a very narrow carpeted corridor and then a door to the right led into a small studio that had been used for broadcasting but now was a dedicated production studio. A couple of steps further along the corridor was the door to the on-air studio. It was very small but extremely compact and cosy. The back of the DJ console was about five feet high, forming a corridor with a porthole to the left. Against the opposite wall was another porthole and to the side, built-in wooden racks just deep enough to slot in all the tape cartridges that had the commercials recorded on to them.

The console was about two feet high and three feet wide, with a swivelling DJ chair just fitting in front of it. It was almost vertical with a row of large pots (volume controls), VU meters (which showed the average volume level of the audio signals) and various switches. Above that was another tape cartridge rack with all the station's jingles. There were three large Gates broadcast turntables, one to the left of the console and two on the right. Above those were other racks with a huge row of singles and above those, a row of albums.

Once seated in the chair, I felt like an airline pilot. All my controls and gadgets were built into beautifully made, purpose-built wooden cabinets and shelves. It was an organic 747, brilliant in its ergonomic design and wonderful to work in. Everything I needed was within arm's reach, including a reel-to-reel tape machine next to the left-hand turntable. For the ads, the jock just swivelled the chair around to pull out the tape carts for each commercial break.

The singles were the latest hits, or about-to-be hits, that made up the Caroline Countdown. This was the station's own chart, which was always a couple of weeks ahead of the national Top Forty that was based on sales. Added to those were the entire current American Hot 100 hits from the Billboard chart. The albums stacked above were a series of American compilation albums containing all the big hits of the last ten years or so. No wonder the Caroline jocks always sounded so happy. This was radio heaven compared to Radio England's radio hell.

The wooden staircase near the washrooms led down into the accommodation section. Off a central corridor, four doors on each side housed the radio staff cabins. Again beautifully made and designed, each had a small table, wardrobes and two wide roomy bunks built into one side. In the ceiling was a metal skylight hatch that opened on to the narrow deck above to let in pure, fresh North Sea air. What a contrast to the dank, dark, smelly hole I'd had to sleep in on Radio England. At the end of the corridor was the DJ lounge/record library. There was a TV in one corner and around all the walls from floor to ceiling were shelves full of singles and albums. On the floor were several large cardboard boxes brimming over with letters and cards from listeners.

For all of us living aboard, it was a warm and comfortable home away from home. The relationship between the on-air staff and the crew was one of mutual respect, support and cooperation. On my old ship, there had been suspicion and resentment between the two sides. DJs on the *Laissez Faire* were just a bloody nuisance to a crew who didn't even want to be there in the first place. In contrast, the *Mi Amigo* was a very happy place to be and within days I'd settled in and was feeling very much at home.

There were six DJs on duty at any one time. When I joined, there was Tom Lodge, Mike Ahern, Robbie Dale, Tommy Vance, Dave Lee Travis, Emperor Rosko, Rick Dane, Keith Hampshire (an Englishman who'd grown up in Canada) and Steve Young (also Canadian), plus a couple of newsreaders, some engineers and the six Dutch crew: the captain, first mate, two cooks and two shipmen. It was a companionable, all-male environment. There were very few, if any, female DJs at the time. It was generally considered that women on board would only cause trouble.

I did my first broadcast, covering for Rick Dane, the night I arrived. He went on leave that day and I sat in that evening. It was all done in a very straightforward way. It was just announced, without any fuss or hype, that Johnnie Walker would be presenting Rick's show that night and off we went. I was nervous to start with, but the sheer enjoyment of being behind a mike soon took over, and the wonderful ease of broadcasting from such a brilliantly designed studio also helped. It was still sinking in that I was now a Caroline DJ, and that the vast audience listening in was now hearing my voice – but I was having too much fun to worry about it.

My first weeks on air were spent filling in for jocks who were on shore leave and gradually discovering my own, more natural style of presentation. Another huge advantage of Radio Caroline was that I no longer had to copy the American DJs. Gone was the need for the frantic approach of the 'boss jocks' and the forced permanent on-air smile. Here I could learn to be more myself and, as a result, I was enjoying doing radio more than I ever had.

My favourite show was sitting in for Rick Dane, who had the nine to midnight slot. Rick wasn't the most popular jock on board; he was very 'me, me, me' and was convinced that everyone on board must be tuned in to every moment of his show. In fact, most off-air staff spent the evenings watching TV, reading listener mail or just sleeping. Rick had an onshore project running a mobile discotheque business and, a few weeks after I joined, he decided to quit the ship and concentrate on that.

Then a memo came out from Caroline House: nine to midnight was now the Johnnie Walker show. I was beside myself with happiness; I now felt on a par with all the other DJs, my rota would be presenting my own show for one week, then on the second week doing my show as well as sitting in for Mike Ahern from nine a.m. to twelve noon while he was on leave. It was a tough schedule. Coming off air at midnight, I'd love to wind down over a bowl of cornflakes and a cup of tea and sit up late talking to the engineers and crew. I learnt so much about radio, life at sea and the ways of the world during those magical hours when the ship was quiet and peaceful. Then, after a few hours' sleep, I was up for a quick breakfast and back in the studio for another show.

I was spending six hours a day on air. I absolutely loved my life on board and even enjoyed the storms and rough seas. Sometimes the metal shutters were bolted over the portholes and the ship would lean at crazy angles as she rode the huge waves. It was more like being on board a submarine then, as it was hard to know whether it was night or day. We had to hang on to whatever we could grab as we stumbled around the ship. In the studio we had a rope fixed on to a desk support, which we could then tie round the back of the DJ chair to stop us being thrown into the commercial racks behind. Two heavy old pennies were taped on to the top of the hydraulically mounted turntable arms so that we could keep playing records in the heavy seas.

Not long after I left Radio England, exactly what I had feared came to pass: on 4th November, Radio England ceased to broadcast. The next day, Radio Dolphin, a new Dutch station, began its life on board the *Laissez Faire*. The English DJs were all sacked. I had got out just in time.

My first winter passed by like a flash on Radio Caroline. Even when the weather was at its roughest, I loved it. And the summer was even better. There were beautiful warm, sunny days when the sea would be calm and as flat as a millpond. We would climb the ladder and sunbathe on the flat roof. Pleasure boats from nearby Clacton offered trips for a pound to holidaymakers keen to 'come and see the pirates'. Often small boats and yachts would surround the ship, the occupants keen and excited to be so close to this famous ship that, in brave defiance of the mighty British government, continued to broadcast to the millions who tuned in every day.

Different captains would do three months on board on a rota basis, and the friendlier ones would allow some boats to tie up alongside and gorgeous girls in their brief bikinis would be helped on board. The problem was that they were always with their boyfriends, who owned the boats. Fortunately we had an engineer who wasn't remotely interested in sex with either gender and we would bribe him with packs of cigarettes to offer the boyfriends a tour of the transmitter and generator rooms. Then we DJs would offer the girls a tour of the living accommodation. Robbie Dale and I were once engaged in making a willing girl feel very much at home in the top bunk of our cabin. After about a quarter of an hour there was a loud banging on the door. We all pretended we hadn't heard it and carried on. Minutes later, there was a more furious banging on the door. It was one of the Dutch crew.

'The girl's boyfriend is worried and wants her to come back on deck!' he called.

We stayed quiet.

'Come out of there, he is getting very angry.'

We carried on. After a few more minutes, there was a really heated banging on the door.

'He says if she doesn't come back on board immediately, there's going to be big trouble.'

'Oh, tell him to piss off,' said the girl.

'You better get back up there,' I said, reluctant to let her go but sensing an ugly incident was developing. 'We'll go up first and you follow a few moments later.'

Robbie and I hurriedly got our clothes back on, went upstairs and back on deck using the hatchway on the opposite side of the ship to where the yacht was moored. Walking round the ship to the other side, we saw the girl getting back on board the yacht. We gave a friendly wave to her boyfriend as he cast off.

'Thanks for coming out to see us. Do come again, anytime!'

When my turn came for shore leave, I'd always follow the same routine. The tender arrived at about midday and I'd come off the ship along with anyone else who was on leave, and start the long journey back to shore. It would be four o'clock before we got into port at Harwich, and then, because we'd come from international waters, we had to go through customs and immigration checks. When we were finally allowed to enter the country, we'd catch the six p.m. train to Liverpool Street. A few drinks on the train would warm us up nicely and then, when we got to London, we'd go straight to a restaurant with our bags for a bit of dinner and then on to a club. It was usually the Cromwellian, which was a wonderful night spot, and we never had to pay to get in; pirate DJs had a bit of status at the time, and a warm welcome was always extended to us. The receptionist would say, 'Welcome back onshore, boys' and wave us through.

Once inside, we'd party hard, drinking, chatting up girls and enjoying the music. On a good night, we'd get lucky with a couple of girls who'd take us back to their place and we'd stay the night there. This was how I met my girlfriends. There was no one really special but I was having a lot of fun.

It was a real rush when I did the Radio Caroline gigs. I always enjoyed them and had a brilliant time. When I went on, the girls would scream, run to the stage and try and clamber up to reach me. The first time it happened I was amazed but, I have to admit, it was a bit of a buzz.

One night in November 1966, not long after I joined Caroline, when I was on leave and in a club, I met Dee, a nice Irish girl with dark curly hair, freckles and beautiful green eyes. She had huge energy and zest for life, and was, to me, quite sophisticated. She was my steady girlfriend for some months, and managed to teach a naive boy from Birmingham quite a lot. She was responsible for one of the most memorable experiences of my life, back on board the *Mi Amigo*.

It was after midnight in my cabin, and fellow jocks Robbie Dale and Tommy Vance had joined me for an important initiation ceremony. We were about to smoke our first joint. I had just got back from a week's shore leave during which Dee was amazed to discover the Caroline boys had yet to get stoned.

'Surely you're all getting turned on out there?' she asked in her Dublin accent. 'How else can you get through the boredom of being stuck on a ship for weeks at a time?'

'No, nobody does,' I replied.

Dee had already introduced me to amyl nitrate 'poppers' while making love the previous evening, and I guess this was the next stage in my drug education.

Handing me three big fat joints, she said, 'Here, take these with you and try them out. If you want some more, just say on your show you've run out of tea and I'll post you some.'

I'd chosen Robbie and Tommy to join me in this experiment and, after some persuasion, now was the time to get high for the first time. I lit one up, took a few drags and passed it to Robbie, who then passed it on to Tommy. There was much coughing and spluttering as the joint went round.

'Well, I don't feel anything,' I said, after the joint was finished. 'Anyone else feeling anything?' No one was. 'Maybe we need to light another one,' I said.

Dee hadn't really given me any instructions and so the second joint was duly lit and passed around. Now things started to happen. Robbie began giggling for no apparent reason. Tommy's face was beginning to go deathly white and all I wanted to do was to lie down and so I climbed up into the top bunk. I was aware of the cabin door opening and the others leaving as I was trying to deal with what was going on in my head. I seemed to have entered a new reality where everything looked and sounded completely different. At times it was quite frightening, at others, I'd be filled with a sense of wonder and amazement. This was like nothing I'd ever experienced before. I decided it was time to find out how Robbie and Tommy were getting on, but first I had to get out of this bunk. I looked over the edge. Jesus, it looked a hell of a long way down and the descent from this safe haven seemed fraught with danger. I got one leg over the edge and stopped. After what seemed about ten minutes, I summoned up the courage to get my other leg out and climb down. I'd lost all sense of time, was grinning like a lunatic and was busy talking complete nonsense to myself.

It felt like it took about half an hour but eventually I was safely down on the floor of the cabin. The next challenge was to negotiate my way out of the door, along the corridor and up the steps to the mess room on deck level. Robbie was there with a few of the Dutch crew who liked to stay up late drinking beers and sharing tales of the sea. Trying to appear as normal as possible, I exchanged a knowing smile with Robbie.

One of the crew spoke to me: his voice was a dull, flat monotone. Then Robbie spoke. His was in the most amazing, ethereal stereo. This was really bizarre – we smokers were somehow connected on a higher level while the others were lower down in the normal world. We had enhanced sound and vision, with the most beautiful colours. It was definitely a 'mini trip' into a heightened consciousness and no subsequent smoking experience ever produced such a profound effect. Poor old Tommy Vance, though, was having a rotten time and had spent the last few hours leaning over the side of the ship heaving into the ocean.

We should have waited for that first joint to take effect before lighting another. As Dee had rolled them pretty strong, we had overdosed somewhat for first-time smokers. A couple of days later Robbie and I shared the third joint and had a great time, and so now I needed to order some more. About half an hour into my nine p.m. to midnight show I casually gave a dedication for Dee.

'This record's for you, Dee, and by the way, we've run out of tea.'

Two days later, a padded white envelope arrived on board via our shipping agency address in Harwich. Carefully wrapped in several sheets of paper were four beautifully rolled joints. Good old Dee – she'd got my message.

The next day I went down to the record library and DJ lounge to look through the latest listener mail sent from Caroline's London office. Out of the sacks tumbled hundreds of packets of Typhoo, PG Tips, Tetley, every kind of fresh tea and tea bags. Our listeners were so kind and supportive and would have been so upset to see so much tea go over the side. Dee and I were going to have to think of a new, more subtle code.

We enjoyed smoking but that was about as hard as it got in those days, in terms of drugs. I found that smoking pot opened my mind and enabled me to get rid of the shackles of my restrictive upbringing at home and school. I wasn't alone – a lot of young people felt like me. Drugs set us free and broadened our whole outlook on life, art, and the way we related to other people. Looking back, I feel that this was the time when I changed the most. Experiencing drugs, free love and swinging London was amazing. I had absolutely no desire to go back to Birmingham – this was the experience of leaving home that I'd always dreamed of.

I felt like I was free at last.

Chapter Fourteen

Radio Caroline gave its DJs a huge amount of freedom to choose the music they played. As far as Ronan was concerned, that's what DJs were for; you hired the guys that had good taste and let them get on with it. The daytime music format was dead simple: we just alternated between 'one in, one out'. The 'in' was a record from the Caroline Top Forty Countdown and the 'out' was anything the DJ chose: a hit from the Billboard Hot 100, or one of the album hits, or an oldie picked out from the record library downstairs. At night-time it was even more relaxed and free-form. The commercial ad log was lighter and there was the space to experiment and try new things.

I introduced the 'Ten O'Clock Turn-On', where I played two of the best up-tempo soul records I could find back-to-back. At eleven o'clock one night I read out a heartfelt letter from a girl listener and played her Percy Sledge's 'Warm And Tender Love'. I got so many letters requesting a special goodnight, it became a regular feature, attracting thousands of letters. I would turn the studio lights right down, turn up the microphone level and speak quietly and intimately to the letter writer as if no one else was listening in. I had to be on my own to do it – if anyone else was in the studio I'd feel far too embarrassed.

One evening I was right in the middle of reading a letter from a girl who'd just been dumped by her boyfriend, her parents didn't understand her and she was really down. I was doing my very best to connect with her and be sympathetic and understanding when I heard the studio door opening. There didn't seem to be anyone there and then suddenly, bobbing up from behind the jingle rack in front of me, was Robbie Dale in full drag: bra and panties, lipstick and hair lacquered up in a bouffant. I completely cracked up and the moment of intimacy across the radio waves between me and my 'goodnight girl' was lost. Somehow, though, I managed to get over the giggles and finish off the letter.

I always used to wonder what people were doing while they were tuned in. I guess no matter what time of day you're on, someone, somewhere, will be making love. If you're on between nine and midnight, the percentage must increase hugely. In the sixties parents were nothing like as liberal as they are today. There was none of this bringing your girlfriend back home and being left alone, and no chance of taking her up to your room. In my teenage years you grabbed what few opportunities you could. A pretty good one was sneaking into a house where your girlfriend was baby sitting, except every so often the parents came back early and there'd be the leap up from the sofa and the frantic readjustment of clothing before they came through the door.

Then, of course, there was the flicks. A whole bunch of us used to occupy the back couple of rows of my local cinema in Olton on a Saturday night. But by far the finest place for what was euphemistically called 'heavy petting' was the car. It is no wonder there are so many songs about cars in rock 'n' roll. They shared so many characteristics with music: glamour, excitement and freedom. In those days it was only the fortunate families that had a car at all but, as there was no annual MOT vehicle check, you could buy an old banger for about twenty quid and just run it until it wouldn't go any more.

I had a feeling that a lot of my 11.30 p.m. audience were probably doing what their girlfriends' mothers would be shocked to find out about. The lucky ones would be in quiet car parks and country lanes, busy steaming up the windows. I thought it was my duty to promote the art of kissing so, putting on Bob Dylan's 'Like A Rolling Stone', I issued the challenge to couples to kiss non-stop throughout the entire record. I sat back listening to the record, thinking I'd set a challenge, and for those who completed it there should be some kind of reward.

I played another long record again the following evening at 11.30 p.m., and suddenly the idea came to me of a special licence for kissing in the car. I remembered a late night with Jenny, when we were parked up in our old car, having the most beautiful snogging session. Just as my hand reached the top of her stocking, there was a banging on the window and outside was a copper with a torch. He managed to frighten the life out of Jenny and ruined not only that moment, but our kissing-in-the-car sessions for several weeks after. Maybe my 'Kiss in the Car' licence would guarantee that couples would be left alone by the Old Bill. I designed a circular licence, much like a tax disc, which entitled the bearer to kiss in the car while listening to the Johnnie Walker show on Radio Caroline. On my next week off I went back home to Birmingham and took my designs in to a local printer.

'I can't possibly print this,' he said. 'It's too much like a proper tax disc.'

'Oh, no need to worry about that,' I lied. 'I've been to the police with it and they say it's quite all right.'

I ordered the first print run of a thousand licences, and asked my mum if she could help me send them out. I couldn't wait to get back to the ship. This was going to be fun.

On my first show back on Caroline, I played another long record at 11.30 p.m. At the end, I announced that anyone who'd managed to kiss non-stop all the way through the record was now eligible for an official Johnnie Walker 'Kiss in the Car' licence.

'Just send a stamped addressed envelope to Radio Caroline, 6 Chesterfield Gardens, London W1.'

On board we got daily sacks of listener mail, and about three days later I got a couple of hundred letters. I was obviously on to something here, and it was a novel slant on the car-sticker idea. I forwarded the envelopes to my mother to fill and send off to the listeners. The whole thing snowballed to such an extent that Mum had to get friends in to help out. All in all, we sent out over 19,000 licences – there was an awful lot of snogging going on.

When my mother saw how many people were listening to my show, and read some of the letters that went with the request for licences, she decided to start a fan club for me. She was intrigued by the fact that so many people wanted to know more about me.

In total, about four and a half thousand people joined my fan club. Mum sent out a photo, a badge and a newsletter to members. It was nice that so many people felt interested enough in me to join. My mother wrote personal letters to so many people that she ended up having pen pals all over Europe, and some of those friendships went on for years.

One clear and peaceful night, an engineer noticed flashing lights on the shore at Frinton on Sea.

'It could be a car flashing its headlights,' he suggested.

With the engineer in the studio looking out of the porthole, I said casually into the microphone, 'If you're listening in a car parked at Frinton, flash your headlights three times.'

'There were three flashes!' said the engineer with great excitement.

We were not allowed ship-to-shore radio on Caroline and there was no such thing as a mobile phone, so we both got very excited at this direct contact with a listener. I told the car driver that we could see him and suggested we use a code: two flashes for yes, and one flash for no. With the engineer's help we got a conversation going.

'Have you been out on a date tonight?' I asked.

Two flashes.

'Is she still with you?'

Two flashes.

'Did you kiss non-stop all through the record?'

Two flashes.

This was huge fun but, stuck in my DJ seat, I had to rely on the engineer to relay the answers, which were slowing down the conversation. I asked the driver if he could come back to the same place at the same time tomorrow and we would try it again.

At the end of the show, after midnight, I was sitting having a cup of coffee with Geoff, the engineer.

'What I need to do is get out on deck with a microphone. Can that be done?'

'Oh, yeah. Piece of cake. I can make two really long leads. One for the mike and the other for your headphones.'

'Would you be OK playing in the records, then?'

'Yeah, no problem.'

The next night, I was in a really extra up mood, because I was so looking forward to getting out on the deck. Geoff kept his eyes on the shore and at 11.20 p.m. saw the lights flashing on and off.

'He's here again.'

'Fantastic.'

I told the car driver that we'd seen him and that I'd be out on deck after the next record. Geoff and I were like a couple of kids, we were so excited. Nobody had ever broadcast from on the deck before and, stepping out into the darkness, I had a whole new sense of the sea at night-time, the twinkling lights along the twelve miles of shoreline that I could see, and all the human life that was going on there. The biggest problem we had on a pirate ship was keeping that connection with the lives that were being lived by our listeners. We did feel very cut off at times, especially when it was foggy or the weather was too bad to go outside. But this night was beautiful. It was over three miles to the shore but I could see all the coloured lights of Clacton away to my left, what was probably a lighthouse way over on the right, and between them various other lights of roads and houses.

And, sure enough, there right in front of me was a bright light that every now and then would flash a number of times. I'd pinpointed our new friends in their car. It was much easier than I thought. Geoff took over at the console in the studio and I chatted to him through the porthole window and told him what record I wanted next. I put on the headphones, and as the record came to an end, Geoff faded up the microphone. Now I was hearing exactly what the listener was hearing and it sounded wonderful. There was the sea gently lapping against the side of the ship and just occasionally a wave would shake one of the tire fenders, rattling its chain. It was so atmospheric.

'This is Johnnie Walker, talking to you live from the deck of the *Mi Amigo* on a beautiful evening, and a couple of friends have come to see us in their car at Frinton. Have you been out to the flicks tonight?'

One flash.

'The pub?'

Two flashes.

'Are you having a good session in your car tonight?'

Two flashes followed by another two flashes, and another two flashes.

'Will you get into trouble keeping your girlfriend out this late?' One flash.

'Ah, so maybe you've been going out with each other for a while. Is it years?'

One flash.

'Is it months?'

Two flashes.

'So how many, then?'

Four flashes.

'Have you been all the way yet?'

Two flashes.

'Is Caroline the best pirate station?'

Two flashes.

And so we went on for about another five minutes, having our 'conversation'. It was odd, I suppose, using a 50,000-watt radio transmitter to talk to two people in a car, but the whole atmosphere of being out on deck, and the direct connection between this ship in international waters and two of its listeners onshore, made it unique and very special.

Needless to say, there were many more cars parked at Frinton the following night. But it was amazing how easy it was to pinpoint one particular car, and we repeated the exercise every now and then. It became known as 'Frinton flashing' but, unfortunately, not everyone thought it was good fun. The residents of Frinton were up in arms about this invasion of cars late at night. They had a point, of course, and we made it mostly just a Friday- or Saturday-night thing.

A BBC TV documentary crew were planning to come out and

do some filming on the ship. I thought it would be a great idea if we could show them how Frinton flashing worked. For a whole week I plugged it every night.

'Come down to Frinton this Saturday night, because we're going to have a TV crew on board. Show them how much you love Caroline.'

From about half past ten we could see lights flashing from Frinton. An hour later I went out on deck and there were miles and miles of lights flashing along the shoreline. It was an incredible sight. I was out on deck, with Geoff at the controls.

'It's great to see so many cars out there tonight, thanks for coming. The TV crew is here filming and it looks great from here.'

I was getting intoxicated on the power of it all.

'Lights off!' I commanded.

In an instant the shoreline went dark.

'Lights on!' and bright illumination shone forth right the way along ten to fifteen miles of coastline. This was my moment of true megalomania. I'd never experienced such power and control. Again I gave the instruction, 'Lights off!'

A few moments of silence and darkness.

'Lights on!'

The TV director and cameraman absolutely loved it. It was the most dramatic proof of the power of Radio Caroline and the commitment of its fans. The two of us together – station and listeners – were united in this opportunity to show authority, as represented by the BBC, that we did have tremendous power.

Enough to illuminate an entire coastline.

Chapter Fifteen

1967

Over the years of Caroline's history, both the press and TV have had a fondness and fascination for the station, seeing it as an embodiment of the freedom they wish they had. The power of our coastline light show was another reminder to the government that we had a free voice, which they were more and more determined to silence. There never seemed to be an opportunity, though, until one day an awful event played right into the hands of the authorities and gave them the excuse they needed to destroy pirate radio.

It involved a fierce argument and a fatal shooting over Radio City, a fort-based pirate radio station. It had originally been owned by Screaming Lord Sutch, who had used it to broadcast extracts from *Lady Chatterley's Lover* over the airwaves. He sold it to a man called Reginald Calvert. It appears that Reg Calvert was not all that straight a businessman and a Major Oliver Smedley became very exercised about the fact that he had not been paid for the transmitter used to broadcast Radio City. After appealing for his money, the major finally took action; he led a raid on the fort and removed the crystals from the transmitter, rendering it useless. Shortly afterwards, Reg Calvert paid a visit to the major at home to remonstrate. What happened next is unclear, but it resulted in Reg Calvert lying dead in Oliver Smedley's hallway, with the major claiming self-defence.

It was a disaster for pirate radio. The tabloid press, which had previously been supportive of our stations, went berserk. There were huge headlines about the 'murderous pirates' and editorial comment saying 'they're just a bunch of dangerous criminals'. It seemed that because the papers had previously built us up, they now wanted to knock us down, and they gloried in our downfall. And it played right into the hands of the government. Within days, plans were announced to silence the pirate stations once and for all with the Marine Offences Bill.

Ever since Caroline had come on the air on Easter Sunday 1964, the government had been huffing and puffing about getting the unlicensed stations off the air. Although we'd heard it so many times before, there was something more sinister about this bill. Having accepted they couldn't legislate over international waters, the government had taken a new tack. This new law was to target individuals, namely British subjects. If the bill successfully passed through parliament, it would become illegal for any British subject to work for, supply, promote, buy advertising time on or in any way support an offshore radio station. That meant that all of us, and anyone who worked with us, would become criminals. Caroline's boss, Ronan O'Rahilly, took legal advice and the consensus from well-regarded and highly respected barristers was that this proposed law was a draconian attack on the rights of the British subject. On board ship we talked about it at length, trying to figure out what the future held and whether or not the government would actually follow through with all of this. There had been over two years of empty threats. Why would this be any different?

But a huge difference was the change in the attitude of the press. The government's case against us had always been weak: they said we didn't pay enough royalties, and that we were a danger to shipping and maritime communications. The pirate stations had always offered to pay royalties but the record companies refused because they didn't officially recognize our existence. And as for our interfering with shipping communications – that was just government spin. Our popularity was always our protection in the past. But now the press had turned against us, taking some of our support with them, and the government seized the opportunity it had been waiting for.

There is absolutely no question in my mind that the pirate

stations and especially the one I knew best, Radio Caroline, did a lot of good. It was obvious from the letters I got and the people I met that Caroline had improved the quality of life of millions of people. Now some of them were really confused. The negative press reports had been extremely effective.

One teenage girl wrote to me and told me that her mother had said this recent story proved that the pirates really were a bunch of crooks and that her daughter mustn't listen any more. 'But I love Caroline, and I love your show and I think my mother's wrong. So I want you to know that I will still be listening with the radio quietly playing under the bedclothes. But I feel so guilty.'

The two major stations, Caroline and London, defiantly announced that they would continue to broadcast regardless of the government's new law. Fans of both stations were delighted at the strong stance and promised to do all they could to help. It was becoming clear that a major battle lay ahead. On one side were the authorities – the government and the BBC – representing the preservation of the status quo and continuing control over freedom of expression. On the other were not only the nation's youth but people of all ages who simply wanted to be able to tune in to a radio station and listen to the music they loved any time of the day or night. Given the number of radio stations we have now and all the different ways people have of being able to listen to music, it's difficult to comprehend what the hell the government was so worried about. But then, that's what the sixties were all about. For years, young people had been ignored but now there was a determination to express thoughts and opinions which challenged society. It's funny how governments love to talk about the great British tradition of democracy and freedom of speech and then, when a genuine free voice is heard, there is panic and condemnation.

In the first few months of 1967, listener letters came flooding in. The government knew that they would be deeply unpopular if they took away the pirate stations and so they announced that they would be asking the BBC to launch a new pop station in September, a month after this new bill was due to pass into law.

This very effectively drew attention away from the destruction of the pirate stations, as everyone got very excited about the advent of a new BBC station. It gradually became clear that, under this kind of sustained pressure, Radio London was backing down from its original defiant stance and that Radio Caroline would be the only station brave enough, or crazy enough, to defy the law and carry on transmitting.

On board Radio Caroline we were now faced with a huge decision: should we stay, in defiance of the government, or should we quit and come ashore? British subjects who broke the law would be liable for a maximum punishment of two years in prison, which effectively meant that if we attempted to land in Britain, we could be arrested and jailed. A decision to stay on board meant we would have to leave Britain for good and, when not on the ship, spend our shore leave in Holland.

Life on board would change dramatically as well. No one would be allowed to supply the ship from the UK, so that would be the end of the daily tender. Supplies would also have to come from Holland, and that would only be possible on a much less regular basis. All our lifelines were being cut off. As well as our basic necessities, there was also the issue of money. British companies would no longer be able to advertise with us and, from a business point of view, it seemed impossible that a commercial radio station could survive without any advertising revenue. When Radio London announced that it planned to close down on 14th August 1967, the day before the bill became law, there was no doubt that this hard business reality was the cause.

But Caroline's founder, Ronan O'Rahilly, whose grandfather was shot by British soldiers in the Easter Uprising of 1906, was absolutely determined that he was going to win this one. He was feverishly drawing up plans to ensure Caroline's survival.

On board we carried on doing our programmes as normal, and did our best to keep up our morale and confidence in the future. Our listeners were desperate for us not to give in and to keep going. During our weeks onshore, we would be buoyed up by the general atmosphere of marches, rallies and the hundreds of fans that gathered outside Caroline House every day. We were still doing our regular onshore gigs at places like the Wimbledon Palais, Chislehurst Caves and the Bal Tabarin Ballroom in Kent. These gigs had always been packed out with Caroline fans who would scream and try and rush the stage when we came on. It was pop-star treatment that now had an added touch of glamour and excitement because we were to be the freedom fighters, facing up to the establishment on behalf of millions of listeners who loved pirate radio and the music we played, and didn't want the good times to end.

When we went back out to the ship, though, things were very different. We were cut off, alone, just a few of us bobbing around on a vast sea in a rusty old ship with too much time to sit and worry about the implications of carrying on after 14th August, when the Marine Offences Bill would become an act of law. What was life going to be like living in exile? When would we see our friends and family again? And how difficult was it going to be broadcasting to a country you weren't allowed to set foot in?

We were still getting a daily tender service, which included the daily newspapers, full of propaganda against the pirates and in support of the 'wonderful' new BBC pop station. I knew this station was going to be an awful replacement for pirate radio. 'Auntie', as she was known, couldn't suddenly raise her long tweed skirts, and there was no way the new station would have a shadow of the energy, excitement and irreverence that Caroline broadcast.

On board, we were one big family and we included our listeners in our life on the ship, talking to them about the day-to-day things that happened to us. DJs would come in to the studio during other people's shows and chat about what was going on. The captain, the cook and other members of the crew would come and say hello. If we mentioned how cold it was, the listeners would knit us pullovers and woolly socks. Little old ladies would bake us cakes. It was intimate, immediate and inclusive. That kind of radio, where the DJs really *live* their jobs, has never been replicated.

I couldn't bear the idea that it would all just end. I was absolutely resolved: if Caroline was going to continue then I wanted to be a part of it. I supported freedom and I was prepared to support it all the way, no matter what the personal cost. As far as I was concerned, the government and the BBC could just fuck right off.

I knew Ronan would be delighted with my decision but I dreaded telling my mum and dad. My father had now come round to accepting my life as a DJ, and I think he had a growing respect for what I'd achieved. My mother worked tirelessly, running my fan club, sending out the 'Kiss in the Car' licences, and religiously keeping every press cutting and photo. I told them about my decision to stay with Caroline and face the consequences. They absolutely understood the reasons why, but both were terribly worried about the possible outcome. It meant I would be a fugitive, unable to return to Britain for two years after my last broadcast, whenever that might be.

I made light-hearted jokes about how Mum could smuggle a file in a cake when she visited me in prison, but my outward bravado was masking my true inner feelings. I don't mind admitting I was scared. I'd seen a film report on Anglia news of the RAF destroying one of the empty offshore forts to ensure that it could never be used for a radio station. One by one, jet fighters swooped low over the fort discharging missiles, each one causing a spec-tacular explosion. It was way over the top but it was a highly effective public demonstration of the government's power and a reminder of just who was in charge here.

During a visit to Caroline House, I talked to Ronan about the future. The London office would have to be closed down and they would open an office in Amsterdam instead. The daily tender service would stop and we'd be supplied from Holland once or twice a week. Getting on and off the ship would involve a twenty-four-hour trip across the North Sea. Life was going to be very different and I knew we were going to feel even more isolated, yet at the same time we would still be beaming Caroline's signal out loud and clear. For the audience, nothing much would change.

Ronan seemed very confident that he had plans to ensure some kind of income to support the station despite the ban on advertising. He said we could do business with American companies and agencies whose products were on sale in the UK; as they weren't British, the law would not apply to them. I went back to the ship to start another two-week stint and found a lot of very worried fellow DJs who weren't at all sure what they were going to do. I was buoyed up from my week off whereas they'd had two weeks of worried isolation. It was a huge decision for each individual to make; meanwhile, it was rumoured that the DJs at Radio London were queuing up to be considered for a job on the new BBC station, Radio One. Tony Blackburn, John Peel, Ed Stewart, Kenny Everett, Dave Cash and others had all been round for talks and auditions.

We were now entering the Summer of Love. The Beatles released their album *Sergeant Pepper's Lonely Hearts Club Band*. It was unlike anything that had gone before and was one of the most important milestones in the history of British music. John Peel, who had built up a huge after-midnight audience with his *Perfumed Garden* show, introduced the new album and it was played from start to finish on Radio London, which was a broadcasting first. The hippy movement was born and in San Francisco anti-Vietnam war protestors were taking to the streets and placing flowers in the rifles of US soldiers. The Beatles performed 'All You Need Is Love' on one of the first-ever worldwide satellite TV broadcasts. Radio Caroline began talking about 'loving awareness', which concentrated on looking for the good in people and situations rather than being suspicious and focusing on the negative.

The successful British group The Ivy League, under the pseudonym of The Roaring Sixties, recorded and released a record called 'We Love The Pirates'. With its flower-power sound, it became a rallying call for free-radio fans and we played the song over and over on Caroline. In London, thousands of banner-waving music fans marched through the streets in a procession that ended up in a huge rally in Trafalgar Square. Despite the huge wave of support, Radio London officially announced that it would be closing down at three o'clock on Monday, 14th August and one by one all the other pirate stations made a similar announcement. Only Radio Caroline did not waver.

The Lady was going to fight the fight and she was going to have to do it alone.

Chapter Sixteen

Friday, 11th August 1967

The Bal Tabarin Ballroom in Kent had never looked so beautiful. Ronan had arranged for thousands of flowers to cover the walls, balcony and stage. Outside was a massive queue of Caroline fans, all of them wanting to be a part of this very special night, the last gig we would ever do. In just three days, it would be illegal for us to set foot in the country. There was a brilliant atmosphere, and the person who booked the bands for the regular Caroline events had the foresight and luck to have booked Procol Harum to play live on the very week that 'A Whiter Shade Of Pale' was Number One in the charts.

Robbie Dale and I went onstage at the start to warm up the crowd. It was like no other gig we'd done before. The place was absolutely packed with more people than it had probably ever had in its entire history. The heady atmosphere crackled with energy, anticipation and excitement. It was like the eve of a great battle and as Robbie and I took to the stage, the whole place erupted with cheers, screams and applause. At eight o'clock we introduced Procol Harum. After a couple of unknown songs they played 'A Whiter Shade Of Pale' to huge applause at the end. As they continued their set of other songs, completely unknown, the crowd started chanting, 'We want Johnnie! We want Robbie! We want Johnnie! We want Robbie!'

I felt really sorry for the band and it became impossible for them to be heard above the noise of the chanting Caroline fans. They had no option but to finish their set early and Robbie and I went back onstage to tumultuous applause. The big moment of midnight, 14th August was so close and the crowd wanted to give us all the love and support they possibly could for the challenging days that lay ahead. They knew from what we had both said on our programmes that we were going to carry on and fight for Caroline's survival. Under the terms of the law we would be liable to arrest and prosecution for a period of two years after our final broadcast. So, if we managed to keep broadcasting for a year, it might be three years before we could set foot in the UK.

The evening ended with a mass singing of 'All You Need Is Love'. Fans swarmed on to the stage and, as one, we and the whole jam-packed crowd swayed together and sang our hearts out. The sound of all those voices in a ballroom bedecked by beautiful flowers was one of the most emotional and uplifting experiences of my life. It was the culmination of a week of incredible highs and lows.

At the weekend, in Hampton-in-Arden, my parents held a farewell party for me. My mother had invited members of my fan club to come and see me off; about a hundred turned up along with various journalists and photographers. It was a somewhat surreal occasion as we served cold drinks and sandwiches to this huge throng of teenagers, mostly girls, on the back lawn of my parents' house. At the end of the day I said thank you to those who had made the journey from all over the UK; then came the time to say goodbye to my family. It was hardest to make my farewells to Mum and Dad. I could sense their feelings of loss, worry and fear. What on earth was their son about to get himself into?

I had no intention of backing down, but I was beginning to become aware of the enormity of all this and just what the implications might be for my future. It was a big thing, defying the government and deliberately breaking the law in such a public way. I was starting to feel just a little bit small.

I picked up my bag and walked up the road to Hampton-in-Arden railway station. I sat on the bench waiting for the train and someone took a photograph of me looking somewhat sad and alone. I felt like Paul Simon at Widnes station when he wrote 'Homeward Bound'. Except, of course, I was leaving home without any idea of when I might be back and the song was actually written at the now-closed Ditton railway station.

As the train approached Paddington, my spirits lifted and I felt that buzz of excitement and energy I always had coming into London. This time it was stronger than usual and it went a long way to dispel the fears that had been building in Hampton. My feelings about the big day on Monday the 14th were now ones of anticipation and excitement. I was boosted even more when I met up with Ronan at his favourite restaurant, Thierry's on the King's Road.

'It's gonna be all right, baby,' he said, with his wonderful smile.

Blessed with the charisma of the Kennedys (JFK and Bobby were his big heroes), Ronan could charm anyone into doing anything. When you were with him problems seemed to disappear and anything was possible. We talked about how I should handle the farewell announcement at midnight and what our first record should be to start the new era of Caroline. 'Can't Buy Me Love' was the record that started it all off back in Easter 1964 so the Beatles and 'All You Need Is Love' was the obvious choice.

On a regular Monday changeover, we had to catch the 8.30 a.m. Harwich train from Liverpool Street. This Monday was different. Extra tenders had been chartered to run out to the ship throughout the day. This was the biggest day in pirate radio history, after the start of Caroline three years before. All around the coast, offshore radio stations were preparing to close down. In the southern half of the UK, journalists, photographers and television crews all wanted to cover the end of Radio London and the defiance of Radio Caroline.

When Robbie Dale and I arrived at Liverpool Street Station, it was a scene of glorious anarchy and mayhem. The station, normally full of conservatively dressed city types, had been invaded by over a thousand pirate radio fans. The whole place was a riot of colour, excitement and noise. The fans were waving their banners and singing, 'We love the pirates.' The police and station staff had been taken by complete surprise. These fans were here both to welcome back their Radio London heroes, and see off us Caroline rebels. Robbie and I were almost lifted off our feet by the hordes who accompanied us to the train. Not bothering with details like a ticket, they all swarmed on to the train with guards and ticket collectors looking on in helpless bewilderment. There had never been scenes like it.

There were similar scenes at Harwich station as we all piled off the train, Robbie and I leading the throng. We were the Pied Pipers of Harwich. In the station car park there were people of all ages, including one dear little old lady who was close to tears.

'You boys out there are the only family I've got. I love you all. Take care, Johnnie, and God bless you.'

They gave us gifts of pullovers, socks, tea bags, chocolate, cakes – anything they thought we might need, as they all knew our lives were going to be a lot tougher with no regular supply boats. Robbie and I fought our way through the crowds to get on the minibus that would take us down to the docks and here again crowds of supporters had gathered to wish us farewell.

There's no turning back now, I thought. At the quayside Robbie and I met Ross Brown, who told us he'd been asked to come out by the Caroline bosses. Ross had been a newsreader on the fort-based pirate Radio City. Why he'd been hired, we weren't quite sure. But we all shook hands and welcomed him aboard the supply tender that was to take us out to Caroline. Joining us were various photographers and journalists, who were going to come out to the ship to cover the story.

We set off. Many thoughts ran through my mind as I looked back at the English coastline. How long would it be before I ever set foot on English soil again? I had put on a brave face for the fans and press but now the reality was beginning to sink in.

We tied up alongside the *Mi Amigo* and were surprised to be greeted by so many long faces. The other DJs who had stayed on board looked distinctly glum. Several of the Caroline presenters, such as Dave Lee Travis and Mike Ahern, had already left the boat to go to the BBC, hoping to be a part of the new Radio One, which was due to start in a month's time. Others, like Canadians Keith Hampshire and Steve Young and the English jock Tom Edwards, had all agreed to stay on to the bitter end. Now here they were in the mess room, bags packed, coats on, announcing that they were leaving. Tom Edwards seemed to be the spokesman.

'It's all right for you guys,' he said. 'You've been gallivanting around London, getting loads of support. We've been sitting out here on our own thinking it all through.' Looking round at the others for support, he announced, 'We've all decided it's not worth the risk.'

I was appalled.

'Fucking hell, guys, you can't pull out now. I do understand that it's been harder for you stuck out here, but you can't let us down now. There are millions of people who are relying on us to keep the music going and show the government what a bunch of bastards they really are.'

Robbie and I pleaded with them to change their minds, but to no avail.

One of the crewmen shouted, 'The tender leaves in five minutes.'

This was the point of no return for them, their last chance to legally enter the UK or be forced into exile and become criminals.

Tom looked at me and said, 'I'm sorry, guys, but our minds are made up. We're going.'

The glorious euphoria of the morning's events evaporated. This was not what was supposed to happen. None of us had anticipated this dramatic turn of events. Journalists on board began scribbling notes. We needed to get away from the prying eyes of the media to figure out what we were going to do.

Once we were safely below and on our own, I asked Ross, 'Have you ever done a DJ show?'

'Not really,' he replied. 'I only ever read the news, but I'm more than ready to have a go.'

I looked across at Robbie and said, 'We're really in the shit here. How the hell are we going to run a twenty-four-hour radio station with two and a half jocks?'

'After the tender gets in to Harwich, word will soon get back to Caroline House. Maybe they'll be able to sort something out,' said Robbie.

It was lunchtime. In the studio, one of our faithful engineers, who hadn't changed his mind about staying, was playing back-to-back records.

Robbie and I worked out a schedule. I'd go on at two p.m., Robbie at six, then I'd come back at nine and both of us would take Caroline past midnight. Ross would spend time practising in the spare studio.

I went on air at two o'clock. I talked about the morning send-off and thanked people for their support, but I was determined not to let them know of the dramatic turn of events on board. We had to keep up a public show of confidence despite all our problems.

Just after three o'clock Robbie came in to the studio.

He joined me at the microphone and, with an obvious lump in his throat and emotion in his voice, he said, 'I've just heard Radio London close down. It was so sad to hear their theme tune for the last time. Radio Caroline is now alone,' he continued. 'But, Johnnie, we should now welcome all the new listeners who have tuned in to us from Radio London.'

The rest of the show went by in a blur. At six o'clock Robbie took over and I went in to the mess room to get something to eat. On the one hand, it was just like a normal day on board, but on the other it was so very different. There wouldn't normally be any journalists on board and every minute was charged with the anticipation of what was going to happen at midnight. I went down to the library to browse through the shelves of records to pick a few of my favourites to take up to the studio for nine p.m. I really wanted this show to be special because I knew there'd be a huge audience tuning in.

Just along the corridor from the library was my cabin where I could be on my own. I lay on my bunk and tried to relax and get a little bit of rest. This was going to be a momentous night.

Meanwhile, back at Liverpool Street Station that morning's scenes were being repeated with even greater crowds, who had turned up to welcome back DJs from Radio London. The scenes of the girls tearing at the clothes of DJ Mike Lennox were front-page news in that evening's newspapers.

Journalist Tom Mangold was in Ronan O'Rahilly's office at Caroline House. He refused to believe that Ronan really intended to go through with the defiant stand he promised.

'Why don't you just openly admit it, Mr O'Reilly?' he asked in a disbelieving tone. 'You have no real intention of carrying on. You're just doing all of this for publicity and attention.'

Ronan just sat there smiling.

'You really can't expect me to believe that you are going to totally defy the government and the establishment. You can't possibly succeed.'

'Of course we're going to carry on,' countered Ronan. 'Why don't you just listen at midnight and find out for yourself?'

It was 11.05 p.m. and I'd just played 'Warm And Tender Love' by Percy Sledge. It was a lovely soul ballad that I played every night at this time, dedicated to a different listener as a special good night. Suddenly I felt a bump against the side of the ship. It usually meant the tender had come alongside. Surely there can't be another one at this time of night, I thought, and leant outside the studio's porthole window. Sure enough, there was *Offshore 1* and climbing on board were even more journalists, plus two strangers. Robbie brought them into the studio and introduced them as two brand-new DJs – Spangles Muldoon and Stevie Merick.

I'd never met them or heard of them before. I found out later that the people in London put out a desperate search for anyone willing to be a DJ and they found these two, neither of whom had any experience. The closest Spangles Muldoon came to being a DJ was that his brother, Barmy Barry, was a Birmingham jock. At the time, I didn't care where they'd come from or even if they'd never seen a record before. They were there and, my God, they were a welcome sight. Now there was a glimmer of hope. We might be able to keep going.

I welcomed them with a big smile of relief and then Robbie took them on a tour of the ship, and to sort out their cabins. I don't think that either Robbie or I had ever been so pleased to see a tender in our lives. The arrival of our new colleagues was certainly a much-needed boost; we weren't quite as alone out here as we'd feared. With all the excitement, it seemed only moments before the clock was approaching the fateful hour of midnight. At one minute past, the Marine Offences Bill would become law and we'd all be criminals.

With Robbie and a couple of journalists crammed into the tiny studio, I announced to an estimated audience of 22 million people all over Europe, 'This is Radio Caroline. It is now twelve midnight.' Then I played the classic folk protest song 'We Shall Overcome'. As it faded away after the chorus, I said, 'Radio Caroline would like to thank Harold Wilson's Labour government for recognizing our right to be here, our right to broadcast to the people of Great Britain. And, as we enter this new phase in our broadcasting history, you have our assurance that we intend to stay on air as Caroline belongs to you and we love you.'

It had been Ronan's suggestion that we thank Harold Wilson and the government.

'What the hell do we want to do that for?' I'd asked.

'Just think about it,' Ronan replied. 'The ship is in international waters over which they have no control. The only thing they can do is try and scare British people from working on it. So therefore it is an acknowledgement of our right to be there.'

That was typical of Ronan's somewhat perverse way of looking at things.

Once I'd made this proclamation, I cued in the Beatles with 'All You Need Is Love'. Someone in the studio produced a bottle of champagne, the cork was popped and we all drank a toast to the future of Caroline, then we sang along to the Beatles. I was on a complete high. Robbie turned back to me from looking out of the porthole, his eyes bright with excitement and enthusiasm.

'I can see the lights of hundreds of cars parked along the coast. They've all come to support us in our finest hour.'

Robbie and I carried on doing the show together and we kept the party atmosphere going for as long as possible. A special boat chartered by the newspapers came along to take off the journalists and photographers. And, as things started to calm down from the

(left to right) Michael, me (the one not smiling), Mum, Maureen, Dad and John

Brother John looking cool on holiday

Mum and Dad with Dad's retirement gifts

Christine and me on Sheringham beach, Norfolk

Robbie Dale and me, ready for a
week's leave

The *Mi Amigo* – the little ship with the
big heart, 1966–8

A   12100

JAN 68

RADIO CAROLINE 259 m.

Johnnie Walker

**OFFICIAL
KISS-IN-THE-CAR
LICENCE**

*This licence is valid
until January, 1968 and
entitles the holder(s) to
kiss-in-the-car providing the
occupants are listening to
the Johnnie Walker Show
on Radio Caroline South*

**NOT
TRANSFERABLE**

FRONT

REVERSE   KISS IN THE CAR LICENCE
David and Karen of Sudbury wanted to know if it was valid for scooters !

One of 19,000 'Kiss In The Car' licences

Radio Caroline's studio

Hampton-in-Arden, August '67 – the fan club farewell

Hitting the headlines – 14th August '67, the day I became a criminal for playing records

All alone at Hampton station (velvet jacket from Granny Takes A Trip)

Robbie and I singing 'We Shall Overcome' just after midnight on 14 August 1967

Frances and me, just married
– December '71

With Sam and Beth in Ramsgate

My first motorcycle
– a 175cc Honda

The luxurious bedroom in my first London flat

Radio 1. Back row *(left to right)*: Jimmy Saville, Ed Stewart, Dave Lee Travis, Emperor Rosko, Alan Freeman, Annie Nightingale, John Peel, me, Terry Wogan
Foreground: David Hamilton, Noel Edmonds, Tony Blackburn

Lunchtime show at Radio 1

Graham North tries to pull the door off my crushed leg, Aldershot

Super stock car sponsored by Orange Amplifiers

Another great coat from Granny Takes A Trip

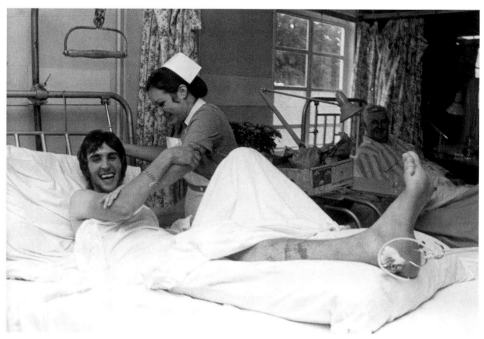

Enjoying the attention on the Orthopaedic ward in St. Peter's Hospital, Chertsey, Surrey

intensity of the midnight moment, we eventually wound up our historic broastcast at two a.m. We came out of the studio completely exhausted.

It had been one hell of a day.

I had no trouble getting to sleep. The moment my head hit the pillow I went out like a light, but now, some five and a half hours later, I awoke with a troubled mind. I hurriedly dressed and went up on deck, fully expecting to see a Royal Navy frigate nearby with a boarding party ready to clap us in irons. Despite Ronan's firm belief that they couldn't touch us in international waters, I recalled the television footage of RAF planes blowing up those forts, which also were in international waters. There wasn't a ship to be seen on the horizon, however, and everything was eerily quiet and normal. It was almost an anticlimax after the intense excitement of yesterday.

Robbie and I had breakfast and as we were working out the on-air shift rota for that day, we were interrupted by a shout from on deck. We went out to see what was up and there was a tiny little inflatable boat alongside with a man standing up in it, hanging on to the rubber tyres slung along *Mi Amigo*'s side.

'I just thought I'd come out and see if you boys needed anything. I think you're doing an amazing job and I just wanted to see if I could help. I'll go to the shops for you if you like. Anything you need?'

'I'd love a fishing rod,' said Robbie, 'and maybe today's newspapers.'

'And I'll have a box of fruit gums!' was all I could think of.

His boat had the tiniest little outboard engine I've ever seen but he started it up and chugged off, shouting, 'I'll see you a bit later.'

Sure enough, a few hours later, he was back with a whole bunch of goodies including Robbie's fishing rod.

I leant over the deck and said, 'Just before you hand this stuff over, you do realize that you're breaking the new law and you could be in all sorts of trouble?'

'Oh, I don't give a stuff about all that,' he replied. 'They can go take a running jump. I just want to do my bit to help. And just think of the tale I'll have to tell the lads back in the pub when I get home. I've taken a week off for a fishing holiday and I'll come out every day if I can.'

We saw him a couple more times, but then he took the captain's advice not to risk the treacherous currents in such a small boat. We were bowled over by his courage and his spur-of-the-moment efforts to do his bit to help. He was a great morale booster during those first few anxious days.

Besides the anxiety, we also had a lot of fun in that early period. We were still riding high on the euphoria of Monday the 14th, and were feeling invincible. We decided to carry on our commercial ad breaks much as before, so beaming out from The Lady were the usual messages extolling the crunchy sunshine of Kellogg's Cornflakes, life going better with Coca-Cola and Maclean's toothpaste giving you a lovely white smile. Back in London, the authorities were wondering what the hell was going on. Surely the whole purpose of this new law was to stop advertising. Little grey men went scurrying around advertising agencies and corporate headquarters, determined to find out why these products were still being advertised. They were usually told, 'We haven't asked them to play the ads, we haven't paid for them. We'd like to get in touch with them to tell them to stop, but you've closed down their London office and we don't know where to contact them. You tell us how to get them to stop.' While feigning anger and indignation, most agencies were probably delighted that their clients' products were being pitched at an even bigger audience while costing them nothing.

Caroline as a company was, of course, desperate to secure whatever money it could to keep the ship out there. Some of the commercials we ran definitely had been paid for, but the majority of our financial support was now to be provided by Philip and Dorothy Solomon, whose main claim to fame was that they managed The Bachelors, a cheesy vocal group from Ireland. Their plan was to launch a new record label called Major Minor, to use Caroline to promote their releases, and to start an organized payola system where labels and managers could buy airplay on Caroline. This sounds pretty outrageous but it was only what Radio Luxembourg had been doing for years.

On the ship, we weren't very aware of this new arrangement. We were still getting used to the changes in our lifestyle, the biggest of which was the lack of a daily tender. Right from the beginning, supply boats would arrive as regular as clockwork at around lunchtime. The listeners always knew when the tender arrived as very often the record on air would jump as the boat banged against the side of the ship. It was one of those highlights of our day that used to break up the monotony. Along with supplies of food and water, there'd also be the day's newspapers, listeners' and friends' letters. My mum could post a letter in Hampton-in-Arden in the afternoon to the shipping agency in Harwich, and by the following lunchtime it would be delivered to the ship. Because of the new law, that was no longer possible. We now felt very cut off without the daily tender visit. Supplies had to come all the way from Holland and there was a much greater chance of weather conditions making it difficult for a boat to get through. Sometimes the delivery would be once a week, sometimes once a fortnight.

Our shifts had changed, too, and now consisted of three weeks on and one week off, the week off being spent in Holland. Instead of an hour and a half to Harwich, it now took twenty to twenty-four hours to cross the North Sea to the port of Ijmuiden. Every time I made the crossing, it seemed the sea was really rough. Below decks there was a large cabin with several bunks, but there was a dreadful smell of diesel oil down there, which made you feel sick anyway, so I would spend the crossing hanging on to the stainless-steel sink in the tiny galley, constantly retching with the most violent sickness. The awful thing about seasickness is that even after you've emptied the contents of your stomach, the retching doesn't stop. You really feel like you just want to die. Every single time I got to port, I swore I would never ever make that journey again. But after a week's leave, I would always go back.

Caroline had opened offices in Amsterdam and also rented a large B&B. Although we had a strict Dutch landlady, our time there was good. But it wasn't a patch on being in London. Robbie and I often talked about taking a chance and flying back to London on our weeks off. The flight from Schiphol Airport to Heathrow was only about forty minutes; we had the idea of announcing on air that we were flying back to London and giving out the flight number and arrival time. We knew (or we certainly hoped) that a huge crowd of Caroline fans would turn up and if the police or customs officers attempted to arrest us, there would be a riot. We both thought this would be a great idea and got very excited about the prospect. However, Philip Solomon got to hear about it. He was aghast at the scheme and managed to talk us out of it.

Philip Solomon, now Caroline's main investor, was very unlike Ronan. He shied away from any kind of rebellion or confrontation, and was a ruthless businessman. All he wanted was for Caroline to continue playing his records. The big problem was that they weren't very good and neither were the records people paid us to put on the playlist. Let's face it, any good records we would want to play anyway. It was the crap ones people had to pay to get on air.

I hated the playlist. I had loved the freedom of the original Caroline format of alternating one Top Forty hit and one free choice. Sometimes I would start the hour by playing all of the playlist crap in a row and getting them out of the way so that I could then play what I wanted. I made no secret of my loathing for this new system – it went against everything that Caroline stood for. One week I ripped up the playlist on air and chucked it out of the porthole, which got me into huge trouble.

I hated playing by the rules.

Chapter Seventeen

The BBC's three networks of the Light Programme, the Home Service and the Third Programme closed down for ever at 6 a.m. on 27th September 1967. Moments later, four new networks were born: Radio Three and Radio Four for classical music and speech, Radio Two for middle-of-the-road light entertainment, and the brand-new pop station Radio One.

Tony Blackburn launched the station with his breakfast show, and the first record was The Move with 'Flowers In The Rain'. The choice of opening song speaks volumes about the difference between a large corporation and a station like Caroline. At an important moment in our history, we chose the Beatles' 'All You Need Is Love'. They chose a fairly average pop hit that spoke of waking up in the morning to something new and contained the bright colours of the flowers – but, appropriately, it was also pissing down with rain. For many, Radio One was a fairly damp and dull replacement for the pirate stations they loved so much.

Back on the ship, we tuned in with great interest as Radio One started its life. We weren't very impressed with what we heard, especially as at nine o'clock Radio One linked up with Radio Two for *The Jimmy Young Show*. But it was impossible to tell how successful Radio One was going to be; after all, it had the might of the BBC behind it and transmitters that were certainly a lot more powerful than ours. And when the weekly tender arrived, we saw the massive newspaper coverage that had been given to Radio One's launch. Caroline never got a mention and we became quite dispirited. It was starting to look as if the government was going to win after all. It seemed that even Mother Nature was against us as the weather took a turn for the worse, and so began one of the toughest winters Caroline had faced out in the North Sea.

Quite by chance, I discovered a record called 'The Ballad Of The Green Berets' by Sergeant Barry Sandler. It was a blatant piece of American propaganda that attempted to praise and glorify American soldiers fighting in Vietnam. On the B side was the instrumental version without the vocal and I liked the way it started quietly and then gradually built up, with layer upon layer, to a crescendo of real power and emotion. I started writing some lyrics of my own that would fit in with the structure of the tune. I called it 'Man's Fight For Freedom' and my story told the tale of Radio Caroline bravely fighting the British government, who, one glorious day, relented and gave permission for Caroline to sail proudly up the Thames to start broadcasting legally. It was an exercise in positive thinking that ended:

. . . The insurmountable odds have been surmounted . . .
We have overcome,
The battle is over,
Free radio becomes a way of life but no man will ever forget Monday
14th August, 1967.

It got a great reaction from the listeners and, although it might have been a little bit over the top, it helped our morale during the difficult days when we felt utterly cut off from everyone and lost in the shadow of Radio One. It gave us, and thousands of listeners, hope that Caroline might, just might, emerge victorious and take its rightful place alongside the other stations.

Caroline listeners at that time will remember hearing Major Minor releases over and over again. There were The Dubliners going on and on and on about their 'Seven Drunken Nights' and the slushy orchestral sound of the Raymond Lefevre Orchestra. Those records and the playlist obviously spoilt the overall sound of Radio Caroline, but there was still enough freedom to play the really good stuff and we all knew it was only Major Minor and the playlist that was keeping us on the air.

My morale was at times really low. Everything seemed to be conspiring against us. The isolation was hard to bear and we would run short of food and water when the tender couldn't make it out because of harsh weather. The creature comforts that had previously been so abundant on the *Mi Amigo* were now gone and sometimes it was hard to feel that it was worth it, or that millions of people still loved listening to Caroline. I missed my old DJ friends, who seemed to have taken all the fun with them when they left. It felt like we were living under siege and I was beginning to get the sense that we couldn't win in the long run. We weren't playing as many commercials as we once had, so we didn't have the revenue we needed to keep going. Our new bosses, who were providing the money to keep us on air, didn't seem as committed to Caroline as Ronan had been. But I was determined to stick with it for as long as it took.

On 3rd March 1968, I finished my show at midnight, walked into the mess room and prepared my usual after-show snack of cornflakes and a couple of rounds of toast and tea. I loved that time of night. The seas were usually calm, the ship was quiet and I'd chat for hours to the Dutch crew member who was on night duty. Eventually, at about three three a.m., I went to bed.

I was roughly shaken awake by someone who told me there was a tug alongside and that I had to get up.

'What time is it?' I asked.

'Five thirty,' was the reply.

'Jesus, what the hell are you waking me up for at this time? I've only had a couple of hours' sleep.'

'I'm telling you, you've got to get up now. We've got a major problem. You've got to come and help sort this out.'

I pulled on my jeans and sweater and blearily climbed up the stairway to find six heavyset big Dutchmen looking pretty menacing. The guy in charge barked out his commands.

'You've got ten minutes to get your stuff out of the studio. Then we seal it up. We have taken over the ship.'

I was completely bamboozled and far too dazed by lack of sleep to understand what was going on. Before I could get my head together and collect my things from the studio, it had been locked up with a couple of men guarding the doors. By now, with all the shouting and kerfuffle going on, everyone was pretty much awake, but no one seemed to know just what was going on. A huge powerful tug had moored alongside us and its crew were arranging towing lines. All we could get out of the tugboat's captain were the words, 'We go to Amsterdam.'

It had long been rumoured that the hull of the *Mi Amigo* was in such a poor state that one day she'd have to be taken into dry dock to have her hull scraped and repainted. One of the jocks suggested hopefully that this was what was happening now – but the menacing attitude of the tug's boarding party made me doubt that. They seemed to be anything but friendly.

What happened next confirmed my worst fears. After securing the towing lines, two of the tug's crew unhooked the anchor chain and let it fall into the sea. The *Mi Amigo* maintained her position thanks to the enormous seagoing anchor attached to her after a night, years before, when she'd run aground. Surely if she were going to return, the anchor chain would have been attached to a temporary buoy.

At that point, my whole world caved in. All the struggle and hardship of the last seven months appeared to have been in vain. All I could think of were the millions of regular Caroline listeners who would be waking up and turning on their radios. Instead of the usual music and chat, there would be silence. There was absolutely no way of letting them know what was happening. Without the power of our 50,000-watt transmitter, we were rendered totally helpless. Slowly, we were tugged across the North Sea and finally the *Mi Amigo* began to make her way up the canal to Amsterdam. We must have looked a strange and sorry sight. And how very different was this scenario compared to the victorious sailing up the Thames that I'd outlined in 'Man's Fight For Freedom'. Was this really how The Lady was going to end? I couldn't believe it.

Pinky Siedenburg, who ran Caroline's Amsterdam office, was waiting at the quayside. Word had spread like wildfire that the famous *Mi Amigo*, home of Radio Caroline, was being ignominiously towed into the harbour. Pinky, like everyone else, seemed to have absolutely no idea what was going on. I stayed in Amsterdam for a few days, hoping the situation would become clear, but there was no more information and there didn't seem to be the slightest chance that Caroline was going to go back on air. So I packed my stuff and caught a cab to Schiphol Airport and flew back to London.

It was risky because I had no idea what would happen at immigration. Would I be arrested? Was I going to face years behind bars merely for going home? I decided there was nothing else I could do.

Sure enough, once I'd entered Britain, I was pulled to one side by an immigration officer.

'You're a pirate DJ off Caroline, aren't you?' he said.

'What on earth gives you that idea?' I asked innocently.

'Listen, son, I 'appen to know you're that Johnnie Walker fella.'

As my passport was in my real name of Peter Dingley, I was amazed that he knew who I was.

'Maybe I am. Maybe I'm not,' I replied with a smile. I had no idea what was about to happen but I wasn't going to show him how scared I was.

'Listen, Johnnie, don't muck about. I know just who you are.'

He reached for an official form.

Uh oh, I thought, my heart sinking. I'm really in for it now.

Turning the form over to its blank side and putting on a huge grin, he said, 'I wonder if you'd be kind enough to autograph this for my daughter? She's a huge fan.'

We both shared a really good laugh. He'd enjoyed his little game and I was so relieved to be back in England without the major hassle I'd been anticipating.

Robbie Dale, as official chief DJ on the ship, eventually managed to find out from Philip Solomon what had happened. None of the regular bills had been paid to the company Offshore, so its owners – the Weissmueller brothers – in a meticulously planned operation simultaneously hijacked Radio Caroline North and South. Now there was a stand-off. They were going to sell or salvage the ships for whatever they could get unless the outstanding money was paid.

Philip Solomon was outraged by the Weissmuellers' cheek and was raving on about their blatant act of piracy, which was very funny when you thought about it. Maybe Solomon's entire plan had been to avoid paying any of the bills, but just to keep Caroline running as long as possible in order to establish his record label, and make a few easy quid selling space on the playlist. He seemed to care very little for Caroline or its listeners.

I was angry with myself for being so naive. As with so much of the idealism of the sixties, a network of 'get rich quick' merchants lay behind the dreams and hopes of many of the artists and groups. They recognized that by paying lip service to the revolution, they could make themselves lots of money. That, I fear, is what did for Caroline. Love was the dream, but in the end, all you needed was money and when Caroline ran out of it, that was the end.

My radio days were over.

PART THREE

'Auntie'

Chapter Eighteen

1968

I was driving down Wood Lane heading towards Shepherd's Bush in a battered old white van. Behind me, someone was impatiently blasting their horn. Roaring past me at breakneck speed was an open-top Jaguar E-type. The driver blasted the horn again and waved to the uniformed commissionaires standing at the gates of the BBC Television Centre. It was that flash bastard Simon Dee. He was riding a wave of incredible success as the good-looking young blue-eyed boy of television, host of the hugely successful show *Dee Time*. He had absolutely everything going for him at that time. I recognized him instantly. And what was his main claim to fame? He was one of the first DJs on Radio Caroline. There he was showing off his fame and fortune and here was me rattling along in an old van delivering a bunch of eight-track stereos.

I had to laugh. The contrast couldn't have been more stark. He got off the ship early, got himself on Radio One, and now had a hit TV show. I had stayed past August 14th and now had nothing except temporary jobs from a drivers' agency. If that wasn't bad enough, the company I was doing this delivery for was right next door to Radio Luxembourg in Mayfair. As I unloaded the van, I deliberately piled up the boxes so that I could hide behind them as I carried them into the office. I didn't want anybody seeing how low I had sunk.

I was in the bizarre situation of recently having been voted Number One in a *News of The World* DJ poll, and yet the only work I could get was as a part-time van and lorry driver. With no commercial radio yet in existence, there was only Radio Luxembourg or the BBC and I doubted I'd be welcome at either.

So I was unemployed. Still worried about what might happen to me if I was known as Johnnie Walker, I worked as Pete Dingley. At first I felt nervous whenever I passed policemen and spent a lot of time looking over my shoulder and wondering if I was about to feel a hand clamp down on me and a rough voice say, 'Johnnie Walker? You're under arrest. Please accompany me to the station . . .'

But it didn't happen. Not even the long arm of the law was interested in me. My fear gradually dissipated. It seemed that the government couldn't be less concerned with chasing up the 'criminals' who'd worked on the pirate stations. Once the pirate stations had been put off the air, the aim had been achieved and it was all forgotten about.

I had enrolled with a company that worked like a secretarial temp agency, only for drivers. I'd delivered crockery to a market stall in the Old Kent Road, worked for a London laundry heaving baskets of linen in and out of the basements of hotels, and now I had this current job – basically anything I could do to make a few quid. I was determined to stay in London, camping on the floors of various friends, and see what happened. I knew that in Amsterdam there was a fully functioning radio ship and I hoped that before too long I would be back on board, broadcasting my Caroline show again. I also hoped that a Conservative government would get in and introduce a proper, land-based commercial radio network where I might be able to get a job. Until then, I just had to survive.

Whenever there was no work, I'd hang out in the offices of Atlantic Records. I had made really good friends with label boss Frank Fenter and his secretary, Janet Martin. Because of my on-air support for their artists, such as Otis Redding and Wilson Pickett, they had made me Honorary President of 'Uptightanoutasight', the Atlantic Label Appreciation Society. In the UK Atlantic Records came through Polydor Records and occupied a wonderful building at the end of Stratford Place, a small cul-de-sac off Oxford Street. It became my second home and I was always made welcome there. I made friends with some great record-business characters including Clive Selwood, head of Elektra Records, who also managed John Peel. There'd always be some kind of session going on with a group recording something. Among others, I became good friends with Gordon Haskell, the bass player of Fleur de Lys.

Frank Fenter and his team ran the whole of Atlantic Records UK from one large office on the fourth floor. Frank was a tall, striking-looking man, always well dressed in his tailor-made shirts and suits, who had come to London from his native South Africa to seek fame and fortune. He'd done an incredible job in launching Atlantic in the UK and no one who saw it will forget the incredible Stax Tour of 1967. (Stax Records, based in Memphis, was home to Booker T. and the MG's, Otis Redding, Sam and Dave, and so on. They were released in the UK through Atlantic.)

Frank was obviously grateful for what I'd done for his artists on the ship; we liked each other a lot and he valued my musical judgement. There was always music playing in the office and Frank was often sent acetate test pressings of the latest recordings from the States.

One day, he opened up a package, looked at the label info and said, 'I don't believe this. Lady Soul' – as he always called Aretha Franklin – 'has gone and done a Bacharach-David song. What the fuck's this all about?'

He put it on the turntable and cranked up the volume to +10 as he always did, and out of the speakers came 'I Say A Little Prayer'. His secretary, Janet, and I both loved it, but Frank couldn't see it at all.

'They must be crazy,' he said. 'What is one of the world's greatest soul singers doing singing pop?'

'It doesn't matter,' I countered. 'It's still Aretha and her voice is still incredible. I think it's great.'

Janet agreed with me, but Frank was still doubtful.

'They want me to put it out as her new single and I just don't think it's a good career move.'

'Play it again, Frank,' I suggested.

It sounded even better on the second play. Janet and I did our best to persuade him to release it.

'I think it would get a lot of airplay, Frank. It could bring Aretha to a whole new audience and I reckon it could be a big hit.'

'OK,' said Frank. 'I'll think about it.'

'I Say A Little Prayer (For You)' was released as a single and, while some soul critics and fans thought Aretha doing pop was wrong, the record shot to Number Four in the UK charts, giving her her biggest-ever UK hit.

Frank was man enough to say, 'You were right and I was wrong.' As a thank you, he put my name forward to compère Aretha Franklin's forthcoming London concert. This was a very brave suggestion as I still had the air of a fugitive about me. Show promoter Arthur Howes was really reluctant to give me the gig, convinced the police would arrest me onstage. Frank told him not to be so ridiculous and eventually he won the day. I was booked to compère this prestigious concert.

It was going to be a huge night. The concert was at the enormous Finsbury Park Astoria Theatre and when I got there at about six p.m. and saw the size of the place, I really started to get the jitters. I wasn't used to working in front of a live crowd, and I didn't have an act of stand-up patter. Instead, I'd done lots of homework, memorizing every detail of Aretha's career, and I thought that I could always pad that out by talking about my love of soul music.

As show time approached I put on my best velvet flares and a green shirt with billowing sleeves. I was exceptionally nervous and it felt very strange to go from being a van driver to striding out onstage in front of three and a half thousand people. The auditorium was rapidly filling up with a sell-out crowd, and soon I'd have to go out there and do my bit. I hadn't been able to eat a thing all day.

The moment arrived. Standing in the wings, I looked at the emergency exit and thought, 'I could just dash out of there now, disappear into the night, and no one would be able to find me.' But, of course, I knew I couldn't do that. After all Frank's efforts to get me on the bill, I had to give it my best shot. Fortunately it seemed as if there were a lot of Caroline fans in the audience and I got a lovely welcoming round of applause. The hardest thing was getting used to being so dazzled by a spotlight that I couldn't see any of the faces in the crowd. Once I'd become accustomed to that, my nerves settled and I began to enjoy myself. The night went off really well: Aretha was fantastic and 'I Say A Little Prayer' got the biggest applause of the show. Everyone was happy – especially my mum, who'd come down to see the show and had been nudging people left and right, front and back, proudly informing them, 'That's my son up there!'

The concert was just a taste of the high life, though, and I soon settled into a routine of a few days' driving and then hanging out at Atlantic until my next job. Janet Martin had been kind enough to put me up at her Bayswater flat, so I didn't need a lot of money to survive. Every now and then, the subject of joining Radio One came up and I always said, 'I don't want to go there.' I'd always publicly said I would never join the BBC and I didn't want to go back on that promise. Besides, I had spent a lot of time taking the mickey out of dear old 'Auntie' when I was at Caroline. I'd often announced that we were the home of free radio, not like that lot over at Radio One. And I'd already burnt my bridges at Broadcasting House after a little prank I'd played on them during the early weeks of our illegal existence.

I'd read in one of the newspapers that the BBC was worried about falling ratings for their daily soap opera *Mrs Dale's Diary* on the Light Programme. It was at the height of my invincible cheeky period and I thought what great fun it would be to rebroadcast an edition of the soap on Caroline, thus ensuring the entire cast had broken the Marine Offences Act and were liable to two years in the nick. So one morning at eleven a.m., I explained that the BBC were in a bit of trouble and Caroline was happy to help up the ratings of *Mrs Dale*, and by a special link with the BBC we were going to broadcast that morning's edition of the show. While talking live on air, I held a transistor radio to my ear tuned to the Light Programme.

Then, just at the right moment, I proudly announced, 'And now, by special arrangement with our friends at the BBC, Radio Caroline is proud to present *Mrs Dale's Diary!*'

I turned up the volume and held the little radio close to the microphone. The quality was very good and it really did sound as though we had some amazing studio link-up. Maybe it was going a tad too far to do it all over again in the afternoon when they ran the repeat, but I couldn't resist it. Although I didn't find out until later, it was a front-page story in the next day's tabloids. The *Daily Sketch* splashed the headline: WALKER REBROADCASTS THE DALES. The BBC were incredibly angry and the strait-laced Jessie Mathews, who played Mrs Dale, thought the whole thing was disgraceful and appalling. Although the newspaper correctly stated that by broadcasting on a pirate radio station the actors had, in fact, broken the law, the Department of Public Prosecutions said they would not be taking any action. It was great publicity for Caroline and Ronan loved it, telling the newspapers that we were only doing our bit to help. But I had a feeling that the BBC would not be keen to hear from me in the near future.

One afternoon Elektra label chief Clive Selwood came bursting into the Atlantic den.

'Johnnie, I've got to play you this new album. It's the greatest thing I've heard in years. If you get a minute, come by my office and have a listen.'

In his office, Clive put on the album he was so excited about. It was called *Accept No Substitute* by a new band called Delaney & Bonnie. And Clive was right. It was really great music. It was a wonderful mix of soul, gospel, country and rock.

'I love it, Clive. It's really good. But it's so frustrating not to be able to play it on the radio,' I said.

'I was going to talk to you about that. You really belong on the radio and the way things look at the moment, Caroline isn't coming back and there's nobody else crazy enough to try and run a pirate station. You're either going to have to give up the idea of radio altogether, or you're going to have to bite the bullet, swallow your pride and join Radio One.' He saw the doubt in my eyes and continued, 'Listen, you know I look after John [Peel]. I could just casually mention that you might be interested and see what the reaction is.'

The truth was, I was beginning to despair about my situation and I was desperately missing the buzz of being on air. My main worry about the BBC was its corporate structure: would they let me be myself, and give me a decent amount of freedom over music choice? I'd heard all sorts of tales of heavy-handed producers with stopwatches. And my old mate Mike Ahern had only lasted a couple of days at Radio One. But I desperately wanted to work again.

After some deliberation, I said, 'Okay, Clive, give it a mention.'

His eyes lit up and he was obviously relishing the challenge.

Clive was a very laconic, droll sort of a guy; it was a few days later that he casually said, 'Umm, Johnnie, Radio One would love to meet you and have a chat, and they're suggesting a lunch on neutral territory so you don't have to go to them.'

Lunch was arranged at The Bark and Bite, a floating restaurant on the canal in Regent's Park. Clive and I went along and met two besuited bods from the BBC. One of them, with a very military air and moustache, looked like a squadron leader in the RAF. It turned out he was Mark White, head of Radio One.

'Well, Johnnie old boy, so glad that you could make it to lunch. We thought we'd come here because it would make you feel more at home,' said Mark in his rather posh accent, as he gestured towards the portholes.

'That's very kind of you,' I replied.

It was perhaps a rather obvious joke, but it was nice of them to think about it, and it certainly showed that they accepted my lawbreaking time with Caroline. In fact, it was a clever way of acknowledging it without having to actually talk about it. The lunch went very well. It was really a mutual getting-to-know-you exercise, and we parted with them saying they were going to put a few ideas together and come back to me.

Clive and I walked back through Regent's Park.

'Thanks very much for setting that up, Clive. If you're heading back to the office, I think I'm just going to wander round the park for a bit, sit and watch the ducks, and have a good think.'

'No problem,' said Clive with a grin, and left me to my ruminations.

I'll always be grateful to Clive Selwood for opening a really important door for me. He asked for and expected nothing in return; I think he just really wanted to see me back on the radio. As I sat in Regent's Park that day, my mind was racing with a hundred and one thoughts. Would Caroline fans ever forgive me for going back on all the pledges I'd made? And, most importantly, would I be able to play stuff like Delaney & Bonnie and all the other music I loved?

But the future was looking a lot brighter.

Chapter Nineteen

1969

Clive Selwood's timing was perfect. Shortly after Caroline went off the air, a memo was circulated to Radio One producers telling them that on no account should they consider using Johnnie Walker for at least a year. The taint of criminality had to subside before the BBC could hire me.

Just over twelve months had passed when Clive nudged open the door, and after that lunchtime meeting, things happened very fast. It seemed that in no time at all I was a new Radio One recruit with the enormous security of a thirteen-week freelance contract. Because the programmes were scheduled in quarters, we got a contract for a quarter of a year, which was then renewed. The money was better than the £25 a week I'd been getting on Caroline – not riches, by any means, but more than I'd been paid before for being on the radio.

They were going to start me off with a Saturday-afternoon show, which traditionally was the slot for trying out new people. Either by accident or design, my first show was on Cup Final day, which in those days was a huge national event when the roads and the shopping centres would be deserted, and very few people would be listening to the radio while the game was on. Actually, I didn't mind too much – a quiet show would give me the chance to get over my nerves and learn the ropes a bit.

Walking into the BBC for the first time was a daunting experience. The huge corporation, buzzing with people, couldn't have been more different from the ships.

Inside the studio, there was no longer the intimacy of the mike, the listener and me. Now a producer and an engineer sat behind

a glass window and while I cued up my own records, I had nothing
to do with setting the levels. Almost at once, I missed the closeness
I had felt when I was on my own with the listener, and couldn't
help feeling inhibited with other people around, embarrassed even.
I supposed that I would get used to it in time, but I also knew it
would never be the same as it had been on Caroline.

I gradually began to get the hang of the new way of doing
things. There were so many differences between the BBC radio
show and a pirate one: I had never had a producer and I had always
played records spontaneously, just going with the flow and the
mood of the day. Now I was expected to spend a whole day sitting
in an office planning with a producer the music we were going to
play several days later. I realized this was the way the BBC did
things, so I just got on with it. But, most of the time, I regarded
producers as a stop on my creativity. Their tastes and ideas had to
be taken into account and I found it very difficult to compromise
on what I thought were the right records.

A new difficulty for me was that I wasn't able to play just records
– my show had to include live music. Because of the power of the
Musicians Union and the Performing Rights Society, the amount
of records – or 'needle time' – was severely restricted. These
entrenched rules and regulations, which the pirates never had to
bother with, came out of the early days of radio, when most of
the music was played live by the BBC orchestra and other bands.
The major record companies were also convinced that if hit records
were played too many times, people wouldn't bother to go out
and buy them. Pirate radio had completely disproved that theory
and the huge music revolution of the sixties meant that sales had
never been so good. In fact, the pirates had helped to stimulate
growth and creativity: the four big labels, EMI, Decca, Pye and
Philips, had lost their stranglehold on the market place and there
were now many, many more labels including small new indepen-
dents like Island Records.

But the union regulations at the BBC meant that we could not
play records all the time, so quite a large proportion of the music
played was by bands who had recorded a session in BBC studios.

They'd only have a few hours to record three or four songs including their current hit, which was nothing like as good as the original. But unfortunately Wilson Pickett or The Doors were hardly about to fly over to record a radio session.

After I'd done the first few programmes of my new show, my nerves wore off and I began to really enjoy being back on the radio. It was not long before I was being offered all sorts of other programmes, including being added to the rota of *What's New*, a daily review programme of new singles, which featured a different Radio One DJ each week. A lot of letters came in from listeners and I was very encouraged by their positive reaction to me – it helped me feel like I was really settling in.

Now that there was a bit of regular money coming in, I found the perfect bachelor pad to rent: a top-floor studio flat in a really unusual building in Belsize Park. It was the brainchild of a dotty professor, who wanted to create something unique that would be perfect for single professional people working in London during the week. He built a restaurant on the ground floor and each of the flats had a dumb waiter lift for delivering food. It was fifty quid a week all in, and for that I got free heating, electricity and a cleaner, who came in every morning to tidy up. Most people weren't there at the weekends and I had the place pretty much to myself, so I could play my music really loud.

My front door opened into a tiny area just big enough for a cupboard, and then a second door opened into the main flat. It was like going through an air lock and I felt as though I was in my own little world. I suppose in a way it was like a bigger version of my cabin on board the *Mi Amigo*. I even had my own balcony, which was just like going out on deck. During the summer weekends I'd roll a massive spliff, play some of my favourite albums like The Eagles or The James Gang at full blast, get wonderfully stoned and dance around the balcony like a mad dervish. Having spent a week struggling with the conformity and the suits at the BBC, I just needed to let off some steam.

★

After a year at Radio One, I'd served my apprenticeship. It was
1970 and I was twenty-five years old when I was offered a daily
show of just one hour at nine a.m. sandwiched in between Tony
Blackburn and Jimmy Young. It was really bizarre doing a one-
hour show – by the time I was getting warmed up and into it, the
show would be over. But my big problem was not being allowed
to play the records I wanted. Saturday-afternoon shows had more
freedom musically, but because this new programme was on a
weekday morning, anything other than mainstream Top Forty hits
scared producers to death. But ever since *Sergeant Pepper's Lonely
Hearts Club Band*, the single had started to be regarded as light-
weight and the album was where really great music tracks could
be found. Inspired by Delaney & Bonnie, and borrowing three of
their band, Eric Clapton had just finished a double album calling
himself Derek and The Dominoes. The album was *Layla And
Other Assorted Love Songs*. Now, I might have been a bit stoned
when I first played it at home but I thought the title track was just
the greatest thing I'd heard for years. I was desperate to play it on
my show.

'I'm sorry, Johnnie. You can't play that,' said my producer.

'But why on earth not? It's fantastic.'

'Yes, it might be, but not for a daytime audience on Radio
One. It's just too heavy for your average housewife.'

Just who were these housewives that we were trying to protect?
If you loved the Beatles and the Rolling Stones, you didn't suddenly become a raving Frank Sinatra fan just because you got
married. My producer was worried about what his executive producer might say, and he was worried about what the assistant head
of Radio One might say, who in turn had a whole layer of managers
above him to worry about. Everyone was so desperate not to take
risks. Playing it safe was entrenched in BBC thinking. But I wasn't
going to give up on Layla. We argued back and forth until my
producer started to lose his temper.

'You're not playing it and that's that.'

It was in the early days of this daily show and I think if I'd gone
ahead and played 'Layla' anyway, they would have taken me off.

It was so frustrating. I spent so much of my spare time listening to all the new singles and albums, reading through all the music papers and going to see lots of bands at gigs. I did it for sheer love and enjoyment, and when I heard something that I just knew would sound great on the radio, but was denied the opportunity to play it by someone who didn't know or understand music, it really rankled.

'Layla' was eventually released as a single two years later and became a massive hit in the UK and America. And Radio One played it quite happily because it was a seven-inch single, and made the charts – so it was now okay. The same thing happened with early records by Rod Stewart and Bad Company, whose album tracks I was not allowed to play as they were considered unsuitable for a Radio One audience. But once they were released as singles and became hits, they suddenly became quite acceptable. I always felt it was our job to play records that were the potential hits of tomorrow, but Radio One was too cowardly to do so.

On the plus side, I was benefiting from the biggest perk of all: free records. I really loved getting all the latest singles and albums and I listened to as many as I could. Tickets to concerts were also a very enjoyable benefit, along with invitations to film premieres, record-company receptions and any number of parties. My social life was part of my job and I had a great time. The money was good and I had the benefits of growing fame without the hassle of recognition.

Around that time I was into stock-car racing. Wimbledon Stadium – now there was a place on a Saturday night: packed stands, pop music blaring out of the PA system and then the lights would dim. There'd be the roar of fifty or so cars racing round the floodlit oval track, skidding, sliding, bashing each other, rolling over, smashing into the fence. It was all the fun of the fairgrounds I'd loved as a kid, but a lot more exciting.

One evening, a team of Radio One DJs were invited to take part in a special celebrity race. It was the most thrilling experience to be strapped tightly in the car and then roar round the track in glorious four-wheel slides, nudging competitors out of the way. It was like dodgem cars multiplied many times over. My car was an old MG Magnette prepared by Graham North, whose whole family had been totally committed to stock-car racing for many years. I pulled into the paddock after the race, my eyes blazing with excitement.

'So, Johnnie, what did you think of that?' asked Graham.

'It was absolutely fantastic. I loved it!'

'You did pretty well out there. Would you like to do some more?'

He didn't need to ask twice. A deal was sorted between Graham and the promoter whereby Graham would supply and maintain a car for me for free in return for the PR value that a Radio One DJ could give the sport. For a while, I also raced every week in the Superstox class for purpose-built, high-speed stock cars. But my real love was the saloons, and also it was a safer form of racing. Everything was removed from the car except the driver's seat, and two RSJ girders ran through the car with special crash protectors front and back. I loved the glamour, the excitement, the noise and even the dirt, and did as many races as I could.

I took part in a big race at Aldershot in Hampshire. I had that extra bit of confidence and self-belief after a recent near win, and as the pack of forty cars built up speed round the track for the rolling start, the adrenalin was in full flow. The great thing about stock cars was that the faster guys started at the back. Based on previous results, drivers were graded to a colour code: red were the fastest, then blue, yellow and white. I had recently been promoted to a blue top and was roughly in the middle of the pack. As the speed built up, I heard the familiar theme tune and the commentator revving up the excitement as the lights went out in the stadium leaving just the floodlights over the track.

All the faster drivers at the back had their toes down and were pushing hard against the slower drivers at the front. Suddenly my car flipped sideways and, stuck in the rolling pack, my car was being crushed by the enormous force of the cars sandwiching me. I had no control over it at all. I was getting incredible pain in my right leg and eventually the car was pushed on to the centre green.

One of the girders that strengthen the car emerged between the pedals and went under the driver's seat, so that it sat between my legs. The driver's door had been squashed right up against the girder with my leg trapped between them. The cars continued to race round and round the circuit, while I sat in the middle, trapped helplessly inside my car in great pain.

Normally the start marshal would always go to any car pushed on to the centre green and check to see that the driver was okay; but the regular guy was on holiday and the reserve marshal didn't come over. I was waving furiously out of the window and pointing down to the door that had trapped my leg. My frantic signals were completely misinterpreted and it seemed an eternity before the race was stopped. It was my pal and team leader, Graham North, who had sensed something was not quite right, and he raced his car over and stopped next to mine. All of a sudden I was surrounded by cars with drivers leaping out, frantically trying to pull the smashed door away from my crushed leg. Eventually they managed to lift me out and I was stretchered into a decrepit old St John's ambulance. My friend, fellow driver (and later my agent) Jimmy Smith accompanied me. The journey seemed to take for ever and every slight bump bounced me around, sending another wave of excruciating pain up my leg. Finally I was carried inside to Aldershot's small cottage hospital.

I lay on a trolley for ages and ages, and, as Jimmy has often reminded me, I wasn't the most polite patient.

'Jimmy, all I want is a fucking fag and a cup of tea.'

'You can't have a fag, but I'll go and see if I can rustle up a cup of tea.'

The nurse quickly put the mockers on that one. I wasn't allowed to eat or drink anything in case an operation was necessary. Eventually a doctor checked out my leg, gave me a shot of morphine and it was decided I should be transferred to St Peter's Orthopaedic Hospital in Chertsey. Jimmy left to go and sort out his stock car and I was stretchered into another ambulance, and so began the long painful journey.

Finally, I was stretchered on to a table in the emergency department where a team of doctors and nurses began cutting off my blood-soaked overalls. The last thing I remember was being wheeled into an operating theatre and the next thing I knew I was waking up in a strange ward, wondering where I was and what on earth had happened. There was a huge cradle over my legs and some kind of pulley system attached to the end of the bed. I tried to get a better look. I could see my foot at the end of the bed and there seemed to be a cord attached to a pin sticking out of my ankle. It didn't make sense that the same pin seemed to be sticking out the other side of my ankle as well until I realized they must have drilled through my ankle bone. I felt sick at the thought.

A nurse approached my bed, wheeling a telephone on a trolley, and said, 'There's someone who wants to speak to you.'

I took the phone and mumbled weakly, 'Hello?'

'Hello, Johnnie,' said a cheery voice on the other end. 'It's Tony Blackburn here and you're on air, on Radio One.'

'Oh. Hello, Tony.'

This was all I needed: I was still dopey from the anaesthetic and not up to a live broadcast. My accident had made the papers and so Tony thought it was a good idea to call me and see how I was. Nice thought, but I could have done with some warning, and it would have been better if he'd asked if I was up to it. I did my best to sound cheery and explained what had happened and that I was okay. Tony thankfully brought the chat to a swift end, as I wasn't making a whole lot of sense.

The surgeon came round to check up on me and we had a chat about my options. 'You've had a nasty compound fracture, but it should heal fine. After you've had a couple of weeks of traction, there are two ways we can go. The traditional way would be to put you in a full-length plaster, which will mean hobbling around on crutches for a few months. Or we could get you mobile as quickly as possible by screwing a metal plate on to the bone, which will require just a knee-to-ankle plaster.'

He seemed keen on the second plan so I decided to go for that. I had the operation to insert the metal plate and after the first few days of intense pain, I gradually began to settle down to hospital life.

I didn't get many visitors as Chertsey is a good way from London. Good old Jimmy Smith and Graham North and family came by to see me and, whenever I did have a visitor, I asked them to bring in some brandy miniatures that I could easily hide in my bedside locker. I soon built up quite a stash and found knocking back two or three about ten o'clock was the best way to get a decent night's sleep. The nights seemed very long and it was rare to get a really decent kip. I liked the atmosphere at night; gone was all the bustle, the lights were dimmed right down and all was quiet apart from the gentle drone of the snoring. Sometimes there'd be a friendly nurse on duty who could be persuaded to make some toast and brew a fresh cup of tea, and we'd enjoy a little chat in hushed whispers.

Sometimes the attention would surpass anything you would expect from an NHS hospital. A really attractive black agency nurse was on duty on a night when I could only sleep in fits and starts. Several times she stopped by my bed to see if I was okay and always flashed me a lovely smile as she checked the other patients. At about three a.m., she drew the curtains round my bed and asked me if I'd like some company for a while. Of course I would, I said. She pulled up a chair to the side of my bed and we talked about this and that. I'd been in the hospital for over a month and apart from my leg, the rest of me was working normally and long days in bed seemed to be making me more and more horny.

All was quiet and peaceful and the dim night lights created an alluring and sensuous atmosphere. Somehow we both sensed the effect we were having on each other. Looking steadily into my eyes, she ever so slowly slipped her hand under the sheet and began gently caressing me. It felt wonderful. It had been a long time since anyone had done that, and the element of risk and the complete outrageousness of what we were doing made it all the more erotic. I wanted the feeling to last and last but couldn't hold myself back, and desperately trying not to make a sound, our oh-so-naughty little encounter came to an end.

'You should have no trouble sleeping now, Mr Walker,' she said softly.

'No, I won't. Thank you very much, nurse.'

She drew back the curtains and was gone, as I drifted off into a very contented sleep.

Chapter Twenty

I enjoyed a fond farewell from St Peter's Hospital. They were either sad to see me go or deeply grateful – probably a bit of both. In any event, it was time to get back to my show on Radio One. No DJ likes being away for too long; there's always the fear that the listeners will start to like the guy sitting in. I would begin to worry even after a two-week break, and I'd been away for nearly two months. The BBC were good to me, though, and my slot was kept open for me. They were no doubt relieved that my motor-racing days were over, for a while at least. The orthopaedic surgeon was as good as his word and, after some adjustment of my knee-to-ankle plaster, I was able to get around, albeit pretty slowly. But I wasn't going to let a broken leg get in the way of normal activities.

I had to conquer the usual 'haven't done this for a while' nerves on my first show back and then soon settled down to the daily routine of a one-hour show from nine till ten. For the rest of the morning, I'd be in the producer's office, listening to music and planning the next day's show. I was still frustrated by the lack of freedom in what records I could play but at least I was allowed to pick my own 'Record of the Week', which was played every day.

A new single on RCA came into the office, by Lou Reed of Velvet Underground fame. 'Walk On The Wild Side' was taken from the magnificent *Transformer* album and the moment I heard Herbie Flowers' incredible bass lines on the intro, I was totally hooked. The fact that the song then went on to deal with trans-vestism and oral sex made it all the more compelling. I loved the female backing chorus of 'doo, da doo, doo da doo' and the glorious close with the really sexy, soulful saxophone solo. One of the great singles of all time.

'I've absolutely got to have this for "Record of the Week" next week,' I told my producer.

He looked doubtful but, noting my enthusiasm and not wishing to get into another 'Layla'-style confrontation, he reluctantly agreed. It sounded so good on the radio and after the first couple of days, people were beginning to talk about this amazing record Johnnie Walker was playing. By Wednesday, the press had picked up on it and were asking whether this was a suitable record for the BBC to be playing on daytime radio. There was a hastily convened meeting of the executive producers to discuss the situation. They realized they were in a bit of a quandary: as it had already been played three times, they couldn't really ban it at this stage; that would make them look a bit foolish. So they decided to let me carry on playing it. Doreen Davies, executive producer and unofficial 'Head of Morals' at Radio One, didn't quite get it and Chris Lycett, a fresh young producer, was summoned to her office.

'I don't really understand what all the fuss is about,' she said. 'It seems all right to me. But one thing *does* puzzle me – what does this expression "giving head" mean?'

Poor old Chris – what an initiation into the politics of Radio One.

The BBC is famous for its many tiers of bureaucracy. Not only did I have to deal with a producer, executive producer and the Head of Radio One, but also all the other jobsworths above them. Coming off a pirate station where there was no one telling me what I could and couldn't do, I found it endlessly frustrating dealing with people who, I felt, just got in the way of doing creative and innovative radio programmes.

For some years I'd been really interested in astrology and soon learnt that generalized forecasts for the twelve sun signs were not the real thing. Proper astrology needed an individual's time and place of birth to draw up an accurate chart. I came up with the idea of inviting listeners to send in their birth details and then leading astrologer Patric Walker would draw up a specific chart for a different person every day. At about twenty past nine, I would read out Patric's chart and then, later in the show, call the person concerned for their reaction. It was a fascinating experiment in bringing real astrology to a mass audience and virtually all the listeners pronounced themselves totally amazed at the accuracy of their chart; only once did someone say it didn't fit them at all.

One morning, the BBC Director of Radio, Howard Newby, was driving in his car with his wife and daughter while listening to Radio Four.

His daughter said, 'Mum, can we have Radio One on, please?'

'Oh yes, Howard, put Radio One on,' said Mrs Newby.

'Why on earth do you want to listen to that station, for goodness' sake?' asked Howard.

Radio One was always looked down on by much of the corporate establishment who didn't think a pop music station was something the BBC should be doing at all.

'We want to listen to Johnnie Walker's astrology feature. We always listen at home when we can,' said Howard's wife.

This was all news to Howard who had no idea Radio One was putting out an astrology feature.

A few weeks later, I returned from a week's holiday to be told by Doreen Davies that the astrology feature had to stop.

'Why?' I asked. 'It's really popular and generates huge amounts of mail. Who's decided it's got to stop?'

'The order has come down from Howard Newby.'

I'd never heard of him.

'Who is he and why has he suddenly got involved with things?'

'Johnnie, he is the director of radio, in charge of all the networks, and he thinks it's completely wrong for Radio One to be dabbling in the occult. As we're the BBC, we should be promoting Christian values.'

I didn't get a chance to argue my case or have a meeting with Howard. The decision had been made and that was that.

This was typical of the way things were done. When the government had told the BBC to broadcast a pop music station as part of the fight against the pirates, there had been a huge number of people inside the corporation who didn't want to do it and who, frankly, despised pop music. But how could Radio One ever connect with its audience when people like that were in charge of it?

Douglas Muggeridge, head of Radio One and Radio Two, once said to me in his clipped, upper-class accent, 'You know, Johnnie, with the benefit of hindsight, I rather think that the BBC under-estimated the impact of the Beatles.' Well, the Beatles emerged in 1963 and it wasn't until 1967 that the BBC considered launching a station for popular music. And it seemed that lessons still weren't being learnt. But why should they? There was no commercial radio, no competition. The BBC had no need to change and it took its huge audiences for granted. The future would bring some big surprises.

In the meantime, at least they didn't stop me playing The Eagles. Their eponymous album had just been released and I absolutely loved it. It was hard to believe it was actually recorded in London; it was brimming with the good vibes of California, sunshine, freedom, cars and girls. The opening track, 'Take It Easy', written by Jackson Browne and Glenn Frey, was a great radio record and so much better than a lot of the pop stuff I had to play. And then there was the song 'Peaceful Easy Feeling' which spoke of sleeping out in the desert underneath the stars. To me, that's the sort of image dreams are made of and I vowed that one day I would live it for real.

My hour-long show went by in a flash. After spending the morning with my producer and chatting with the record-promotion guys, who were invaluable for news and information, there would be the choice of a good lunch with a friendly promo guy or, more often, beer and sarnies in the pub with a producer or two and my good friend, executive producer Teddy Warrick. He did so much to help me deal with the frustrations of trying to do a spontaneous pirate-style show within the conservative, corporate environs of the BBC.

The record promo people, or pluggers, were a big part of day-to-day life in Radio One's headquarters, Egton House. Their job was to make sure producers and DJs had copies of all their companies' new releases and, if possible, to establish a friendship with those in a position of power. Charisma Records famously had an annual day at the races, and almost every evening some record company or other threw a lavish reception. These were the days when the big companies were awash with money and we were always being invited to functions. Some nights there was more than one reception, so I would start at EMI – this was usually a bit boring, with the same old duffers and predictable food – and then move on to another one, ideally given by a more fashionable label like Warner Brothers. This would be much vibier, often in a really unusual venue and with a hip crowd.

One morning after the show finished at ten, I was back in the office with my producer when Roger Bolton from President Records knocked on the door. After the usual preliminary chat and the handing over of new releases and reminders about their current releases, we were invited to one of his regular parties.

Roger said, 'It's a good night out, plenty of booze and there're always some really pretty girls there. Why don't you come along?'

My producer and I looked at each other. Both of us thought it sounded a bit dodgy and we politely made our excuses. But the same invite would be repeated every week and he was becoming a bit of a bloody nuisance. Eventually I decided it was time to get Roger off our backs and when he came in, all smiles and invitations, I said, 'Maybe I'll come this week, Roger. Where is it? What's the form?'

Roger looked delighted.

'It's Wednesday night over in Notting Hill. I could come round and pick you up.'

'OK, I'll be ready at seven o'clock.'

It can't be that bad, I thought, and if it is, I'll just leave early.

I persuaded my producer to come with me and, together with three other Radio One producers, we were driven to a little terraced house in Campden Hill Road, Notting Hill Gate. I'd expected some sort of club and was quite surprised when we were invited into an ordinary house. We were ushered into the sitting room and our blonde hostess, Janie, offered us a drink.

Having made a note of what we wanted, she shouted down the stairs, 'Arthur, come and get the drinks order.'

Moments later, a meek, sad and put-upon man with hunched shoulders hobbled into the room. He eventually returned with the tray of drinks and stood there, looking helpless.

'Put them on the table, Arthur!' she commanded. He put them down and shuffled away. She looked at us with a sweet smile, and enquired demurely, 'Would you like some ice in your drinks?'

'Yes, if it's not too much trouble,' I replied.

Stepping to the doorway, Janie again shouted down the stairs, 'Arthur, you forgot the ice, you bloody idiot! Bring some up here immediately.'

This whole scenario was starting to look very bizarre. Once again, poor old Arthur climbed the stairs, this time carrying a bucket of ice cubes.

'Come on, get a move on,' snapped Janie. 'Put it down on the table!'

I was beginning to feel really sorry for Arthur, and said, 'Thank you very much, Arthur. That's very kind of you.'

'Don't be nice to him,' said Janie. 'He hates that. He's my love slave, and he only gets his rocks off if I'm really nasty to him.'

This was becoming a weird, uncomfortable scene, but I was intrigued as to what might happen next.

'Come on, boys, bring your drinks. Let's all go upstairs. There's something I want to show you,' said Janie.

We all looked at each other somewhat nervously and then followed Janie up the stairs. For me, still in plaster, it was a slow and painful climb up the narrow stairs. We crowded into a little room and Janie stood next to a pair of curtains hanging on the wall. It looked like she was about to unveil a plaque.

'Gentlemen,' she said proudly, 'you might be interested in what's going on in the next room.'

She drew back the curtains to reveal a large rectangular window. This was the first time I'd ever seen a two-way mirror. In the next-door room was a large bed and two naked girls were on it, simulating lesbian sex. It was such an incongruous scene that I think we were all slightly embarrassed at being there. We were supposed to be surreptitiously spying on these girls and their 'impromptu' sex act, but they were obviously quite aware they were being watched.

Janie said breezily, 'Come on, boys, follow me.'

She led us into the bedroom where we all sheepishly stood round the bed, not knowing what to do next.

'Come on, then,' urged Janie. 'Get your kit off and get stuck in. These girls are here to give you a good time.'

There was much shuffling of feet and exchanging of nervous glances. Was anybody going to be brave enough to actually get undressed and go for it? Seeing all this hesitation, Janie started to tease us all.

'Gawd, what a bunch of wimps you BBC boys are. Isn't there a man among any of you?'

Now she'd touched a raw nerve. Here was my chance to save the good name of the corporation. I began unbuttoning my shirt and trousers. Sitting on the edge of the bed, I pulled off my boots and socks and looked at the others.

'Well, are any of you going to join me or am I going to have to do this on my own?'

They all decided to go back downstairs for another drink. I was joined by a third girl (which was a first for me) and despite the handicap of my leg in plaster, we all romped around on the bed giggling and laughing and I had a bloody good time. I just hoped there weren't any producers or, even worse, cameras, on the other side of the mirror – and then I forgot all about it. I left the house exhausted but happy.

The next day everything was back to normal and at our daily meeting, neither my producer nor I mentioned the previous evening. It was as if it had never happened. About ten days later, a call was put through to my producer's office. He passed me the phone.

'Hello, is that Johnnie Walker?'

'Yes.'

'Hello there,' said the cheery, friendly voice at the other end.

'This is Detective Inspector Giles from Scotland Yard. I'd like to have a little chat with you.'

I wondered what all this was about; I didn't expect what he said next.

'We're doing a little investigation which involves a premises in Campden Hill Road. I believe you've been there. I'd like you to come to the Yard and have a little chat.'

'Is that a voluntary chat?'

'No, I rather think it's compulsory. When can you come down?'

We arranged an appointment for a couple of days later. It never occurred to me that I should take the precaution of arranging for a lawyer to accompany me as I didn't think I'd done anything illegal.

In the DI's office, the atmosphere was very non-threatening as we chatted over our cups of tea.

The detective inspector said, 'We're doing an investigation into alleged payola at the BBC. Tell me about this party that you went to in Notting Hill.'

I recounted the persistent invitations and how I had eventually decided to go, not knowing we'd end up in Janie Jones's famous show-business brothel.

'Were you aware that President Records picked up the bill for this particular evening?'

'I don't really know. I imagine that as it was their plugger who had made the invite, they probably did.'

'As a result of going there, have you been asked to show favour to one of their records?'

'Absolutely not. I just saw the evening as an extension of the usual record-company hospitality. I admit this was somewhat different, but no one would ask for a direct favour because it just doesn't work like that. Actually, I feel pretty angry that I was duped into going there in the first place. I was invited to what I thought was just another record-company party.'

'Well, you seem to have made the best of it once you were there.'

'Maybe, but the real issue is that I'd never play a record I didn't think was any good just as a favour for somebody. I care too much about my show and my reputation to risk it all for a few quid or a bit of fun.'

DI Giles seemed happy enough with that explanation and it appeared our chat was over.

'Is this investigation likely to lead to a court case?' I asked.

'Quite possibly, but you won't be asked to appear in court. A witness who makes a voluntary statement like yours has their anonymity protected. If your statement is submitted as evidence, you will just be referred to as Mr X or Mr Y.'

We said our goodbyes and I hoped that would be the last I'd hear about it. Not so. Rumours started to circulate of an impending court case involving a payola scandal at the BBC. When the court case did start, it was front-page news in the tabloids and, as each day went by, I got more and more worried. Finally, one morning came the details of the record-company party at Janie Jones's house in Notting Hill. One of the girls gave evidence to the court of romping on the bed with Mr T.

'I remember it very well,' she said. 'I knew he was a Radio One DJ, and he had his leg in plaster.'

So much for anonymity. Now the cat was really out of the bag. I had no idea what the reaction of the BBC hierarchy would be to this but, putting on my bravest face, I headed in to my morning show. When I got there everything seemed perfectly normal and no one, not even Tony Blackburn, made any reference to it. Maybe they were going to politely ignore it. So I put the matter to one side and started my show.

At Radio One, the two studios and the engineers' control rooms were all in a line, divided only by glass so that you could see through to the other studio. As soon as Tony Blackburn finished, Jimmy Young would go into the other studio to start prepping his show and reading the day's newspapers. At about twenty past the hour, I heard this bright and cheery voice through the intercom.

'Good morning, Mr T!' said JY, sounding very pleased with himself.

Chapter Twenty-One

May 1971

After my experience with Janie Jones, any invitations from pluggers for anything other than a lunch or a gig were approached with extreme caution. That's why I turned down flat an invitation for an evening drink at a pub, even though the guy was a good friend of mine and we'd been out for drinks many times. This invite was for me to make up a foursome with his girlfriend's best friend. I really hate blind dates – they never seem to work out – but my friend made this particular invite sound all very relaxed.

'Just come along and have a casual drink, Johnnie. I'm sure you'll get along, but if you don't it won't be a big deal.'

I still didn't want to go. But what did kindle my interest was that the pub he suggested was the Red Lion off Curzon Street in Mayfair, the regular drinking haunt of all the pirate radio DJs. Having fond memories of it and not having been there for years, I was quite fascinated to see how the old place was. So I eventually agreed.

I turned up at the pub as arranged and was introduced to my blind date. My worst fears were confirmed; conversation was difficult and I just knew we weren't going to click. Fortunately, I noticed Mike Lennox, an ex-Radio London DJ, leaning against the bar. I excused myself as politely as possible, saying I was going to chat to an old friend.

I shook hands with Mike and he introduced me to the girl he was drinking with. Her name was Frances and within seconds I was completely mesmerized by her. With short blonde hair framing a lovely face, she was very beautiful, full of life and laughter, and had a stunning figure. But she was with Mike.

The three of us joked and laughed together and then, not

wanting to overstay my welcome or spoil Mike's evening, I reluctantly said goodbye to them both and headed home. But I just
couldn't stop thinking about Frances. I'd never met anyone before
who had had such a strong effect on me. Mike had introduced her
as 'my friend Frances'. What did that mean? They seemed more
like friends than lovers, but there was nothing I could do about it
as I had no number for her and hadn't a clue where she lived. All
I knew was that I was desperate to see her again. I felt as though
I'd been hit by the proverbial thunderbolt. All evening I was
thinking of Frances and reliving the moments I had spent close to
her in the pub. I could not get her off my mind. Thinking about
her kept me awake most of the night.

The next morning I knew I had to get her phone number and
make contact. Maybe she wouldn't want to see me, maybe she
was in a relationship with Mike. Whatever, I had to find out
otherwise my head was going to get no bloody peace at all. I could
hardly ring Mike Lennox, but I knew he was a good friend of Ed
Stewart – they had worked together on Radio London – so I
decided to give Ed a call.

After the usual exchange of pleasantries, I said, 'By the way, Ed,
I bumped into Mike Lennox last night in the Red Lion.'

'Oh, yeah.'

'And he was with this girl called Frances. Do you know her?'

'Yeah, I know Frances.' He was being very cagey and not
making this easy at all.

'Are she and Mike a bit of an item, or what?'

'They're just good friends, there's nothing heavy going on. And
anyway, why do you want to know?'

'Well, she had an incredible effect on me and I'm just desperate
to get in touch with her and maybe see her again.'

'I can't give you her number,' said Ed.

He was enjoying this; I should have played it much more casual.
Too late now.

'Oh, come on, Ed. Do us a favour. You said they're just friends,
what's the big problem? Surely it should be up to Frances to have
some say in this.'

Again, Ed refused to give me the number and this verbal tennis went on and on. I had to wear him down. Eventually he realized I was being deadly serious and that I would keep on and on unless he gave in.

'Oh, all right, then, if only to get you off the bloody phone. I'm still not going to give you her number but she works at a theatrical agency at the top of Regent House.'

What a coincidence. My agent, Jimmy Smith, worked for London Management, whose offices were in Regent House, just a few yards down Regent Street from Oxford Circus. I went in and out of there several times a week.

'Thanks, Ed, you're a star. You'll never know just how much this means.'

I called Jimmy, who gave me the name of the agency and directory enquiries had the number. Gathering all my courage, I dialled it, and asked for her. She came on the line with a beautiful, 'Hello?'

'Hello, Frances, it's Johnnie Walker. I met you in the Red Lion with Mike Lennox last night.'

'Yes, I remember.'

She sounded great on the phone. Me, I was quivering with nerves. I knew I mustn't blow this.

'Well, I, um, er, just happen to have a couple of tickets for a Cat Stevens concert tonight. I know it's a bit short notice and you might have something already planned but I'd love it if you came with me.'

Small pause.

'Well, it just so happens I was going to stay in tonight so, yes, I'd love to come with you.'

Wow, I couldn't believe my luck. Now I was trembling with excitement. 'How about if I pick you up in the car after work, say about half six, would that be okay? Maybe we could have a quick drink before the gig?'

'Half six would be fine.'

'Parking is a bit tricky there, so I could stop opposite Regent House.'

'That's okay, but how will I know it's you?'

'I'll be in a white Jaguar XK 120.'

I tried to make it sound as casual as possible. For me, the XK 120 was one of the most beautiful cars ever made. My ex-boss at Patrick Motors, Ben Martin, collected old cars. When he managed to get one of the last XK 150s made, he sold his 120 to my old sales partner, Vernon Ryland. When, years later, Vernon called me up and said he was selling it, I practically bit his hand off to do a deal and I was immensely proud of being its new owner. I usually gave it a run at the weekends and for special occasions. This was certainly a special occasion.

Nervous, excited and keyed up with anticipation, I stopped opposite Regent House at 6.25 p.m. My heart leapt as I saw Frances coming out of the entrance and crossing the road towards me. All the agonizing after meeting her at the pub, wondering if I was ever going to see her again, was over. Frances was my date for the evening. I got out and proudly opened the passenger door to allow this beautiful girl into my car.

It was a magical evening. Everything seemed to go right: there were no traffic problems, an easy parking space at the gig and a lovely vibe inside. It was those first heady moments of love beginning to grow, and I sensed that neither of us wanted the night to end. Frances accepted my invitation to come back to my flat in Belsize Park for coffee.

The night was ours and tomorrow was Saturday, so neither of us had to go to work. We played music, smoked a little grass and talked and got to know each other. We spent a magical night together and fell into a blissful and contented sleep.

In the morning I brewed up some tea and toast and we chatted away like old friends.

'Where did you say your flat was?' I asked.

'Earlham Gardens, Earls Court.'

'We may as well go over there and pick up your stuff. You could move in today'

'All right. Sounds like a good idea. You're on,' said Frances.

That was the beginning of an idyllic seven months during which we were together pretty much all the time. I went down to Sandwich in Kent to meet her folks: Mum Ivy and Dad Alec, loads of sisters and two brothers. They were a close, wonderfully crazy sort of family. Alec was the local PC Plod who had never wanted promotion. He was happy riding his bike and doing his bit to keep the peace, which in a quiet little place like Sandwich wasn't too hard. Together he and Ivy raised eight kids, which in itself was an amazing achievement. Ivy loved her music, always called me 'son' and always had a treacle tart and custard on the go when we visited. Alec made his own wine in a shed in the garden and it was a pretty lethal brew. We'd all have a few glasses and then, with Ivy's favourites like 'Rivers Of Babylon' by Boney M on the record player, they'd try to outdo each other doing headstands and cart-wheels in their front room. They were all a bit mad but knew how to have fun and a good laugh together. It was never like that in my house – we just didn't have the freedom to feel at ease and be ourselves. They were such a great family and I loved it.

Frances confided to me that one morning, before we were together, she had been listening to my show and had heard me play a Ray Charles song that had contained the words 'I need someone to watch over me'.

'Sounds wonderful, that's just what I need,' was my off-the-cuff comment after the song.

'Yes, you do. And that someone is me,' she had told the radio.

Now fate had brought us together and I never wanted it to end. But both of us were the types who had always sworn that we'd never get married. As the sixties ended and we entered the seventies, life was about trying new things and enjoying freedoms our parents never had, not fretting about the future. Now, though, having met Frances, I really wanted to get married. But she was dead against it.

'It's great as it is, why change it?' was always her view.

And, in the past, I would have agreed but this was different – *she* was different. I didn't want to lose her.

I tried to persuade her.

'It doesn't have to change anything. We'll be the same as we are now but there'll be a greater depth and meaning to what we have.'

She wasn't convinced and I let the subject drop – for a while, at least.

The year sped by as we both were on such a high. A new love is such a wonderful feeling and everything about life was perfect. Radio One offered me a new slot and instead of an hour at nine, I was now to present a two-hour lunchtime show and, for the first time, could play all records. The BBC had negotiated a new agreement, which meant extra 'needle time' and, for this new show, no more musician sessions. This was fantastic news. Now I would be able to do a music show more like the one I did on Caroline. This new slot had the potential to be really something special and my brain was churning away with ideas.

The only snag was the producer they had allocated to the show, the dreaded Ron Belchier. He had a fearsome reputation for being a really nasty bastard, especially when he'd had a drink. Secretaries lived in fear of him and he often reduced pluggers who dared to knock on his door to quivering wrecks. Now I was lumbered with working with him. I needed some advice and went to see my trusted ally and friend within the BBC, Teddy Warrick. He was one of three executive producers at Radio One and the only person who could explain and make sense of the vagaries and inconsistencies of the strange world that was the corporation.

'Teddy, I'm really grateful you're giving me this new show and I'm very excited about it. It's a perfect slot and I've got two hours of needle time. Then you go and spoil it all by lumbering me with Ron Belchier. I've heard he's really difficult to work with. I could do with some advice.'

'Well,' said Teddy, after careful thought. 'I'd say, do all your work with him in the morning and forget the afternoons.' And that was it.

I took Teddy's advice and Ron and I gradually built up a good working relationship, based on mutual respect. We thought up various ideas for the show, mostly based around music. We played a different Number One at one o'clock each day: Monday's would be an oldie; on Tuesday, following some new entries and a run-down of the chart, I'd play the new Number One; Wednesday's was an album track, Thursday's the American Number One and on Friday a Number One from a different country around the world.

The management at Radio One were totally obsessed with singles. The playlist for the daytime shows was made up of the current Top Forty, previous hit singles and a few new releases, but always on seven-inch 45rpm records. I'd already tried to explain to them that there was a huge number of albums being released with great tracks on them that would eventually be released as singles. Some bands, like Led Zeppelin, refused to release singles in the UK, with the result that Radio One never played their music. To try and get round this, Ron and I devised a feature called 'The Family Album' where members of a family could pick three album tracks that we played over the two hours of a show.

All our ideas seemed to work pretty well and I soon settled into the routine of the new slot. It's one of the best, really. I was finished at two o'clock and there's no need to get up early for a show that starts at midday. We got a lot of mail, the ratings were very good and the suits upstairs seemed pleased with the new show.

The offices in Egton House were like rabbit hutches and we DJs, all being freelancers, never got our own offices and were lucky if the producers gave us any space at all in theirs. I could be much more productive at home so once the show was over, I headed back to my little flat in Belsize Park, rolled up a nice joint, had a cup of tea and listened to some music. There was always a stack of new singles and albums that I never managed to get to the bottom of. Trouble was, when I got stoned they all sounded great, so I'd have to check them out again the next day when I was straight to see if they were really as good as I thought.

It was in October 1971 that I again raised the subject of marriage with Frances.

'Don't you think it would be lovely to get married at Christmas? What about Christmas Eve? There's always such a great feeling at that time, people are being nice to each other, and it'd be a lovely day to get hitched. We could go to the registry office on Haverstock Hill. There'll be a Christmas tree all lit up outside – it would be so romantic.'

To my huge delight, Frances turned to me and finally I heard the words, 'Yes. I would like to marry you.'

We kissed, hugged and looked into each other's eyes, and then started laughing and dancing. We were very much in love and now had a whole lifetime to look forward to.

Neither of us liked having to act or behave in ways dictated by convention, so, rather than have a big bash, we decided to keep our wedding a complete secret, not even telling our families but just going ahead with no guests except the minimum two witnesses. I arranged the marriage certificate and asked Teddy Warrick if he'd be my best man and witness. He agreed, as did Frances's friend Pat Hayley, so we had the two necessary witnesses for our secret wedding. An ex-journalist called Mike Housego was my unofficial press guy and I asked him not to try and get any press coverage for the wedding. We both wanted it to be a private event just for us.

There was no hen or stag night; we were together the night before the wedding and the day itself started as any other except that I had a large brandy after breakfast. Both Frances and I were really nervous. Frances looked absolutely stunning in a skirt and white blouse. The ceremony was over in a couple of minutes and all I remember is trying really hard not to laugh when the famous lines 'Do you take . . .' were said. It was like something out of a movie.

Our marriage had stayed a secret and been quiet, with no fuss. We came out of the registry office with its two illuminated Christmas trees and, arm in arm and blissfully happy, walked down Haverstock Hill to our parked car.

Suddenly, from nowhere, a man jumped out of a shop doorway and snapped us walking down the street. Mike Housego was also there, hiding behind a tree.

He said cheerily, 'Had to do it, Johnnie. It's my job, after all.'

My anger at being tricked disappeared when I later saw the front page of the *Evening Standard*. There we were, my gorgeous wife and I, newly married, both looking so happy. It was a great photo.

Frances, Pat, Teddy and I went to our favourite pub, The Green Man, where we shared a bottle of champagne and played some bar billiards. The hardest part for me was leaving them there celebrating while I went to do my lunchtime show at the BBC. In the studio, I chose Gilbert O'Sullivan and 'Matrimony' as my first record and I announced at the end that I'd just got married. The two hours went by in a happy blur. Frances joined me at the end and we called our respective parents to tell them the news.

My mum was not pleased.

'I feel really left out. Why didn't you invite me and your father to be there?'

'I'm sorry, Mum, but I didn't think it was worth it for you and Dad to come all the way from Birmingham. The ceremony only lasted about five minutes and you've already had three proper white weddings with Maureen, John and Michael.'

By contrast, Frances's dad simply asked the question, 'Are you happy, girl?' Hearing a definite yes, he said, 'Then we're very happy for you both. Have a wonderful future and look after each other. Come and see us soon and we can drink your health.'

We went home to Belsize Park and it all felt a little bit flat – we had wanted nothing to change by getting married and it seemed as if nothing had. The next morning it was Christmas Day and we were both quiet and muted, as though we were thinking, 'What the hell have we done?' We'd been so focused on our secret and unconventional wedding that we hadn't planned a honeymoon or even how we were going to celebrate Christmas. Neither of us really knew what to say and we sat there staring at one another. It couldn't all be going wrong on day one, could it?

Then, out of the blue, the phone rang.

'Hello, Johnnie, it's Joe Brown here. What you doin' today?'

'Well, Frany – with a long 'a' – [Frances was always Frany to me and her friends] and I are just asking ourselves the same question. We're just realizing that it's the first day of our married life together and we hadn't planned anything.'

'Then jump in your motor and come and have Christmas with us. There's just me and Vicki and the family here – and me mum's with us, she'll embarrass us all but take no notice. We'd love to see you both, get yourselves over here.'

To this day, I have no idea why Joe Brown should have called us on Christmas morning, totally out of the blue. I had met Joe only a few times and we weren't what you'd call close, but I'd always loved him. Way back in 1961, lonely, broke and homesick in Gloucester, I'd go to the local coffee bar and my last coins would go in the jukebox to play Joe's 'A Picture Of You', which always gave me a lift and made me feel good about life, as it still does today.

We drove to Joe's lovely house in the Essex countryside. There, all was good food and wine and lots and lots of laughter. Joe was the same cheerful bloke in real life as he was on stage and TV, maybe more so. He and his wife gave us a tour of the house and passed on some advice for a happy marriage.

'Always have a bottle of lemonade by the bed. When you've 'ad yuh great sex an' are dyin' of thirst, it saves the argument about who's going to get up and go for a glass of water.'

Frany and I had such a good time there, one of our best-ever Christmases, and now we'd be stepping into New Year as Mr and Mrs Walker.

Chapter Twenty-Two

1972–4

At a time in my life when things couldn't have been brighter, a terrible blight began to turn everything sour. It took me to a point where, despite my happy marriage and beautiful wife, my fantastic job, my youth and good health, I considered ending it all.

Like so many others, I'd always been looking for some kind of meaning to my life. Our good friends Tony and Andrea were the same, and we'd often get together at each other's houses for dinner, smoke a little grass, play music and have long conversations into the night about books, philosophy, religion and politics. We had all been hugely influenced by the cultural changes of the sixties and early seventies – we'd read Jack Kerouac, Khalil Gibran, Linda Goodman's *Sun Signs*, the *I Ching*, Robert Pirsig's *Zen and the Art of Motorcycle Maintenance*, all that kind of stuff. We played endless games of backgammon and mah-jong, had challenging intellectual and philosophical arguments and generally encouraged each other on our journeys of discovery.

So it wasn't a great surprise when, at a dinner party over at their place with about half a dozen friends, one of the guests, Rupert, suggested a Ouija board session. He was apparently psychic and had experience in this sort of thing. There were differing reactions among the others to this suggestion. Some seemed excited by the idea, others were a little wary. I felt a mix of fear and fascination. I didn't know much about Ouija sessions. I'd heard there were risks involved but the sense of stepping into the unknown was too big a pull for me to resist and, after some discussion, we all agreed to go ahead.

Our 'expert' cut out small squares of paper and wrote a letter of the alphabet on each, plus numbers 1−10 and then two more with the words yes and no on them, and arranged them all in a circle. Then an upturned glass was placed in the centre and the lights were dimmed.

'Just lightly rest a finger on the glass, don't push, just let it move by itself,' said Rupert. Then he addressed the air. 'Is there anybody there?'

Nothing happened.

Again the question was asked, 'Is there anybody there?'

Still nothing; I wondered if this was just a waste of time.

And then the glassed moved − tentatively at first, then with a stronger and stronger pull. Rupert started asking some basic questions, such as 'What's your name?' and 'Where were you born?' and the glass was now rushing from one side of the table to the other. We were all astounded at first but it was amazing how soon it all seemed perfectly normal and natural. Whoever was in touch with us seemed to be enjoying the communication enormously and was in a rush to spell out answers.

Naturally we suspected that someone could be pushing the glass so, one by one, everyone removed their fingers until just Rupert and I were touching it. I used the lightest touch, just resting my finger on the top − and still the glass rushed around with incredible force. There was no way Rupert was pushing it because at one point he removed his finger and it made no difference.

Despite Rupert being the so-called 'expert', I didn't think he was handling it right at all. He was asking mundane questions and testing the spirit. I felt very strongly that somehow I had a better understanding and connection with the spirit, who I felt was starting to get fed up with Rupert's silly questions. He asked if there was a specific message for anyone present and the glass went straight to 'j' and then 'w'. Suddenly this had become personal and I was a bit freaked out.

'Go on, ask a question,' said Rupert.

I felt embarrassed and didn't want to voice in public the one deep issue that had been bothering me for some time.

'I haven't really got a question,' I stammered.

So Rupert asked the spirit, 'Do you have a message for Johnnie?'

The glass began to spell out a message that said simply, 'It's going to be okay.'

I said, 'Thank you.'

With that, the mood in the room changed, the energy was no longer there and that was the end of our Ouija board session. It left me deep in thought. It was both reassuring and a little frightening at the same time. I was the only person who'd been singled out by name, and what had been a fairly light-hearted experiment had ended with something very deep and personal.

I felt that the spirit knew my big problem was depression. In my teenage years, it had been particularly acute, and seemed to be more than the usual adolescent angst. Life for me was often extraordinarily hard, while for others, it all seemed so easy and straightforward. With no one to talk to, I spent a lot of time brooding and looking inward rather than outward. During my years on the pirate ships, I'd been busy and absorbed and my depression had receded. Now, though, just when life should have been at its brightest, the depression was returning and I couldn't understand why.

At least the spirit had given me a positive message but, as the days went by, I grew more and more disturbed by it. I couldn't stop thinking about it. Was this what they meant by the dangers of Ouija boards? Had I invited some strange spirit into my life? I needed some help and advice and I thought maybe a priest would be the person to turn to. Recently, a young vicar had taken part in my radio quiz 'Pop the Question' and, as we kept records of who had been on, I contacted him and arranged to go and see him, desperately hoping he would be able to reassure me and give me some answers.

The vicar was a nice-enough bloke but within minutes it became obvious he was way out of his depth on this one. He had no knowledge or belief in a world of spirit and could only give me the usual Bible stuff about not dabbling in the occult, living a good life, going to church, having my sins forgiven, and going to heaven. But I had experienced a contact from a world outside the material one we live in; this spirit knew my name – or at least my initials – and that I was going through a hard time. I left my friendly vicar none the wiser and more frustrated than before.

Meanwhile, I had to do something about this depression. I simply couldn't understand what was wrong and why I was feeling this way. The radio show was going really well with good listener response and ratings. Frany and I were getting along fine and we were now living in our own little house in West Acton near Ealing. I had every reason to be happy and content. So why was I so terribly depressed a lot of the time?

My local GP just put it down to my being in a high-profile media job.

'Don't worry about it, happens all the time to people in your profession. It's stress, I get lots of people like you in here with the same complaint. The latest tranquillizers are very good, they'll sort you out, and the fact you know there's an answer will reduce the future possibility of depression.'

I've always been wary of prescription drugs and the selling tactics of pharmaceutical companies. For every positive benefit of a drug, there are always side effects they don't tell you about. But I was getting desperate, so I decided to try them out. They were a disaster. On the first day of taking them, I went in to do my lunchtime show and my mouth was so dry I could hardly speak. I chucked the pills straight in the bin. I would have to find another route out of this black hole.

I eventually found the name of a psychiatrist and began weekly sessions at his consulting rooms in Knightsbridge. Stephen would sit in his comfortable easy chair, contentedly puffing away on his pipe, while I tried to put into words what I was feeling. I tried to articulate the horrible sense of hopelessness that engulfed me, the feelings of being a terrible failure and unworthy of anything, and of everything in the world being wretched. I felt as though every-one would be better off if I weren't around, even my beloved Frany.

A great deal of time was spent talking about my parents and childhood experiences. Sometimes Stephen seemed to be nodding off and it used to annoy me intensely that he would never comment on anything. He would sneak glances at the clock every now and then and just when I felt we were really getting somewhere, my time would be up and that would be it for another week.

Occasionally he would try some kind of 'truth drug' injection, which was supposed to help me bring out deep feelings. I usually just felt really woozy or would end up in floods of tears. This went on for about eighteen months and I didn't seem to be getting any better. Frances did her very best to understand and to help. But as I couldn't find any reason for feeling so down, it was very hard for anyone to help – even my wife, who knew me best.

One Saturday morning, my depression was so bad that I started to think seriously about suicide. Frances was away in Greece on a holiday with a girlfriend and had no idea why I was so very down. I managed to get Stephen on the phone and when he realized I was in a pretty bad way, he told me to come straight over. It was a grey day with moody dark skies and driving rain. I took a taxi over to Stephen's consulting rooms to get there as quickly as possible. He sat there as I tried to explain that things were at their absolute lowest point. There was dead silence for what seemed like an age. Was he going to come up with a magical answer? God, I hoped so. Eventually, he spoke.

'Well, there's always ECT. We could try that.'

I was totally unprepared for that suggestion. Did that mean I was going mad? I didn't know much about electroshock therapy but what I did know filled me with horror.

'No fucking way am I going to let anybody fry my brains!' I told him. 'I'm getting out of here now.'

I stormed out and started walking, not knowing where I was going or what the hell I was going to do next – I only knew that I had to get away from there. Instead of a friend, Stephen now seemed like an enemy. I wandered through Hyde Park sobbing uncontrollably, getting absolutely drenched in the pouring rain. I'd tried drugs, I'd tried a psychiatrist. Neither had worked. Now I was on my own with this problem and I had to find a way out of it somehow.

I eventually got back home and the feelings of gloom and desperation became heavier and heavier. The answer seemed so very simple. I didn't have to struggle with the decision at all. It was the obvious thing to do. I could end all this pain so easily, I thought. I'll just leave this world that is so very hard to live in. I can find a peaceful place of perfect bliss and my worry and depression will be over.

I drove my little Citroën 2CV up the narrow access road to the garages at the back of our row of houses. It was mid afternoon now. The sky was leaden and dense with dark, ominous grey-black clouds and still the rain poured down. The access road was deserted, no one seemed to be around. I got the green garden hose from the garage and put one end into the Citroën's exhaust pipe and the other into the back window. I couldn't fully close the window because of the hosepipe but hoped it wouldn't make any difference.

I started the engine and held the revs fairly high, thinking: This shouldn't take long and then all my troubles will be over. The minutes dragged on and I was still conscious. Come on, hurry up, I thought. If only I had a bigger pipe that would fit right over the exhaust, it would be all over by now. I revved the engine harder and still I wasn't slipping away. Then I started to get angry: Why isn't this working? Why am I still here?

I'd taken the big decision and now I'd found that I couldn't even get suicide right. What a useless prat I was! Then I started to laugh at the sheer silliness of it all. Sod this for a lark, I thought. I switched off the engine, got out of the car, pulled the pipe out of the exhaust and chucked it back in the garage. I was glad I was still here but I was feeling pretty woozy. I knew I couldn't get in the house from the garden as the back door was locked so I started to walk along the access road towards the exit. My legs felt like jelly; I stumbled a few yards and then they just crumbled underneath me.

Oh God, I hope I haven't damaged myself in some way, I thought. Now I really wanted to live. I picked myself up and tried walking again. Another few yards and I collapsed again. I called on God again: Please help me get into the safety and warmth of the house. I was drenched through, cold and shivering, but I kept on, staggering, falling, picking myself up and trying again. After what seemed like an eternity, I was at the front door, fumbling the key into the lock and, at last, I was safely back in the house. It felt as though Providence, or an angel or a spirit guide, had stepped in to save me.

Soon afterwards, I heard of a doctor called Shyam Singha. He sounded the most amazing doctor, who could completely turn your life around and make you feel better than you had for years. He'd done wonders for others, so maybe I should go and see him. Dr Singha did acupuncture, homeopathy, naturopathy and was a chiropractor as well. He had a practice in Gordon Road, Ealing and I decided to give him a call and book an appointment.

Back then, over thirty years ago, alternative or complementary medicine was unheard of and the few practitioners around were regarded as quacks, to be avoided at all costs. But I'd tried the conventional route and got nowhere. I had nothing to lose and maybe a lot to gain. I was determined to give it a try.

I sat across a wooden desk from a striking and charismatic Indian man with locks of flowing dark hair and brown eyes. His manner was curt and businesslike and I felt somewhat nervous and intimidated.

'So, Mr Walker. Why have you come to see me?'

I gave him a brief rundown of how I was feeling and the failure of both my GP's treatment and eighteen months of psychoanalysis.

His penetrating brown eyes stared into mine. It was as if he could see right through my outward layer to the spirit and soul deep within.

'If I take you on, you must do exactly what I tell you. You'll be wasting my time and yours if you don't follow my instructions.'

'Okay, I understand. I want to give this a try.'

He then proceeded to ask me a lot of questions, many of which didn't seem to have any relevance to either my medical or mental state but he frantically scribbled copious notes with his fountain pen. Then he looked me in the eyes with another of those penetrating stares.

'Who told you it was your responsibility to carry the entire troubles of the world on your shoulders?'

I looked down, mumbling some sort of reply to the effect that I didn't know I was.

Shyam let out a deep sigh, 'Take all your clothes off and lie face up on that table.'

He undid a packet of new acupuncture needles and, with great skill, identified points on my feet, legs, stomach, hands and head and deftly inserted the needles. There was the slightest pinprick as they went in; some produced an ache but as they're so thin it was fairly painless.

'Breathe deeply, just breathe,' said Shyam, and promptly disappeared into another treatment room next door.

I lay there, thoughts rushing through my mind, wondering what on earth I'd got myself into. This was all very weird and foreign to me. I tried to just concentrate on my breathing, letting the lungs fill naturally, expanding the stomach and then the chest area, and then emptying. Gradually my mind-chatter quietened down and I began to feel as if I was floating gently in a place of calmness and beauty. I felt completely safe and so relaxed, I never wanted this serene state of being to end.

Dr Singha came back into the room after what I guessed to be about half an hour.

'How are you feeling now?'

'Wonderful, thanks. Really nice. Wish I could feel like this all the time.'

He expertly whisked out the needles and then stood at the bottom of the treatment table, looking at me. He put his hands on my feet and dug his thumbnail into the side of my big toe.

I let out a yell and shouted, 'What the fuck did you do that for?'

I couldn't comprehend why on earth he'd want to hurt me so much just when I was so wonderfully relaxed and at peace. And then he did it again. The pain was so excruciating that my eyes welled with tears. He dug his nail in a third time and now the floodgates opened. My body convulsed with sobbing and the tears poured out of me. I don't remember ever having cried like that.

The doctor said, 'Let it all out, don't control. This room is the safest place in the universe, just be.'

With that he left the room.

Now there was no stopping the flow. I sobbed my heart out and cried until there was nothing left: all the pain from feeling unloved as a child, being criticized by grown-ups, being bullied and put down at school and having my heart broken by Jenny, all of it just came out. Gradually the sobs and the tears lessened and stopped. I felt drained and completely exhausted. As I was getting dressed, Shyam came back in the room and gave me my instructions.

'I want you to stick to a diet of fruit for a week, drink plenty of water and do meditation every morning for two weeks. Go to the Bell Street clinic on Monday at seven thirty.'

There were about a dozen of us gathered in the basement at Bell Street, some dressed in orange robes with mala beads round their neck containing a small photograph of a bearded Indian man. The meditation leader welcomed me and explained that we were going to do dynamic meditation and to just follow the instructions. Stripped down to my underpants and with a mask over my eyes, I first had to exhale through my nose as fast as possible for ten minutes while frantic Indian music played. Just when I thought I could go on no longer, it all stopped and instead we were urged to rush about and scream, shout, cry or do whatever we wanted.

What on earth am I doing here? I wondered. Bodies cannoned into each other and from every direction there were screams, yells, people sobbing, swearing, shouting. It was total mayhem and a really frightening thing to experience for the first time.

After a while, the noise and chaos subsided; a different kind of music came on and now we were urged to shout from deep within, 'Hoo! Hoo! Hoo!' It was a technique to release more energy. Shouting was harder work than I expected, and when eventually we stopped, there was a wonderful 'blissed-out' feeling as we relaxed completely and soft music played. Eventually I could hear movement as people got up and left the room. I followed suit and later, dressed and minus the eye mask, joined the others next door and sipped mugs of hot, spicy Indian tea. We were all relaxed, content and smiling. We had just been through something profound.

The meditation was pioneered by Bhagwan Shree Rajneesh and was based on the principle that emotional hurt and pain are stored in the body, blocking natural energy flows and disrupting the body's natural functions of digestion, chemical balance and strong immune system. I was never one for joining clubs, groups or organizations – I valued being a free spirit too much – but the meditation made me feel good and I went every morning for the two weeks Shyam suggested.

By the end of it, I had a flat stomach from all that breathing and hooing and felt really fit. But, most important of all, the depression had gone and I felt happy and at peace with the world. I had spent eighteen months with a psychoanalyst and felt worse at the end of it. In two weeks of meditation and Shyam's acupuncture, fruit fast, plus vitamin and mineral supplements, I knew what it was to be really well, to feel better than you can ever remember feeling, and to be able to deal with the stresses and strains of modern life without being beaten down by them.

Frances could see what a huge difference it had made to me and I suggested she might like to think about becoming a patient of Shyam's as well. Her first appointment was in October. I eagerly awaited her return and asked her how she'd got on.

'Really good, thanks,' she said. 'But he says what I really need is to have a baby and that I'll be pregnant by Christmas.'

So accurate was Shyam Singha's prediction, the joke among our friends was that Frances would give birth to a baby with Asian colouring and Shyam's deep-brown eyes. But when the baby arrived in October 1974, he was obviously our little fella. Because of his little snub nose, we called him Mr Magoo for the first few days until we got to know him a bit and then the name Sam just seemed to fit. He'd come into the world at about twenty past nine in the morning with just a gurgle and a little whimper, in contrast to his mum, who had made a hell of a lot of noise during the long twenty-two-hour labour. He was born at home with midwife Kate and the local GP in attendance using the Leboyer method of delivery.

Frany and I had come across the book *Birth Without Violence* written by French gynaecologist Frederick Leboyer, which set out a philosophy of sensitivity and gentleness to a new human being at their time of greatest vulnerability. So the room where Frany gave birth was dark and very quiet, Dion's album *Peaceful Place* playing softly in the background. After he'd emerged, Sam was gently put face down on his mother's stomach, which was a natural resting place that gave him warmth and close contact with his mum.

Kate persuaded the doctor to wait until the pulse in the cord had stopped beating and, after about ten minutes, gave him the okay to cut it. This was to give Sam's lungs time to begin working naturally rather than being shocked into premature action by a sudden deprivation of his oxygen supply.

The next part of the calming process was to bathe him. I lifted this tiny new life gently in the palm of one hand and lowered him into a rectangular washing-up bowl filled with tepid water. It was wonderful to see him, calm and relaxed, in a similar environment to the one he'd just left. We watched as he tentatively began to stretch out his arms and we could sense his wonderment that now there were no restrictions to his movements. He gradually began to explore his new world and actually started to play, kicking his legs and stretching out his arms.

Frances was totally exhausted after such a long delivery and I asked Kate if it was okay for us all to sleep together in our bed.

'Of course it is,' she said. 'You'll be very aware the baby's there, it will be fine, don't worry.'

I woke about lunchtime from a deep and beautiful sleep and there, lying next to me, was our son. It was an indescribable feeling. I got up and went off to the shops to buy some food and each shop I went into, I just had to announce, 'Hey, I've just become a dad!' I felt like standing on the rooftops and announcing it to the world. Such is the pride of a new father.

I'd been looking forward to being a father from the moment Frances told me she was pregnant and the arrival of Sam changed our lives completely. It gave me a whole new impetus for getting up and going to work each day. Now I had the little man's future to think about and each day meant the joy of getting home to my little family and immersing myself in its world and the day-to-day progress Sam was making. Frances was a natural at motherhood and I did my best to be an involved dad; I became expert at nappy changing, bath times, reading the goodnight story and taking endless photos. Frances found a wonderful old coach-built pram in a charity shop, the sort nannies used to steer through the parks in the forties and fifties. We'd proudly wheel Sam around the neighbourhood every day and then park him in the back garden for his afternoon nap. He seemed to love being in the fresh air and always went straight to sleep, giving us a little break from looking after him. Much as we loved and doted on him, he could be a demanding little chap, always in need of attention and stimulation.

One afternoon, Frany and I were playing a game of pool on the scaled-down table we'd found that fitted perfectly on top of the dining table. Music was blaring out from the Bel Ami jukebox in the corner that Frany had bought me for Christmas. All was well with the world and I was playing beautifully. I was just about to pot the black, when Frany suddenly said, 'Where's Sam?'

I gasped, 'Oh my God, we've forgotten all about him!' I looked at Frany in horror and then out of the patio window. 'Fuck me!' I said. 'It's been snowing!'

It was now almost dark, the garden was a carpet of white and there in the gathering gloom stood Sam's pram with a four-inch coating of snow on the cover and hood. We rushed out and looked anxiously inside. Well wrapped up in warm clothes and blankets lay our little man, fast asleep and without a care in the world. He was none the worse for the experience but loves to recount the story about the night his cruel and neglectful parents left him out in the snow.

I was so lucky having the job I had. I could be there in the morning when Sam woke up and on most weekdays, I'd be there for bath and bedtime as well. Weekends were different. On Friday and Saturday nights I'd be somewhere like Wolverhampton or Taunton, doing gigs at clubs and discotheques, which was a great source of extra income, especially as they paid in cash.

I'd send all the paperwork and receipts to my accountant and stuff the wads of cash in a little drawer in the gorgeous roll-top desk, which was another great gift from Frances (I'd seen them in western movies and always hankered for one). I had a fairly carefree attitude to money. When it came in, I spent it. I liked buying things and making sure life was nice and comfortable for us all. When the booze cupboard was empty I'd just open the desk drawer, take out an inch or two of fivers and tenners and swan off to the off-licence up the road to stock up on bottles of Beaune and Château Neuf du Pape. If it wasn't booze, it was clothes or more of my beloved gadgets. I had to have the best and latest equipment and the newest things. In the mid seventies, I owned one of the first video recorders, which was an extremely rare thing back then. When the television stopped broadcasting at ten o'clock during the winter of discontent, I could go on watching for as long as I wanted, as I'd taped hours of programmes.

My financial acumen could be summed up as easy in, easy out. 'I'm helping small businesses and keeping the economy going' was my lame excuse for spending merrily with never a thought of saving for a rainy day. I was also no good at stashing away money for tax at the end of the year, but somehow I always seemed to get through – a job or a gig would come up and get me out of a hole.

I was enjoying living in the present too much to think about the future.

Chapter Twenty-Three

1975

While my family life and outside work were going well, I was finding things a big struggle at Radio One. There was frequent criticism, both externally and internally, that playing pop music all day was hardly the sort of public service broadcasting the corporation had built its reputation on. The management believed they could fend off some of the complaints if they improved the news service on Radio One, so back in 1973 a fifteen-minute programme called *Newsbeat* had been introduced twice-daily into the weekday schedule, at twelve thirty and five thirty. Not only had they nicked the name from the old Caroline hourly bulletins but I also hated the fact that it landed right in the middle of my programme. Why couldn't it be broadcast at the beginning or end? My show started at twelve and just as I got a rhythm and atmosphere going, it would all stop at half past twelve and I'd hand over to Richard Skinner or Laurie Meyer for fifteen minutes of speech.

While I was off the air, I'd pace round my studio, trying to keep my energy up and impatiently waiting for the minutes to tick by. They would hand back to me at a quarter to one and, despite my best efforts, it felt like starting the show all over again – it was very hard to get back into the 'feel' of the first half hour. *Newsbeat* was a very inventive and groundbreaking show, fast-paced, slickly produced and presented. I just wished it hadn't landed where it did.

With the hour and three-quarters I had left on the air, I was still managing to get in some good album tracks and singles. Artists like Steely Dan, Fleetwood Mac, Steve Harley, Bad Company, Led Zeppelin, Doobie Brothers, Doors, Eagles, J. J. Cale, Lou Reed were blended in with the best of the current hit singles. It was the naff production-line pop like the Bay City Rollers that I tried to avoid playing. Maybe I was trying to impose my personal taste on listeners but the feedback I got through letters and meeting people at gigs was that they liked the chance to hear something new and a bit different. Research showed the appreciation indices for the show were sometimes in the upper nineties, the highest figure for any daytime show. Ever since my club days in Birmingham, all I'd ever wanted to do was discover something really good and then share it with others. Most things are all the better for being shared and it was especially true for great music.

I was one of the very few daytime jocks who would listen to all new singles and albums. Every spare moment was spent listening to new stuff and when I found something that really excited me, I wanted to rush into Broadcasting House, play it on that day's show and share my excitement with the audience. But the system didn't work that way. Anything new I discovered from Tuesday afternoon onwards I would have to give to my producer. He would then take it into the playlist meeting the following Tuesday (a meeting I wasn't allowed to go to) and, if the group of producers decided it was suitable for the playlist (unlikely), I'd have to wait until the following Monday before I could actually play it on the air.

Jesus, it was so frustrating. Radio is such a spontaneous medium yet the BBC system, so safe and conservative, took all the energy of immediacy and the thrill of the moment out of it. Oh, for the days of rock 'n' roll in America, when someone like Buddy Holly would turn up at the local radio station with his latest record and the excited DJ would put it straight on the air. He and the station wanted to be first with something hot, to beat the competition and be ahead of the game. But in the early seventies there was no competition and Radio One was just that, the one and only national music station. There were beginning to be rumbles from above that my show was becoming too different to the other daytime shows and that I should be made to play more pop hits and cut out the newer, less familiar stuff.

This rigid conformity was like being back at school and I was getting more and more fed up and pissed off. I had no way of venting all this suppressed anger and resentment, so it just festered away inside, waiting for something to trigger its release. The safety valve blew off in spectacular style one glorious, rebellious day in March 1975.

It was a Tuesday, and, as usual, I had the brand-new chart to unveil before the waiting millions. I gave out a precis of all the important statistics and then played a selection of the new entries and big climbers. Just before one o'clock, I slotted in the tape cartridge with Booker T. and the MG's 'Time Is Tight' on it and got ready to announce the rundown of the entire Top Forty chart, culminating with the big, Number One chart topper at the end.

'And get ready, here it is, the moment you've been waiting for!' I said, sounding as though something really special was about to happen. Then, as the tempo and energy of 'Time Is Tight' was building up, ready for the big announcement, my tone changed to one of huge disappointment and boredom as I announced, 'This week's Number One is yet again, for the sixth week running, the Bay City Rollers with "Bye Bye Baby".'

I sounded as if each word tasted horrible: well, it did. I was sick to death of that record and on again it came, the same old song I'd been having to play for over a month. This was the group that the Fleet Street press had been hailing as the new Beatles. What utter, ridiculous nonsense. Once the record was finished, my enthusiasm returned and I carried on with the show. About ten minutes later producer Ron Belchier came into the studio from the cubicle next door.

'We've got a problem, the duty officer's just been on. Apparently loads of Bay City Roller fans have been complaining.'

'What the hell's the matter with them?' I countered. 'I played the bloody thing, didn't I?'

'Yes, but it was the way you played it and your sarcastic introduction. Maybe you'd better say something.'

I think Ron was hinting that I apologize, but he knew better than to make the suggestion outright. The fact that I'd played the

Rollers' record, albeit with much less enthusiasm than their fans would have liked, and yet still the complaints were flooding in finally tipped me over the edge. The record on the air was coming to a close and I faded up the microphone.

'Apparently there have been lots of calls coming in from Bay City Roller fans complaining about the way I introduced the Number One. I don't know what it is you want – I can't pretend to like the Bay City Rollers or get excited by the fact their record is Number One for yet another week. If you really want to know what I think, I'll tell you. I can't stand the Bay City Rollers. I hate that silly little record and I think they're musical garbage.'

Ron rapidly disappeared, probably off to the pub to avoid the fallout. Me, I bloody loved it and was high as a kite on the adrenalin rush of the moment; months of frustration were liberated in one glorious moment of freedom. Bollocks to 'em, I thought. If I get the elbow for that, so be it. At least I'll go down in a blaze of glory. There were millions of people who were as sick to death of the whole Rollers phenomenon as I was, and they probably enjoyed my outburst almost as much as I did. However, there was no immediate fallout and the day finished much as any other, and I thought no more about it. The next morning my home phone started ringing. Various friends were all saying the same thing.

'God, have you seen the papers this morning? You're all over the front page.'

Oh Christ, I thought. What's happened now?

I dashed up the road to the newsagent's and bought all the tabloids. I was headline news in nearly all. A typical banner read: WALKER SLAMS THE BAY CITY ROLLERS. The story ran on to the effect that hundreds of the group's fans had besieged the BBC switchboard with complaints about Johnnie Walker saying their band produced musical garbage. I thought it was all a good laugh, and I always enjoy upsetting the apple cart now and then, but I was shocked and surprised that the press had made such a big deal of it. I wondered if I was going to get fired for this. But towards the end of the story they quoted Radio One boss, Derek Chinnery, who seemed remarkably unfazed.

'It was just an off-the-cuff, ad-lib comment and Johnnie Walker is entitled to his opinion.'

I was pleasantly surprised at how supportive he was but also suspected that he was just trying to defuse the row and show some solidarity, and that behind the scenes, he was more than a little pissed off. I had a reputation as a bit of an awkward customer at the BBC, not one prone to sucking up to the management or quietly accepting the way things were. My show was still popular enough to keep my quarterly contracts being renewed, but my card was marked and my BBC file grew a little thicker.

Nearly thirty years later I was discussing future guests with the production team of my *Drivetime* show on Radio Two.

'I don't suppose you'll want ex-Bay City Roller Les McKeown on?'

'Yeah, why not,' I replied. 'Maybe it's time to bury the hatchet.'

Les and I shook hands warmly and exchanged smiles when he came into the studio, and we chatted off air before the interview.

'There's something I've been wanting to tell you for years, Johnnie,' said Les.

'What's that, Les?'

'You were absolutely right way back then, we did make musical garbage.'

We shared a really good laugh and then chatted away on air like old friends.

I was beginning to think more and more that I was a round peg trying to fit in a square hole. I was often embarrassed at the style and antics of Radio One. The station was Top Forty jukebox during the day and more of a real music station during the evenings. I envied John Peel's freedom to be himself and play the music he believed in. He and I had always got along well. We were old mates from the pirate days and, thankfully, John never saw me as one of the grinning, 'Isn't this all fun?', shop-opening DJs. We'd exchange knowing and sympathetic glances at the really embarrassing events we had to go to, and he knew the struggles I had to get anything other than mainstream pop on the air.

My problem was that I was neither a daytime nor an evening-style DJ but somewhere in the middle. I believed in presenting a show that was entertaining and played the hits that people wanted to hear (minus the really naff ones, of course); but I was also desperate to introduce listeners to music and artists that were rarely heard on daytime shows, yet who really deserved the exposure. This, I was never able to do.

The extremes of the two sides of my life as a DJ can be illustrated by two significant events in 1975, one highly embarrassing and the other absolutely the opposite. The first I witnessed with John Peel whose vivid description graces the pages of his autobiography, *Margrave of the Marshes*.

I think Radio One had underspent its annual budget and needed to splash out in grand style in order to ensure a similar budget the following year. A 'Fun Day' was organized at the Mallory Park motor-racing circuit in Leicestershire. No expense was spared. DJs were flown in by helicopter, as were Desmond Dekker, Noddy Holder from Slade, The Three Degrees and, here we go again, my favourite band, the Bay City Rollers. Rollermania was in full swing and the tartan army was there in such vast numbers that it caused a massive security problem. Someone had the brainwave of putting the group on top of an observation tower at one end of a boating lake inside the circuit. They would obviously be safe there and the fans would be able to catch a glimpse and wave at their heroes.

Glimpses were not enough for the hordes of teenage girls who were whipping themselves up into a mad frenzy of excitement. Police manning the barriers were unable to hold back the hordes who broke through and began wading and swimming across the lake. Why they were there, God only knows, but to the rescue came members of the BBC Sub Aqua Club, who hauled the fans back to the bank where, joined by others, they promptly jumped back in the lake again. Noddy Holder voiced his fears for their safety in an interview with David Hamilton. One would think the limits of surrealism had been reached, but no, there was one more element to make this a day that would be etched in the memory for ever. Roaring into view came Tony Blackburn in a speedboat with a huge furry Womble at the wheel.

John Peel turned to me: 'Johnnie, look at this and marvel. You will never see anything like this again.'

On Midsummer Day 1975, another event took place that was memorable for all the right reasons. I got a call to say that Elton John was organizing an all-day music festival at Wembley Stadium and he had specifically asked for me to DJ and compère the whole day. Wow – what an honour. There would be seventy-five thousand people there. The idea thrilled and excited me but, at the same time, scared the pants off me. Would I be able to do it? I never really thought about the huge numbers that listened to my radio shows; they were unseen and it wasn't that hard to be bold and extrovert in a room on your own. Okay, so there'd be a few hundred in clubs at gigs but after a couple of drinks to steady my stage fright, I'd just stride out there and get on with it. This was different, this was big. But I had to say yes, especially when I was told who was going to play. Elton had chosen the bands himself – and what a line-up.

The day was to start with the wonderfully eccentric West Country band Stackridge, who were now on Elton's label, Rocket Records. Then Rufus with Chaka Khan, Joe Walsh, The Eagles, The Beach Boys and then Elton would close the show. These were all people whose music I had played on the radio for nearly ten years and whose albums I put on for pleasure at home. This had the potential to be one amazing gig and I was so lucky to have been asked to take part. I rushed out and bought more album cases, then spent hour after hour sorting out which records I was going to take. With half an hour or so between each band, I was going to need a lot of music.

I was up early on the big day after a night when excitement meant sleep was nigh impossible. It was such a great feeling arriving backstage at Wembley Stadium. The place was buzzing with activity and there was a sense of anticipation in the air. Riggers, soundmen and lighting technicians were all frantically putting the finishing touches in and around the huge stage at one end of the stadium. They had constructed a great DJ platform for me, just in front and slightly below the main stage. From there I could look out on the entire stadium and also have the best view of the bands on the stage.

I began playing records just before midday as the crowds started to file in and grab the best spots on the pitch. All the elements needed to make a music festival really special came together on that Midsummer Day at Wembley. The skies were a beautiful blue with just a few fluffy white clouds above seventy-five thousand happy music fans basking in the sunshine.

Stackridge and Rufus were the perfect opening acts and then on came Joe Walsh, who played a great set. I was loving my role providing music during changeovers. I had half a dozen boxes of albums I'd lugged on to my platform, which seemed like plenty of material so I hadn't brought the singles boxes I used for clubs and discos. How very wrong I was. The huge arch over the stage provided shade for the bands but I was out front under the blazing sun, which shone relentlessly down on the mixer and turntables. Within about twenty seconds of putting an LP on the deck I watched in horror as the vinyl disc warped and buckled with the heat. I was patched into the main sound system and it was going to sound dreadful if the stylus started jumping. I increased the weight on the pick-up to maximum and said my prayers. Amazingly I got away with it, but there were many scary moments.

The Eagles came onstage and the crowd rose as one as Wembley became California and the packed stadium danced to 'Take It Easy' and swayed to 'Peaceful Easy Feeling'. Halfway through the set, Glenn Frey announced they had a surprise and he and the others dragged onstage a huge aluminium flight case. They opened the lid and out stepped a long-haired musician from Kansas, who took a bow and plugged in his guitar as the band kicked off 'One Of These Nights'. Joe Walsh had joined The Eagles.

And then a really good day turned into one of those sublime, unique experiences that stay etched in the memory for a lifetime. The Beach Boys came onstage, took the stadium and its massive crowd into the palm of their hands and lifted us up to a place of superb joy and happiness, a place where the sun always shines, where there are no worries and troubles, where people's smiles come from the heart and where complete strangers feel total love and connection with everyone around them. Arms stretched up high to the heavens, we sang, we danced and clapped our hands to a Beach Boys greatest hits collection. Mike Love stood centre stage looking like a god in a shimmering gold shirt that reflected beams of sunshine all over the stadium.

By this time I was at the other end of the stadium, down with the crowds on the pitch, dancing and enjoying the fun. I became so caught up in the joy of it all, I never made it backstage in time to introduce Elton. He and his new band came on and Elton announced they were going to play the new album *Captain Fantastic And The Brown Dirt Cowboy*. There were groans from people around me and I heard someone say, 'Oh God, I hope it's not a double album.'

All around the pitch, groups of people began leaving the stadium. It had been a long hot day, the energy had peaked with The Beach Boys and, for many, there was a long journey back home. It was a cruel time for Elton. Having organized the whole event and watched so many people enjoy a wonderful day, he was then rewarded with the sight of them walking out on him. It was a brave and bold decision to play the new album and one he now admits, with hindsight, was a mistake. A hard way to learn the lesson that there are times, especially at festivals, when it's best to give fans want they want and play the hits.

I went home thinking that I really did have the most fantastic job in the world.

Chapter Twenty-Four

We celebrated Sam's first birthday in October 1975 and then, a month later, we had another positive result on a pregnancy testing kit.

We'd had an extension built on the back of the house, and Frances had found all the special bits and pieces she wanted from various antique and second-hand stores. Our house was complete and so would our family be with a second child due in July 1976. Home life couldn't have been better; I wished I could have said the same about my working life. The frustrations of trying to work within the confines of daytime Radio One didn't only involve music; there was the spiritual side as well.

Ever since I had met Dr Shyam Singha, I had more of an interest in the spiritual side of life, and particularly Eastern approaches. I had been on a two-weekend Silva Mind Control Course, which sounds ominous but was in fact very positive. I learnt how to relax, meditate and lower the brain frequencies to the 'alpha state'. Here, I became more in touch with my own intuition and learnt to 'programme' positive affirmations that would improve my life. I also learnt that we all have mental abilities and intuitive or psychic powers that, for the most part, lie dormant all our lives. Francesco, the course leader, added his own spiritual element to the course and, on the final weekend, passed around copies of a letter, said to have been written by Chief Seathl of the Suquamish tribe of Native Americans in about 1854. It was to the president of the United States in response to the government's request to buy the tribe's remaining land.

There has been much controversy about the authenticity of this now world-famous letter. Whatever the origins and authenticity, the letter was a moving and powerful statement about the environment, mankind's connection with the land, his hopes and dreams for his children, and respect and tolerance for another race's beliefs and way of life.

Coming back on to the air, I had the strong urge to share my experience, especially the Native American letter. Maybe, I thought, I could read the whole thing on my show. But how would it be received? Would people think I was starting to lose the plot? Was this something I should broadcast on a pop music show?

I split the letter into five roughly equal sections, thinking that perhaps it would work if I read a little each day. I stuffed the paper in my bag and set off for the studio, still unsure what to do. Then, throwing caution to the winds and summoning up all the courage I could muster, I decided to go ahead and do it. I told the audience that I'd come across an amazing document that I'd found profoundly moving, and that I wanted to share it with them; I read out the first section. That afternoon in the office, producer Ron mentioned there'd been quite a few interested calls about 'that Indian letter'. I read the second part the next day and by Wednesday morning the few calls had turned into an avalanche and letters were arriving asking for copies of the letter.

Ron commented on the amazing reaction, 'It's really good that people have responded so well to this. After you read today's part, mention that listeners who want a copy of the letter should send in a stamped addressed envelope. I'll arrange to get a load of copies printed off.'

I was grateful for his support and pleased that he thought reading the letter on air was a good idea. I hadn't consulted him, partly because I hadn't made up my mind to do it until the last moment and partly because I had learnt long ago that if you came up with any unusual idea at the BBC, the answer was always no. Better just to go ahead and face the flak afterwards.

On Thursday and Friday I finished off the reading and reminded listeners to send in an SAE. The Radio One mailroom helped by siphoning off all the copy requests into separate bags as we just didn't have room in Ron's small office. The whole thing was quite amazing and I felt vindicated for taking a chance and trying something out that was a bit different. Then, the following Tuesday, I got a call from the Radio One controller's office. Would I please come to Derek Chinnery's office immediately? This was a rare event. Derek had a face like thunder and lost no time in ripping into me.

'What the hell do you think you've been doing?'

'I don't know what you mean.'

'This bloody Indian letter – what the hell is that all about? Where on earth did you get it from, and who is this bloody Chief Seattle?'

'I got it at a course I did recently. I thought it was an amazing document and it was something people might be touched by, so it was worthwhile reading on my show.'

'It's just a load of mumbo-jumbo poppycock,' fumed Derek.

This really got my blood up. Now it was my turn to vent some anger.

'Bloody hell! I'm amazed at your reaction. I thought it was a great success and that as boss of the radio station you would actually be pleased that BBC transmitters had been used to spread such a good message. Something worthwhile. It makes a change from Terry Wogan's "Fight the Flab" and Jimmy Young asking, "What's the recipe today, Jim?" That's what I call mumbo-jumbo. You're just typical of the narrow, closed-minded attitude of the BBC – all you want is silly inconsequential stuff. Something real comes along and touches thousands of people and you just dismiss it as poppycock. I can see I'm wasting my time talking to you because you're just never going to understand.'

With that, the meeting was obviously over and I left his office fuming. All the glowing letters and phone calls from people who had thought so much of the piece were now trashed by his attitude. The whole thing was typical of my working life at Radio One. While many of my listeners seemed to appreciate what I was doing, the management clearly didn't. It was all very demotivating and soul-destroying.

★

A month or so later, I was back in Derek's office. We were discussing extending my contract on the lunchtime show. In the early days of Radio One, all DJs, as freelancers, were on contract and the most they would give you back then was a thirteen-week stint. But, with the advent of commercial radio, things were changing. LBC started in 1973, followed a month later by Capital Radio, and DJs now had an alternative to the BBC. The BBC acted quickly to hold on to its talent, extending contracts to one and sometimes two years. My contract was due to end in July 1976 and Derek was offering me a further two years. But there was a catch.

He said, 'I'm afraid we can't extend you the freedom to play album tracks and other music not on the playlist.'

My face fell.

'We want your show to be in line with Tony Blackburn and David Hamilton. It's not right that one show in the day is different from the others,' he explained.

I felt the usual burst of frustration, 'You mean I've got to play more chart stuff like the Bay City Rollers?'

'Yes, if it's in the Top Forty. You'll have to.'

I groaned, and then I suggested a possible solution, 'Why not think about giving me a year or two off daytime? Let me do a weekend show where I can have more musical freedom.'

Derek couldn't believe what he was hearing.

'You mean you actually want me to demote you from a peak daytime show to the weekend? You must be crazy.'

Back then, weekend jocks were always thought of as being in the second division. New recruits were tried out at the weekend, especially on the Saturday-afternoon slot, where I'd started. A weekday daily show was first division and Derek just couldn't understand why I would volunteer to come off lunchtime. We talked about things like musical freedom and job satisfaction, but the conversation was going nowhere when Derek came out with a wonderful statement that I'll always remember.

'You know what the trouble is with you, Johnnie?'

'No, what's that, Derek?'

I was fascinated to hear what might come next. Derek gathered himself up to give me the benefit of his great wisdom and make his important pronouncement.

'The trouble with you, Johnnie, is that you're *too into the music, man.*'

He said the last words with maximum sarcasm. I sat there speechless and stared at him. I was a DJ who was 'too into the music'. I thought back to all the times when my enthusiasm for music had been quashed, when I had to read letters from listeners who thought I was slacking by not playing some new record that I was in fact desperate to play and not allowed to. I remembered executive producer Doreen Davies telling me I had to learn the art of compromise – in other words, do it our way. And now I was being sneered at by the head of the station, who thought my love of music was an actual disadvantage. It seemed he wanted me just to turn up, indulge my ego, be a 'poptastic' DJ and not really care about what music I played.

Derek and I continued to glare at each other, the silence heavy and menacing.

'Johnnie, what I'm offering you is a two-year contract on the lunchtime show. It's that or nothing.'

Did he want me to go? I wondered. Or was he convinced I would never turn down such a high-profile show, that I would stop being concerned about the music content and toe the line? Here was the moment of truth. I looked him straight in the eyes.

'Well, in that case, it had better be nothing.'

Chapter Twenty-Five

1976

I left Derek Chinnery's office in a complete daze. Oh my God, what had I done now? This was history repeating itself. I'd walked out on my motor-trade job in Gloucester, the promising future I had at Patrick Motors in Solihull, and I'd left Radio England on an impulse. Now here I was doing it again, except this time it was really big. I was throwing away a top-rated, high-profile show on the nation's biggest radio station plus lucrative side earnings at gigs – just like that. Bloody hell.

And just how was I going to break the news to Frances? I had a mortgage, a son and a second child on the way. I had minimal savings in the bank, credit card and tax bills to pay and had absolutely no idea what I was going to do or where I was going to work.

'You did *what*? What the *hell* are you thinking of?'

I tried my best to explain but Frances took it really badly, and who could blame her? It was a bolt right out of the blue. She had just got our house finished and had two children's future and security to worry about.

'You must be completely mad! You're crazy and you're a bloody fool. Always you, you, you. You put your career first every time. What about us? What about your responsibilities? What about this house, about Sam and our unborn child? What's their future going to be like now? Go back and tell them you've made a big mistake.'

'I can't, Frany, I just can't. They wanted another two years of lunchtime and I'd have to stick totally to the playlist. I just can't do that, it would do my head in, it's just not me. I would have to drag myself in every day and pretend I'm enjoying it when I'm not.

'I can't face another two years of that. I've got to love what I'm doing otherwise there's no point. I asked Derek if I could do a weekend show with more musical freedom and he just wouldn't hear of it.'

We argued back and forth, getting nowhere. She could see it was hopeless and that my mind was made up. A heavy silence filled the room.

'I'll work something out, you'll see,' I said.

I had to try and seem positive, even if inside I was a quivering mess. But inside was also the glimmer of that steely determination that had seen me through similar dramas. I had followed my intuition; it had worked before, and somehow I'd find a way to make it work again. Ten years before, on Radio England, DJ Ron O'Quinn had planted the idea that one day I might go to the USA. Maybe, just maybe, it occurred to me, there would be a chance to build a good new life for us all in America.

A music-business manager named John Stanley had got Alan Freeman an American radio show that he recorded in London, and, in the previous autumn, I'd asked him to try and get me a similar show. I was now without an agent, and John agreed to manage me. We came up with the idea of creating a unique promotional tool and got radio producer Tim Blackmore to craft a demo tape. Along with excerpts of my lunchtime show, there were clips of radio producers and music-business figures, who talked about me and my place in the UK radio and music scene. James Fisher, then the head of RCA Records in the UK, said I was the most influential jock in the UK and had single-handedly kicked off Lou Reed's career in Europe. Ron Belchier, Doreen Davies and even Derek Chinnery waxed lyrical about my radio skills and status in British radio. Derek even said when it came to the really important DJs in Britain, Johnnie Walker was right up there in the top three. What sweet irony that his contribution towards finding me a part-time extra job might now turn out to be one of the important keys to my making a successful escape from the BBC.

Instead of using tape or cassettes, John came up with the idea of pressing a number of copies of the finished piece on to twelve-inch vinyl.

'You're an album jock, after all. Now you've got your own album, a great showcase for who you are and what you can do. We'll just leave it with a blank label and a covering note, and send it to the major stations in New York and Los Angeles. They'll be intrigued by the mystery of it all and are bound to give it a listen.'

The album served as a great calling card and John set up a visit to the US in January of 1976, which would help me make contacts and get known in the States. I loved America from the moment I arrived. Seeing the famous Manhatten skyline as we approached New York was incredible – at last, I was finally in America, home to the music I'd adored for so long. Once I was there, it exceeded my expectations. The energy of the place was amazing.

In New York, John and I sat on panel discussions about the disco explosion at a *Billboard Magazine* convention and, as a thank you for making the trip, the magazine presented me with the International Disco DJ of the Year Award in New York. I visited key FM rock stations like WPLJ and WNEW, home of DJ Scott Muni, a legendary pioneer of FM rock radio. I was interviewed by Jim Lowe for his AM talk show and was a guest with Doctor Jerry on WPIX.

Here was a whole new world of radio where jocks were admired and valued for their love and commitment to music. What a difference to Radio One and being 'too into the music, man'. Every spare moment, I was searching the dial, tuning in to the huge choice of radio stations playing great music. This is radio heaven, I thought.

After New York, John and I flew to Los Angeles. We left behind icy blizzards and sub-zero temperatures and arrived in another world: the sun was shining, the air was balmy and warm, the skies were blue and it was eighty degrees. Here I was in California, home to The Eagles and all those other wonderful West Coast bands. I could hardly believe it.

My 'demo album' had got through and had pricked interest at the radio stations. I went off to meet DJ Thom O'Hair at KMET.

He was a tough biker sort, a very cool guy with a renegade moustache, long hair and cowboy boots. His first job as a teenager had been in a mechanic's workshop where he kept the guys entertained by picking the records to play on the hi-fi system. We had lots in common and we hit it off straightaway. He showed me around the station and then we went for a drink.

We went into his favourite bar and he became the first guy I ever heard order a 'JD on the rocks'. He was fascinated to hear about my life in England and the fact that I knew people like Robert Plant, Roger Daltrey, Elton John and Peter Frampton. Quite a few JDs later, we headed back to his flat, which was wonderfully messy with records everywhere, and Thom expertly skinned up a neat grass joint and we smoked it together. I had never been so stoned – I was used to warming up and crumbling up a little black or Moroccan hash or sprinkling grass in a joint that was mostly tobacco. This was a one-skin neat joint of California's finest, the sort Jo Jo smoked in the Beatles' 'Get Back'.

'I want you to come in on my show tomorrow afternoon,' said Thom, seemingly unaffected by the strength of the grass. 'We'll have a bit of a chat, then you can do an hour of your favourite stuff.'

'Wow, that would be amazing, I'd love to.'

'There's one condition, though.'

'What's that?'

'You gotta do it stoned.'

'No, no, I don't think I could do that,' I replied nervously. 'I've never gone on the air high before, that's not exactly the BBC way.'

'Well, that's the deal, Johnnie.'

'Do lots of jocks have a smoke before going on the air in LA?' I asked.

He looked at me with a sort of pained expression.

'It'd be easier to try and find the ones that don't.'

I tried to convince him that, in my case, it wasn't such a good idea but he wasn't having it. Eventually he wore me down and I agreed, thinking, Well, it's his town and his show. When in Rome . . .

The next day we smoked a joint in the engineers' workshop at the back of the station and headed into the studio. With casual, laid-back cool, Thom presented the first hour of his show and, at the end of a set of three tracks, turned on the mike.

'And now we're going to have a real pleasure. Johnnie Walker, a top DJ from England, is here at KMET. Johnnie, I'm just gonna turn it over to you for the next hour. It's all yours.'

He put on the track I selected and got up out of the chair. I was petrified and my hands were shaking so much, I could barely cue up the next track. For me, it was a big enough challenge to go on air in LA, to who knows how many people, but to do it stoned was really freaking me out. The effect of marijuana is so dependent on mood and environment. If you're really relaxed and feeling good anyway, it just heightens the mood. Stripped of reserve and inhibition, you can feel free to laugh, have fun, dance, be outrageous. Here I was, in an unfamiliar nerve-wracking situation, and the reverse happened. Paranoia set in and I could barely summon up the courage to speak. My mouth was also desperately dry. But I did my best and managed to sound as cool and as relaxed as Thom had.

Then halfway through my hour, I decided to do something a bit different. In my stoned-out haze, I resolved that what LA needed that afternoon was a bit of a treatise on love. I was very much into Khalil Gibran's *The Prophet* at the time and had marked up a passage to read out. So I duly did so, and followed it with a suitable track, and then struggled through the rest of the hour. Thom came back into the studio and I rather got the impression that my whacked-out 'spiritual' moment had gone down like a lead balloon. I think he'd been convinced that a smoke would lift all the constraints of my BBC conditioning and I would suddenly discover a new, freer radio style. Well, it hadn't and I'd blown a big chance to make an impression on LA radio.

My next stop was KLOS, which couldn't have been more different. The station manager gave me a tour and we went into the on-air studio. A tall, lean black guy was sitting at a small round table in front of the mike. They played soft rock and the jock gently announced the tracks just played, current time and station ID, then gave a signal for an ad break. There wasn't an album in sight. He just had a list of songs, which were all played by an engineer in a cubicle next door. It was all so laid-back, it was like Radio One on Valium.

'Wayne's big thing is learning to fly light aircraft,' explained the manager as we left the studio. 'I like my jocks to have an outside hobby so their show isn't the most important thing in their lives.'

No wonder, I thought, mentally crossing KLOS off the list.

A few more visits and then, to my regret, it was time to go home. But I left America inspired, feeling sure that this was a place I could really be at home. The radio was incredible: the sheer amount of stations and choice amazed me. The kind of music I wanted to play was freely available all the time. I knew I wanted to come back sometime soon. I'd made important contacts and got to know some key radio people, so perhaps something, sometime, would come of it.

Back in London, I really didn't know what I was going to do. A job in America was still just a dream. I needed some help and rang medium Don Galloway. I'd come across him during my search for some meaning to the Ouija board experience. Don had calmed my fears, explained about psychic phenomena, and introduced me to the concept of life after death and the existence of a spirit world. Don hadn't heard about my impending departure from Radio One and knew nothing about my future plans. He is a very gifted medium and clairvoyant and very well respected in his world. He asked for my wedding ring, which he held in his hand. After a minute or so of silence while he tuned in, he began talking about travels abroad.

'I can see you poring over maps and planning a trip. It's definitely overseas and I'm pretty sure we're talking about America.'

There was much more in the reading about job frustration, a search for more fulfilment and then, as he was about to return my ring, he paused.

'I don't know why I feel the need to say this, but you wouldn't want to lose this ring, would you?'

'No, of course I wouldn't. It means an awful lot to me. I'd be devastated if I lost it.'

'Well, make jolly sure you don't,' said Don, passing it back to me.

The closeness of the reading to my own plans was very reassuring and welcome support at a time when I was still feeling pretty wobbly about the future. I did my best to reassure Frances that things were going to be okay and that all would be well. I was inundated with letters from listeners saying they felt sad I was going to leave but many of them saying they understood why I felt the need to move on. Brian Eno and Dave Gilmour were kind enough to drop me a note wishing me good luck for the future.

Now I had to plan for my last show and try to have confidence in the future. I knew there was no changing my mind and staying with Radio One; I intuitively felt I was on the right course but I was under incredible stress trying to keep positive for Frances and our family as well as sounding my usual happy self on the air.

For my last show on 2nd July 1976, I decided to do a bit of a retrospective look back on my radio years. I played the Radio Caroline theme tune and the Beatles' 'All You Need Is Love' – the song played at the big moment, midnight on 14th August 1967. I also mentioned how hard it was to get away with playing the occasional album track at Radio One, and the battle I had lost in 1970 to play the title track from Derek and The Dominoes' *Layla And Other Assorted Love Songs*. I put the record on and within thirty seconds a red light starting flashing on the studio wall. It was the emergency phone. I'd never known it ring before. I picked it up and on the other end was a very irate Derek Chinnery, the head of Radio One.

'Johnnie, I've given you the freedom to be able to do your last show and I hope you're not going to spend the rest of the programme slagging off Radio One.'

I reassured him that I wouldn't and that he had nothing to worry about. Anyway, the engineers had tipped me off that there was a technician in the control room with the express job of cutting me off if I got really out of order.

I revisited some of the special personal moments I'd shared over the radio: meeting Frances, getting married and the birth of Sam. At the end I announced we were all heading off for a new life in America and put on Led Zeppelin's 'Going To California'. I said my goodbyes and ended with The Eagles' 'I Wish You Peace'. The record faded out and on came the time signal for two o'clock.

I had done my last show for Radio One. I gathered up my records and headphones and headed out of the studio. There were a few people outside who'd come to say goodbye. I couldn't say much, I was too choked up. I had to go away and be on my own for a while. As I left, I looked back at Broadcasting House, an imposing building often likened to a huge white cruise liner. I'd come from a little ship with a tiny transmitter bobbing around in the North Sea to a massive, all-powerful one that broadcast to the entire United Kingdom.

And now I was turning my back on it and leaving it forever.

PART FOUR

Stateside

Chapter Twenty-Six

The most important thing now was the safe arrival of our second child, due the Sunday after my last radio show for the BBC. All our attention was focused on the impending birth. Kate was back as midwife and we elected to go for another home birth. This time Kate offered me the chance actually to deliver the baby.

'I'll help you,' she said. 'Once the head is clear, you take over.'

It was not to be, however, as the baby had the umbilical cord wrapped round its neck and, for a while, things were all very tense. But the delivery went fine and a beautiful, healthy baby girl was born on 14th July 1976. I did the bath routine again and when all was calm and peaceful, Sam came up from downstairs to meet his sister. We named her Beth.

As before, the bedroom filled with flowers from friends and well-wishers and again, a beautiful aura of peace and tranquillity surrounded the new arrival. You could sense it so strongly from halfway up the stairs and everyone automatically walked on tiptoe and spoke in whispers. It was no less a miracle the second time around and it was a wonderful event to take our minds off the future. We were truly blessed.

And then something else rather wonderful happened: manager John Stanley called me to tell me he'd just heard from KSAN in San Francisco – only the premier and most highly respected FM station in the States. We'd had a brief visit there in January and now they wanted me to go over and do their breakfast show for three weeks while DJ Terry McGovern took a vacation in Europe.

Bingo! Eureka! God bless my intuition and willingness to take a chance. I could relax for a short while, the panic of what I was going to do next over. All I had to do was be so bloody good on air they wouldn't want me to leave. When I told Frances, she was in two minds. Of course she was pleased that I had some work: she was still very frightened about our having no security at all, so any job was a reason to be happy. But she knew that my ambition was to get something permanent in America and she was very reluctant to make such a big move, away from our comfortable home, our familiar world and our families.

The other downside to this job was that it would take me away from her and the children for at least six weeks. I would do the breakfast show for three weeks and then stay on to record some specials. That meant leaving Frances to cope alone with a toddler and a newborn, and missing nearly two months of Beth's babyhood.

'This is my big chance,' I told her. 'I have to go.'

She could see that I wasn't going to change my mind, so she gave in gracefully. Perhaps she hoped I'd get America out of my system if I went for a short stint.

I arrived in Berkeley, California to a balmy summer's evening. Queen Ida and Bon Temps Zydeco Band were playing great Cajun music in the restaurant and out on the sun-drenched terrace at the back were a whole bunch of KSAN people mingling with movers and shakers from the city's media.

Sales guy David Bramwick had picked me up from the airport in his blue BMW. The trip was amazing. We drove into the city of San Francisco and then east towards Berkeley, over the Bay Bridge, which was eight miles long and took twenty minutes to cross. But there were wonderful views of San Francisco and the bay along the way.

It was a music-business reception and people were milling around with drinks, indulging in cocktail chat – something I've never been very good at. But they seemed keen to meet me and find out more about this jock from England. I'd start to answer the friendly questions directed my way and thought I was doing okay until more than one person turned away from me as I was in mid sentence to start another conversation with someone else.

Fuck me, I thought. I must be really boring. Either that or they're incredibly rude. What's it going to be like broadcasting to people like this? I started to get the horrors. Was I really this dull? I was due to go on air in a couple of days and I started to wish I'd come out much earlier to acclimatize myself to the Californian culture. This was my first introduction to the well-known American short attention span; I was going to have to learn to be interesting and snappy.

I was at the radio station bright and early at five a.m. on the Monday morning to be greeted by newsman Dave McQueen looking every inch a San Francisco hippy. He had a moustache and long hair tied back in a ponytail. He was ripping news stories from the teleprinters and at the same time was expertly rolling up a neat little pure grass spliff. I was a bit surprised.

'Is this your regular way to start the day, Dave?' I asked.

'Oh yeah, nothing like it to kick the day into gear,' he replied, passing the spliff in my direction.

My LA experience of being stoned on air came back into my mind and there was no way I was going to risk screwing up day one of such an important show. So I politely declined.

The KSAN studio was two or three times bigger than those at Radio One. All along one wall were shelves stacked floor to ceiling, full of albums: they were the 'Red Dot' collection, all the albums that had been played a lot on the station over the years. Along the back wall were various pieces of equipment that sent the studio output to the transmitters. Various readings had to be checked hourly and noted in the broadcast duty log. In the centre was the DJ console with three turntables on the left and, behind, all the tape carts containing the commercials. To the right of the DJ chair was space for guests and, alongside, a small trolley containing new and current hit albums. In front was the mixing desk and a window to the library beyond, which contained a massive collection of all kinds of music: jazz, rock, classical and comedy.

I loved the freedom of being on a station where the toughest decision was deciding which record to start a programme with; after that the record on air seemed somehow to suggest the one to follow, and so on. Elated, I reversed my Radio One music style.

At the BBC, I had played a majority of pop singles with occasional album tracks for flavour. Here, good rock LP tracks were the staple diet of the output and I added in great classic pop singles like Ben E. King's 'Stand By Me' and Fats Domino's 'Blueberry Hill' alongside tracks by The Grateful Dead and Led Zeppelin.

It was too early to get feedback from listeners on my first show, but it seemed to go down well with the station staff. One by one, they passed the studio window and gave me grins and thumbs-up signals. David Bramwick stopped by the open doorway and congratulated me on a great first show. My nerves had gradually eased after each link and the four hours went by in a flash. I had done my first full show on a Californian rock station and it felt great.

Compared to the BBC, this was so much more relaxed: no producers or executives to worry about, and the studio door left open most of the time so that the general atmosphere of the radio station would be part of the broadcasts. It was very like the old Radio Caroline days and I loved the informality of it all.

When I wasn't at KSAN broadcasting or preparing for the next show, I got to know San Francisco, and completely fell in love with it. Thanks to Tony Bennett, I'd always thought 'little cable cars that climbed halfway to the stars' were like ski lifts and was surprised to discover they actually ran on the streets, gripping onto moving cables that ran just under the road surface. The San Francisco hills are incredibly steep and the cars slowly climb to the summit where there would often be the most perfect view of the 'city by the bay': the waterfront of Pier 39, the island of Alcatraz, the Golden Gate bridge in the distance and the bay itself, its shimmering blue waters reflecting the Californian sunshine.

I envied those who lived and worked there in this wonderful place. Did they get used to the beauty of it, or did it still take their breath away? At night, nature's air conditioner would cleanse the city's air as the fog gently rolled in from the Pacific. Then high-rise buildings would pierce through the swirling mist, giving the impression that the city was floating on clouds. It was unlike anywhere I had ever been and I wanted to stay forever.

The next three weeks just flew by. I spent a lot of time preparing for each show, picking unusual tracks and assembling sets of songs based on various themes. It was a very creative place to work and I often blessed the memory of the late Tom Donahue, the founding father of KSAN and its free-form format. He really was the man who began the whole FM rock radio movement that swept across America in the late sixties and seventies. On my final breakfast show, newsman Dave McQueen said on air how much he'd enjoyed working with me and that he admired my style, which he thought was unique and a real breath of fresh air.

It was warm and generous praise that came right out of the blue and was tremendously reassuring. I was very much in awe of the KSAN jocks: they had vast musical knowledge and could pick out individual tracks on hundreds of albums. My background was much more Top Forty singles, and I just hoped I had somehow made up for my limited experience of programming albums. I was introduced to so much music I'd never heard before and discovered that my love for American rock was a two-way street. They had enormous respect for English bands and a group like The Who was probably more loved and venerated by Americans than they were back home.

Having finished the breakfast-show stint, I devoted my energies to producing a series of documentary specials on the English/ British music scene. I had brought over some tapes of various interviews with artists and I also had some cassette tapes of documentaries on pirate radio. With a bit of EQ (equalization) I could get good-enough quality for broadcast and decided to do two one-hour shows on the pirates and three one-hour programmes on British music, so delivering a week of specials. I virtually took up residence in a small production studio and spent hours and hours on dubbing, editing and crafting the very best programmes I could make. The specials ran in the early evening and the reaction to them was really good, especially the pirate and Caroline story. The switchboard was flooded with calls from listeners who'd had no idea of the battle for free radio and were fascinated to hear what had gone down in the sixties.

On my last day at the station, programme director Bonnie Simmons called me into her office.

'Well, Johnnie, this is the end of your time with us.'

'Yeah, I know. I've really enjoyed the whole experience.'

'We've kinda got used to having you around and we like what you've done. How do you feel about joining us full time?'

I looked at Bonnie in amazement. My dream had been to get some kind of job at a good American radio station. I'd genuinely thought I would have to start much lower down the scale in some small-town station until I got more experience. Here I was being offered a job on the West Coast's second most important market. Only Los Angeles or a station in New York could beat working for KSAN – and I knew both the station and the city of San Francisco was far preferable to LA or the Big Apple.

Bonnie added, 'I've talked to our legal people and we think there should be no problem in making a good enough case to get you a green card.'

'That's brilliant news and I would love to work here full time. The only problem is, I've got a lot of things to sort out back home and I haven't seen my kids, especially my new daughter, for ages. I need to think things over for an hour or so.'

This was a fantastic offer. I had hoped something would come from my temporary stint there but hadn't thought too hard about it in case nothing happened. Now I had a major decision to make. I had geared myself up to catching a London flight the very next day and was so looking forward to seeing Frances, Sam and little Beth again. I could hardly ring Frances and tell her to pack everything up and get over here. It just wouldn't have been fair. There was so much to do and she had two young children to care for.

I knew that from a career point of view, I should stay. But if we were going to make a new life out here, I had to go back, consult Frances and then we could sort it all out together. Anything else would be selfish and extremely unfair. So I told Bonnie I needed to go back, but that I'd return as soon as I could.

'But I hope you'll keep that job offer open for me.'

Bonnie smiled.

'I can't make any promises, Johnnie. But you'll always be welcome here at KSAN.'

Chapter Twenty-Seven

November 1976

It was wonderful to see Frances and the children again, and in many ways it was brilliant to be back home. But I had itchy feet. If Frances had thought that my time in America would quell the desire to go there permanently, she was wrong. My ambition to get there and start a new life was stronger than ever. Now I had the confidence of my spell at KSAN and the possibility of a proper job, I was sure I could make a go of a life and a career out there. But when I started to make the preliminary moves, it became clear that it was not going to be as simple as I'd imagined.

Then, completely out of the blue, I had a visit from a guy I'd met briefly in San Francisco. I told him about the KSAN job and their offer to help me get a green card. He was immediately quite negative about their chances. According to him, it was getting harder all the time to prove that an individual had skills that were unique and unable to be provided by a resident US citizen.

'Imagine if you and your wife and children are over there and then they decline your green card application. You'll be instantly deported and will find it very hard to enter the US in the future. Your only way to be absolutely sure of success is to do an investment petition. If you can bring $40,000 dollars into the US, start a small company that employs just one US citizen, you'll get a green card guaranteed. I've got a lawyer friend of mine who specializes in this area. I'll put you in touch.'

It would have been so simple to ring Bonnie Simmons at KSAN to ask her if there might have been any doubt about my getting a green card, but I didn't do that. Somehow the whole impetus of what I'd built up in San Francisco had faded away. I'd had a great time out there on my own but back in London Frances had been really struggling with a toddler not yet two, and a new baby just a few weeks old. There seemed to be a mountain of problems and obstacles to be overcome before we could start a new life on the other side of the Atlantic. The idea of an investment petition sounded like a guaranteed green card, so that was the course I decided to follow. It meant selling the house, and there was another problem. There was a Labour government at the time and there were strict laws about the amount of money one could take out of the UK. I was told it was £4,000 – but in order to qualify for the investment petition, I needed to arrive in America with $40,000. The exchange rate was two dollars to the pound, so I had to find £20,000 to take out of the country.

That's okay, I thought. There're four of us, that's sixteen grand I can take out. Just another four to try and find. But no. The allowance was £4,000 for an individual or for a family. How could a family possibly move to a new country to set up a new life with just £4,000? It was crazy. There must be a way round this, I thought. If somebody buys, say, a foreign car like a BMW in the UK, then surely the money had to find its way back to Germany. So what if I purchase an American motorhome through a London dealer but I arrange to pick it up in the States . . . ? Maybe that was the answer. So I hatched a plan and *London Freebird* was born.

Officially I was starting a company that would equip a motor-home with a studio, travel around America recording interviews and live music, and then sell the shows back to UK broadcasters. I would be helping export American culture around the world, which was something I felt sure US immigration would be impressed with. In reality, the built-in studio didn't exist and, once in the USA, I'd sell the motorhome and I'd have my money back. But, most importantly, because I was investing in a business, I would have the vital green card, which would give me and the family the legal right to live, work and earn money in America.

I found a dealer in London who imported American RVs (recreational vehicles) and after a few days of making inquiries, he agreed to take my small motor caravan at a low price and sell me an RV, which I would pick up in America. Now I had to find one. He had names and addresses of manufacturers and dealers and I wrote off for some brochures. I narrowed it down to two choices. One I totally fell in love with. Made by a small company in Indiana, it looked very much like a Silver Streak caravan but with an engine in front. Bullet-shaped, made from shiny aluminium with a split windscreen, it was stylish and beautiful, very thirties and art deco. The other was a regular big fibreglass RV called a King's Highway and was on the lot of a dealer in Nashville. I decided to fly over, take a look at both and clinch the deal.

I rented a car at the airport and drove up to Indiana via the legendary Indianapolis Motor Speedway, home of the Indy 500. What an incredible place it was, steeped in the history and tradition of America's most famous motor race. The aluminium motorhome was even more beautiful in reality – it was stunning. There were two single beds in the back, a living area and kitchen up front with a sofa that converted to a double bed. I asked the guy if he could fit some doors to separate the bedroom at the back so that we could put the kids to sleep at the normal time, close off the doors and Frances and I could have some privacy up front. The answer was no and there was nothing I could do to persuade him otherwise. I said I'd let him know and set off for Nashville.

The King's Highway was bloody enormous, thirty-three feet long, with two air conditioners on the roof, a built-in vacuum cleaner and a fridge-freezer bigger than our one at home. It had the same front-to-back layout but this time my idea of fitting doors was readily accepted.

'No problem, sir. We'd do that for no extra charge.'

I had to decide. My heart wanted the aluminium one but the practical side of me said it had to be the King's Highway. Practicality won and we shook hands and closed the deal. He didn't see any problem about being paid by a dealer in London and said that as soon as the transfer cleared I could come in and drive it away.

The RV cost $33,000 and the imaginary built-in studio $10,000. I was over the $40,000 needed for an investment petition and

Hank, one of the engineers I'd befriended at KSAN, had agreed to be listed as my US employee. With all the necessary criteria covered, I got back in touch with Joel Turtle, the LA lawyer who'd been recommended to me.

'It could take forever if we apply through the US Embassy in London,' said Joel. 'Come over on a visitor's visa and we'll make the application here. It will be much quicker and simpler this way.'

The cost would be $6,000: $4,000 for me and Frances, $2,000 for the kids. I arranged to pay him $3,000 up front to start the ball rolling. Now the only problem was to find the money to pay for the RV. The London dealer wouldn't make anything on the American one; his profit would come from the resale of my caravan, so I had to let it go very cheaply. Now we had to put our house on the market. For Frances, this whole plan was getting crazier by the minute and the last straw was selling our much-loved home, the only stability and security we had left. We talked long into many a night going over our options, which weren't many.

I could stay in the UK and, with a huge loss of face, try and get a job with Capital Radio, so we could hang on to what we had. But I had enough experience to know how tough it can be to get a job when you're out of work, and my heart was set on America and making a success out of a new life there. I've always been a hopeless romantic when it comes down to travel and freedom. The only job I ever wanted as a kid was to drive a lorry. The open road, seeing new places, meeting new people, embracing the unknown – these are the things that get my blood flowing.

Frances had her dreams and adventurous spirit too, but these were tempered by her practical side and the fact that she was the mother of two young children. She had worked so hard to create a happy and comfortable home and was now being asked to chuck it all up for something that could so easily go wrong. We had some terrible rows but I was determined to follow my dream.

Christmas came and went and with each passing week, the contact with KSAN was fading. Would they still have a job for me when I got there? If not, could I get another one somewhere else? I told Frances that we could travel west from Nashville, calling at stations along the way and applying for work. If nothing came of that, I felt sure KSAN would give me something, especially if I had the green card by then. She was gradually warming to the whole idea and I used all my old skills as a salesman to sell her the concept of success in America and a good lifestyle for us all.

The UK was having its fair share of problems. The economy was struggling and the government seemed to be in hock to the all-powerful unions. The music business was also in the doldrums. A handful of major record companies had a virtual monopoly over the UK scene. Formulaic, production-line, cheesy pop records from faceless session men were dominating the charts. When they had a hit, they would hastily manufacture a group to go on *Top of the Pops*. Record companies were reluctant to sign anything new and different, moaning that it cost so much money to launch a new band, they couldn't afford to take risks. Either they didn't sign any new groups at all, or if they did, it was a band that sounded exactly the same as ones currently enjoying success.

There was a glimmer of hope, though. Just before Christmas, quite by chance, I was watching the ITV magazine show hosted by Bill Grundy. On came the Sex Pistols, a bunch of scruffy, anarchic wasters with no musical talent. So thought Mr Grundy, who seemed to have convinced himself that by giving them enough rope, they would show themselves for the no-hopers they really were and hang themselves in the process. Instead, what we got was the most wonderful slice of anarchic television I had ever seen. I was jumping up and down, loving it all. I shouted for Frances.

'Come and look at this – you won't believe what's going on here. It's fantastic!'

'*We've got a few seconds left,*' said Bill. '*Go on, show us how clever you are, say something outrageous.*'

So they did. There had never been such extraordinary behaviour and so many four-letter words going out on safe ITV at teatime. Viewers were appalled and hundreds rang in to complain. The following day's newspapers whipped up the anti-punk frenzy. It was all wonderful publicity for the Sex Pistols. Manager Malcolm McLaren was beside himself with delight and it was Bill Grundy, rather than the Pistols, taking all the flak not only for allowing it to happen, but for positively egging them on. Instead of the Pistols hanging themselves, it was Bill Grundy's neck in the noose, and that was the end of his TV career.

Was this punk thing the beginning of something really good for the music scene? Could the Sex Pistols really play? Were they any good live? No one really knew but 'Anarchy In The UK' soared to Number One and, sure enough, was banned by the BBC. The *New Musical Express* carried a full double-page feature on a guy called Jake Riviera, who had just launched Stiff Records. He was boasting about how he could make great records for £30 a time and the article had pictures of the labels of his first releases by Nick Lowe and Elvis Costello. He reckoned he'd sell his records to the stores out of the boot of his car. I was fascinated and called the *NME* to get a phone number for Stiff Records.

Jake answered the phone, 'Yeah, what d'ya want?'

'It's Johnnie Walker here, Jake. I've just read the article in the *NME*, I'd love to hear those new singles. Any chance you could post them to me?'

'No, I can't, we don't do free copies. You could come over and buy 'em if you want.'

This was a new and novel way of promoting records.

'OK, I'll be right over.'

I thought Jake's style was a breath of fresh air. Producers and DJs at Radio One had got so spoilt by record companies falling over themselves to hand out all the new releases you wanted. I bought copies of Nick Lowe's 'And So It Goes' and Elvis Costello's 'Less Than Zero'. Jake was right. You didn't need massive advances and huge production budgets to make good records. These had cost only £30 to make and were recorded in a couple of hours. They were raw and exciting with a great energy to them. I headed home, proud and excited at getting hold of these fantastic records, much more satisfying than getting half a dozen copies of something pretty lame from the majors.

Then I went to see The Jam in a small club in Shepherd's Bush. They were absolutely mesmerizing. They, too, were loud and raw with an amazing energy. The crowd went nuts – it was one of the best gigs I'd been to in years. The Jam were stunning, much like The Who had been back in the early sixties. There certainly was something new and exciting going on. The A&R guys and the staff at major labels, ensconced in their fancy offices with their glass-topped, chromium-plated coffee tables, hadn't a clue what was happening on the street. It seemed ironic that just as it looked as if the UK scene was coming to life, I was planning to leave.

But more musical freedom was what the big move was all about and I knew if I was still at Radio One, there was no way I'd be allowed to play any punk-rock. Playing music on any radio station was still only a theory, however. I had no firm job offer in the States – I was going to take a huge chance going over there with nothing solid set up. But that wasn't going to stop me now.

Meanwhile, we had a huge amount of things to sort out: a house sale to arrange, the furniture and all our belongings to store somewhere, a garage full of disco equipment and a Ford Transit van to dispose of. The disco and sound equipment was soon snapped up and I placed an ad in *Melody Maker* for the Transit. It was more truck than van with its big Luton body and nifty electric tail lift, which made loading and unloading so much easier.

A young musician named Tom Robinson came round for a look. We did a test drive and then I invited him for a cup of tea. It seemed only polite to offer him a joint to celebrate the sale and I rolled up some Thai grass into a neat, one-paper spliff, California-style. After much giggling, more cups of tea and various munchies of Mars and Kit Kats, Tom set off in his newly acquired vehicle, grinning from ear to ear. Could the reliable miles up and down the M1 in my trusty blue Tranny have been the inspiration for his massive hit '2-4-6-8-Motorway'? I like to think so.

A German couple fell in love with our house and insisted we sell it with all the furniture, fixtures and fittings – a terrible wrench for Frances, who had laboured so long and hard to find the perfect pieces for our house. But we had to look forward, not back.

There was an adventure to embark on and *London Freebird* was about to conquer America.

Chapter Twenty-Eight

1977

Roger Cook and I were kindred spirits. With songwriting partner Roger Greenaway, he'd left Bristol in the early sixties to seek fame and fortune in London. It wasn't long before one of their songs was in the charts, 'You've Got Your Troubles' recorded by The Fortunes. Success followed success, including a spell in the group Blue Mink with singer Madeline Bell. As songwriters, the two Rogers racked up hit after hit but, as the seventies wore on, Cooky was becoming more and more disillusioned with the British pop scene. It was almost too easy to turn out yet another, innocuous, catchy pop song that was virtually guaranteed a chart placing. Where was the challenge any more?

So in the mid seventies, the Cook family relocated to Nashville, Tennessee. Roger opened an office in a house on a tree-lined street known as Music Row and bought a farmhouse a few miles out of town.

It was there that a tired and weary Walker family arrived in May 1977. Roger and his wife Joan had been kind enough to offer us accommodation while the money transfer from London to the Nashville RV dealer was going through. We were all pretty knackered, having had to change at Boston, go through immigration on our three-month visitors' visas, collect all our bags and head to a different part of the airport for the internal flight to Nashville. But once we were there, we all felt better and after a day or two had recovered from our journey. Sam and Beth played with the two Cook children, Frances and Joan got along fine and Roger was glad of the male company. We'd go off and play pool together and, at night, spend time indulging in what Roger called 'grinning competitions', sampling his primo grade grass.

Roger had struck gold in Nashville with a Number One hit he'd written for Don Williams and was respected and appreciated in what was essentially a songwriters' town. His day would start with the school run, followed by nine holes of golf with his pal Charles Cochran, one of Nashville's in-demand session musicians and songwriters. They'd call by the office on Music Row to check in, then it was usually lunch at Brown's Diner – a funky greasy spoon bar and café housed in an old railway car. After a few beers, bar chit-chat with the likes of John Prine and Don Everly, Roger would feed his favourite blackjack gambling machine. From there, it was back to the office for a couple more beers, a spliff or two, some backgammon and then Roger would pick up a guitar or mandolin and, with a bit of luck, a new song would be born.

He always said songwriting for him was the most natural thing he could do. It seemed like a pretty idyllic kind of life to me. I'd either hang out with him or stay back at the farmhouse, doing my best to help around the place to earn my keep. Sam loved to sit on the ride-on mower with me and there was also a swimming pool to help the idle afternoons pass by. Soon, the days turned into a week and then two weeks. Every day I'd check in with the RV dealer for progress with the bank transfer, which was infuriatingly slow.

'Roger had to wait months for his house money to clear through the Bank of England,' said Joan, somewhat ominously one afternoon.

'They promised me it wouldn't take more than a couple of weeks,' I replied anxiously.

We were very aware of our intrusion into their family home and were desperate not to overstay our welcome. But until the money arrived, we were stuck. Towards the end of the third week, the RV dealer called. The necessary funds were now in his account and we could pick up our new RV at our convenience. The King's Highway motorhome was ours and now *London Freebird* could take to the highway and our adventure could begin in earnest. I spent the afternoon with the dealer getting a complete tour of this amazing machine. It was full of every kind of gadget and there was a lot to learn.

The dealer explained, 'Drivin' this is as easy as drivin' a car. Jess remember that when ya turn a corner, you've got thirty-three feet of vee-hear-cle behind ya'll.'

With the power steering and automatic gearbox, the RV *was* much easier to drive than I'd anticipated and I gingerly steered the huge machine out of his lot and headed for Roger's place. I'm a truck driver at last! I thought, as *London Freebird* cruised majestically up the highway. Better not crash the bugger, everything we own is on these wheels.

Sam, being as much a gadget freak as his old man, loved it. Beth and Frances were not so sure. I could see Frany thinking: We gave up our beautiful little house in Ealing for this fibreglass monstrosity. God knows what the future holds for us. But, after packing all our stuff on board and Frances doing her magic, the place was soon looking like home and we planned to set off early the next morning. With big hugs all round and our profuse thanks for the generous hospitality, we waved our farewells to the Cooks and set off down the drive.

We weren't going to go far. I'd decided it would be sensible to stay around the Nashville area for a while, spend a night or two on local campsites to give *London Freebird* a good shakedown test. Better to discover any teething problems or faults before we hit the road proper. We found a state park campsite overlooking a lake, booked our pitch and I reversed carefully into our space. I hooked up running water, mains electricity and the sewage pipe. Outside, I extended the built-in awning, put up some folding chairs and a picnic rug and we settled down to enjoy the view of the lake and the impending sunset. This was going to be okay.

'Hi there,' said a cheery American voice. 'Would you like to join us for a drink? It's after six o'clock, you know. Come and join my wife and me at our trailer.'

He was a tall, striking-looking man in his sixties with grey hair, suntan and a friendly smile. We were still not used to the American openness and the way strangers treated each other like old friends. Accepting their invitation, we all went up to his RV, similar to mine but with various iceboxes and fishing tackle dotted around his pitch.

'What's it to be?' he asked. 'We're on sour mash and ginger ale.'

Not really knowing what the hell sour mash was, or wishing to show our ignorance, we said that would be fine, thanks. He poured out two enormous tumblers and fixed some soft drinks for Sam and Beth.

'Cheers. This is Tennessee's finest, you know.'

We clinked our plastic tumblers and enjoyed our first tall glass of Jack Daniels and ginger ale. Our new friend was a business adviser to the country music stars and took every opportunity to spend time by the lake and do a little fishing. He and his wife were fascinated by our plans to journey across America with such a young family. We spent a very pleasant evening with our neighbours.

The next day, as we packed up, the radio announced the death of Elvis Presley. I had worshipped Elvis in my teens and was shocked and saddened by the news; it was hard to believe that the King was no more. The news announcer spoke of the hundreds of fans beginning to gather outside Graceland and I immediately considered making the journey. By American standards, Nashville to Memphis is a short drive and I felt incredibly drawn to go down there. But on reflection, I decided not to – it seemed a somewhat ghoulish trip to make. That's a decision I've often regretted. It was a huge milestone in the history of music and the scenes and experience would have left a lasting imprint on our memories.

I wanted to press on. It was an ambition of mine to visit Macon, Georgia, the birthplace of Otis Redding. Where Elvis was raw excitement and the epitome of the handsome rock 'n' roll legend, Otis touched me deeper within. I felt I had learnt much about love and emotions from his records, and his voice had warmth and real humanity. I'd seen him in concert, watching both from the stalls and in the wings on the Atlantic Stax Tour in 1967, but had never met him. From Macon, the plan was to go via Atlanta, continue south into Louisiana to see New Orleans and then head west across Texas, north into New Mexico and then west again through Nevada and on into California.

In Atlanta I stopped by the offices of Kent Burkhart and Lee Abrams. Together they had set up a hugely successful consultancy business, advising radio stations on everything – from which DJs to hire to which jingle packages to buy, and, most controversially, the music for the playlist. There was no doubt that stations who paid for their advice were rewarded with higher ratings, but critics accused the company of dumbing down radio and creating stations that all sounded the same. I'd written to Lee, sent him some tapes and my CV, and mentioned that I would call by if we came through Atlanta.

Even though I turned up out of the blue, he was very welcoming. We got on well and he left me to go and talk with Kent and make some calls. He came back into the office with some good news.

'Johnnie, there's a job waiting for you in Seattle at a really good rock station. How soon can you get there?'

Wow, I hadn't expected this. This was all too soon into our trip. What should I do? I knew nothing about Seattle.

'It's a good city,' said Lee. 'Like San Francisco but instead of the fog, it rains quite a bit.'

'Let me go and talk to my wife about this.'

I tried to analyse what I really thought about this job offer. I'd said I'd try and get work along the way and here I was, successful so soon with a firm job offer on the table. But I knew nothing about either the city or the radio station. I went back to the RV in the car park and gave Frances the news.

She said, 'It's entirely up to you. It has to be your decision.'

If I'm honest, I was perhaps just a little bit frightened about going to a strange city and to a station where I was unknown. The other consideration was their strict playlist policy. Although I would certainly be playing a lot more of the music that I couldn't play at Radio One, it was nothing like the freedom of KSAN.

Besides which, I didn't want our trip to end so soon and I really wanted Frances to see the beauty of San Francisco. I went back to Lee's office and thanked him, but declined the offer.

As the days of our trip went by in a routine of freeways, truck stops and camping sites, the romantic idealism of the journey was wearing a bit thin. Our camping choices were either state parks, which were very beautiful and lovely to stay in, or, if we wanted to visit a city, an urban campsite in a not particularly nice part of town. You can hardly park a 33-feet-long motorhome downtown, and so we found ourselves confined to the RV every night, as we obviously couldn't leave Sam and Beth on their own. Being in an exciting town like New Orleans yet unable to enjoy all it had to offer was incredibly frustrating. And big as *London Freebird* was, being stuck up front in the living area at night led to a general feeling of dissatisfaction. We couldn't even have a decent argument for fear of waking up the kids. I was starting to wish I'd taken up the job offer. We could have sold the RV, rented ourselves a house and years later I'd have been sipping coffee with Frasier in that Seattle café he hangs out in.

But the upside was meeting new and fascinating people, and seeing amazing places. The journey continued across Texas, which seemed to take forever. The people we met along the way were incredibly friendly although they couldn't understand why we wanted to go to California: 'They're all mad out there. If you want a good life you should settle here in Texas.' These were words of advice we heard over and over again, but we weren't ready to settle yet.

Our journey took in an Indian Reservation; I was shocked at the poverty and degradation, and the dreadful state of the land they'd been given to live on. At one point in the history of white settlement, they'd been told all land to the west of the Mississippi was theirs, but that only lasted until gold was discovered in California. Although we tried to journey on the smaller back roads, most of the miles were on the freeway system and with McDonald's, Best Western, Kentucky Fried Chicken and Burger

King at every stop, one place looked much the same as any other. As we got nearer to San Francisco, I was starting to get more and more worried. The American dream has to come true in California because there is no further west to go. It was now nine months since I'd done the breakfast show and documentaries at KSAN. What sort of welcome would I get there? And what were the chances of being able to get on-air work?

With brilliant timing, the price of oil doubled as a result of Middle East crises and the bottom dropped out of the market for gas-guzzling motorhomes like mine. There wasn't much we could do about it except hope things would improve. Once we reached San Francisco, I parked on the outskirts of the city and called my friend Hank, one of the engineers at KSAN. Had he any advice, I wondered, as to where was the best place to park up when we got to SF? He suggested an ideal spot would be right outside his apartment.

'You'll have Golden Gate Park on one side, my place on the other and you can even run a power cable into the house. And you'd have a phone number for contact. You'd be breaking city ordnance of course, but I don't think anyone is going to give you any hassle.'

That was a really kind offer and, as luck would have it, there was space right outside his house big enough for our 'vee-hear-cle'. It was a bizarre living arrangement but I have to say that we had some of our best times there. The house could have come straight out of Sesame Street with wide wooden steps down to street level, where we'd sit and hang out and pass the days. We were just a five-minute walk away from Haight and Ashbury Streets, birthplace of the hippy movement back in 1967, the area that prompted songs like Scott McKenzie's 'San Francisco' and The Flower Pot Men's 'Let's Go To San Francisco'. Although those days had long gone, it was still a vibey area full of eccentric characters and weirdos.

After a hassle-free week outside Hank's apartment, there was a knock on the door. I opened it to be faced with a cop. Uh oh, this looks like trouble, I thought.

'I guess you know you're breaking city law, but I'm not here to hassle you. I just wanted to take a look at this amazing rig.' He looked around, then gave us a warning. You're right alongside the Pan Handle area of Golden Gate Park and there are some pretty strange characters that you get around here. My advice to you would be to keep your door locked at all times.'

We thanked him for his concern and continued with our open-door policy. Sam used to love sitting on the step chatting away to the various characters that passed by. When I'd taken him for walks back home in Ealing, he'd say hello to crusty old military types, who would completely ignore him. He always looked so hurt when that happened. Now just about everyone would stop and say: 'Hi, little fella. How are you doing? What's your name, young man?' Beth had learnt to walk in the corridor at the back of the truck using the single beds for support, and she also loved life on the park.

I wasted no time in going to see Bonnie Simmons at KSAN and, although I sensed I didn't have the same status as before, she did promise me I could do fill-in and weekend work, but she wouldn't be able to pay me until I had my green card. I hoped that wouldn't be long as my lawyer told me the application was going well, and soon I'd be called into the embassy for an interview. Just a formality, he told me.

'After that, they'll issue you a green card. And can you send $2,000 on account?'

I fervently hoped my card would come soon, as our visitors' visas had expired two months previously. We'd been in the States for five months, making our way across its vast terrain, and now we were all illegal aliens. Lucky that the cop who'd paid us a visit was a friendly one.

There was one major drawback to living on the side of the street. After about a week, the septic tank would be full and I'd have to drive down to a site south of the city to drain it. Whether or not our space outside Hank's was still there when I got back was a lottery. Often it wasn't, which meant parking on the opposite side of the road next to the park. I had to get the nearside wheels up on to the kerb on a one-way street with four lanes of traffic. Worse still, the door opened the wrong way so you could see what had gone past but not what was coming. We had to develop the real skill of waiting for the traffic light one block to the east to turn red, then gingerly open the door, get the all clear and make a dash across the street to the safety of the sidewalk (we were starting to get Americanized by this time). Sometimes we'd be two or three days in this situation and the moment 'our' space became free, I'd take off round the block to nab it again.

This was no way to live and raise two small kids, and it certainly wasn't the dream lifestyle I'd promised Frances. She'd coped magnificently so far, entering into the spirit of our adventure and finding as much excitement in this strange new country as I did. But the motorhome was supposed to be a temporary arrangement, not a permanent one, and Frany was getting understandably more anxious about our immigration status and the fact that I couldn't earn any money. The cramped conditions we were surviving in weren't helping. We had to get a house or apartment but, as we were just about broke by this time, we couldn't afford deposits and up-front rent. The money was all tied up in the motorhome and we couldn't sell that because we were living in it. A classic catch-22 situation.

One evening, during rush hour, a guy knocked on the door.

'Hi,' he said. 'I've been passing this RV every night on the way home. Can I have a look round?'

He said he wanted to buy it as a Christmas present for his wife and he offered me $20,000 cash.

Twenty grand! With extras, I'd paid going on thirty-five thousand for it just five months previously. Surely I could get a better price than that.

I said no and he didn't up the ante, so that was that.

I reckoned the answer was to get a loan using the RV as collateral. I tried every bank I could find and the answer was always the same: a guy with no fixed address and collateral that was mobile? No way. Then, by luck, I read a feature in the entertainment section of the *San Francisco Chronicle* on the early struggles of

Fantasy Records & Films over in Berkeley. They had Credence Clearwater Revival on their roster, were desperate for finance to film *One Flew Over the Cuckoo's Nest* and were having about as much luck with the banks as I was. Then they bumped into a cool black dude, who was a bank branch manager. He took a chance when no one else would and advanced a loan. He became known as the rock 'n' roll banker. Now there was a guy who might just give us a break.

The article named the bank where he worked, so I called him from Hank's and set up an appointment for the next day. Taking all the paperwork with me, I told him our whole story. He gave us our break.

'I'll keep the title to your RV and loan you $12,000 for six months.'

God bless that man. We shook hands on the deal and, in no time at all, we found a little place to live in Berkeley. Okay, so we were across the Bay Bridge in the suburbs – but we would never have found a house we could afford in the city and here the kids had a garden to play in. We now had our family home just in time for our first Christmas in California. Now I just had to spruce up the RV and get our money back.

How come, with my five years' experience in the motor trade, two of which were as a salesman, I do such lousy deals buying and selling motors? Winter was no time to get a good price for a motorhome and *London Freebird* eventually went to a dealer for $16,000. With hindsight, when that guy came round with his cash offer, I should've bitten his hand off. Instead of losing fifteen grand, I'd lost nearly twenty, over half our precious house money. We would all have been much better off if I'd let Frances do the deals, she's so much better at handling money than I am. But at least I could walk into the bank with my head held high. The bank manager's confidence in me wasn't misplaced and I could pay off the loan.

Now if only the green card would come through, I could start earning money and maybe the tough times would be over.

Chapter Twenty-Nine

Despite letters and repeated assurances from immigration lawyer Joel Turtle that everything was going ahead, it had become obvious that he was bullshitting. He had his dollars and I had been taken for a ride. I was never going to get a green card. So I wangled something that was the next best thing. I went into San Francisco's immigration office and, declaring myself a British businessman making frequent trips to the US, told them I wanted to open a bank account to deposit some funds to cover expenses. To open a bank account I needed a social security number.

'I'm sorry, sir,' said the clerk, 'I cannot issue you with a number unless you have valid immigration documentation. Do you have a green card?'

'Not at the moment, my application's still being considered.'

'When you have your green card, sir, come back and we'll issue you a social security number.'

So that didn't work – another catch-22. A friend suggested trying in Berkeley because 'they're more laid back there'. I walked into the immigration office to be greeted by a warm smile from a friendly and helpful assistant. I was halfway through my spiel about needing a bank account when she interrupted me.

'Ah, you'll need a social security number, sir. Please fill in this form with your name and address and we'll post one to you. It should only take a couple of days.'

Three, actually, and I now had a card that enabled me to work and be paid, so I could do something to earn money even if I still wasn't able to work at KSAN. I took a driving test and then I had a driver's licence. Now I had the all-important photo ID and a social security card, I was as legit as it was possible to be in my situation. My only problem would be leaving and re-entering the States, and I had no plans to do that anytime soon. To keep our

family going, I started working as a cashier in a gas station at night
– earning money was becoming something of a priority. But during
the day, I was at KSAN, doing whatever work I could for the
love of it, and becoming a part of the family there.

Richard Gossett was the tall, laconic DJ who did the six p.m.
to ten p.m. shift on KSAN. It was said Clint Eastwood took a lot
from Richard when developing his character for the film *Play
Misty for Me*. Richard played the coolest collection of American
and British FM music, which he presented in a wonderful, laid-
back style. I used to hang out at the station whenever I could and
I loved to stay around while Richard was on the air, watching him
while he drank beer and smoked spliffs throughout his show.
Visitors popped by with coke much as people take a bottle of wine
to a party, and Richard would gradually get more and more wasted
as the evening wore on, which was fine really, as most of his
audience were doing exactly the same. This was a far cry from
Radio One, and I loved it all.

Some jocks at KSAN – Richard Gossett, Beverly Wilshire, Sean
Donahue and librarian/DJ Vincenta Licata – loved punk-rock and
championed the new music. KSAN broadcast lots of concerts and
selected some of the best live tracks for dubbing on to tape cartridges, which were racked up in the studio for playing at the
jock's discretion. They loved the English 'don't give a fuck, let's
have a laugh' attitude, and the casual use of words like 'wanker'.
It was a real breath of fresh air. The jocks knew what 'wanker' was
all about, but most of the audience and management didn't, which
added to the fun. Same for the Sex Pistols' *Never Mind the Bollocks*
album; the title and the music on it were no problem for KSAN.

Most of those at the station embraced punk-rock, sure in the
knowledge that freedom and anarchy and stirring things up were
part of what KSAN was all about. But there was a problem. Lots
of the listeners hated it and so did station manager Jerry Graham.
The Metromedia Corporation, owners of KSAN and other
stations like KMET in LA, had sent him from New York to take
over after Tom Donahue, the station's founder, had died from too
much partying, booze and cocaine. Jerry was a bookish, intellectual

guy who liked his life in the Berkeley Hills, hosting dinner parties with Joni Mitchell and Fleetwood Mac playing softly in the background. One couldn't really blame him for being worried about ratings as he struggled with the balance of maintaining freedom for his on-air staff while fending off negative listener reaction.

And then the Sex Pistols came to town. They had been working their way across America, playing all kinds of sleazy clubs and bars, creating mayhem wherever they went and polarizing opinion. New York, the true birthplace of punk, loved them but in middle America, they were anathema to music fans. In Texas the Pistols had to dodge a hail of beer bottles from angry rednecks. Promoter Bill Graham completely underestimated the degree of interest and booked them into a small venue called California Hall. Demand for tickets was so great that he twice had to change the venue, and the show ended up scheduled for 14th January 1978 at the famous Winterland Auditorium, where all the great bands have played.

Good old KSAN decided to broadcast the concert live and the Pistols came into Bonnie Simmons' morning show for an interview. She handled them very well. They weren't as outrageous as on the Bill Grundy show but there was a spattering of 'fuck' and 'wanker'. I went to the Winterland gig that evening. The place was packed and heaving for the show. The excited atmosphere was almost on a par with the Beatles' gig in Birmingham all those years ago. Anticipation was building throughout the evening and by the time they came onstage we knew we were in for something special. Yes, they could play: Steve Jones knew his way round a guitar, Paul Cook kept it all hammering away on drums at the back and Johnny Rotten prowled and scowled his way round the stage, constantly hurling insults at the audience. Sid Vicious stood full on and faced the huge crowd – come and get me if you dare. With blood and painted tattoos and swastikas smeared all over his bare chest, his bass slung low, he was so out of it, I expected him to fall off the stage any moment.

It was complete mayhem but I loved all of it. The crowd and the band became one heaving mass of glorious rock 'n' roll rebellion. There were lots of boos, jeers and catcalls, and coins were constantly being hurled on to the stage.

Johnny said, 'Thank you very much, we love money, chuck some more,' and collected up coins between songs.

They blasted out 'God Save The Queen', 'Holidays In The Sun' and ended with a blistering version of 'Anarchy In The UK'. I'll never forget Johnny Rotten's final words: 'Na, na, na, ner, ner — ever get the feeling you've been cheated?' The others left the stage but Johnny prowled around picking up more money.

Like the Beatles at Candlestick Park Baseball Stadium before them, the Sex Pistols had played their last ever gig in the city of San Francisco. Was Johnny's final comment about that night's show or the whole Sex Pistols phenomenon? Probably the latter, as he was intelligent enough to know how Malcolm McLaren had manipulated the whole thing from start to finish: the great rock 'n' roll swindle, indeed. It wasn't really pure anarchic punk, it was show business. It had been a fun ride but it was all over.

McLaren and Rotten weren't speaking to each other; Malcolm hadn't even bothered to arrange a hotel room for Johnny and he left town right after the show. Sid went up to Haight Ashbury to hang out with the heroin crowd and get blitzed. I went backstage as part of the KSAN crew and met Paul and Steve; they knew who I was from my Radio One and pirate days, and a bunch of us went out and got drunk at some club or other. Paul and Steve had to go to San José for a radio interview the next day and they asked me if I'd give them a tour of San Francisco and then drive them down there. Of course I would.

The next day I picked the boys up and we did all the usual sights and then headed south for San José. I liked them a lot and enjoyed their company tremendously. I hadn't realized how much I'd been missing English humour. We got to the station at about eight o'clock and were shown into the studio. Kate Ingrams was a young slip of a girl in her early twenties; tonight was her first-ever radio show and her guests were two of the Sex Pistols. Talk about a baptism of fire. She played a track and opened with a few questions about the concert and the US tour and then invited her listeners to call and chat with Steve and Paul.

FIRST CALLER 'You guys suck, you're total rubbish and you can't play.'
STEVE 'Why don't you just fuck right off, you fucking wanker?'
PAUL 'Yeah, just fuck off, will ya?'

Kate was visibly trembling but she had to keep going and as more calls came in, her confidence increased. For an experienced broadcaster she was doing well; for a person doing their first live radio, she was totally brilliant.

FEMALE CALLER 'Hey, am I really talking to a Sex Pistol? I think you guys are really cool.'
STEVE 'Well, thank you.'
PAUL 'Have you got big tits?'
FEMALE CALLER Giggles of embarrassment.
PAUL 'I bet you have got big tits, we only wanna talk to girls with big tits. Get 'em out, we wanna see 'em.'
FEMALE CALLER 'You guys are just too much.'
STEVE 'Can we come round later and play with your tits?'
FEMALE CALLER 'Yeah, sure thing, come on over.'

And so it went on. Even male callers offering praise were insulted: 'You Americans, you're all a bunch of tossers, you're all half asleep, you wanna bleeding well wake up.' With the female callers, it was all about the size of their tits.

There are seven words that the FCC (Federal Communications Commission) say cannot and must not be broadcast. Between them, Steve and Paul said most, if not all, of them. But what did they care? They were the Sex Pistols, after all. They weren't going to change for anyone. When the band imploded a few months later, it was no surprise to me. It was all too intense to last: once the Sex Pistols had outraged the world, they ended as quickly as they had started, leaving their infamy behind.

Things quietened down and got back to normal after the Pistols left. Then programme director and DJ Bonnie Simmons decided to take up an offer to work in the promotion department of Warner Brothers Records in LA. Jerry Graham put an ad in *Billboard* magazine, the music and radio industry bible, advertising the job of programme director at KSAN. The best and finest radio people from all over the States must have replied to that ad. KSAN was known and respected all over, and to be programme director there was a high spot in anyone's career.

So Jerry hired his secretary, Abby, who, in terms of radio experience and musical knowledge, had to have been the least qualified person for the job. Obviously Jerry wanted a yes person in charge. Now he could get that damned punk-rock off the air. Abby called a meeting to inform us that a playlist was going to be brought in and that we were going to 'play the music our listeners want to hear'.

Richard Gossett protested, 'But, Abby, they don't really know what they want to hear. It's our job to tell 'em, to play the best new music we can find. We play the records they're going to want to buy and hear tomorrow.'

There were other muted murmurs of discontent around the room. I was surprised by how meek they all were. Even Radio One meetings were a lot more spirited than this. But we were in America. Employers are ruthless: step out of line and you're fired. There're always plenty of others who would just love your job.

A couple of days later, Beverly Wilshire, now presenting the morning show, put on a track by Chuck Berry. Thirty seconds later, Abby marched into the studio.

'This isn't on the playlist, who the hell is this?'

Beverly gave her a withering look.

'It's Chuck Berry.'

'Who the hell is Chuck Berry?'

'Abby, why don't you just fuck off out of my studio?'

The story went round the station like wildfire.

At the next weekly meeting with Jerry Graham in attendance, I decided to speak out. Even though I wasn't on the payroll, I was very much a fixture at the station and a part of the KSAN family.

My experience and my connections with the English music scene – which was all the rage – made me a valuable addition to the station, even if I wasn't exactly staff. I thought that was enough to qualify me to express an opinion.

'It's such a shame that a great station like this, which has pioneered FM rock radio and been brave enough to try new things, play new artists and groups, should now just give all that up and bring in a bloody playlist.' Richard and the others were shooting me warning glances, but my blood was up and I wasn't going to shut up. 'And to cap it all, after having the choice of any one of America's finest programme directors, you've hired someone who has never heard of Chuck Berry.'

There were sharp intakes of breath around the room. I had challenged the station manager in front of his staff – not exactly the fastest route to job security. Jerry fixed me in his gaze. He didn't raise his voice, he was all very calm but his voice was cold.

'Johnnie, I think I've had about enough of you. We don't need you round here. In fact, I wanted to get rid of you when you ran that interview from one of the Pistols but I thought I'd give you another chance. But I *am* getting rid of you now. Collect your stuff and go.'

The Pistol reference was to Steve Jones, who had said in an interview: 'KSAN – sounds like a lavatory cleaner.'

Well, in fairness to Steve, when you're used to names like Radio One or Capital, KSAN does sound like a lavatory cleaner. But, together with my challenging comments, it was enough. I was out.

The meeting was over. People came over to offer their sympathy and support. A bunch of us went out to the nearest bar so I could drown my sorrows. It was mid evening by the time we returned to the radio station. I still wasn't quite ready to face Frances and tell her the bad news. I was just so bloody angry with the whole sorry situation. The Californian dream was over, dead and buried. What the fuck *was* I going to do now? How was I going to earn a living and support my family? The idea of going back to England a failure was too awful to contemplate.

I had to vent my rage and frustration on something. I went

round the station corridors, bashing all the posters and paintings on the wall and, in an act of mindless vandalism, grabbed a bottle of Coke and poured it into their main switchboard. Not my regular sort of behaviour, and not something I'm proud of, but I was in the depths of despair. I had given up a top daytime show on Radio One, sold the house we'd worked so hard for, lost half of all we had, hoping to find a place where a DJ's knowledge and enthusiasm were valued. I had found it, and it was wonderful, but what I didn't know was that I had caught the last wave. KSAN's great era of freedom was over. When it came to major markets, it was all over for that style of radio. It would be consultants, testing and research that would decide the music that people in cities would hear on the radio.

The same few, tried-and-tested artists and tracks would be played on high rotation over and over again.

Chapter Thirty

1978

Robert Hanrahan was gazing through the window of the Mexican restaurant on Valencia Street in the heart of San Francisco's Mission District. We were having our usual lunch of burrito, his with beef or chicken, mine with rice and refried beans with a generous helping of sour cream and avocado. It was our main meal of the day and cost us only $1.60 each – an important consideration when you're unemployed.

After being banished from KSAN, I moved our little family back to the city. Things were too quiet and remote in Berkeley and we were twenty minutes' drive from downtown. Now I had to live on my wits and get work where I could, I needed to be back in the city where there was much more going on. We found an apartment on Guerrero Street, just one block from the busy, bustling main thoroughfare of Mission Street. Apart from cockroaches in the kitchen, it was a good-enough place and suited us well.

This was the Mexican part of town, the wrong side of Market Street, which was a real dividing line and frontier in San Francisco. The advice was to always lock your car doors when you crossed over Market Street and not to drive on your own. But like that cop's warning about the pan handle, the advice was ill-judged and born out of fear and ignorance. As long as you treated the Mexicans with respect, they would treat you the same way, although Robert and I got jeers and catcalls of 'Hey punk rocker, hey Johnny Rotten' when we walked down the street in our uniform of engineer boots, black trousers and shirts.

The whole area was vibrant with colour, noise and atmosphere, especially on a Saturday night. The Mexicans would take over

Mission Street and cruise their open-top cars low and slow up and down it with sound systems playing. Girls, dressed in their finest, would strut along the sidewalk, hoping to catch the eye of the guys with the coolest car. The Mission district was also home to the punk community; rents were low, and, like the Mexicans, the punks weren't really accepted by mainstream society so the two sides had a natural affinity. Now it was our home too.

Frances had been horrified when I'd told her what had happened at KSAN. Once again, a dream had been shattered and everything was turning out to be very different from what I had promised her. The only upside was that we would be moving back to the city: Frances had missed the vibrancy of being in the centre of things and we had both found the suburbs a bit stifling. But even though we were now central, the precarious nature of our existence still put us both, and our relationship, under a lot of strain.

Living in the Mission was great. A short drive away was the little hippy enclave of Noe Valley, home to lots of young families. Sam and Beth went to a pre-school daycare centre there, where the parents all took turns to help out so as to keep the costs really low. It was a kind of cooperative and worked very well. There were quite a few Brits in the Mission and Frances and I had a wide circle of friends, both English and American.

Robert Hanrahan was one of my American friends. He managed bands, ran Walking Dead Records and taught film at San Francisco State University. He and I were always making plans about how we were going to make money together. He was still staring across the street. Something had obviously caught his eye.

'I've just seen something interesting,' he said, getting up. 'I'll be right back.'

He was gone for ages but when he returned, his always-twinkling eyes were now burning bright with excitement.

'I've found the place, the perfect place. Now we can put on shows.'

'Where?'

'Right across the street. It's a Deaf Club. That's why it took me so long trying to communicate with the guys over there. It's absolutely perfect; they get no help from the city or state, so they're desperate for funds. We can rent the hall on Fridays and Saturdays. We can be as loud as we like 'cause they won't hear a thing and there's no neighbours to worry about, just shops that'll be closed. There's a stage at one end, a bar at the other. We can get ourselves a PA system and mixing desk and you can set up your gear and play records between the bands.'

Perfect. I'd been looking for a way to re-establish myself on the music scene now that I didn't have my KSAN job – and this was it. There was a whole scene developing fast in the city with new bands being formed all the time, groups like The Mutants and the Dead Kennedys. There was only one venue where these bands could play: the Mabuhay Gardens on Broadway, right in the heart of SF's equivalent of London's Soho district. A Philippino restaurant by day and early evening, late at night it transformed itself into a punk-rock club. Promoter Dirk Dirksen enjoyed and exploited his total monopoly of the live scene. An alternative was badly needed. Maybe the Deaf Club was it.

In the absence of radio work, I'd turned to my other skill of live DJing to make money. I had contacted an old friend in London, Roger Squires, who ran a small equipment company, and I'd ordered a neat little mixer and twin-turntable mobile DJ deck. I also arranged for my boxes of singles to come out of storage and be shipped over. I was the only DJ with such a set-up and soon I was getting more and more jobs playing records at concerts.

Instead of poor-quality cassette tapes that roadies would chuck on the sound system between bands, I could provide good-quality sound with all the latest records, which made a show much more professional. I even did a major seated theatre show with Talking Heads one night but my regular gigs were at the Geary Temple, an old Jewish synagogue. All the well-known British punk/new-wave bands on a US tour would play there: Gang of Four, The Clash, Nick Lowe, Dave Edmunds, Elvis Costello and from the US, Blondie and The Go-Go's. But for local bands and groups from LA like X and Black Flag, the Deaf Club became the coolest and hippest venue in the city.

Robert and I went into partnership to hire the club and get the word out. Once we'd paid all the expenses and the bands, we split what was left, which wasn't much but it was a start. The sheer excitement of being in on such an amazing venture was worth it, anyway. Gigs at the Deaf Club were like a secret rave. You had to have your ear close to the street to know who was playing when. Then you went up some rickety old wooden stairs from the small street entrance and you were in a funky little club. Seedy and run-down, it was the perfect place for San Francisco's unofficial punk HQ. Early in the evening, people would wander in, get a beer at the bar and exchange news and gossip. In no time, the place would be full with a couple of hundred people squashed in together. Then the bands would start and the crowds at the front would mash up to the small stage, pogo-ing like crazy, while lead singers often just launched themselves into the masses, being passed around over the heads of the crowd and thrown back on to the stage.

It was all wild, wonderful mayhem and we had some truly fantastic and memorable nights there, even recording a *Live At The Deaf Club* album. There was never any violence or trouble. Opposite the stage at the other end of the small room, the deaf folks would down their beers and chat away in manic sign language. They loved all the energy and excitement as the floor bounced up and down from all the leaping about. And the money coming in was great for their club – the best thing that had ever happened for them.

It was, of course, all too good to last. The crowds milling outside eventually attracted the attention of the cops cruising by in their patrol cars. A couple of times they came up the stairs to check out what the fuck was going on up there and, after closing time, they'd hustle people and move them on. Dirk Dirksen was not happy about the Deaf Club's success. Crowds had dwindled at the Mabuhay Gardens and his place seemed very ordinary and run of the mill, just another part of the Broadway scene. The Deaf Club was in the Mission, the cool part of town, and the Deaf Club was where it was at. Rumour has it that Dirk tipped off the SF Fire

Department, who came round one Friday night to inspect the premises. There were no emergency exits, no emergency fire escape, and the room was licensed for a maximum of a hundred people. We were packing well over two hundred into a wooden building with just the narrow staircase for an exit. They took notes and left.

The following night, we had bands booked and opened as usual. At about nine o'clock, teams of cops carrying drawn nightsticks forced their way up the stairs, pushed through the crowds and got up onstage.

'This place is now closed!' they declared. 'The show's over, there ain't gonna be any more. If you wanna spend a night in the cells, stick around. If you don't, leave now in an orderly fashion.'

There was a bit of pushing and shoving. The cops hated the punks and the punks hated them. I looked over at Robert, who shrugged his shoulders and forced a wan smile. Game's up, it's over.

But, boy, was it good while it lasted.

All the ups and downs and setbacks and disappointments had put a huge strain on Frances and me, and on our marriage. Although she seemed happy in the States and had coped very well with our life in San Francisco, the unstable nature of our life took its toll and we found ourselves arguing more and more frequently. We did our utmost to stick it out and support each other come what may, but eventually we reached the point where we needed to get away from each other for a while.

We each found an apartment in houses just a mile apart on Folsom Street, not far from our old place. Frances shared with two American women, one of whom had a daughter around Beth's age. Mine was on the top floor and I shared with three other English people, all of whom were happy for me and Sam to move in. Somehow Sam had always seemed closer to me and Beth closer to her mum, so this arrangement, though somewhat unusual, seemed to be the fairest and best way to share our responsibilities. We divided equally what money we had and agreed to share the

Chevy estate car. Living so close, the kids could see each other most days and they didn't have to suffer our arguments and bickering. It was sad that Frany and I didn't feel we could live together any more but I think we were both relieved to have found a solution that seemed to suit us all.

My problem was that most of my work was in the evening. My three flatmates, two men and a woman, were very helpful when it came to babysitting Sam but often there'd be times when none of them wanted to stay home for the evening. I had to turn up for my gigs or I'd soon lose them and, if Frances couldn't take him, sometimes I had no option but to take Sam with me. At Geary Temple I would set up a little bed for him underneath my DJ desk. We were on a small balcony above the stage, so it was a safe spot. Amazingly enough, despite the sound level of the music, he'd go straight off to sleep with a contented look on his face, while below bands would be thrashing it out with a wild pogo-ing crowd leaping all over the place.

If Sam was really tired before the gig, I'd make up a bed for him in the estate wagon, which was parked in a safe, secure area in the artists' car park. While the bands were on, I'd go down to check all was well. During the days he'd go to pre-school and at weekends we often took a trip out to the zoo and the beach. I saw Beth as often as I could, usually a couple of times a week, and before long the children settled well into their new routines.

We were all still missing the Deaf Club but then another space became available. A mate of ours called Joe ran the company Target Video, and he lived and worked in a huge warehouse space not far from the Deaf Club. He filmed all the bands that ever came and played in San Francisco and had built up an incredible archive of the birth and development of the whole West Coast punk movement. His space was big enough to put on a late-night party and after a big group's gig, the whole crowd would head down to Target. He took a few bucks on the door, which included tokens for beer, thus getting around the problem of his premises being unlicensed. With Sam being looked after at my place or up at Frany's, we'd start about midnight and party through till four or five in the morning. Often I would have already worked at the Geary Temple and then packed up to set up again at Target, so they were long and tiring nights but I loved being the guy to keep the party going and the atmosphere was fantastic.

One night The Clash dropped in after their show at the Geary. I was playing my usual mix of punk, old R&B and reggae. Word soon spread that they were in the place so I thought it would be a good idea to put on 'London Calling'. It hadn't been playing for long when their roadie came up onstage.

'Johnnie, the guys are here to relax and unwind, they don't really want to hear one of their records.'

I muttered an apology, embarrassed at my lack of cool and went back to reggae.

After a night at Target with daylight not far off, I'd head off down to my favourite all-night bar and restaurant. It was run by black people for black people but I always felt welcome and never out of place. Their jukebox was full of the finest soul and R&B, they had a pool table and could rustle up one of the best break-fasts in town: two eggs over easy, wonderful real hash browns and fabulous crispy bacon (my one lapse from vegetarianism). Then a couple of JDs and black coffee and a few games of pool. I usually won – my opponent one night was convinced I was a pool hustler in town to make a fast buck. Quite a compliment in a way.

Those all-night raves went on most Saturday nights until, once again, crowds outside attracted the cops. A patrol car cruised by, slowed down for a good look and then slowly drove out of sight. It seemed as if all was okay until the next weekend's rave.

It was two a.m. when the doors burst open and a whole squad of cops flowed into the warehouse, nightsticks drawn and looking very much in the mood for some aggro. Their nasty attitude worsened when they spotted a poster on the wall. It was a shooting-practice target but instead of the usual outline of an anonymous figure, this one depicted a police officer. It was just Joe's idea of a cool poster for his company.

'What the fuck is this?' said the guy leading the raid.

He called his buddies over to have a look and now the atmosphere took a definite turn for the worse. Fuck me, here we go again, I thought, imagining all sorts of dire consequences if they roped me in and checked out my immigration status. The chief cop stepped on to the stage and grabbed the microphone off me.

'There're two ways that we can do this – the hard way and the easy way. The easy way is for you guys to just get out of here and go home. Or there's the hard way, where you don't wanna go and we crack a few heads and take you downtown.'

I decided meek cooperation was the way to go, and so, keeping my head down, I immediately began packing up my records and making it obvious that I'd accepted the fun was over. He glanced at me, saw what I was doing and then directed his attention elsewhere.

By the time I got outside there were half a dozen squad cars and three paddy wagons filling up with punks seemingly picked out at random for a night in the cells. Leaving my gear to pack up later, I headed off home for some much-needed sleep.

The police and the city had nothing to fear from the punk scene. It was all part of the usual rock 'n' roll game – we wanted to be different, get noticed and be a bit outrageous, have our own clubs and music. The cops gave us aggro because we didn't look like normal people. But that was the end of Target all-nighters. Another wonderful venture over with.

I was back to DJing at concerts to get by, and wondering when I'd ever work on the radio again.

Chapter Thirty-One

1979

Sam and I made a new move, this time into a warehouse in a semi-industrial area behind Market Street. We were a bit further from Frances, but not much, and now we had more flatmates sharing the vast space with us. It was an unusual, exciting place to live that was also ideal as a workplace. There were some very talented people in all forms of the arts, who contributed to the vibrancy of the SF scene, and we all helped and supported each other. Robert Hanrahan, who had opened the Deaf Club with me, was one. My pal Brad was another.

Brad, a highly educated and talented journalist, launched and edited the city's own punk magazine called *Damage*. We became good friends and together discussed the idea of a radio version of the magazine. I had access to visiting UK bands that knew me from my Radio One days, Brad had all the info on the local scene and so *Damage on the Air* was born. It was a two-hour monthly show of interviews and music featuring UK bands breaking into the States as well as hot new local groups. I recorded it in the warehouse where I lived and it was distributed by the National Federation of Community Broadcasters based in Washington DC. They duplicated copies and sent them to all university and small radio stations all over the US. We built up a network of sixty stations. My fee was 10 per cent of the $12 they charged each station, so it wasn't much, but at least I was doing radio again.

Damage on the Air won an award for Best Independently Produced Programme, which I was very proud of. Not bad for a home-made effort produced on a mobile DJ desk, old Revox tape machine and cassette recorder, plus a sucker thing on the phone to record telephone interviews. I spent hours and hours putting it together, editing the old-fashioned way with a razor blade and splicing tape. But I was very proud of the show and the award.

In 1979 the ever-changing music scene was undergoing another moment of evolution. A bunch of friends decided to form a band, one that would combine far-out spacey music with weird visual images. They rented a warehouse in a nondescript industrial area just south of San Francisco. With security fencing round their compound and a guard dog, their valuable equipment was safe and there were no neighbours to complain about noise. They then had a meeting to decide what would be the band's drug of choice. I guess every movement has its drug: grass and LSD for the hippies during the sixties, ecstasy for the dance generation in the eighties and for the punks in the seventies, speed – or cocaine as a special treat if you had the money.

The band considered the options. Grass or pot was out, they'd never get anything done. Speed – no, that was no good, too detrimental for their health. Cocaine – similar to the above and too expensive. They wanted to be creative and produce an audio-visual experience the like of which had never been seen before. There was only one drug that met all the criteria – LSD. One of them managed to track down a source of pure, unadulterated LSD, being legitimately manufactured by a pharmaceutical company in Europe. The drug had been made illegal but there were analysts using it in therapy and it's said the US military were researching its effect on soldiers under interrogation. Knowing a member of the group, I was often gifted with a couple of tabs of Sandoz's finest: tiny little pills, the beautiful blue of a Caribbean sea, their effect was unlike anything I'd experienced before.

Frances and I had had a couple of amazing trips in our little flat in Belsize Park, usually on a Sunday when the block was virtually empty and we knew we wouldn't be disturbed. We'd plan the day carefully, unplug the phone, have enough snacks and drinks we might need and then embark on an eight-hour journey of dis-covery. Frances was a very good guide: if anything started to get a bit weird, she'd change the music and the mood and off we'd go down another little side road of amazing sounds, colour and always, a lot of laughter. This stuff was so much better. The purity ensured the body had no adverse chemical reactions and half a Sandoz would give a very gentle little trip, similar to really strong grass.

I knew what a bad trip was. I'd been in New York with Robert Hanrahan, helping road-manage his band The Offs, who were doing an East Coast tour. It was a Saturday night and drummer Robert Steele had a one-off gig with Jorma Kaikonen's band at the Palladium. Robert warned us not to drink anything from an unsealed bottle, as Jorma loved to play tricks. Without thinking, I tucked into some cheese and crackers in their dressing room and will always remember the sly look on Jorma's face as he saw me eating. An hour later, standing in the wings watching the band, the stage lights began to swirl all over the place and my body felt incredibly hot. Thank God I had some experience of LSD as I realized the food had been spiked. Oh Christ, an acid overdose, this is going to be tough. There was no escaping its effects; for the next eight hours I had to try and keep a grip on reality and find the group's apartment.

I knew I had to get out of the theatre so I fought my way out of the stage door where masses of people were fighting to get in. It was a really ugly scene, made all the worse by the acid. I knew I'd taken quite a lot. I was hallucinating way more than I'd experienced before. I was out on the street, on a Saturday night in downtown Manhattan and I couldn't get my bearings. I sat down on the step of a shop as hordes of people were rushing back and forth. People went by and complimented me on my bright orange Converse baseball boots, which seemed to be glowing in the dark.

My brain was playing Stevie Wonder's 'Living For The City' on an endless loop. The scenario in the middle of the song of a shoot-out and the arrival of the cops, an arrest and jail was freaking me out. Maybe this was going to happen to me. If the cops came by I was convinced they'd know I was totally out of it. I too would be arrested and thrown in the pen with God knows what kind of characters. That would be no place to deal with an eight-hour acid trip. I eventually got it together enough to hail a cab, though I was then convinced that the strange little bald-headed driver was kidnapping me and taking me God knows where. I made it back to safety and fell on my bed, sobbing with relief. The next day I had the white dove of peace tattooed on my left forearm as a memento of my having survived an acid overdose in such a manic city.

And so, after nine months of hard work, the group (whose name I forget) decided they were ready to launch their new experience to the outside world. Friends, journalists, DJs and assorted members of the San Francisco underground were sent an invitation to attend the unveiling at their warehouse compound. Fires were lit in oil drums to keep off the evening chill and we all milled around sipping beers, waiting for the big event.

There was the sound of rattling chains as, very slowly, a huge metal shutter began to lift. Smoke and dazzling red lights poured out from inside as the sound of weird, spaced-out music grew steadily louder and louder. With the shutter now fully raised, four musicians were standing in front of a huge wall of electronic gadgetry, various lights, dials and meters blinking and flashing. All along the top of their stacks was a row of video screens showing a bizarre mix of geometric shapes, colours, news and war footage, and naked bodies.

The whole experience was a total affront to the senses and, as one, the crowd moved backwards, almost in fear of this incredibly powerful and mind-numbing audio-visual assault. After twenty minutes the performance ended. There was a shocked silence and then the assembled crowd burst into tumultuous applause and cheers. What a way to launch a new band, a showcase to end all showcases.

The party continued long into the night. I sampled all that was on offer and, by midnight, my friend Jim and I were flying high and ready to take on the world. We staggered out of the compound and began the long walk home, passing through a parking lot full of Greyhound buses.

'Hey, Jim, check this out. None of the doors to the buses are locked. I bet you don't need a key to start 'em up.' I went from one to another, some with manual gears, others with automatic. After fiddling around for a while, I got one started. 'Come on, Jim,' I shouted, 'let's go for a ride.' The bus was so easy to drive, what a fantastic lark. 'Tell you what, let's go round to my warehouse, wake everybody up and go down to LA.'

It seemed like such a good idea at the time. I parked the bus in the street directly opposite the warehouse and ran in. Everyone was fast asleep. I roused them all awake, including Sam.

'Come on, guys,' I said, excitedly. 'I've got a Greyhound bus, we're going to LA.'

'Walker, you're fucking crazy.'

'Leave me alone, I was asleep.'

Others were up for it. Bleary-eyed, Jackie, Sam and a couple of others crossed the street and climbed on board.

'Okay, everyone on board? LA here we come,' I yelled. I hit the starter button. The engine whirred a couple of times, then slowed and stopped. 'Shit! It was going a treat before.'

I tried it again. Nothing. Not a sound. My passengers muttered and grumbled their way out of the bus and headed back to bed.

What was I going to do now? Why hadn't I parked it up the street a bit? Here was a huge Greyhound bus parked directly opposite our place. Nothing much I could do at one o'clock in the morning. Might as well go to bed, and see what happened tomorrow.

I woke about nine and rushed to our kitchen, hoping a miracle might have happened overnight and the bus would have disappeared. Or maybe it was all just a dream.

Unfortunately, there was no miracle and it wasn't a dream.

There it was, directly opposite, resplendent in its grey aluminium livery, one enormous Greyhound bus. I was teased by flatmates as, one by one, they woke up and came into the kitchen.

'Woah, Walker, you're in for it now. How are you gonna get out of this one, then?'

'Nah, no worries,' I said, doing my best to sound braver than I actually felt. 'There's nothing to connect it with us. It's on a yellow line, the cops will probably report it to Greyhound, and they'll come round and take it away.'

That's what I desperately hoped would happen. But all morning, every time I looked out of the window, the bloody thing was still there.

As I brewed up yet another cup of tea I glanced across the road. There was some activity going on. A van had arrived and two blokes in grey overalls were walking round, inspecting the bus. One disappeared inside and, after about half an hour, I heard the engine roar into life. With never a glance across the road at our warehouse, and with the van leading the way, he drove the Greyhound bus up the street. I breathed a massive sigh of relief and rustled up some eggs, bacon and toast to celebrate. A close call. I'd been dead lucky to get away with that mad escapade.

Then things in San Francisco began to change. A table lamp caused a small fire in the apartment Frances and Beth shared. Though not their fault, the landlady blamed them and things got a bit sour. Frany's friend Jane, the one with the little girl, had met a guy and they decided to set up home together somewhere up north. Their other flatmate was also making plans to leave town and Frances decided that, for her, the American experience was over. Homesick for England, she wanted to go home and take Beth with her. Now four years old, Beth would soon be starting school and Frances wanted that to be at home, in England.

With no place to live, Frany moved into the warehouse where there was plenty of space, and we talked over all the various options. Sam was in a good school he loved, I was making *Damage on the Air* and was getting plenty of DJ gigs. Maybe, having been in the States long enough, I might qualify for the precious green card. If I left now, I would never get one. It was too soon for me, I wasn't ready to go back yet, but Frances definitely was. As she made plans to get a ticket and book a flight, it was obvious she had no desire to stay and was positively elated at the prospect of going back to London. I realized that she was determined and I knew that she wouldn't be happy unless she went home. Did it mean the end of our marriage? I wasn't sure. We both knew that our relationship had taken a battering and it needed some time to recover. Maybe this move would help us both.

The desperately sad part for me was how much I would miss Beth. We sat the children down and explained to them what was going to happen and that it didn't affect how we both felt about them. They took it very much in their stride, as children often do. They were already accustomed to living apart and I think that the idea of living in different countries didn't mean a great deal to them. For me, it was very hard to think of my little girl being so far away. I only hoped that it wouldn't be for long.

I drove Frances and Beth out to the airport, dropped them off at the entrance to the terminal and headed off to find the car park. There were building works going on all over the airport and confusing diversion signs took me far away from the terminal. I was getting more and more desperate. I hadn't said proper good-byes and unless I found the right car park, they'd be gone. I wanted to give Beth a final goodbye hug. Round and round I went, feeling more and more panicky and overcome by emotion. I eventually found a space in a multi-storey car park and Sam and I ran desperately back to the terminal, hundreds of yards away.

I had worked myself up into such a state that I couldn't stem my tears. I was rushing blindly around in all the wrong directions, but we eventually found the right terminal and dashed inside, heading for departures and the security gates. Frances and Beth were still there, totally relaxed.

'What the hell's the matter with you?' asked Frances, seeing my tear-stained, panic-stricken face.

'I had to park miles away, I couldn't find the right terminal and I was so scared you'd leave without a proper goodbye.'

'It's all right, we're all here now.'

Frances had a wonderful ability to calm a desperate situation, but there were now tears in her eyes as she gave Sam a huge hug and kissed his cheeks. We hugged and kissed and I wished her all the luck in the world, hoping that friends would rally round and help her when she got back. I knew it wouldn't be easy for them both. I turned to Beth; she was nonchalantly swinging on a barrier, without a care in the world. She had no idea what was happening but must have found her father's behaviour strange and confusing.

I picked her up and held her in my arms. I had so much love for Sam and Beth, they meant the world to me. Saying goodbye to my little girl was horribly painful. I squeezed her tight, kissed her cheeks and told her I loved her. Sam and I held hands and watched them walk through to the desk and on into the departure hall. We waved and waved again. I wanted to rush after them, to get on the plane and for us all to be together. But I knew in my heart of hearts that it wasn't meant to be; they now had their own adventure ahead of them.

For now, at least, our destinies were on different paths.

With a final glance at their disappearing figures, I squeezed Sam's hand.

'Come on, little fella, it's time to go home.'

Chapter Thirty-Two

1980–81

The wind lifted up the frisbee and Sam ran to chase after it. We carried on playing for a while but the gusts of wind were blowing stronger.

'Let's get back in the car,' I said.

We clambered back into the safety and shelter of my beloved old, white Chevrolet estate car.

'Dad,' said Sam. He looked at me, his eyes alive with excitement. 'This has been the greatest day of my life.'

I smiled and gave him a big hug. I started the car, which was running low to the ground with the weight of all our stuff, and we set off again on our journey across America. I looked at Sam sitting there next to me and felt so strongly that my dad was with us and that all three of us were connected. He had died only a few weeks ago, on 11th February 1980.

My mother had called me at the end of January to tell me that Dad was seriously ill. He had been diagnosed with lung cancer but his treatment had seemed successful until the doctors discovered a brain tumour. I immediately said I wanted to come home but I was broke and in the States illegally. If I left, it was possible I wouldn't be able to get back in, and Frances and the children would be stranded.

My mum said, 'I don't think he would recognize you, Peter. His memory is all but gone and he doesn't really know where he is or what's happening. He's in a hospice and they are doing all they can to care for him but I don't think he'll be with us much longer.'

I was about to lose my father. I was six thousand miles away and he was going to die without my being able to say goodbye and 'I love you' one last time. I had learnt so much from him about the value of honesty and decency; I had never heard him speak badly of anyone and I felt so proud of him on those journeys we shared together in my school holidays – it was so obvious that everyone respected and admired my dad.

The next call from Mum was to tell me he had died. I had never felt so sad or cried so much. The funeral was to be later in the week – not only was I denied a final farewell, I wasn't even going to be at his funeral.

Gradually, as the weeks passed, I was able to accept what had happened. In quiet, gentle moments when I thought of my dad, I began to feel some sense of connection. I began to realize that our father–son relationship had changed to a different level: it now had a wonderful freedom to it. There was none of the old baggage of misunderstanding and criticism. Dad now had complete under-standing of me and knew my true feelings for him. It seems a strange thing to say but my relationship with him was better now than it had ever been when he was alive.

I never had what you might call proof until one evening in 1985. The man they called the psychic detective, Keith Charles, had been a guest on a radio show I was presenting and he invited me to introduce him at his evening show at a hall in Stroud. He was with my old pal Derek Robinson, who ran the Wimbledon Spiritualist Church and put on shows with psychics all over the country. We always called him Del and he liked to think of himself as the Del Boy of the psychic world.

'Come and intro Keith on his dem and we'll go and have a ruby after,' said Del.

I'd followed them in my car and we'd just pulled into a car park near the restaurant. Suddenly the passenger door opened and Keith jumped in.

'Johnnie, just before we go into the curry place, let me sit here a minute. I just felt drawn to getting in the car and us having a quiet moment.' He paused for a moment and then said, 'There's a man who's been impressing himself on me. I've got a feeling it's your dad. He's telling me he has such admiration for you and all the many things you've done in your life that he would have loved to do but just didn't have the opportunity.'

Keith carried on telling me more things that I could imagine my dad saying. And then a small but wonderful thing happened.

'I can feel your dad starting to draw away from me now as he's getting quite tired. It takes a lot of energy for him to break through this dense level we're in. But just as he's going, he says I'm to tap your leg and ask, "How's your leg, son?"'

I could feel tears at the back of my eyes. Now I knew Dad had been with us. Every time I visited him after my stock-car accident, he'd playfully tap me on the thigh and ask, 'How's your leg, son?'

Sam and I continued on our journey, leaving San Francisco and the beautiful bay far behind us as we headed towards Washington. Even after a year apart from Frances and Beth, I still wasn't ready to return to England. Instead, we headed east.

My friend Jim Dunbar had moved to Washington DC to take up a political internship on Capitol Hill and had phoned repeatedly, imploring me to consider a move to DC. According to Jim, the whole new music scene there was expanding fast. There was a really happening punk/new-wave club in the city, radio stations were embracing more adventurous programming and he was convinced these developments represented great opportunities for me. Jim had a big place, so accommodation would be no problem.

I decided to go. We packed up our car and took off for Washington. As I hadn't worked in so long, we hadn't the money for motels and so slept in the car at truck stops. Now that it was late autumn, the nights were cold and we were cramped together, snuggled in our sleeping bags on the bench front seat. Behind us, every inch of space was occupied by my DJ and studio equipment, records and clothes. Everything we owned in the world was in the car.

We awoke one morning shivering with cold. Snow lay on the ground and on the bonnet and roof of the car. After breakfast of cornflakes and toast in a nearby diner, we got back in the car. I was anxious to get under way in case the weather worsened. I turned the ignition: the starter could hardly turn the engine over, so thick was the oil in these low temperatures. Getting the jump leads out of the back, I opened the bonnet, connected them to the battery and trailed them over the front. As each car and truck pulled out of the parking lot, I gave the driver an imploring look and within ten minutes a good Samaritan stopped to give us a jump start.

I knew the car needed a new battery and I just didn't have enough money to buy one. The situation was pretty desperate. There was only one hope. I was about a day and a half away from Nashville. Much as I was reluctant to impose myself on Roger Cook again, maybe he could help.

It was lovely seeing Roger again and if he was surprised to see me without Beth and Frany, he didn't say anything. With a little persuasion, dear old Rog eventually agreed to buy my Revox tape machine off me for $100. I bought and fitted a new battery and we set off again for Washington.

I had called Jim a couple of times along the way to check that it was still okay for Sam and me to stay at his place. He assured me it would be absolutely fine, no problem. We got safely to Jim's place in Arlington, Virginia, and he gave us a warm welcome and introduced us to the others sharing the house, who all seemed friendly enough.

Sam and I had the basement to ourselves and with our army sleeping bags, with their built-in groundsheets, we managed to make ourselves a reasonable cosy sleeping and living space on the concrete floor. Apart from going upstairs at mealtimes, we kept ourselves pretty much to ourselves in our little basement, anxious not to impose on the others.

I really hit the ground running in Arlington, determined not to waste a moment in trying to build a new life there. Within three days, Sam was booked into the local school and I had made a valuable contact with a guy running a record shop and magazine. He offered me some work as a weekly columnist for the magazine and advised me to go and check out radio station WHFS in nearby

Bethesda, Maryland. So I went round there and introduced myself.

The station was owned and run by a family and operated out of two large apartments in a tall high-rise block. Their transmitting antenna was on the roof, sales and admin on one floor and studios, production and library on the next floor down. I got on really well with their programme director, who was amazed that a former KSAN jock was knocking on the door looking for on-air work.

'I'd love to give you the breakfast show,' he said, 'but I've got a black woman doing it at the moment. That's double points with the FCC.'

We were well into the era of positive discrimination and employers were under great pressure to raise their percentage of female staff and members of ethnic minorities. He did, though, offer me a show on Saturday afternoons. The money wasn't great, but at least I would be back on the air live, and on a pretty good radio station.

Things were looking really good and I was amazed at how well it was all going in the space of only a week. Then, about four o'clock one afternoon, Jim came down into the basement. It seemed his girlfriend had a problem with us being there. Back in SF, Jim had been so into the whole punk scene, and had spent hours round at my warehouse chatting about music and playing his favourite records on my DJ mixer. His girlfriend no doubt saw me as a bad influence from the old days.

'Johnnie,' he said, 'I'm going to have to ask you to go.'

This was very unexpected and a bit of a shock, to say the least.

'But, Jim, I checked and double-checked with you on the journey over and you said it would be fine. I've achieved so much in a week, I just need a bit longer to get the deposit together on a place and we'll be gone.'

'Yes, I know all that. But I'm sorry, you're gonna have to leave.'

'Well, if that's what you want, okay. But at least give me a couple of days to find somewhere else.'

'I can't give you a couple of days, you're gonna have to go right now, tonight.'

I looked at him incredulously.

'For fuck's sake, Jim, do you realize what you're doing? Are you really willing to chuck out someone with a five-year-old kid, with absolutely nowhere to go?'

The look on his face said that he was.

'Well, I hope you're happy to live with that kind of karma. I know I wouldn't be.'

Jim looked pretty shamefaced.

'Come on, Sam,' I said. 'We're going to pack our stuff back into the car.'

'Where are we going, Dad?' asked Sam, surprised that we were on the move again.

'I'm not sure. Don't worry, I'll find us somewhere.'

We drove up to the nearby 7–11 store and got some food for supper. Then I drove round and round Arlington's leafy suburbs until I found a quiet, remote little street and parked up. I hoped and prayed the cops didn't patrol here and that we'd be safe for the night.

After a fitful night's sleep, thankfully without any hassle, we drove back to the 7–11 and parked outside, waiting for them to open. With some fruit and yoghurt for breakfast, I helped Sam get ready for school.

'Now, listen to me, Sam. This is very important. I know this is difficult, living in the car, but please, don't mention anything about it to your teacher at school. Just keep it our little secret for now and I will do my best to find us a place to live as soon as I can.'

'Okay, Dad, I won't say anything,' he assured me.

We had grown so close through all our little adventures and now we needed each other more than ever. I was so terribly afraid that if the school got wind that we were homeless, they would inform social services and Sam might get taken into care. Then the authorities would investigate us, with all the implications of my illegal alien status and possible deportation. I had a few hours till the end of school and racked my brains as to what to do next. It's at times like these, despite feeling so desperately alone, that, maybe, help is given from the unseen world of spirit. Don Galloway had talked about the powerful spirit of a Native

American who, pleased with my interest in his people's life and history, had chosen to be one of my spirit guides or helpers. And there was also my dad, who was now in the world of spirit. I still had all the letters he had written as we made our original journey to California and I was sure he was aware of my predicament and doing his best to offer some sort of support. An idea came to me: the kindest soul I'd met during my short time in Arlington was the guy at the record store and I felt inspired to head over there. The shop was closed. I scribbled a note with a brief outline of my situation and said I'd come over tomorrow morning.

I was waiting outside the school at three o'clock. Sam came running out and headed for the car.

'All okay, son? Did you have a good day?'

'Yeah, it was good, thanks, Dad. Where are we going now?'

'Let's go and get some food and then we'll go for a little drive.'

I had fish and chips while Sam munched his way through some KFC chicken and fries.

'Hey, Dad?' His voice had that questioning tone. I wondered what was coming next. 'Dad, the teacher wanted me to tell you something.'

'What's that, Sam?'

'She said there are places we could go and we could get a bed for the night and it wouldn't cost us any money. She said it was called a hostel or something like that, and we wouldn't get into any trouble if we went there.'

He spoke with such wonder and innocence, there was no way I could be angry that somehow the teacher had found out the truth of this little fella's living situation. Maybe he had spoken of his adventure in the car, who knows?

'Ah, bless you, son, she is doing her best to try and help us. I think, though, that it would be best if we slept in the car again tonight and we won't need to go to the hostel place. I'm sure I can find a home for us tomorrow.'

He seemed happy with that and after a walk and frisbee session in the park, I started the evening cruise again, looking for a different place this time. We followed the same routine next morning and, after dropping Sam, I headed back to the record store. My lovely man (I wish I could recall his name) greeted me with a smile and said he might have some news for me. He knew a couple called David and Diana who had a place and they had a spare room that might just be suitable for me and Sam. We could go over tonight to meet them. My heart and hopes lifted with joy. Please let this one work out, I thought. I couldn't thank my record-shop saviour enough. What a great guy.

We had our usual fast-food meal after school and, around six o'clock, I headed over to Dave and Diana's place. They were in their late twenties, they both had jobs in Washington and shared the ramshackle old wooden house with Eric, a skinny writer who stayed in his room all day, chain-smoking full-strength Camels and pounding away on his typewriter. Their spare room was perfect. There were a couple of mattresses on the floor and a wardrobe and chest of drawers for our stuff. We all got on really well. Diana obviously warmed to Sam, as did everyone, especially the women. With his gorgeous blond hair, charming manners, cheeky smile and his wonderful spirit and zest for life, my little Sam was irresistible. If we were happy with a rent of sixty dollars a week, the room was ours and we could move in straightaway.

Life was good again and we had new hope for the future.

Chapter Thirty-Three

1982

The coming months were blissfully happy: Sam was thriving at school, my weekly radio show was going well and I was DJing one night a week at the 909 Club in the city. I soon got known and was accepted into the Washington new-music scene. But I needed more money. I got an interview with a company selling office stationery over the phone and was offered a job. There were about fifty of us in a room in a soulless place housed in an office block on an industrial estate. A hi-fi system blasted out a local rock station at high volume to keep the energy up and our telephones were fitted with special devices to filter out background sound. Supervisors would pace up and down, occasionally picking up the small speaker on each desk to listen into both sides of the conversation. We worked to a script and it was thankless, relentless work. If we got a sale, we'd go up front, ring a bell and chalk up the amount on the blackboard.

My English accent was a help and one of my gimmicks was to call up as Patrick Fortescue-Smythe, private secretary to Prince Charles. It was around the time of Charles and Di's marriage and, putting on my best hooray accent, I'd inform them that HRH would like to invite them to his wedding to Diana. It would break the ice and always got a laugh, and then I could try and sell them stationery they didn't need.

I made reasonable money and the hours fitted in with Sam's school day, so it was okay. Then school was out and the long summer holidays began and, with horror, I realized I now had to look after Sam every day. As a single parent in San Francisco, I'd had a lot of help from local services. Sam would come out of school and go upstairs to a free childcare facility in the same building. I could pick him up from there anytime up until six o'clock. It was open all day, every day, even in the holidays. Now I was in the state of Virginia, a Republican stronghold and deeply conservative. Single parents were rare and looked upon with some suspicion, and there was no provision for daycare in the holidays, certainly not at a price that I could afford. But I had to do my shift at telephone selling as it was our main source of income.

Every evening I would frantically call on neighbours with young children and ask if they could possibly have Sam over to play for a few hours next day. One kind woman next door was especially helpful but couldn't do every day. I was in a bind. Then I got a phone call. It was Vincenta, an old DJ friend from KSAN. Had I seen an article in *Variety* magazine that spoke of a relaunch of the pirate station Radio Caroline? I hadn't, but it sounded fascinating and immediately she had my full attention. It felt like such a long time since Frances and I had split up and she'd left America with Beth to go back to England. It was time Sam saw his mum again and I so wanted to see Beth. I had missed her terribly and I knew Frances felt the same way about Sam. We had kept in close touch, sending each other audio cassettes of ourselves talking to the other half of our family – they couldn't believe Sam's American accent – but that wasn't really enough. I was longing to hold my little girl again, not just hear her voice.

I also had the sense that the American adventure was over and the time was right to go home now. It had been amazing – nothing like I'd planned, of course – but I realized that I could never live full time in America. There were many things I loved about it, but I missed England, the English humour and its wryness, and I couldn't get away from the fact that my roots were there. Maybe it was time to think of going back, and to arrive as a jock again on Radio Caroline would be a fantastic way to return.

I made a few calls from the information Vincenta gave me and eventually tracked down Vincent Monsey, who was working out of an office in an advertising agency in New York and helping to set up the new venture. When I called, he told me that, yes, it was true. Ronan O'Rahilly was involved in resurrecting his station and plans to re-launch Caroline were at an advanced stage. He was delighted I'd got in touch. They'd love to have an original Caroline jock back on board, so to speak.

I talked it over with Vincenta, who was very keen to get involved. She was a total Anglophile, loved the music and was full of enthusiasm at the possibility of being a DJ on a pirate station. There was a friend of hers named Mitch Parker, who'd worked on campus radio, and he was also very enthusiastic and prepared to make the trip to the UK.

I left Vincent my phone number and a week or so later he called and suggested I come to New York. I mentioned the others in San Francisco and he thought they should come as well. I told Sam that we were going to England and he would see his mum and sister again. He was beside himself with excitement, but also sad that he'd have to say goodbye to a school he loved and all the friends he'd made there. But give that boy a new adventure to dream about and he was always raring to go.

Dave and Diana agreed to look after my records and stuff, which I hoped to ship back at a later stage. Without a decent-sized suitcase between us, Sam and I packed what stuff we'd need for the trip into loads of small bags and rucksacks and I put all my most valuable things into my favourite leather Gladstone bag. There was my passport, early photos of the kids, the first present Beth had ever bought me and, most valuable of all, my wedding ring.

When I'd decided to go home, I'd written a long, long letter to Frances expressing the hope that maybe, when we got back, we could try all being together again. I knew Frances was tentative about the idea but I felt very strongly we should try if we possibly could, and this was a way of reaching out. If our reunion was successful, then I would put the ring back on, so it would have greater significance.

Dave and Diana gave us a lift to Washington railway station. There were hugs and tears all round as we said our goodbyes. They were so very good to us and had come to our rescue in an hour of need.

I owed them a great deal and, wherever they are today, I hope they're doing well.

We caught the Amtrak to New York Grand Central Station. I had a sense of foreboding about the trip and was worried about being in New York with such a young child. At least we would have a place to stay – an old friend of Mitch's had agreed to put us up in her apartment. Sam and I both loved trains and all seemed to be un-eventful on our rail trip to New York. Then the train came to a shuddering stop and didn't move again. We stayed like that for over half an hour before the conductor made his way through our carriage.

'There's been a fatality on the line, we hope to get going again soon.'

With others, I looked out of the window. Why, I don't know, and how I wished I hadn't. There, jutting out from the front of the locomotive were the remains of a human head, the hair blowing in the breeze. I felt sick and tried to hide my shock from Sam. Thank God he didn't see it. The train eventually starting moving again but for the rest of the journey, I was haunted by that awful sight. It was not a good omen for the beginning of this new chapter in our lives.

I was very thankful to see Vincenta and Mitch, who'd had the patience to wait and meet us off our delayed train. They helped us carry our crazy collection of hand luggage and we went out of the station concourse to hail a cab. Grand Central is a pretty mad place at the best of times, and this was rush hour, with hordes of people running for trains to get home, or standing on the kerbside trying to get a cab. There were plenty of taxis but they wouldn't come up to the kerb, instead stopping one lane into the street, afraid they would never be able to pull out again into the queues of traffic. We set up a chain to ferry all our bags from kerb to cab and, safely loaded, headed off to the apartment, down in the SoHo district. We climbed the stairs up to the tiny two-room apartment and slung all our bags on the floor. There was no sign of my leather

Gladstone bag. I frantically asked the others if they remembered picking it up. No one did.

In the haste and confusion of trying to load the cab, we hadn't arranged for one of us to stay with the bags and guard them while others did the loading. Within seconds someone had spied the expensive-looking bag and made off with it. The blood drained from my face. Please, any bag but that one. All the little things that I treasured were in the bag. My passport was in there – that was going to be a major problem – but worst of all, my wedding ring. Don Galloway's words all those years ago at our psychic reading came back into my mind: 'You wouldn't want to lose this ring, would you? Well, make jolly sure you don't.'

I phoned lost property at the station and trudged round the next day to various police stations, but I knew it was hopeless. It had been stolen and I would never see it or the contents again. I felt so incredibly sad. I cried and cried over the ring, not only its loss but what it represented. Would my heartfelt hopes of reconciliation come to nothing? Two bad omens in one day. I was wishing Sam and I had never left our safe, secure home from home in Arlington with Dave and Diana.

Kind as it was of Mitch's friend to put up three and a half people in her tiny apartment, it was not a good place to be, especially for a young child. Our hostess showed all the signs of being on heroin. The place was in a real mess and was infested with rats and cockroaches. I hoped it was only for a day or two at most.

I applied for a temporary passport for the journey back to London and was told that it would be through in a couple of days. And things looked considerably brighter when I called round at the advertising agency to see Vincent Monsey and find out what was happening with the relaunch of Radio Caroline. He was just full of it. They had a ship being fitted out at a secret port and everything promised well. Vincent showed me the video they'd been using to try and pre-sell advertising space to US companies with products in the UK.

'But, Vincent,' I said, 'all the footage on the ship is old sixties stuff on the *Mi Amigo*.'

'Ah, can't possibly film the new one, Johnnie, all very hush hush. But trust me, the new ship is great.'

The place was buzzing with activity, phones ringing off the hook, people dashing in and out. If it was a con, it was a bloody good one.

'Johnnie, just fantastic you're available for this project,' said an ever-excited Vincent. 'The punters and the press are just gonna love it – Johnnie Walker returns to the North Sea on the new Radio Caroline. I can see the headlines now.'

I couldn't help but be caught up by Vincent's energy and enthusiasm. I so wanted it to be a reality; I loved Caroline and all it stood for and Caroline was going to take me home to England and to Frances and Beth. I had never dreamed that Caroline could or would ever happen again but, seemingly, it was. Mitch and Vincenta were in Pinch-Me-I'm-Dreaming land. To go to England, where all that great music and those brilliant bands came from, to become a famous DJ on the most famous radio station of them all . . . it was just amazing. They couldn't stop grinning.

On the journey home, as the New York skyline and America's East Coast were left behind, I reflected on the great adventure we'd embarked upon in the spring of 1977. Travelling right across the USA is something many Americans dream about but never accomplish. We had done it and we had seen America in all its vast and staggering beauty, alongside the ugliness that blights the land: the scars left behind by strip-mining, the waste dumps, the chemical factories belching out poison, the litter. No wonder the Native Americans (or First Americans, as many called themselves) couldn't understand the white man's ways. For them the earth was Mother, to be loved, nurtured and respected. For the early white settlers and their descendants, land was to be conquered, divided up, and bought and sold. We had known some wonderful times, as well as deep sadness. Things hadn't gone according to plan and we didn't exactly live and enjoy the Californian dream of my imagination. But, by God, we'd had one hell of an adventure.

I had no regrets at all about leaving our safe, secure existence in

London, no matter what we'd lost by coming away. We'd met some wonderful people, were shown great kindness and hospitality, and had learnt to stand on our own feet and face some tough and challenging times. Somehow, in America, we felt free. I know I did, and I think it was also true for Frany. We were able to discover who we were without the constant pressure to conform and fit in that is part of the English way of life. Perhaps being English in another country in itself gives you permission to be different – or perhaps freedom is an essential strand of the American way of life, to be preserved and cherished at all cost. It was probably a combination of both.

I was returning to my homeland a very different person from the one who left. How would England and the UK have changed since I'd been away? More to the point, how much had Frances and Beth changed?

How would we all get on together after living apart in such different cultures?

PART FIVE

Riding High

Chapter Thirty-Four

We arrived in the cold grey light of an English dawn and piled on the Heathrow bus for London. It was such an odd feeling to be back home: everything felt very different and yet completely the same. But I felt very happy to be back, even if I could tell already that there was a lot to learn about how the culture of my homeland had changed. I'd left in 1977 and it was now 1982. Everything had moved on and I'd been completely removed from it, locked away in my American experience. Not only did things look different, but there were new sounds, new music, new TV shows . . . a totally different scene to the one I remembered.

Once we got to London, we took a cab to the Caroline office in Beauchamp Place, South Kensington, just down the road from Harrods. We checked in there and announced our arrival but I was too keyed up to stay around for long. All I could think of was getting a train to Luton to where Frances and Beth were staying with an old friend of ours. I was desperate to see them both, but I needed particularly to see Beth again.

Sam and I arrived about three in the afternoon and I knocked on the front door. My heart was pounding and I was so, so nervous. How would Beth look? How big would she be now and would she remember me? She hadn't seen me for such a long time. And I knew Frances would be pleased to see Sam – but would she be pleased to see me? Was this the beginning of our reconciliation and our new life together as a family?

It was all very, very weird. I don't think Beth really remembered me at all, but she was very friendly and she and Sam got on well right away. Frances seemed wary and unsure about my sudden arrival back in her life. She and Beth had had some really tough times but now seemed settled. Frances was doing some part-time work and Beth was in a local school and doing well. They were making a new life for themselves and it was far too soon to be talking about all living together. We needed time to get to know each other again and to see how this madcap notion of the return of Radio Caroline would pan out.

My hope was that once my Caroline job was under way and I was at sea for two weeks and home for one week, we would have a gentle reintroduction to family life with the right combination of space and intimacy to get to know each other again and see if our marriage could be reborn. I really wanted us to have another chance – and I wanted Sam and Beth to be together. Happily, Frances agreed that we should give it another chance and restart our life.

The next few months were difficult. At first, Sam and I stayed with friends and I spent time hanging out at the Caroline offices, trying to find out what would be happening. Money was very tight, and I spent a lot of time trying to cadge advances on my salary out of Ronan whenever I managed to pin him down, which wasn't easy.

Eventually we all took up residence together in a small cottage in the grounds of a country house in Kent. It was owned by one of Ronan O'Rahilly's backers in his new venture. Both Frances and I hated imposing ourselves on another family; it was all too similar a situation to being at Roger Cook's home in Nashville. It felt like we'd stepped back in time instead of moving forwards, so we decided that we'd do whatever we could to be on our own.

We ended up in a small flat over a fish and chip shop in Albert Street, Ramsgate – I'd been tipped off that Caroline would be tendered from near there. But I was getting desperate. There was still no firm date for the relaunch and money was in short supply. Despite my vow never to take government handouts, I signed on the dole. Thanks to Frances's brilliance at eking out the pennies, we survived on a monthly giro. Vincenta and Mitch were living in a cheap B&B in Bayswater, and surviving on an occasional hand-out from Vincent Monsey. This wasn't an auspicious start to the dream of returning to Caroline.

We spent a lot of time in the office on Beauchamp Place, getting

in touch with record-company promo people to blag records for
a new library for the ship. Chris Mason from Polydor Records was
incredibly helpful and supportive. I was to be programme director
– that is, until Ronan met Annie Challis. On discovering that
she used to produce Gerald Harper's show on Capital Radio,
he promptly gave her the job. I was disappointed and disillusioned
and my enthusiasm began to ebb away. My faith in the whole
venture was undermined and I stopped believing it was going to
happen. Gradually, I went to London less and less and, eventually,
the whole project just faded away and disappeared, like the dream
it was. Vincenta and Mitch went home and I contemplated my
future.

It was a sad end to my dream of a triumphant return on board
Caroline. With hindsight, I don't think there ever was a new ship.
I think the plan was to pre-sell advertising space in New York and
then buy a ship with the money, but the Americans were far too
canny for that. And that meant there was no cash to get started.

There has always been a huge amount of blag and bluster sur-
rounding pirate radio – the original Radio Caroline would never
have got on the air and survived as long as she did without it – but
it didn't work this time. Perhaps times had changed too much for
a crazy plan like that to work the way it had in the sixties.

At least I was back in England. I was so pleased to be home, even
if times were harder than I'd anticipated, and it was a great joy to be
reunited as a family again. I spent many happy hours in Ramsgate
walking down to the harbour, watching the boats coming and
going and playing on the beach with Sam and Beth.

The weeks rolled into months. Christmas came and went and,
with the start of a new year, my thoughts turned to the future. It
was time to get on with something. We were all getting along
okay as a family but it wasn't ideal scraping by on dole money.
Chris Mason from Polydor Records would often call. He was
doing regional promotion now and travelled around the UK,
calling on various radio stations.

'Walker, it's time you got back on the bloody radio instead of kicking your heels down there in Ramsgate. You should really go down and take a look at Radio West in Bristol. Your old mate Dave Cash is doing the programming down there. I bet he'd love to have you doing a show.'

I wasn't very keen; maybe I was too frightened to take on a new challenge. Being on the dole, turning up to sign on – it was all such a dispiriting experience and my confidence was at a very low ebb. It seemed an absolute age since I'd done a live radio show. Maybe I just couldn't do it any more. Chris, bless his heart, was not giving up that easily and kept up with the calls.

'Come on, Walker, you lazy bastard. Give old Dave Cash a call.'

He gave me the phone number and I promised him I would give it some serious thought. I finally plucked up the courage and made the call. I don't know whether Chris had prepared the ground, but Dave was full of enthusiasm about Radio West and the possibility of a show for me down there.

'Johnnie, come down and have a look around, I'm sure you'll love it,' he said.

So I decided, What the hell? I may as well go and see what's happening.

Dave, who'd made his name on pirate station Radio London with the legendary *Kenny and Cash* shows with Kenny Everett, was there waiting for me at Temple Meads Station. We zoomed through the city centre. Bristol seemed so spacious, big and bustling, full of life and such a contrast to sleepy old Ramsgate. He negotiated a small roundabout and headed up a narrow street into the dock area, pulling up at the rear of an old warehouse building. The whole dock area had been refurbished, yet retained the original charm of cobbled streets, and I loved it straightaway. Radio West was at the end of a long warehouse block that housed the Arnolfini Arts Centre. There were shops and cafés and a pedestrian walkway looked directly over the water. It was a great location.

Dave proudly gave me the tour of the modern studios on the ground floor and a vast open-plan office space upstairs where sales, admin and programming departments were located. He introduced me to all the staff, who were relaxed, open and friendly. The place had a very good vibe about it. I met Tony Kelly, a bearded Irish musician, producer and now presenter. He and Dave were good friends and together were doing an excellent sales job on both the station and the lifestyle that Bristol could offer.

'Come on back downstairs,' said Dave. 'Let me show you the engineers' workshop.'

Full of the usual paraphernalia of cables, soldering irons, old meters and stuff, the workshop occupied a small and discreet space right at the rear of the building.

'The least we could do is to give you a warm Radio West welcome,' said Dave as he produced a packet of Rizlas and starting rolling up a joint.

'Our little relaxation cubicle,' said Tony. 'No one will disturb us here.'

The joint was passed back and forth and we chatted away, catching up on our life and times since the old days on the North Sea and our drinking sessions in the onshore pirate hangout, the Red Lion off Curzon Street.

'Well, that's put a nice new perspective on the day,' said Tony. 'Do you think Johnnie's ready for our next surprise?'

'I reckon so,' said Dave as they grinned at each other, and we headed out of the convenient fire exit at the back of the workshop and out into the cobbled street.

It was less than a hundred-yard walk along the dockside before we came to a large ship moored against the harbour wall with roped gangways at either end. I followed them on board, round the deck and down a stairway that led into a vast lounge. We walked up to the bar.

'Three pints of Guinness, I reckon,' said Dave.

'I think so, Dave,' said Tony.

We clinked glasses.

'Johnnie, cheers! Welcome to the Lochiel, the finest floating pub you'll ever see, Radio West's official watering hole and the place where we tend to have all our meetings.'

A couple of pints later and I didn't need any further convincing that Bristol and Radio West was the place to be. Dave felt sure that managing director Chris Yates would support the idea of getting me on the team and, at the end of a really good day, Dave dropped me back at the station. I couldn't wait to get back to Ramsgate and tell Frances the good news: I was coming off the dole and going back on the radio.

A good future in the West Country beckoned.

Chapter Thirty-Five

1983

'This is the modern world.'

Paul Weller spat out the words with venom and aggression. The words followed the seven o'clock news every weekday evening on Radio West. I'd edited The Jam's record to create an opening jingle to my new show and it set the tone for the programme's mix of new, alternative music, together with news and features aimed at a younger, more student-based audience. Produced by a journalist from the newsroom, it had a harder, more direct style than other Radio West programmes. Tony Kelly used to refer to my interview technique as coming from the 'Johnnie Walker charm school', which he illustrated with a loud grunt followed by a pretend headbutt. There's no doubt my years in America had given me a more assertive style and the show was new and different, and making a great impact.

Frances had been pleased and relieved when I'd told her about my new opportunity at Radio West: at last, it looked like I might be on my way back, and anything was better than being on the dole. Not only that, but the package I'd been offered was a good one. We didn't want to uproot the children immediately, however, so we decided that I'd go to Bristol alone at first and stay with Dave Cash in his flat while I looked around for a place where we could all live. Once that was organized, Frances and the children would come and join me.

Dave's flat was up in Clifton, on the Royal Crescent, and I soon settled in there. I was loving being back on the air – being in front of a microphone again was a brilliant feeling – and I worked hard on preparation and research, but I also played hard. Suddenly, after a year languishing on the dole, I was the hot new guy in town with the money to score some grass and buy a drink whenever I wanted. There was only one problem. All of us at the station were caught up in some glamorous time warp that wasn't based in reality. We came on the air in the wake of a highly successful TV series; based in Bristol, it starred Trevor Eve as private detective Eddie Shoestring, who worked at a fictitious local station called Radio West. It was decided to adopt the same name for the real radio station, so capitalizing on a name already well known and established in the public's mind. MD Chris Yates swanned around town in an expensive two-seater Lotus sports car, but the business community was unimpressed and Radio West was never a well-run or profitable company. Everyone was too busy having a good time.

Meanwhile, Frances was phoning to find out what was going on and ask yet again when she and the children were going to be able to join me. Weeks had gone by, she was getting fed up and wondered what the hell was going on. I was making a great effort to find us a place and tramped around all the flat-letting agencies with absolutely no success. Every time I found the ideal place, the moment I gave them our details, I'd hear the words: 'Sorry, no children.' The answer lay in widening the search away from Clifton and Redlands and I finally found a three-bedroom house for rent in Brislington, a suburb just outside the city. The house was now owned by a vicar, the son of a couple who had lived there together for virtually all of their married life. According to the neighbours, they were a deeply devoted couple and did everything together. Sadly, the wife passed away after an illness and her husband, distraught and unable to face life without her, threw himself into Bristol docks just days after her death. The house was still full of their lives together: their furniture, their paintings on the wall, and their old clock on the mantelpiece.

It was three months after I'd started at Radio West that Frances and the children arrived at our new home. Although it had enough room and a garden, it wasn't somewhere we wanted to settle permanently, but the local school, which was excellent, was a big draw. It would more than satisfy us in the short term. We got two

The studio at KSAN, San Francisco

Me and Mick, looking rather pleased with ourselves

Elton hands over a Sony Gold Award for lifetime achievement

With Roger Daltrey, lead singer of The Who

With Ben E. King (and is that Brian Epstein in the background, maybe?)

Eric and I model our Christmas sweaters

Elaine Page and me at the Radio 2 Christmas dinner

Tiggy and me in Venice

A very happy couple at Ashmore
Church, Dorset

Sam on the back of my yellow
Harley-Davidson Fat Boy

A post–hospital hug from Beth

Me and 'Hedge', my HD
Heritage Softail Classic

Tiggy and me with Sam and Beth – MBE
day at Buckingham Palace

Proud dad Sam with my
grandson, James

I think maybe it's time to quit

Tiggy, looking very much at home in the Hotel Splendido, Portofino

Nashville singer Pat Green, me and Sally 'Traffic' Boazman

Celebrating forty years on radio in May 2006 – Fiona Day, Lynn Bowles, myself and Ralph Jordan

In Dorset, struggling to finish the book

Recuperating in Jamaica

Post-cancer – me with Tiggy and Fergus
in Dorset

Pure happiness – a day on a boat in Majorca

beautiful white cats after hearing that Curt Smith of Tears for Fears had a litter living in the bottom of his wardrobe, at his house in nearby Bath. But despite all of Frances's skill in making a house into a home, it wasn't feeling like *our* home. It was almost as if we were intruders there. I was convinced that the spirits of the previous couple were still hanging around.

I was in the small kitchen one Saturday morning and I felt we had to make a stand.

'You know, Frany, it's time we claimed this house for us. Okay, so it was theirs for many years and they knew great happiness here, but they've had their time. It's our turn now. We should take all their old paintings and pictures off the walls and start putting our own up. Make the place a bit more ours.'

A split second after I finished speaking, there was an almighty crash from the dining room, just next to the kitchen. We rushed in, wondering what the hell had happened as the room was empty. One of the large paintings that dominated the whole room was now standing on the floor. The hook was still firmly in the wall, the cord at the back of the heavy frame hadn't come undone. Amazingly, despite the huge crash the glass was perfectly intact with not the slightest crack.

It was a turning point. From that moment on, the entire atmosphere of the house changed. From being dense and heavy, it became lighter, happier. There was more laughter and now, at last, it felt like our home. The previous occupants had decided to leave, but not without making a statement of their displeasure at my telling them it was time to go.

Although Brislington wasn't the ideal place for Frances and me, Sam and Beth seemed very happy there. They loved the local school, where Beth was getting into playing table tennis, and it was great to feel like a normal family again, all living together. At Radio West, MD Chris Yates was getting his money's worth out of me and I was now doing two shows a day, *Modern World* at seven p.m. and a mid-morning show from ten a.m. till one p.m. One morning, the legendary medium and psychic Doris Stokes was my guest on the morning show. We talked for a while and then opened up the phone lines for callers to talk to Doris. A young housewife and mother came on the line and chatted for a while.

Doris then said, 'I've got your dad here, love. He's so happy to make contact with you like this. He wants you to know he's doing fine and he's very pleased with how well you're living your life. And he says for me to tell you, he's with you much more than you realize.'

'Really?'

You could hear the lump in the throat of the caller on the other end.

'He says you're sitting on the stairs and you've just kicked off one of your shoes. Is that right, love?'

'Yes, it is,' came the astonished reply.

'Well, he told me that, love, just to let you know he can be here with me but also with you at the same time. He's telling me there's something blue in the hall. What's that, then?'

'I don't know, Doris. There's nothing blue here.'

'Oh yes, there is, love, he's adamant about it. Now what's in the hall that's blue but is not usually there?'

'Oh my God,' said the caller. 'I couldn't see it from where I was but there's my husband's blue Black and Decker workmate here. He was using it in the front garden and meant to take it back to the garage but left it in the hall. That's just incredible.'

'There you are, dear,' said Doris. 'Spirits don't usually get it wrong.'

I put some music on and dashed upstairs to get a record I'd left on my desk. Upstairs, normally a scene of noise and bustle, was uncannily quiet. All work had stopped. Usually blasé about the station output, everyone was near a radio, fascinated by what was going on. No one wanted to miss a moment.

All phone lines into both the studio and main switchboard were jammed. I decided to keep Doris on into the next hour as I'd never known anything like it. Again and again, she demonstrated her amazing gift with callers taken at random from the hundreds who'd dialled in. It was only after the show that I met Doris's manager. It was my old mate Laurie O'Leary, who used to run the legendary Speakeasy Club on Mortimer Street back in the sixties. He was the last person I expected to be involved in the world of psychics but he believed Doris was something special and needed a bit of protection and looking after. There was a great deal of opposition to her work from the Church, and Christians had recently demonstrated outside her show at the London Palladium.

I asked Laurie what he thought about all this negative opposition.

'Oh, they're just bloody jealous because Doris can sell out the Palladium and the churches are empty. I think religions are just like any organization, like companies or unions, just interested in power and self-preservation.'

He told me Doris had felt a good connection with me and asked if I would consider being onstage with her and hosting her big show in Bristol that night. I took it as a great honour and agreed at once. We had a wonderful evening. Doris was so loved by the crowds who flocked to see her and, once again, she demonstrated her great gift of clairvoyance and her ability to connect people with loved ones now in the world of spirit.

About eighteen months after I'd joined Radio West, I got a call from a man called Ralph Bernard.

'Johnnie, I'd like you to consider coming to work for us at Wiltshire Radio.'

I was puzzled. Wiltshire Radio was a much smaller station — surely this was a step backwards.

'I'm flattered by the offer, Ralph,' I said, 'but why would I want to leave a big station in the media centre of the South West to come to your much smaller station with far fewer listeners?'

Ralph insisted that he was acting in my best interests and wasn't taking no for an answer.

'At least come up and have a look round. I'm certain it would be a good career move.'

I agreed to go and listen to what he had to say.

Ralph had moved from print journalism to Radio Hallam in Sheffield where he became head of news and produced an award-winning documentary on alcoholism called *Dying for a Drink*. He was now programme director and acting managing director at Wiltshire Radio. He showed me around the station, based in an old house in the small village of Wootton Bassett, just south of the M4. It was a far cry from the buzz and energy of Radio West's location in Bristol city centre. But there was something about the place that interested me, and Ralph's enthusiasm was infectious. He was convinced that I could develop more speech-based broadcasting skills and said that, if I were to move, I would do more interviews and some news presentation.

Ralph had developed a unique format and structure at Wiltshire Radio. Traditionally, music presenters and news journalists loathe each other and never really get on. Here they worked together and shared each other's jobs. DJs read the news headlines on the half-hour and the breakfast and drivetime shows were double-headed by a DJ and news journalist – although the term DJ was rarely used. We were now 'presenters'. Ralph did enough to convince me I should give serious thought to joining his station and I went back to Bristol to talk it over with Frances.

Frances agreed with me – the move seemed like a good idea. It was becoming obvious to us that Radio West was in a shaky way. The Independent Broadcasting Authority had recently forced the removal of the MD, and the future was not looking good. So I followed my intuition and formally handed in my notice. Staff at the station were incredulous, but I never regretted the move. I fitted straight into the scheme of things and relished the challenges of a more intelligent style of radio. Within a matter of months, Wiltshire Radio merged with Radio West and the two stations together became GWR. Not only was I now broadcasting to Wiltshire, I was also back on the air in Bristol as my programme was networked on both stations.

This was the beginning of my 'straight' period when I began wearing a suit to work and Ralph had visions of me becoming more involved in the overall planning of things, maybe rising to programme director and senior management one day. The only snag was my fondness for the Cross Keys pub just up the road.

With newsman Steve Brodie and others, we became some of landlord Len Sara's best customers. There would be the occasional 'lock-in' at two o'clock and, instead of being back at my desk planning future programmes, I would be knocking back pints of Flowers Original and glasses of port up at Lenny's. A former sergeant in the paratroopers, Len was one of life's great characters. He was a big fella with a heart to match and we became great friends and drinking partners. But when it came to my new life as a potential company executive, he was not a good influence.

'Got some of that Harvey's Special Port coming in, John, rare as rocking-horse shit, you're gonna love it.'

Word soon spread of the riotous Keys sessions and Ralph called me in for 'a little word'.

'I rather think you're spending a little too much time in the pub, Johnnie. In fact, I'm thinking of declaring the Cross Keys off limits for you.'

'That's a bit drastic, Ralph,' I said, with my best disarming smile, 'but I will try to have afternoon meetings here rather than there.'

Sessions were reduced for a while to one a week. Ralph couldn't fault me on the shows, though. They were going really well. I'd start at eleven a.m. with a general hour of music and the odd small feature, and at twelve I'd be joined by journalist James Cameron for the news hour. The normal behind-the-scenes news planning discussions were presented live on air, giving the listener an insider's view on how news gathering worked. Then there would be a degree of suspense and anticipation as James went off to try and line up the names in the news for a live interview later in the hour. It was ground-breaking stuff and well ahead of its time. Years later, the technique was used very successfully on television on Channel Five's news shows.

Every Wednesday my show contained an hour-long feature called 'The Fourth Dimension'. I'd gather unusual stories from esoteric sources like the *Fortean Times*, and there would be the occasional guest clairvoyant. This was pretty controversial stuff at the time. The Doris Stokes appearance on Radio West had caused quite a stir and the Radio Authority (in which the Church had a powerful voice) banned her from all commercial stations. As the public interest in life after death, reincarnation and psychic phenomena grew, so did the pressure from the authorities to keep such subject matters off the radio. The Radio Authority put a lot of pressure on Ralph to get me to stop. I told him I felt really passionate about it and, as there did seem to be growing listener interest and reaction, perhaps it was also good for ratings. He was really in a cleft stick on this one.

But we were now battling over something else. In order to work in a journalistic capacity, I had become a member of the NUJ, the National Union of Journalists. As I recall, an edition of Granada Television's highly respected *World in Action* documentary series was censored by Mrs Thatcher's Conservative government. The banning of the programme caused enormous uproar and all journalists and their unions in both print and electronic media called for a national one-day strike in protest.

There were meetings in newsrooms across the UK. Our father of chapel (shop steward) Steve Brodie met with Ralph, who agreed that GWR would not attempt to broadcast any news for that day. It really was the strangest day: on every television and radio station, there was absolutely no news whatsoever. At twelve o'clock on my show there would normally be a five-minute bulletin.

At midday I announced, 'It's twelve o'clock and the news today is that there is no news.'

I carried on playing records and then at twelve fifteen, head of news Linda Couch came into the studio with a tape cartridge and a sheet of paper.

'Ralph wants you to run this,' said Linda.

I was immediately suspicious.

'What is it?'

'It's a news item. Ralph says you're to run it.'

'But I thought it was all agreed that there would be no news at all today. I'm not going to use it.'

Linda stormed out and, within five minutes, was back.

'Ralph insists you are to run this item. I'm telling you to put it on air.'

'Well, I'm telling you, I'm not going to. Tell Ralph I categorically refuse.'

Linda's face turned a deep shade of red.

'Johnnie, you must run it. It's Ralph's direct order to you. There'll be big trouble if you don't.'

By now I was getting exasperated. This was a national no-news day right across the whole of the UK and Ralph was putting me in an impossible position. But Linda wasn't giving up.

'Johnnie, I'm telling you for the last time, you will run this news item.'

I'd had enough.

'Linda, you can tell Ralph to fuck off. And while you're at it, you can fuck off as well and leave me to do my show.'

I was boiling with anger and yet had to carry on playing records as if nothing was happening. I finished the show at one o'clock, went out of the studio and was walking through the newsroom when an announcement came over the tannoy.

'Will Johnnie Walker please report to Ralph Bernard's office immediately.'

Here we go, I thought. Well, if he wants a fight, he can bloody well have one. I knocked on the door and went into Ralph's office. He was sitting at his desk, glowering.

'Sit down, Johnnie,' he began his ranting speech. 'I've never been more angry with anyone than I am with you and your complete refusal to follow my instructions. You have challenged my authority as managing director of this radio station and blatantly disobeyed me. The entire staff is aware of what has happened and you have completely undermined my position here and made me look a bloody fool.'

My turn.

'Ralph, it's entirely your fault. Why the hell did you want me, the only person on this whole station, to run a piece of news when you had reached complete agreement with Steve Brodie and the NUJ that this was a day when there would be no news, no news at all? You've put yourself in this position – why, I don't know – and you've only yourself to blame.'

'Johnnie, you work for me, if I give you a direct order, it is your job to carry it out. You have blatantly and publicly disobeyed me. I have been in touch with the AIRC [Association of Independent Radio Contractors] and by disobeying me, you have broken your contract and I'm quite within my rights to fire you, right now this instant.'

'Go ahead, Ralph, fire me. It'll make a great story. I can see it on the front page of *The Sun* tomorrow: "DJ Johnnie Walker fired for refusing to break nationwide strike."'

He stared at me, I stared back. I hadn't a clue how to place a story with *The Sun* newspaper and there was no way they'd put such a story on the front page. But it was a good bluff and I think Ralph was rattled. It was a battle of wills and I was determined not to back down. The staring competition continued for well over a minute.

'It's a game of bluff, isn't it, Johnnie? You're gambling that I won't dare fire you.'

'Yes, I guess it *is* a game of bluff, Ralph.'

I was secretly rather enjoying the stand-off. This was like a really big game of poker and the stakes were high.

Ralph reached for the phone.

'Brenda, tell Steve Brodie to come in.'

Steve came in and sat down.

'Johnnie has totally disobeyed my orders, Steve, directly challenged my authority and I'm quite within my rights to fire him.'

'Well, you can fire him if you like, Ralph, that's your right – but I must tell you, the union will back him one hundred per cent and you may well have a much longer strike on your hands if you do.'

I was beginning to feel a little bit sorry for Ralph.

'All right, Steve, you can go.'

Steve left and Ralph and I went back to our staring competition. The room was silent. Finally Ralph stood up.

'I'm going for a walk in the garden.'

I remained seated and watched him pacing up and down outside. He eventually came back through the patio doors.

'Johnnie Walker, you're a fucking bastard and I hate you.' He reached down and opened the door of a cupboard in the corner. 'What will you have? A brandy or a scotch?'

'I think a brandy would be very nice, Ralph, thank you.'

He called Steve back in. We clinked glasses, drank each other's health and laughed. The stand-off was over and, from then on, our working relationship deepened. Perhaps Ralph now had a greater respect for me and he began to trust me with confidential ideas and plans for the future.

Oh, and by the way, he did allow me to continue having spiritual and psychic features on my programme.

Chapter Thirty-Six

1985–6

I was still commuting between Wootton Bassett and Brislington every day and we were keen to get out of rented accommodation. The problem was that Ralph wasn't sure whether GWR's network centre would be in Bristol or Bassett. The desire to find a home nearer to work was heightened by a journey home one evening.

It was winter and dark and the long stretch between junctions 16 and 17 was crowded with commuters keen to get home. I was in lane three, keeping up with the traffic flow at about eighty-five miles an hour. Suddenly, a hundred yards ahead, all hell broke loose.

A car swerved into the central reservation, tore up the crash barrier and ripped up an enormous cone-shaped lump of concrete that flew upwards and landed in the middle lane. Cars were now crashing into each other, with others swerving all over the place, taking to the hard shoulder to avoid the collisions ahead. It all happened in a split second, as these things do. All I could see ahead were red brake lights and other cars shooting by on the inside. I hit the brakes hard, thankful I'd left a decent space between me and the car in front. I came to a stop with just a few feet to spare.

Thank fuck for that, I thought. That was bloody close. Then I remembered the cars behind me. I looked in the rear-view mirror. A pair of headlights were coming towards me at incredible speed. Nothing I can do about this, I thought. I braced my arms against the steering wheel and my head against the headrest and waited. An instant later there was an almighty bang and my car was thrown forwards into the one in front. Everything stopped and suddenly, after all the screaming and the screeching of metal being ripped apart, there was silence. It was uncannily quiet.

I got out. My neck ached and I was wobbling a bit with shock but, apart from that, I seemed to be okay. My car, a GWR staff Triumph Acclaim, was a write-off and there was total chaos everywhere, with cars all over the road in various states of damage and people wandering about in a daze, some injured. The emergency services arrived almost at once, and began to deal with the situation. I watched from the hard shoulder as what was left of the car was craned on to a tow truck. The police took all the usual details, work crews arrived to tidy up the motorway and traffic started flowing again. Apart from the few cars left on the hard shoulder it was as if nothing had happened. I got chatting with a driver who'd stopped to see if he could offer help. He kindly gave me a lift to Brislington, where a very worried little family was waiting for me at home.

We had a babysitter booked that night as it was the GWR annual NUJ dinner. On previous experience, I knew it was an evening not to be missed. I was in two minds whether to go or not but decided it would be a good way to take my mind off the dreadful pile-up on the M4. We dressed for the occasion, took a taxi to the hotel and made a grand entrance. News of my narrow brush with death had spread and as we walked in, everyone took to their feet and gave us a standing ovation. It was a wonderful moment. We bowed and took our places at the table. Splendid food and copious amounts of wine were enjoyed by all and the evening descended into a drunken riot of appalling behaviour. But we had a great time.

The near-miss on the motorway was a catalyst to get us moving. Eventually Frances and I found a lovely old house in a sleepy Gloucestershire village near Cirencester, roughly halfway between Wootton Bassett and Brislington. The village was the northern point of a triangle equidistant with Bristol and Wootton Bassett, so it didn't really matter which place was chosen for the GWR network centre. When the removal lorry had left and we were on our own in our new home, I walked up the stone steps to the upper level of the garden and looked back at the house. After all the trials, tribulations and losses that had been part of our adventures

in America, the four of us were back together again in a home of
our own. I felt proud that I'd managed to get us back into roughly
the same position as we had been in back in 1976.

So why, then, was I getting this very strange feeling as I looked
back at the house? A thought impressed itself on my mind: 'You're
not going to be here very long at all.' I couldn't figure it out: I'd
only just moved in, I wanted to put down some roots and now
here I was, feeling as though this was just a step on the journey
towards a different destination. I didn't want that. I decided to just
put the thought out of my mind and pretend I hadn't had that
feeling. I was ready to feel more settled; I was now over forty years
old with two wonderful children and a great job. Beth and Sam
seemed happy and were growing up to be fine people.

However, the relationship between Frances and me was deteri-
orating. She still felt a lot of anger and bitterness towards me over
the past, and this wasn't a good basis for trust and intimacy. We
rowed all the time and the arguments dragged on until it was hard
to see where one stopped and another began. When things were
going badly at home, I sought affection elsewhere; Frances found
out and, once again, damage was done to our relationship. I wasn't
proud of it, but the more sour things became at home, the more I
craved warmth and companionship. It was a destructive cycle that
kept repeating itself and caused Frances to feel justifiable anger
towards me. Her additional resentment that this sleepy village
wasn't a patch on life in London fuelled tremendous rows between
us. It was a situation that I knew would eventually have to be
resolved.

One day something very weird happened. I'd done my daily show
at GWR as usual and hadn't even gone to the Cross Keys for
lunch. I was just sitting at my desk thinking of possible guests for
my Sunday interview programme, *Johnnie Walker Meets*, when my
mind was suddenly taken over by one thought: 'Go back to Radio
One.' It was like the opening sequence to a Monty Python episode,
as if the top of my head had been sliced open, the thought put in,
and the top put back on. This one thought drove out everything

else. It kept repeating in my head like some sort of mantra: 'Go back to Radio One, go back to Radio One.'

I started walking around the station with this thought sounding over and over in my mind. Eventually I began to accept it and, the moment I did, the feeling began to change. From 'Go back to Radio One', it now became 'I'm going back to Radio One'. I went back to my desk, feeling as though the words were flashing like a neon sign above my head. GWR and my life there suddenly looked small and limited; a new vista had been given to me and it felt so completely right. I decided the only thing to do was to grasp the bull by the horns and act upon the thought. I lifted the phone and dialled the old familiar number of the BBC main switchboard.

'Johnny Beerling, Radio One, please,' I said to the operator.

A female voice answered his extension. I did my best to sound calm, but inside I was feeling pretty wobbly.

'Hello, it's Johnnie Walker calling, I'd like to speak to Johnny Beerling please.'

'Hold on a moment.'

Seconds later, the Radio One controller came on the line. He sounded very cheery and actually pleased to hear my voice. We swapped the usual 'hellos' and 'how are yous'.

Then I said, 'Johnny, I thought it might be an idea to meet up for a chat. It's been a long time.'

'This is the weirdest thing, you calling out of the blue like this,' he said. 'I've been thinking about you. I've got something in mind I'd like to talk to you about. Can you come up on Thursday morning about eleven o'clock?'

It just so happened I had no programme that Thursday, because of local election reports.

'Okay, that's good for me, see you at eleven.'

It was all so natural and easy. After having accepted a life in regional radio, with no thoughts at all of ever returning to a national station, I had changed everything within twenty minutes. It was uncanny. I'm often accused by friends of reading too much into little things that happen. 'Oh,' they say, 'here he goes, wait for it, Walkerism coming up – it's a *sign*.' Well, I'm sorry, but this time there was a synchronicity going on that couldn't be denied.

In the event, Johnny Beerling's welcome couldn't have been warmer. He proudly gave me the tour of Egton House. Little had changed, except for one major difference. There had been some little-used production studios on the third floor. I once suggested to Derek Chinnery that we convert them to on-air studios and he mocked me for having the temerity to suggest such a stupid idea. Well, they were now indeed Radio One's own dedicated studios.

'That was one of the first changes I pushed through after becoming controller,' said Johnny. 'We're like a proper self-contained radio station now. This whole building is now Radio One.'

It was a really good change. I'd often felt stranded over in Broadcasting House, cursing myself if I'd left a record back in the office. Now it would be easy to run down the corridor, grab what you needed and be back in the studio before the end of the record playing on air. Brilliant.

My old producer from the one-hour morning show, Stuart Grundy, came over to shake my hand.

'Have a wander round with Stuart,' said Johnny, 'and come back to my office for a chat.'

Stuart was now an executive producer, responsible for several programmes.

'So where's the local watering hole now, Stuart? Is it still the Green Man or do you go round to the Yorkshire Grey?'

Stuart looked at me somewhat blankly.

'There isn't one, really. We tend to stay at our desks and have a sandwich. No one does lunches much any more.'

Hmmm. Not a good sign, I thought.

Back in Johnny Beerling's office, I listened while he outlined his idea. Radio One was still on the old medium wave or AM band with all its problems of poor-quality mono signal and interference from other stations at night-time. Radio Two had the use of the FM stereo transmitters, despite having a much smaller audience than Radio One. But on Saturday afternoons, Radio Two broadcast sport and Radio One 'borrowed' the FM frequency.

'We really have been wasting the FM capability,' said Johnny. 'Soon, more and more of the country will be able to get Radio One on our own stereo transmitters and I want to flag up all the advantages of FM to our audience. I'm planning a high-profile sequence that will run for four and a half hours from three p.m. to seven thirty p.m. It will contain a documentary, an American chart show, a live concert and we'll play high-quality album music. It's the kind of show you always wanted to do in the old days and I can't think of anyone more qualified to present it. I'd like you to consider coming back to Radio One. How about it?'

I couldn't quite believe what I was hearing. An FM rock show – the kind of radio I'd wanted to do, and that had got me in so much trouble in the seventies; the sort of programme I had been doing during my early days at KSAN in San Francisco. Now, here was Radio One asking me to present such a show. It sounded perfect, this was all too good to be true. I knew that when the formal offer came through, I would accept immediately.

Johnny gave the project to Kevin Hewlett, a highly skilled and meticulous producer, who was often given the task of launching new programmes. In October 1986, we secretly recorded a pilot programme at the studios of BFBS (Forces Radio) in Paddington. Kevin and I were both pretty happy with the pilot and I went back to my life with GWR to await developments. Some weeks later, an executive meeting was convened at Radio One. It was agreed that the concept of the stereo sequence was good and should go ahead, but there was disagreement over who should present it. Kevin and Johnny wanted me to do it; the others didn't, and were against the whole idea of me returning to Radio One. Finally, when no agreement could be reached, Johnny pulled rank.

'Well, I'm the controller of this network and I agree with Kevin. Johnnie Walker is the right man for the job, so he's coming back.'

What was good news for me was bad news for Ralph Bernard. I told him of the offer from Radio One and my desire to go back.

'Ralph, this is my last chance to return to national radio. If I don't take it, there won't be another one.'

'Johnnie, don't be hasty. I tell you what, do you like walking?'

'Well, sort of. Why?'

'Let's you and I get away from the office and all its distractions and on Thursday we'll go and walk the Ridgeway and have a chat.'

On Thursday, the skies were grey and ominous. It was pissing down with heavy rain and we trudged along Wiltshire's famous walkway in squelching wellies. Ralph was outlining all his ambitious plans for the future. He talked about a massive advertising campaign to relaunch GWR in Bristol.

'You'd be at the heart of the campaign, Johnnie. Huge posters of your ugly mug all along the M32 into Bristol. It's going to be huge and if you leave now, you'll bugger up all my big plans.'

'Ralph, I'm sorry for the timing and my throwing a spanner in the works. I've loved working for you and you've helped me develop new skills and become a better broadcaster. I don't want to be ungrateful, but I just feel this is a big opportunity and I would be crazy not to take it.'

'How much are they gonna pay you? Two hundred and fifty quid per programme top whack, I bet.'

I said nothing.

'There you go, I was right. How are you going to manage on that? I can throw more money in the pot for you here if you stay.'

'Ralph, it's not a question of money. You know I never let money come into a decision. It's whether it feels right or not, and this Radio One offer feels right.'

'I'll give you forty grand.'

'Makes no difference.'

We walked on. Every twenty yards or so, the dosh went up another ten grand. Finally we stopped, leant over a gate and cast our eyes over the view beyond. Ralph and I were playing another game of bluff; the stakes were high but this time he was determined to win.

'I suppose you're trying to tell me money's no object and no matter what I offer you, you'll still say no.'

'That's about the size of it, Ralph.'

'Walker, you're fucking mad, you really are.'

I laughed.

'Listen, I'll pay you seventy grand a year. That's more than I'm getting, for Christ's sake. Don't be so bloody stupid. You'll never get an offer like that from anywhere. Go home and talk it over with Frances.'

Maybe he was right, but he couldn't make me deviate from the course I knew was the one for me. Ralph knew that Frances would give the sensible advice to take such a generous offer. The trouble was, I was determined to go back to London and to Radio One. This caused huge problems at home. Frances and I hadn't been getting on very well for a while and now here I was planning to change it all again just when we'd got settled.

Our rows got more frequent and more heated. Early one morning we had an awful argument over breakfast, which ended with Sam and Beth leaving the house in tears. It was no way for two children to start their day. I felt so, so guilty and on my journey into work I realized there was no other choice. I knew I had to leave. On the way home that evening I called by a pub in Tetbury to see if they did bed and breakfast and arranged a weekly rate. I told them I'd be back later.

Then I went home and told Frances I was going to leave. I chucked a few clothes and belongings into a suitcase and went to talk to Sam and Beth. I tried to explain that I needed to live apart from them for a while as I just wasn't getting on with their mum. I promised them I would do my best to see them as often as possible and then I said goodbye to Frances and walked out of the front door.

We had been together on and off for sixteen years, had two wonderful children and had been through so much together. There was such a deep, strong love between us but we seemed incapable of maintaining a steady, harmonious relationship. I knew an awful lot of it was my fault, and I was truly sorry for the hurt I had caused her, but for both our sakes, and for the children, I knew we had to separate again.

It broke my heart to leave Sam and Beth. Next to losing my father, it was the worst emotional pain I had ever known. Sam had been my little rock in America. He had never complained or lost his gorgeous smile and love of life and people. Beth and I had grown very close after the two-year gap in our lives. Where Sam was the one with great intellectual abilities, Beth was the sensitive one and we had a strong, unspoken spiritual bond. I knew she would be crushed by my absence from her daily life and feeling her pain and unhappiness added to my own deep misery.

I hoped and prayed that the time I was missing with them now would somehow come back to me in the future.

Chapter Thirty-Seven

1987

The first stereo sequence went out on Saturday, 17th January 1987. After the Adrian Juste comedy hour, I went live on air on Radio One for the first time in ten years and introduced the sequence, which began at two o'clock with a documentary. At three, I began my part of the show and we opened up with Talking Heads' 'Radio Head' followed by Blue Oyster Cult's 'Don't Fear The Reaper'. After having been away so long, and conscious that I was launching a major new flagship programme, I was incredibly nervous. Kevin sat with me in the studio with the running order in front of him, constantly consulting his stopwatch. It was very different to the laid-back KSAN style and I felt tense and on edge.

At five, I had to move into the next-door studio for the American chart show, which featured a live link-up with presenter Laura Gross in Los Angeles. Radio One engineers had been in since one o'clock setting up complex technical procedures to eradicate the delay and so enable us to have a normal conversation without annoying pauses. Everything worked and, although it wasn't easy doing a two-way presenting job, we got through it okay. Then it was back to the original studio, another hour of mainly music, and then I introduced the final part of the sequence, a one-hour live concert till seven p.m.

Reaction to the show was good and I was soon in a regular routine of spending two or three days a week preparing the show and doing interviews, then broadcasting live on a Saturday afternoon. Jeff Griffin took over producer duties from Kevin Howlett, who, having successfully launched the programme, was now concentrating on new projects. Jeff and I got along really well. A lovely man with huge radio and music experience and knowledge of life, he'd roll into work around ten and then proceed to read all the daily papers. And then he would start to talk, and talk and talk. Hind leg off a donkey doesn't come anywhere near it; I soon learnt to shut off and it all went in one ear and out the other.

Then suddenly Jeff would announce, 'Right, Johnnie, we've got to go and do that interview now.'

'Interview? What interview? You never told me we had an interview today – blimey, I haven't done any research for it.'

Jeff would adopt his best tone of wearied resignation.

'Johnnie, I told you last week we had an interview today.'

'But, Jeff, you're always talking. How am I supposed to know when you're going to tell me something really important? Why don't you wear a hard hat in the office with a flashing red light? You could switch it on when something I really need to hear is coming up.'

We had a great time working together. Everyone in the radio and music business alike loved Jeff, and he was a wise and steadying influence on me.

I couldn't really afford my own place in London and old friends Harry and Cindy Barter were kind enough to let me stay in the top room of their house in Ealing and Harry, once again, guided my career as manager. He got me a nice little earner fronting up the US edition of the *Wired* TV music show. It involved dashing around London doing links to camera standing in front of all the usual landmarks like Big Ben and Tower Bridge. We'd tape about three shows' worth of links in one day and I was constantly getting in and out of our van, changing outfits. I got all the money up front and, following Harry's bricks and mortar advice, put down a deposit on a little flat in Colville Terrace, just off the Portobello Road in Notting Hill.

I was also doing the occasional programme for Radio London, the BBC station for London. I interviewed a great character called Richard La Plante, then husband of the writer Linda La Plante. A karate master, he once walked across America barefoot and was also a huge Harley-Davidson fan. He parked his black Sportster in the mews at the back of the station and after the show he proudly showed me the bike.

'Take it for a spin, Johnnie, you'll love it.'

I hadn't ridden a bike since owning a 175cc Honda in the early seventies. I was instantly hooked and became determined to get a Harley. I enrolled with a training school, passed my test and went straight round to legendary Harley dealer Fred Warr on the King's Road and rode away on a second-hand red Sportster. It was just the best way to get around London. I made a lot of new friends and we'd meet up at a café on the King's Road and go off for the day on rides out. It helped keep my mind off how much I missed the children and not being a part of their everyday life.

If I hadn't been so keen to take up any offer from Radio One, maybe I could have negotiated a better financial deal than the one I had. I was being paid a programme fee of £250 despite spending three, sometimes four days working on the show. I was sending money down to Frances and the children and trying to keep up the monthly payments on two mortgages. Interest rates were going up and things were getting pretty desperate. I got away with alternate mortgage payments for a while – one month Gloucestershire, the next month London – but soon the arrears mounted up. Harry's advice was to sell the Harley and hang on to the flat. I thought about it for all of five minutes. Riding my Harley gave me huge pleasure; I decided to keep the bike and let go of the London flat. I found a cheap little basement to rent, cleared my stuff out of the Colville Terrace place and went down to the Halifax Building Society in Berkeley Square.

I went up to the cashier's window.

'I'd like to give you the keys of your new flat,' I said, sliding the keys under the glass partition.

I was asked to take a seat and wait for the manager. She eventually appeared and informed me that my action did not absolve me from the arrears. I would have to sign all the relevant documentation and then ownership would revert to the bank and they could sell the flat to regain their money. Fine by me. I signed whatever they wanted and that was that. The flat is probably worth well over a million by now, but there was no way I would have been able to hang on to it, not without risking the family home. I had promised Frances that, whatever happened, I would make sure she and the children could stay in their home.

We had now agreed that our separation was permanent, and we began arranging for a divorce. It was a very sad time and for long periods I didn't see Sam and Beth anywhere near as much as I wanted. A divorce always has its pain and it would take some time before we could begin to put that behind us and rebuild our relationship. Still the money problems piled up. There was tax due on my freelance earnings and I hadn't put the money aside. It was tough enough getting by on what I had without trying to save some for tax.

Then I got a call from Harry Barter.

'Richard Branson's starting a new satellite radio station called Radio Radio and they're offering you big money to leave Radio One and join them. We should get together and talk about it.'

Richard's idea was to offer an overnight service for all the independent local radio stations around the UK. They could take any or all of the programmes, which would run from ten p.m. till six the next morning. They'd already signed up big names like Jonathan Ross and Ruby Wax and they were offering me something like £70,000 to sign for one year. That was Ralph Bernard sort of money, enough to solve all my problems. Harry and I had a meeting with MD Rob Jones and we went away to talk about the deal and decide what to do. I was reluctant to leave Radio One again, especially after Johnny Beerling had stuck his neck out to get me back. I'd been there only eighteen months and I loved it, but I couldn't cope on what they were paying me.

There was something about Radio Radio that didn't feel right, but then anything Richard Branson touched seemed to turn to gold. So what was I worrying about? For the first time in my life I made a career decision based solely on money. Harry and I went into their office to sign the contract. As we were walking in, workmen were coming out carrying furniture and office equipment.

I said, 'Harry, this is not a good omen. I don't like the look of this.'

A smiling Rob Jones greeted us from a bare office with one telephone on the carpeted floor.

'Hi, guys. Come on in. Sorry about the mess but don't worry, we're just moving across the road to a bigger place.'

I still had a weird feeling about the whole thing but I felt it was too late to turn away now and, after sorting out various details, I signed the contract. Now I had to go round to Radio One and inform Johnny Beerling.

'Johnny, I've got some sad news . . .'

'Don't tell me, you're leaving to join Radio Radio.'

His grapevine was obviously very good.

I said, 'I'm very sorry, Johnny, I've just signed a contract with them. I couldn't manage on what you were paying me.'

'You should have come in for a chat. We could have worked something out.'

I really should have. I felt very ashamed that I hadn't come to see him. I'd made a big mistake, but now it was all too late.

'I just hope the cheques don't bounce,' were his parting words.

I stopped by Radio Radio's new offices off Charlotte Street a couple of days later. There was a reassuring buzz going on and it was good to see familiar faces like freelance producers Phil Ward Large, Chris Vezey and Christine Boar there from Radio One. Other names on the production side included Chris Evans, John Revell and Carole McGiffin. Also signed up for shows, though not there that day, were Bob Harris, Nicky Horne, Phil Kennedy and soul-music freak and snooker champion Steve Davis. At six o'clock Rob Jones suggested we all go off for a meal as a sort of celebration and 'getting to know each other' exercise. We trooped into an Indian restaurant on Charlotte Street and Rob took charge, calling over the waiter and ordering wine and beers.

We had a very good evening but then, as the dishes were cleared away, Rob muttered something about having to go off to a meeting.

'Terribly sorry, got to dash. You guys carry on without me, see you in the office tomorrow,' he said, and with a cheery wave, he was gone.

We had coffees, chatted on for a while and made ready to go. The waiter came over and put the bill on the table. It was well over a hundred quid.

'This hasn't been taken care of by the gentleman who left earlier?' I asked.

'No, sir, it hasn't.'

After definitely intimating he was taking us all out for a meal, Jonesy had done a bloody runner. There were long faces round the table. Most of those present wouldn't have come into such an expensive place if they'd known they were going to have to share the tab. I felt very sorry for them and put a credit card down.

'I'll sort it with him tomorrow.'

Rob never did cough up for the dinner, though, and it was just the first example of a management technique the like of which I'd never seen before, or since. From one day to the next, we never knew what the hell was going on. According to Rob, we had over twenty stations signed up, then we found out it was barely a dozen. The producers were expected to be in the office during the day and then produce the live transmission in the early hours of the morning.

As more stations did sign up, the problems increased. Every individual station programme director had their own idea of music content and style of approach and it was a total nightmare. Sometimes one programme director is one too many – twenty was a recipe for complete mayhem. There was constant bitching and griping and, in the end, I just lost heart with the whole thing and wished desperately I'd never left Radio One. Roger Scott, one of the best music and on-air jocks we've ever had in the UK, had taken over the slot, glad to leave the restrictions of tightly formatted Capital Radio. His wife told me every time Roger got home from a show, he'd be grinning from ear to ear.

'It's radio heaven. Why Johnnie Walker would ever want to leave such a show is beyond me,' he would say.

I was beginning to agree with him. We broadcast the Radio Radio shows from BFBS in Paddington; their studios were unused at that time of night and they were glad of the extra business. I presented a straightforward music show from midnight till two in the morning, and I can't say I enjoyed it. It was turning into a miserable summer, but I'd made my choice and now I'd have to see it through.

I'd only been at the station a few weeks when I started to get written warnings of petty contract infringements, things like being five minutes late for rehearsal, smoking cigarettes in the studio and then finally one for smoking a joint in the engineers' workshop. That was the fourth; the next one would be written dismissal with no severance pay. When it arrived on my desk, I wasn't surprised, or particularly upset. I'd had the sense for some time that something was going on. It was becoming obvious that the station bosses had signed up as many well-known names as possible to launch their new venture and to lure in the independent stations, then planned to shed them. Gradually everyone around me was leaving or being fired, so I got my things together and left without any sense of regret. I was better off out of it.

Johnny Beerling was so right: all that promise of a fantastic amount of money and, in the end, they cancelled the contract with no pay-off.

Chapter Thirty-Eight

1988–95

I didn't have time to feel depressed about losing another job – opportunities seemed to be thick on the ground. My brief stint at Radio Radio had hardly lasted the summer but, by the autumn of 1988, I was back on air with my own show.

Good fortune prevailed in the shape of a revamp of the BBC local station for London. Matthew Bannister was brought in to change everything radically, including the name, and so, in 1988, Radio London died and GLR was born. It was to be a hip new station for sophisticated Londoners in the 25–45 demographic. I was approached to join, along with Tommy Vance (an old mate who'd briefly worked with me on Caroline) plus Annie Nightingale, Emma Freud, Nick Abbott and Dave Pearce. Producers included names from Radio Radio – Chris Evans, John Revell and Chris Vezey, who put together some really good all-music tapes to be run for the test broadcast. Journalists started commenting in the tabloid entertainment pages that the GLR test broadcasts were the best radio going. I remember saying to Tommy Vance that if they thought the non-stop music was so good, we'd be on to a loser when we started broadcasting properly.

In October I started a weekly lunchtime show that ran from twelve till three o'clock. They were really good days: starting a new station is always a great buzz as everyone is so enthusiastic and keen to make it all work. We had guests and live music sessions and, after the dreadful times at Radio Radio, it was fantastic to enjoy doing radio again. Producers, researchers, news people – we were a very close-knit team, all enjoying working hard to make the new station a success. In the evenings, there'd always be a gang of us in the pub having a real laugh together.

I had two really good years at GLR. Emma Freud had left and I now presented the mid-morning show from ten till one. And then, out of the blue, I was approached by Jude Howells, a producer from a BBC department that mostly made programmes for Radio Four. They had been commissioned to do a daily programme for the brand-new national BBC network, Radio Five. I'd heard Five was going to concentrate on sport, some science and programmes for schools, so I couldn't understand why on earth they would want me to do programmes for them. The idea was for me to present a show called *The AM Alternative* – a sort of Radio One and a Half meets a younger Radio Four. Jude wanted me to do Mondays, Wednesdays and Fridays, while Angela Rippon would present Tuesdays and Thursdays. There would be a huge team of producers, researchers and reporters working on the show and it would be quite unlike anything I had done before.

Something new always gets my creative juices flowing – and there was the added incentive that I would be heard not just in London but the whole of the UK again. I struggled with the choice for a few days and then made up my mind to accept the Radio Five offer. Now I had to go and talk to Matthew Bannister. I explained how much I had enjoyed being in at the launch of GLR but, now that the station was well established, I would like to take up Radio Five's offer. It was another chance to be in at the birth of a brand-new station and I wanted to go for it.

Matthew Bannister looked at me in complete shock.

'But, Johnnie, you can't possibly leave us.'

'Why on earth not? I've helped you get GLR going, now I'm being offered another challenge on a national network. Surely you can understand it's a good career move for me?'

'Johnnie, you mustn't leave GLR. It would send all the wrong signals to the staff and be terrible for morale here.'

GLR, like Radio London before it, seemed to be under permanent threat of imminent closure or change. Audiences loved the station but the ratings were terrible and the commercial lobby constantly accused the BBC of wasting the excellent frequency and signal. Matthew and I argued back and forth and seemed to be getting nowhere, but eventually Matthew came up with a plan. As my Radio Five show would be three mornings a week, perhaps I would consider doing a daily show from seven till nine in the evening, where I could have complete musical freedom to play whatever I liked? Canny Matthew: he knew exactly what would tempt me to stay. I told him I'd check with Radio Five to see what they thought. Five were slightly concerned that eight shows a week might be too big a workload but, in principle, they had no objection to Matthew's plan. And so, somewhat reluctantly, I let Matthew persuade me to stay on at GLR.

Radio Five began broadcasting in August 1990. I have enormous admiration and respect for controller Pat Ewing, who, with very limited resources and time, set up and established a ground-breaking new radio network. Its style and tone were unique and her adventurous spirit opened the door for radical new programmes and presenters, many of whom were eventually poached by Radios One and Four. *The AM Alternative* took a little while to bed itself in, partly because separate teams produced each programme, making continuity across the week difficult, but I enjoyed this new style of presentation and, within a few months, I was offered all five shows. As radio goes, it veered a bit too much on the 'straight' side for me but fortunately I had the contrast with the GLR evening show. There I could be more myself and I was having the time of my life. I was playing eight-minute Neil Young tracks like 'Over And Over' from the *Ragged Glory* album and having huge fun on the phones.

Most of the other BBC local radio stations had up-to-date equipment; at GLR, our stuff was really old. But we got a beautiful sound from the old analogue broadcast desk and I discovered a new trick with the antiquated phone system. Ten lines were con-trolled by a box within easy reach. The top row of keys was for answering each call off air. Putting the top key down would put the call on hold and the key on the row beneath would put the call through the desk and on the air. One evening, I discovered by accident that if I just flipped down the lower key, the call was put straight on air. Wow, this could be serious fun. Calls were supposed to be answered by a producer in the control room next to the studio. They would find out what the caller wanted to say and judge whether they could be trusted to go live. Then the producer would hang up, ring them back and set them up to go on the air.

Instead, every ten minutes or so I'd announce, 'Lines are open for your calls' and within thirty seconds all lines would be flashing. The caller would hear the usual ringing tone and then, without any warning, they'd hear me say, 'Hi, this is GLR, you're live on air.'

Of course we got loads of nutters and loonies, but that was all part of the fun. I could spot 'em straight away and always had one hand on the fader to cut them off in a split second in case they went too over the top. In all the hundreds of calls I put straight to air, the worst word broadcast was 'pissed'. In commercial radio, phone-in shows work on a seven-second delay, giving producers plenty of time to dump a caller if necessary.

No one had ever done phone calls like this and the listeners loved it – it was so spontaneous and off-the-wall, it was compulsive listening. Matthew Bannister was not amused and called me to his office.

'Johnnie, you've got to stop putting callers straight to air. It's absolutely against BBC policy.'

'But it's real live radio, Matthew, and no one's ever abused it. They respect what's happening and the fact I trust them.'

'I don't care, it's got to stop.'

'But I only agreed to stay because you promised me freedom to do the show the way I wanted.'

'You know damn well I meant freedom on the music. No more answering calls on air and that's that.'

I didn't do any calls that night, as I knew he'd be listening, but gradually I began to put them live on air again. One night I mentioned I could murder a pint of Guinness. Twenty minutes later a burly biker walked in the studio with a full pint of Guinness. His name was Dave, he ran a small courier company and had been listening in his office. How on earth do you deliver a pint of Guinness on a motor cycle? He had, of course, parked his bike outside and bought a pint from the pub across the road. Very enterprising.

We had a chat on air and I raised the glass to drink his good health and to toast life in Great Britain without Maggie Thatcher. She was over in Paris and had failed to secure the necessary majority to keep her position as Conservative party leader. She had vowed to fight on but the word was out that she didn't stand a chance and her thirteen-year reign was over.

'Can you imagine life without Maggie Thatcher? Some people have never known another prime minister. There're going to be street parties all over the country.'

A few days later Matthew Bannister called. He wanted a meeting. I suggested tomorrow or Wednesday and he said no, it must be this afternoon, in a small, virtually unknown BBC tearoom in Broadcasting House. We met at four o'clock.

'I have some bad news, Johnnie. You have flagrantly defied my instructions about putting live phone calls on air, you had a pint of Guinness delivered to the studio and you suggested there would be street parties and national celebrations when Mrs Thatcher was no longer prime minister. Therefore, I have decided to terminate your contract with GLR. You can consider yourself fired.'

This was a bolt from the blue.

'But, Matthew, it wasn't that long ago you were begging me to stay. "Be bad for morale" and all that, if I left.'

'Yes, I know all that, but there have been complaints. You have to go.'

'All right. When will I do my last show?'

'Johnnie, you've done your last show. You won't broadcast on GLR again.'

Now I was seriously pissed off. I hated the idea of disappearing without some kind of farewell. Matthew knew he could trust me to leave in a professional and dignified manner, but he was denying me that opportunity.

He said, 'Someone else will do your programme tonight. Pack your stuff and go.'

And that was that. Matthew had abruptly chucked me off the station. Perhaps he was fine-tuning his skills as a career executioner in readiness for the big challenge that lay ahead at Radio One.

As the GLR door closed, another was about to open. After I'd given up the stereo sequence on Radio One in 1988, Roger Scott had moved from London's Capital Radio to take over the show. He did it brilliantly but illness intervened. He was diagnosed with lung cancer and, despite a brave fight, he tragically lost his battle with it in 1991. Richard Skinner took over the show and then, to my complete surprise, Johnny Beerling got in touch with me to ask if I would consider going back to my old job. Absolutely I would. It was so good to know he'd forgiven me for going off to Radio Radio.

I carried on with the Radio Five show that I was enjoying so much, which meant three hours on air on a weekday. In addition, I broadcast the stereo sequence for four hours on a Saturday afternoon. It kept me hugely busy but it was absorbing and enjoyable radio and I was in my element. Despite what had happened at GLR, I was back in the BBC family.

It was a family undergoing radical change. John Birt was now director general and introduced the internal marketplace. BBC departments would now charge for everything and producers would be free to buy their skills and services, or go outside the BBC for production facilities. More and more BBC programmes were going out to independent production, and I'd been thinking for a while about starting up my own company. Before leaving as controller of Radio One, Johnny Beerling tipped me off that the Saturday-afternoon show could go to an indie. Phil Ward Large and I quickly formed a company called Wizard Radio, wrote up a proposal and sent it in to the new controller, one Matthew Bannister. We pitched up at his office in black jeans, engineer boots and leather jackets looking like we meant serious business. We pitched Wizard's plan for the Saturday show and, to our great delight, we were awarded a year-long contract with the promise of a rollover for a second year if the programmes were satisfactory.

Wizard rented a small office in the Canalot Building, Kensal Road, West London. The place was full of units housing small creative businesses and it had a great atmosphere. And so began a year enjoying the freedom, challenge and opportunity of independent production. We recorded great sessions with Thom Yorke and Jonny Greenwood from Radiohead, as well as Dodgy, Gun, Rumpelstiltskin, David Gray, Soul Asylum and many others. We got exclusive interviews with Bob Seger and Kate Bush and were the first BBC show to broadcast live from the now-famous South By South West Festival in Austin, Texas. We also did a couple of shows live from Nashville.

It was heady and exciting stuff and gave me a taste of the kind of control over my shows that I'd always longed for. It seemed to be a successful format that appealed to the listeners and, at the end of year one I was given verbal assurances by Matthew Bannister and Andy Parfitt (now radio controller) that our contract would be renewed for another year. On the strength of that, we moved into bigger offices, which included our own studio space for recording, and waited for the contract that we were assured was on its way.

Meanwhile, Harry Enfield and Paul Whitehouse's portrayal of 'poptastic' DJ's Smashy and Nicey had had a profound effect on Radio One. One by one, Simon Bates, Bruno Brookes, Gary Davies and Mike Read were all given their marching orders. Dave Lee Travis famously resigned on air from his Sunday-morning show and the cumulative effect of all these changes meant that Radio One began losing millions of listeners at an alarming rate. Most would agree that Radio One was in need of modernization but it was the rapid speed of the changes that turned listeners off.

Producer Chris Lycett assured me that I was safe, that Radio One didn't consider me to be in the Smashy and Nicey mould. That was all very well, but I was now several weeks into a new twelve-month period of independent production and, despite constant verbal assurances, I still had no written contract.

For all I knew, I might be making programmes for which I'd never be paid.

Chapter Thirty-Nine

It was March 1995 and the occasion of my fiftieth birthday. The last few years had been some of the busiest and most productive of my life and I was proud of what I'd achieved, particularly with Wizard Radio. We had a really good team and we made excellent radio shows.

I was expecting to meet a few friends in a restaurant for a birthday dinner when my mate Adrian Williams called and asked me to drop by Sony for a quick birthday drink before my night out. When I got there, he said he had something to show me and led me into Sony Music's restaurant and function room. The place was heaving with people and, as I walked in, they burst into a huge round of applause. I was immediately hauled onstage to be confronted by well-known radio producer and executive Tim Blackmore. He was holding a red book and did his best Eamonn Andrews routine.

'Johnnie Walker, you thought you were meeting one or two friends for a quiet evening meal, but tonight – *this is your life!*'

The Wizard team had pulled out all the stops and a succession of amazing guests turned up. Roger Cook was there all the way from Nashville; Johnny Beerling strode onstage to relate one of many stories about our time together; and then on strode Matthew Bannister. He proceeded to go way over the top with his tribute to me.

'Johnnie Walker is one of the finest broadcasters in the country and I am proud and honoured to be head of a network that he is on. As long as I'm in charge at Radio One, there will always be a place for Johnnie Walker.'

It sounded like my future was secure, but somehow I didn't feel convinced. Sure enough, only a week or two later, I got a call from Matthew Bannister.

'Johnnie, we're making some changes to Saturday afternoons and we won't need Wizard to produce any more shows. Jo Whiley will be taking over the slot.'

'Oh, really? How interesting,' I replied. I had suspected as much by now, but it was still a shock. 'And when will you be making these changes?'

'In two weeks' time.'

He hung up.

Bastard, I thought. What an absolutely bloody bastard.

That was now the second time he'd fired me. The first time there was no notice, and now there was just two weeks. I had premises, staff, bills to be paid and, in two weeks, no more money.

Then the truth began to emerge. Bannister had foolishly taken Steve Wright off his hugely successful afternoon show and put him in the breakfast slot to try and stop haemorrhaging listeners. Steve's style didn't really work early in the morning and now Radio One was losing millions of his afternoon listeners. Steve left and soon joined Radio Two.

Matthew decided that Chris Evans was the man to save Radio One. At GLR, Chris had moved from producer to doing his own show and he was brilliant on air. He was bursting with innovative ideas and his show was fresh and new. Matthew began courting Chris for the Radio One breakfast show. Chris knew Matthew was desperate for him to sign up and that he, Chris, could name his own figure. How about a million a year? It was an awful lot of money for a BBC network to find. Bannister raided every Radio One budget he could find in a desperate attempt to raise the loot. My independent production must have been an easy target, hence the lack of notice.

We checked Wizard's current account. There was enough to give the team a couple of months' money each, pay off the bills and wind down the company. I should have done. Instead we carried on in the hope of securing other BBC commissions but, within a few months, the money was gone. I gave the team the bad news, paid them what I could and then settled all the accounts with the small local businesses we owed money to. Now the only creditor was the local council for the business rates. I decided the only answer was voluntary liquidation; for two thousand pounds, Wizard Radio was wound up. We'd reached the end of the road.

Now I was unemployed and had to find some work. I called my old friend Ralph Bernard and soon joined the likes of Paul Burnett and Dave Lee Travis on GWR's Classic Gold Network on the AM band. I went up the M1 to Dunstable each Saturday lunchtime for my show from midday to two o'clock, which was heard on twenty or so stations all over the UK. I also managed to get hired by LBC, the London news and talk station, and presented Saturday and Sunday breakfast shows from six till ten a.m. There was no music at all and it was a big challenge not to have a record on standby for when I ran out of things to say – but I really began to enjoy talk radio. My good friend Alan Freeman used to call me up and congratulate me on the shows. He was always up early and a keen listener to the station.

Although I enjoyed my work, I couldn't help feeling that I was, to some extent, in radio wilderness. Then I heard that someone at the BBC had studied Radio Two's listening figures and had done an audience projection into the future. At current levels, the Radio Two audience would continue to decline until about 2015 when, finally, the last listener would switch off the lights and die of old age. What about all those millions of disaffected Radio One listeners? I wondered. Surely the time must come when Radio Two decided to change and appeal to a younger audience – those who'd grown up with the Beatles and the Stones, the post-war baby boomers whose vast numbers were being ignored by BBC Radio. I was interested to see what would happen.

Cancer had taken my father from us in 1980 and now, in 1996, it struck the Dingley family again. My brother John developed a cancerous growth in his colon. He had an operation and the surgeons were confident they'd got it all and he'd be okay.

John and his wife had emigrated to Canada many years before and I hadn't seen much of him in recent times. I flew over to Vancouver for a visit and we had a great week together with his wife Ann and children Sean and Trudi. We all went to the Molson Indy Car Race in downtown Vancouver. They closed the streets and made a temporary motor-racing circuit. John, Sean, Trudi and I went on all three days of practice, qualifying and then the race itself. The only downside was the obvious pain John was still in.

A little while later, I went back over to Canada with my sister Maureen to help out as John was to undergo a week of intensive chemotherapy and radiation treatment. I drove him to the hospital each day, as slowly and carefully as possible, because each bump in the road gave him terrible pain. He and Ann had not asked the doctors for full information about his condition. They had decided that, after his treatment, he would have another scan and they would take it from there. I found the most senior staff member I could and explained that as I lived in London it would be very helpful to me to know exactly how ill my brother was. She wouldn't give me any information, explaining that one of the few areas of control a cancer patient had was knowledge of their condition and it would not be ethical for her to tell me any more.

At the end of the week Maureen and I flew back to England. John had a raised temperature and was to spend the night in the small local hospital just down the road. I didn't know then that the lack of white blood cells after chemo means that the slightest infection is extremely dangerous. Trudi seemed to sense something was wrong and she desperately wanted me to stay. I so wish I had. A week later my brother was dead. It is one of my greatest regrets that I didn't cancel everything and stay in Vancouver. None of us had any idea just how advanced the cancer was: it was everywhere – in his liver, his pelvis and bone marrow.

Maureen, Michael and I went back to Vancouver for his funeral. As family, we were allowed into the chapel before the service and we were all shocked to discover his coffin was open. There was my hero, still and at peace, with his comb in the top pocket of his shirt as it always was when he was alive. Michael and his wife Jane found it very hard, but I knew John wasn't there. His spirit was alive and well and my diary entry for the day he died was: 'Brother John flies like an eagle.' I felt his presence so strongly as the funeral cortège journeyed from the chapel to the graveyard. He was in a magnificent long grey limo. I was travelling in a car behind and watched as all the lights seemed to be green and we cut a fine dash through Port Coquitlam. In my mind, I sensed John saying: 'Look at this motor, bro, what a way to go! This limo's just like the one Elvis had.'

My mum was too poorly to make the journey to Canada. She was devastated by John's death and told me she never expected one of her children to go before she did. I vowed that, come what may, I would be with my mum when her turn came. She suffered terribly from osteoarthritis and was virtually bed-bound in her little flat in Hampton-in-Arden. She had done so much in her role as a councillor to make sure sheltered accommodation was built for the elderly people of the village. In return, social services made sure she was well looked after and she had very good helpers, who visited often, especially a wonderful woman named Sue.

On visits to my mum, I gently raised the subject of what lay ahead. She told me she was convinced she would see Dad again and I told her that I believed the world of spirit was a beautiful place and that her life would be so much better there. I felt she was ready for the ultimate 'letting go'. It was as if John's passing had paved the way and given her permission not to fight on any longer.

Just a few weeks after John's funeral, Sue the carer called me to say Mum wasn't feeling too good at all. I told her I would be there right away. I was halfway up the M1 when Sue called me on my mobile.

'Peter, I think you'd better come straight here.'

'I'll be there in about forty minutes. Tell Mum I'll be there soon.'

I arrived at ten o'clock that evening and spent some special time with Mum. It gave Sue a break and she took over again at about midnight while I went to rest on the sofa. At about four a.m. Sue shook me awake. 'I think your mum's gone.'

I went into her bedroom, there was Mum, propped up in bed by pillows on either side. Her face was grey and lifeless. She had indeed passed on, almost exactly a month since John's death in Vancouver.

We said a prayer for her and the next morning I called Maureen, Michael and Christine to tell them the sad news; then called the undertaker to make the arrangements. Sue was wonderful and such a great help. I decided to walk up the hill to the parish church where Dad was buried. A service had just started, so I sneaked into a pew at the back and did my best to sing along with the hymns. I felt shattered and, as the service ended, I let go and began sobbing. After being away for both my dad and brother's passing, I was relieved that I had managed to honour my vow to be with Mum at such a profound time. Now it was all over, my strength was gone and I was exhausted. The other churchgoers that morning were so kind. They all knew my mum, of course, and were understanding and supportive.

I'm very grateful for the experiences I have had that have taught me that death is not the end, just the beginning of the next chapter in one's eternal existence. The Ouija board experience started off the search, and I explored Native American history and philosophy. Trusted psychics and clairvoyants have also deepened and strengthed my knowledge of the unseen world of the spirit.

Many years after my mother's death, by chance, I visited a clairvoyant I had never seen before. She mentioned a spirit she'd been aware of all day, so keen was the person to make contact. It was dear old Mum, who wanted to pass on her thanks.

'Please tell him he was so right in what he said. This is such a beautiful existence. I have never known such freedom and peace.'

Chapter Forty

1997

There was the usual Friday crush of drinkers spilling out on to the pavement outside the Crown and Sceptre pub just one block away from Broadcasting House. Known as the 'Hat and Stick' to BBC drinkers, it was a favourite haunt, especially on a Friday evening. It was like a madhouse inside, with a blaring jukebox and a crush to get to the bar. I was glad to get outside when I was suddenly accosted by a rather portly gent, with a round, jolly face.

'You know what, Johnnie,' he said. 'I always think you missed your vocation in life. You would have made a wonderful bingo caller. Maybe it's not too late. I'd be happy to put a word in if you think it would help.'

'Well, that's very kind of you,' I replied. 'Shame you weren't around earlier in my life when such guidance would have been so helpful.'

He grinned, extended a hand and said, 'Hello, I'm Jim Moir from Radio Two. It's very nice to see you.'

I knew very well who he was, of course, but was surprised he recognized me.

'Listen, all joking aside, old son, I just want to say I'm very aware of you and your work and have great respect for your broadcasting skills. You take good care, old son.'

And with that, our chance meeting was over.

I had wondered when I might meet the man who had been a legend in his time as head of light entertainment at BBC television, and who had now been brought in to revitalize Radio Two. He had put down a marker for change by bringing in Steve Wright on Saturday mornings but, despite the compliment he'd paid me, he gave me no indication that I might feature in his plans. Quite the reverse: I understood 'take care' to mean 'good luck without us' and felt pretty crushed as I slowly walked home. With my father, brother and mother gone, life felt empty and impermanent and I seemed to be constantly moving.

Eventually I found a place I was able to settle for a while. I discovered a flat on Delaware Road in Maida Vale. The owners were moving abroad and I could have it on a long let. Fantastic. Now all I needed was the job of my dreams.

It was a fairly discreet, out-of-the-way Italian restaurant, not one you would call flash or expensive. No point blowing valuable expenses on what was, after all, just an interim get-together to check out the lie of the land.

Lesley Douglas, as assistant to Jim Moir, had been putting my name forward for quite some time. Jim was not so sure that I would be right for Radio Two. A bit risky, too rock 'n' roll and 'not quite one of us' – those were Jim's reservations. All three of us enjoyed several glasses of red wine and the lunch went well. We strolled back down Great Portland Street and passed Yalding House, the new home of Radio One.

'You know,' said Jim, 'people think all I want to do is crush Radio One. Nothing could be further from the truth.'

Then, with an impish grin, he aimed a V sign in the direction of Yalding House. With that one gesture, I knew he was someone I would like to work for. There would be no bullshit, you would know exactly where you stood and there would never be a dull moment.

So, here I was, back in the old familiar slot of a Saturday-afternoon show with a free choice of the music I played. I was on Radio Two, a national radio station that was going from strength to strength, enjoying myself hugely and all was looking good. Sam had got a job in a merchant bank in London and moved into my flat in Delaware Road, right opposite the famous BBC Maida Vale Studios. It was great having him with me. Although it took many years, I was getting the time back with him I'd lost when I left the family home in Gloucestershire in 1987.

A few months later I got a call from Radio Two producer Gary Bones. Would I be interested in sitting in for John Dunn on *Drivetime*? He was to take some weeks off to go and prepare a series of live broadcasts from various countries in the booming economic region of the Asian Pacific. I couldn't believe I was being asked to sit in for 'Gentleman' John – our styles were so very different. Saturday afternoon is one thing but a peak daytime show is something else again. I was amazed, scared and excited all at the same time. I told Gary I would love to do it and a lunch meeting with Gary and the production team was arranged. At least five of them turned up at Sergio's cheap and cheerful pasta eaterie opposite the Crown and Sceptre. I thought they were a fantastic bunch and really felt that we could make a good programme together. I left the lunch on a high, looking forward to my *Drivetime* stint, even if it was only temporary.

John Dunn was a meticulous broadcaster. He'd been doing the show for about fifteen years and came in every day on the dot of one o'clock, spending hours going over his research notes. He would often pre-record the interviews so any fluffs could be edited out. This was not spontaneous radio, but it was his show I was deputizing on and I did my best to adapt to the style. Jim and Lesley must have been pleased with the shows because when John retired due to ill health in September 1998, they offered me *Drivetime* on a permanent basis. I would do Monday to Thursday, continue with my Saturday show, and Des Lynham would present the Friday edition of *Drivetime*. A big marketing campaign swung into action and photos of Des and me appeared on billboards and buses all over the country – often on the back of a bus, which prompted the inevitable jokes.

We kept pretty much to John Dunn's format: news and features in the first hour and a more relaxed second hour with an in-depth interview spot. One of the things I felt really needed changing was the travel news. It was gathered, typed up and then eventually faxed over to the hospitality area outside the studio. By the time I finally got the sheet of paper to read on air, the accidents and hold-ups were way out of date. We decided it would be a good idea to have a dedicated travel newsreader to collect and announce the information twice an hour. Jude Howells, who had produced *The AM Alternative* with me on Radio Five, remembered how well I'd got along with Sally Boazman on GLR. We'd never actually met as Sally broadcast down the line from a studio in Scotland Yard. A meeting was set up and we hit it off straightaway. Blonde, full of life with a great personality and sense of humour, Sally was blessed with a wonderful radio voice. The try-outs went so well, it was obvious she'd be a great asset for the show and arrangements were made for her to leave GLR and join Radio Two on a full-time basis.

Not only did we now have faster and more accurate news, we also set up a dedicated phone line for listeners to call in information virtually as it happened. The listeners took to Sally instantly – especially the truckers, who soon formed themselves into 'Sally's Army', rushing to her defence whenever they thought I was sending her up too much. Sally is what's known in the trade as 'a good bounce'. No matter what crazy idea or comment I came up with, she always had a reply. It seemed nothing could phase her and our two-way banter got ever wilder and more outrageous. There's no doubting the chemistry between us really worked and many were convinced there was an off-air relationship going on as well. Not true. Besides, Sally lived for Fridays and Des. Now those two did flirt outrageously on air; one little lift of Des's eyebrow and Sally would melt.

John Dunn was hugely loved and respected by his audience and when I took over his show, I was worried my very different, energetic style would alienate listeners, so I was pretty cautious to begin with. Fortunately the feedback suggested John's audience were willing to accept me in the slot and after a couple of weeks I passed Jim in the foyer.

'It's going well, son,' beamed Jim. 'It's all yours now. Just go for it.'

And go for it I did. I was on a roll in my new slot and my confidence was steadily building. I was having a great time on the show and, if I was enjoying it, so too were the listeners. I was the new blue-eyed boy of Radio Two and all was well in Walker's world.

All may have seemed fine on the outside but, privately, it was not so. As my professional life went from strength to strength, my personal life was going in the opposite direction.

When I wasn't on air I felt very unhappy and depressed. I put everything into my shows and it was in the studio that I really came alive: emails and text messages to be read and selected for broadcast flooded in, and CDs had to be cued up ready to go on air. I used to change my mind at the last minute and was often to be found scanning through my filing cabinet of favourite CDs just seconds before the record on air ended. I was flying by the seat of my pants and I loved it. When the show ended at seven o'clock, the team would all rush off home and I would be left in an empty studio. I would put Radio Four on the studio speakers and listen to *The Archers* as I packed up my stuff. Then I'd head back to my empty flat in Maida Vale.

After a few months of sharing, Sam had left to set up his own place with his girlfriend and I really missed his company. The place felt dead without him. The contrast between the two sides of my life couldn't have been more stark. The more I got out of work and being on a top-rated daily radio show, the flatter and emptier my private life became. I'm sure my listeners thought I was living some glamorous life of non-stop parties and nights at trendy restaurants. The reality was a sad empty flat, a Chinese or pizza takeaway swilled down with a bottle of wine and then an evening slumped in front of the TV, waking at two or three in the morning feeling dreadful, before undressing and dragging myself off to bed.

My life was just sleep, eat and work. During the week, as well as *Drivetime*, there would be interviews and music sessions for the Saturday show; Fridays would be spent sorting music and finalizing things for the next day. Sunday was laundry and housework – and that was my weekend. In no time at all, it was Monday again and time to get back on another week's merry-go-round. I never really got a break or a rest from the gruelling routine.

I started to buy the occasional gram of cocaine to help get me through. The drug was rife in the music business and media and there were so many slang names for the stuff: charlie, blow, nose candy, Peruvian marching powder and rocket fuel were just a few. It gave an extra edge to a night out and, for many in high-pressure jobs, the odd loo visit here and there was an essential part of getting through a day.

In the past I had accepted the odd line when it was offered, but had never really bothered to buy my own stuff. In no time at all, though, I was following a new daily routine. Up after ten, leisurely shower, coffee and a fag for breakfast, and a skim through the daily newspapers. At about twelve, I'd drive into work, park my car under Broadcasting House and wander round to Sergio's Restaurant to meet Celia Toynbee for lunch. Through working together on *Drivetime*, we had become good friends and lunching partners. We'd chat away and, in no time, a bottle of red was emptied. We'd order another to go with the main course and I'd round off the lunch with a double espresso and large Amaretto.

Celia would go back to the office and I'd dial up one of a couple of numbers in my mobile's memory. A call to either one could produce a gram of coke in my hand within ten minutes. Then it was back to the programme office to study research notes and then, an hour before going over to the studio, I'd nip into the Gents and chop out a couple of large lines to set me up for the programme. With the booze from lunch and the charlie, I'd be flying high on the show with masses of pizzazz and energy, and I thought I did a great job on air. Others who knew me well thought otherwise. Frances later told me she could always tell when I'd had coke before a show as I lost my warmth and sensitivity to the callers and guests I was interviewing. Celia did her best to persuade me to stop using coke but I always shrugged off such advice. I believed I could handle it.

After the show there might be a music gig to go to – otherwise, it was back home for more wine and to finish off the rest of the gram. Some people can make a gram of coke last for several days. Not me. If I had some in my pocket, I couldn't resist it and I would keep taking lines until there was none left. The result meant no appetite for an evening meal and sleeping was impossible until the early hours of the morning. Unable to sleep, I would waste hours trying to get my jollys off from big-tit soft-porn sites on the web. Cocaine is a frustrating drug as it stimulates the sex area of the brain but makes the achievement of sexual satisfaction more difficult.

No one was more aware than me of the pathetic figure I had become, and the shame of it all meant I needed even more booze and coke to blot out the reality of the situation. I would wake the next day vowing that I would make this new day one in which I would not buy any coke. Trouble was, I usually felt lousy and run-down and the only thing that made me feel better was more of the same. So, after my usual lunch, the warm, woozy feeling from the wine meant resistance and resolve were out of the window and I'd reach for the mobile. The same old inevitable cycle would start all over again.

Except it wasn't quite the same cycle; I had added a new twist. I tried a cocktail of a one-skin joint of neat grass sprinkled with some coke. Smoking it produced a wonderful feeling of euphoria and soon it became a nightly ritual. I guess I was as close as you can get to smoking crack without actually doing it – but what I was doing was taking me inevitably along the road to addiction. Even I had accepted I now had a serious problem. I couldn't go on this way. Something had to happen to make me realize that this pattern of destructive behaviour had to change.

I was in danger of losing everything.

PART SIX

Trying Times

Chapter Forty-One

Saturday, 24th April 1999

Cerys Matthews from Welsh band Catatonia had sung like an angel that afternoon. It was a great show and one to be proud of. We all went round the pub for a drink as usual and laughed and chatted. It was a normal Saturday like any other. I went home, made some pasta and was looking forward to my day off the next day.

At eleven p.m. the phone rang. It was Trevor Dann, the head of the music entertainment division at the BBC with responsibility for Radio Two. I never normally had any dealings with him. Why on earth was he calling at such a weird time?

'Johnnie, you're on the front page of tomorrow's *News of the World*. It doesn't look good. My advice to you is to pack a bag and get out of town before the media descend on your front door.'

My whole body froze in complete panic.

'What the hell's happened? Go away? How long for?'

'Is there somewhere you can go? You need a quiet bolt-hole well out of London.'

'I don't know, I'll need time to think. What about my show on Monday?'

'You can take it that, as of now, you're suspended.' He hung up.

The clue had been in an advertisement in that day's *Sun* newspaper. Promoting a story for the next day's *News of the World*, they referred to a BBC star in a cocaine scandal. I'd assumed it was someone off the telly. I wasn't even worried when Radio Two's publicity officer Hester Nevill had called at lunchtime.

'There's a rumour going round that a big BBC name is going to be on the front page of the *News of the World* tomorrow in a coke story. It's either you or . . .'

She mentioned the name of a BBC TV personality.

'Yes, I saw that in *The Sun*. It mentioned a "star". I don't think that's going to be me.'

She sounded reassured.

'OK, don't worry, we'll see what tomorrow brings.'

I wasn't a 'star'. I'd never considered myself in that way at all. Movie actors are stars. Household TV names are stars. I just presented radio programmes. I could walk down any street and never be recognized. Surely this story couldn't be about me. But now it looked like it *was* me.

I hurriedly packed enough clothes for a few days and tried to think. Where the hell was I going to go? There was someone who lived way out in the country in a little cottage miles from anywhere who might be willing to let me stay for a few days. I called up the number. Thank God, they were at home. I quickly explained the situation and asked if I could come down right away. They said yes. I drove off immediately.

First thing the next morning I went down to the village news-agent's and, keeping my head bowed low, bought two copies of the *News of the World*. My hands were shaking as I walked back to the car and only then did I look at the front page. There was a full-page photo of myself leaning over a mirror, snorting two enormous lines of cocaine. It looked to me as if they had found an actor who looked very much like me and dressed him in a similar shirt to one I had worn years ago for a Radio One photograph. In my mind, with the aid of computer enhancement, it would have been easy to make it look as though it was actually me leaning over the mirror.

Inside the paper there were some old publicity shots they'd dug up, including one of me leaning back in a chair, boots up on the table, arms behind my head and a huge grin on my face. The caption made it seem as if that photo was my reaction to the allegations made in the story. According to their reporter, not only was I a regular user of cocaine, but I was also a dealer in the drug, and a pimp who could arrange for prostitutes to attend parties.

I looked in the rear-view mirror. My face was white, all colour had drained out of it, and now my whole body was shaking. I imagined millions of people reading all the lurid details and being shocked to discover the person they thought they knew was, after all, a shady, grubby and evil man. It was a complete character assassination and I felt absolutely destroyed. As well as the double-page story, the editor weighed in on the leader page, asking how the BBC could ever think of continuing to employ Johnnie Walker after the revelations they had printed.

After all my struggles in America, losing my dad, then my brother and my mother soon after, the final breakdown of my marriage to Frances and now this – shamed in front of millions. I was at the lowest point I had ever been. It was the absolute injustice of it all that I found so hard to take. I had never denied that I was using coke, but to be accused of being a dealer and a pimp was deeply unfair and untrue, and I felt powerless to do anything about it.

All day long my mobile phone kept ringing with calls from concerned friends wondering how I was. I had to turn it off for a while as it was all getting just too much. I was trying to gather my strength, but it was hard. It felt as though the *News of the World* had all the power: everyone would read it and everyone would believe it. I was so grateful to be out of London, far away, where no one could find me. Then a couple of things helped me get some perspective on it all.

I was always a big fan of *Breakfast with Frost* and never missed a show if I was at home. This morning I was watching, and was dreading his regular trawl through the front pages of the Sunday papers. He came to the *News of the World* and quickly scanned it.

'Ah, a BBC person in a cocaine story. They've made a mistake there, he was obviously drinking Coke through a straw,' said David Frost, and then he casually tossed it to one side.

Good old David, I thought.

Later on, fellow Brummie Frank Skinner went one better. He was doing his usual stand-up routine at the start of his TV show.

'Here, did you see that story about Johnnie Walker? Hey, he's a bit of a lad, isn't he? How about that – he supplied cocaine and good-time girls for a party. Well, I'll tell you what. I'm booking him for my next bash. I mean, you've got your DJ and your music and the drugs and the girls, all for one fee. Now that's value for money.'

Big laughs from the studio audience, and I finally smiled and managed a laugh myself. It made me feel better and I began to think I might be able to get through all this, after all. Thank you, Frank.

I got a call from my BBC boss, Jim Moir. He was very supportive and sympathetic.

'Johnnie, my son, you've been well and truly stitched up. I think it's desperately unfair and I really feel for you, but we have to decide what to do next. As you can imagine, there are discussions going on at a high level but I would like to arrange a meeting to hear your side of the story.'

That was good news. At last I was going to get the chance to have my say. I also heard from friends within Radio Two that the listeners were beginning to rally round. Some were angry that the *News of the World* seemed to be calling the shots and deciding who Radio Two should or shouldn't employ as broadcasters. Some said they didn't care what I did in my private life, that was no one's business but mine, and all that mattered was whether I was any good at my job or not. That was a laudable, liberal attitude but it still made me sad that people might actually believe that dealing coke and pimping hookers was what I did in my spare time. There were a few 'Disgusted of Tunbridge Wells' types, who thought I should be instantly dismissed and never allowed back on the air again. But, thankfully, they seemed to be in the minority. In fact, I think Jim Moir was surprised at the reaction from Radio Two listeners, who turned out to be far less shocked than he anticipated.

A meeting was arranged at Durrants Hotel, a small discreet location in Marylebone, and now I sat across the table from Jim Moir and Jenny Abramsky, director of radio for the BBC. I thanked them for arranging the meeting and for the chance to have a face-to-face chat. I apologized for the mess we were all in and for bringing Radio Two such bad publicity. Jenny was the more worried of the two, still very shocked by the whole thing. She seemed to believe all she'd read.

'Johnnie, how can we possibly have you on the air? What on earth are our female listeners going to think? I mean, the way you've treated and exploited women . . .'

'Jenny, I haven't been acting as a pimp, for God's sake. That's the *News of the World* ramping up the story for more effect. Do you really think that's how I spend my free time?'

Jim could see the temperature heating up and spread out his calming hands above the table. Whenever there's some kind of drama going on and all around are panicking, Jim is always there, unflustered, steady as a rock and offering good advice.

'I think we should let Johnnie tell his side of the story.'

Well, it's here that I have to admit to being mug enough to fall for the 'fake sheikh' scam, perpetrated by *News of the World* investigative editor Mazher Mahmood. My name was now to be added to a list that included the Countess of Wessex, Sven-Goran Eriksson, Richard Bacon and John Alford.

It had all started weeks earlier with one of the junior guys on the *News of the World* team pestering me to make a pilot for a monthly radio programme that would be played in the rooms of a chain of hotels in the United Arab Emirates, owned by an Arab prince. I tried to ignore the faxes, phone messages and emails but eventually decided the only way to get rid of him was to get in touch. When he explained what it was all about, I told him I thought it was a wind-up. Pity I didn't stick with that opinion. The deal he laid out was something like two grand a show and a free holiday once a year in one of their hotels. I eventually agreed to make a pilot and, after a couple of weeks, heard back that it had been accepted. They were very pleased and I had the job if I wanted it.

I then met up with a more senior member of the sting team during a birthday lunch at Sergio's Restaurant. A suited business type, he introduced himself as the Arab prince's UK representative. He had a very impressive gold-embossed business card and was constantly fiddling with two mobile phones. One of them, I later discovered, was a recording device. He told me the prince had confirmed that I had the gig to produce twelve shows a year, and they would like to meet me for lunch to get to know me and welcome me to their operation.

A date was arranged at Claridge's Hotel. I'd had a couple of pre-lunch glasses of wine and a line or two and was feeling cocky and invincible – typical charlie delusion. Mr Business Suit met me in the foyer and I followed him into the lift and up to a really expensive hotel suite. Standing outside the door was a vast man with gold teeth – obviously a bodyguard. It was so surreal that, paradoxically, it seemed absolutely genuine. I was welcomed into this huge and sumptuous suite and there were two wealthy-looking Arab princes, resplendent in their robes, puffing away on hookah pipes.

They were extremely welcoming.

'Johnnie, you must come out as our guest. Please bring as many friends as you like. It will be all expenses paid, you'll have a great holiday and you will see how wonderful our hotels are. We'll fly you all out business class, of course.'

They continued to effuse about all the wonderful hospitality that would be shown to me on my visit. Then one of the princes took some pills out of his pocket. 'I have a very bad headache. I had some poor-quality cocaine last night.'

'Are you interested in cocaine?' I asked, surprised that they would even mention it, let alone be users.

'Oh yes, you know what it's like. At home, things are very strict. My brother and I, we love to come to London where we can go to parties and have some fun, all the things that are forbidden in our country.'

Still the penny didn't drop. It all seems so bloody obvious now but at the time it appeared absolutely real.

'Can you get us some cocaine?' asked the prince who was doing all the talking.

'I would have thought you could get whatever you wanted,' I said.

'Ah well, we can get cocaine but it's not very good. Can you get us some really good cocaine?'

It seemed rude not to match their generosity with something in return. But there was no way I was going to get them some cocaine, and I told them so. They kept on and on asking me to get them cocaine and I kept refusing. Eventually I got so fed up with it, I reached into the little Levi stash pocket in my jeans, pulled out the wrap and chucked it on the table.

'If you're so desperate for some cocaine, have some.'

The two princes jumped to their feet, whooping and yelping with delight. I chopped out four lines on the coffee table: two big ones for them to have one each and two small ones for me. They said they would save theirs for later as they didn't want to spoil their appetite. I wasn't worried about that so I took a twenty-pound note out of my wallet and snorted my two lines. Talk about a lamb to the slaughter. I later found out they had video cameras in a briefcase and at least two others built into the wall.

Despite the gift of a couple of lines, they still kept asking me to get them some coke and once again I said I couldn't. They were very persuasive, so I finally told them I would give their business representative a phone number and they could sort it out for themselves.

'We've got a party happening on Saturday. Do you know any girls who enjoy a good time who might like to come along?'

This was starting to get very tacky and I just wanted to get away. I'd heard rumours that the guy from whom I got my cocaine used to have contacts with hostesses. I told them that it was possible that the same person whose number I would provide could also help with girls as well. The princes said they were going to change into Western clothes for dinner and they would meet me downstairs. Mr Business Suit led me out of the suite and we made our way down to the restaurant. Back in the suite, Mazher and his mate were, of course, bagging up the coke to send to a lab for analysis and then keep as evidence.

Downstairs in Claridge's, dinner with the 'princes' was a horrible experience. Now they had their evidence, they didn't even try and make conversation. Both were fairly sullen and monosyllabic. The junior team member who, weeks ago, had made the initial approach to me, had been in the suite and was also at the table. He delighted in making some smart in-joke to the others about how Johnnie had originally thought the idea was all a wind-up. I thought about going to the loo and just buggering off. I'd now pretty much sussed that there was something very weird about the whole thing. I left as soon as I could and, once outside, called the dealer concerned and apologized for giving out his number without first getting his permission. I suggested that he might be interested in doing business with them, but I wanted nothing to do with it. From the newspaper story it would seem he then arranged for some 'good-time girls' to be available for a party. Of course, this all could have been my little scam: go into business with a dealer, pretend to have nothing to do with him apart from buying cocaine, drum up business for him and then share or snort the profits behind the scenes. I guess that was the scenario the *News of the World* was portraying.

I have never dealt drugs or been a pimp but, to use the old cliché, why let the truth get in the way of a good story?

Jim and Jenny patiently sat through my explanation. Jim thought it was all very unfair and that I'd been badly stitched up. Jenny still seemed worried about a Radio Two name being involved in a coke scandal. All this was happening in the climate of a promise by the *News of the World* that they would expose a celebrity, politician or otherwise well-known person every week. I felt passionately that the BBC was setting themselves up for this sort of thing by trying to maintain their famous squeaky-clean image.

'Jenny, the BBC is made up of people, the same sort of people who work for ITV or commercial radio. Some of those people have a drink problem, some of them take cocaine. If you try and keep up this pretence that the BBC is somehow different, then the *News of the World* will continue to target your people. When Richard Bacon was caught in a similar sting, the BBC should have helped and supported him by encouraging him to go into rehab.

He could have become a very effective spokesman for *Blue Peter* to warn young people about the dangers of drugs. But no – you did the usual BBC thing, and hung him out to dry by giving him the boot. You just give the *News of the World* the satisfaction of having all the power by reacting in such a predictable way.'

Jenny came from a news background that was pretty straight and conservative; mine was rock 'n' roll and rebellion. Jim Moir was the guy in the middle, trying to find common ground and calm the troubled waters.

'Johnnie,' he said, 'you'll have to stay off the air for now. We've got to let the dust settle on all this rather than act in haste.'

I left the meeting feeling pleased that I'd had a chance to put my side of the story. Now I had to wait and see how events would unfold.

Two weeks after the original story, the *News of the World* put the boot in again with another double-page spread. The basis of it was Janie Jones retelling the tale of my visit to her house, which had led to the Mr T story in the tabloids. I heard a rumour that she was paid £10,000 for the story. Other rumours were that an insider at the BBC was paid to inform the *News of the World* of any cocaine users at the BBC and that the budget for my sting was in the region of £50,000. Once again, the newspaper's editorial demanded that the BBC sack me. All their evidence had been passed to the police, who were being urged to take action against me.

About three weeks after the original story, the police called.

'Mr Walker, no doubt you've been expecting a call from us. I wonder if you'd care to come down to West End Central for a little chat.'

They're always so infuriatingly polite, especially when they have the upper hand.

I needed to find a good lawyer. It was Ronan O'Rahilly, founder of Radio Caroline, who advised me to engage Keith Schilling and we both went to West End Central to be interviewed. We were taken to an interview room and questioned by a detective sergeant and detective inspector. Not so much soft cop and hard cop, but wise old cop and young, keen-for-promotion cop. They had various pieces of evidence given to them by the *News of the World* including a VHS video tape. We all sat down to watch it. I was amazed. My incredulous question when the prince mentioned he took cocaine – 'Are you interested in cocaine?' – now started the video. Where was the opening ten minutes or so of the meeting? It looked just as if I was a dealer propositioning for business.

Keith sent a sideways glance at me which seemed to say, 'They've got you banged to rights here.'

I told the same story I'd related to Jim and Jenny: admitted I had used cocaine and was in possession on that day but emphatically denied dealing drugs and having anything to do with procuring prostitutes.

The wise cop was very friendly and helpful.

'Johnnie, we're not after people like you. We're after the big guys, the big dealers, but the trouble is that the *News of the World* have goaded us into action. If we don't do something, next thing they'll be accusing us of being soft on drugs in London.'

Young, keen cop with his shiny shoes, immaculately pressed shirt and impeccable haircut, now took over and formally charged me on two counts, one of possession and one of intent to supply.

It was like being in a movie as I was photographed holding a card with a prisoner number on it, front and profile. They took my fingerprints and used a swab to take a DNA sample from the inside of my mouth. All very degrading. Years ago, I'd joked I was a criminal for playing records on Caroline after the Marine Offences Bill became law; now I really was one and it felt bloody awful. We walked down to the station sergeant's desk and keen cop gave him the details to type up the charge sheet. I suddenly had a thought, motioned Keith to step away from the desk and whispered to him.

'Get the amount on the charge sheet.'

Keith casually walked up to the sergeant.

'I wonder if we could just specify the amount here. I mean, are we talking about suitcases full of cocaine, a van load or what?'

The sergeant duly obliged and typed in the words: 'In possession of 0.06 of a gram of cocaine.'

That was the two lines I'd put on the table for the princes and it was a tiny amount, worth about £5. Here was I, having the bloody book thrown at me for a ridiculously small amount, all because of what the newspapers had written and might write in the future. I was bailed to appear in a couple of weeks at Horseferry Road Magistrates Court. The fact I'd been charged was in London's *Evening Standard* and on the radio and television news. At least I'd got the amount of coke into the public domain. It made the police action look a bit heavy handed, but then there was the secondary charge of dealing that was really worrying.

If they made that stick, I'd go to jail.

As if all these troubles weren't enough, I was about to be made homeless again. The owners of the Delaware Road flat I was renting were returning from America and wanted their home back. It was time to call my earthly angel and good friend, Angela Donovan.

'Angela, I'm in a bit of a fix.'

I explained the situation. She was her usual positive, smiley self down the phone.

'Well, darling' – she always called me darling – 'we've got a little caravan in a field that's empty. It's not what you'd call five-star accommodation, but you're very welcome to use it. It's a roof over your head and you can come and have meals with us.'

A friend in need is a friend indeed.

'God bless you, Angela. I'll be down tomorrow.'

I crammed my stuff in the back of my trusty old Alfa and headed down the M4. I put my boxes in an old barn and set about making the caravan home. It was at the back of the farmhouse and looked over a green field and trees beyond. On the one hand I was now trailer trash, on the other I had a home in the country with a beautiful view. I put up some shelving units for my CDs and plugged in my ghetto blaster, thankful that there was electricity.

As long as I've got my music, anyplace can seem like home. Then I caught a train back to London to fetch my Harley.

It was a glorious sunny afternoon as I took the slip road off the M4 at junction 15 and headed north. A couple of miles up the road, the old Roman Road stretched downhill in front of me for as far as the eye could see. I screamed a cowboy style 'Yeeeeeeee haaawwww' at the top of my lungs as the speedo hit 95mph. I felt gloriously free. Thank God for bikes and my beloved Harley-Davidson Fat Boy. No matter how bleak a situation looks, as long as I can get on the bike and feel the wind in my face, I still feel alive and full of hope. It's what Lou Reed calls 'Harley therapy'.

There was a rather prim-looking magistrate in charge for my first appearance at Horseferry Road Magistrates Court. She looked at me over the top of her reading glasses and went back to her notes. I stood in the dock in my best suit and began to realize just how powerless the accused is in this situation. I was allowed to speak only to confirm my name and address; then I had to sit back in silence while lawyers on both sides took over. The magistrate asked for a copy of the *News of the World* and we all sat back while she read it. I can't remember her exact words, but they were something to the effect that she considered it to be an appalling piece of journalism and she stated her concern that its publication seriously hampered the possibility of my having a fair trial.

I was quite happy to plead guilty to possession, but was determined to fight the other charge of intent to supply. The lawyer for the Crown Prosecution Service asked for more time to prepare their case and the hearing was adjourned to a later date.

Needless to say, from the moment I read the first *News of the World* article, my use of cocaine stopped. But I knew I needed help and some form of rehab was the obvious next step. I wanted to get away from it all, to find some peace and quiet where I wouldn't be harangued by the media. After some time on the Internet, I found Crossroads in Antigua. It had been founded by Eric Clapton, someone who I had always felt an affinity with, partly because we were born on the same day in 1945.

Eric had conquered his problems and even managed to stay clean and sober through the dreadful pain of losing his son, Connor. He knew that his continued sobriety could be strengthened by giving help to others, hence Crossroads. It was also a gift to the island he loved; Antigua has a real problem with crack, which is cheap and plentiful. The centre was open to all, treatment fees were kept as low as possible and it was free to residents of Antigua.

I got in touch with Crossroads' UK representative, Carol. After a long telephone interview and subsequent meeting, I was accepted into their rehab programme. The dates clashed with my next court appearance so my lawyer arranged for a hearing before another magistrate, who granted an adjournment.

Antigua was my best chance for rehabilitation away from the stress and pressure of media scrutiny.

Chapter Forty-Two

I missed the flight from Heathrow.

I was in a hell of a state. Physically wrecked, nervous, confused and tired, I just couldn't get it together and went to the wrong terminal. By the time I got to the right one, I was too late and the gate had closed. I was so crushed at being a failure. Here was my big chance and I'd blown it. I got back home, dumped my case, lay on the bed and burst into tears. I felt so alone and helpless.

I'd left Angela's caravan and found a basement flat to rent in London and right now I found the world outside it such a big frightening place that I just didn't feel I had the strength to deal with it any more. Eventually the tears did their healing and I felt a little better. I called Carol to apologize for missing the flight. There was no condemnation; she was so understanding.

'Don't worry, Johnnie. Lots of people have mishaps trying to reach a rehab centre. See if you can get on the next flight and I'll let them know at Crossroads.'

A couple of days later I was back at Heathrow, at the right terminal and in plenty of time for my flight. I was told to look out for Dean Martin at Antigua airport, who'd be holding a card with my name on it. This Dean Martin turned out to be a warm and friendly young Antiguan with a sunshine smile. He drove me across the island in a white minibus and we chatted along the way.

'I used to work in a bar serving alcohol and helping people get drunk. I've seen so much misery, I decided to help those with problems instead,' he said.

We passed small wooden houses and shacks along the bumpy roads. They looked a bit dilapidated but outside many of them were shiny new Japanese cars and trucks, some being washed and polished by their proud owners.

'We're nearly there,' said Dean.

The pride that was obvious in his voice should have prepared me for the sight that followed.

We rounded a corner at the top of a hill and I caught my first glimpse of Willoughby Bay. It was staggeringly beautiful. Below me lay a lush, green valley and the low, one-storey modern white buildings housing the Crossroads Centre nestled into the hillside behind as if for protection from the world beyond. In front lay green gardens that ran down to small rocks and, beyond, the bay itself. I had never seen a blue so beautiful; the waters shimmered and sparkled in the bright sunshine. As we got to the bottom of the hill, the image was somewhat shattered by the sight of a high security fence and a guard house at the gates. The uniformed guard waved us through and, at last, I had arrived at Crossroads.

I went through the admission procedure, was checked by a doctor and shown to my room in the east wing. It was a small, comfortable room with two beds and an en suite bathroom with patio doors leading out to the covered veranda that overlooked the garden. I headed out to the meditation gazebo and there I fell to my knees, shed tears of relief and gave thanks to the Great Spirit for helping me reach this haven of peace and serenity.

The main reason I had wanted to come to Crossroads was for its unique holistic approach to helping people with drug problems. They treated not only the physical body but also the emotional, spiritual and mental areas. The centre was still very new and they were still 'road-testing' their treatment programme. The patients consisted of myself and only three others: Bill from North Carolina; Sindy, an American living in the US Virgin Islands; and Pat, a local Antiguan woman. We later came to refer to ourselves as 'The Fortunate Four' as we obviously had more attention and help than could be given to a full quota of nearly forty.

The day would start at seven o'clock when breakfast, like all our meals, was eaten in the separate restaurant building with a veranda and beautiful view out to the bay beyond. I'd complete my daily journal by eight a.m. so that it could be read by my counsellor, Nancy. The day was then packed with lectures, work-shops, group therapy, massage, yoga and one-to-one sessions with counsellors, all of whom had previously had their own problems with drink or drugs. We'd have a break in the afternoon when we could spend time on our own or swim in the outdoor pool. Then more lectures, supper and the end-of-day meeting with Hicks, a wise and gentle Antiguan with great experience of people, life and addictions.

We'd form a circle of chairs and each take turns talking about our day, trying to find the positive aspects of what we were going through. Yes, we were in beautiful, serene surroundings but it was far from being a holiday. Rehab is tough. There are tears, anger and deep depression as you face your demons at last, as well as all the sadnesses and disappointments of life that get buried deep down in your memory.

It took me a long time to accept the fact that I was possibly an alcoholic in addition to my cocaine addiction. I couldn't under-stand why they kept asking me about my drinking history when I'd come to get my coke problem sorted. The centre's philosophy was to treat addictive behaviour, and so all mind-altering substances were lumped under the same umbrella. Being clean and sober was the aim. Nancy helped me to rediscover the person called 'Peter' who had been lost when Johnnie Walker took over. Her one-to-one counselling, the group therapy and the many essays I wrote about the past, brought back all the painful memories of a childhood spent feeling misunderstood, unloved and rejected.

One evening, sleep was impossible. I was churning over in my mind all that had been brought out and it all became too much to bear. I really didn't want to carry on with rehab, or with living, and was at my absolute lowest point. About two o'clock I got up and went outside. It was a hot, humid night with bullfrogs croaking loudly from the undergrowth. I walked round and round the grassy compound, spent some time in the meditation gazebo, and then walked again.

I cried like never before or since. From deep within poured all the sadness and pain and my whole body was convulsed with grief and tears. I felt that I was at the bottom of some deep, dark pit and that I would never be able to get out of it.

I glanced at the swimming pool and thought of the blessed relief I might find in drowning. Watching me from the other side of the compound was the security guard on night duty. He did his job very well that long, dark night, never intruding but also never letting me out of his sight. His strong, quiet presence helped me get through that long night of pain. Eventually, exhausted from expressing all that emotion and sadness, I gave my quiet friend a nod of recognition and thanks and headed back to my room where, mercifully, I fell into a deep, healing sleep.

The next day, during our mid-afternoon break, wanting to be on my own to think, I walked along the edge of the compound and found a secluded little space just behind the restaurant building. I looked out to sea. All was calm, small waves gently breaking on the rocks that lined the shore. Way out on the horizon, the deep blue of the ocean melted into the lighter hues of the clear blue sky. The world was at peace. All my senses were touched by the beauty and serenity of my surroundings. A few hundred yards out to sea, a narrow reef of rocks just broke the surface of the water. White-crested waves broke gently on to the rocks. From that distance they looked like a row of beautiful white teeth. It was as if the ocean was smiling.

The four of us – Bill, Sindy, Pat and myself – had all been having our own personal struggles with the concept of God, or a Higher Power, which is a vital element of the twelve-step programme that was part of our treatment. At that instant I experienced, for the first time, being 'in the moment'. All time had stopped. This was Nirvana, that place I had read about in books on Eastern philosophy and meditation, the ultimate place where all thoughts ceased and there was complete connection with everything around me.

I looked out at the sky and the ocean and said, 'You're there, aren't you? You're in everything: the blue sky, the fluffy white clouds, the gentle breeze and in the bay with its broad smile.'

As the words formed in my mind and I felt an overwhelming

sense of connection and understanding, two waves, close together and stronger than all the others, broke on to the rocks and distinctly whispered the word, 'Yeee . . . ssss.'

I stayed very still, spellbound. In that moment I knew I had experienced the existence of God. I didn't want that feeling of complete connection ever to end. I stayed at the spot for over an hour, trying to assimilate and come to terms with what had happened. I felt I had been given a gift, one that I knew was not meant for sharing. I could never find the right words to do justice to the magnificence of that moment and, at the time, I knew that if I tried, I would certainly lay myself open to ridicule. I didn't want anyone or anything to diminish what I experienced that afternoon. Now, seven years later, it seems right to talk about it; the gift is still there as strong as ever and nothing can take it away.

As I left that special place, I noticed a small rock on the path. I picked it up and was about to throw it to one side when I looked at it. It was gnarled, bashed and battered with ugly holes and grooves in it. Just like my life, I thought. I walked to the water's edge and with all the strength I could muster, hurled it far out into the ocean. That's got rid of all that pain, hurt and anguish, I thought. And walked back to the centre.

The long dark night of despair and the amazing afternoon experience were the turning points for me at Crossroads and everything began to look brighter for my future. I was feeling stronger and, although I knew there were great difficulties ahead, I felt I would be able to get through those challenges without going back to the escapism of alcohol and cocaine. Then I got some bad news. Nancy, my counsellor, called me into her office.

'Johnnie, I'm sorry to tell you this, but we think you should know. Two reporters from the *News of the World* are on the island.'

My face fell.

'They've been going around bars and clubs trying to find out who works at Crossroads and offering them money to talk about you. But don't worry, none of the people who work here will say anything.'

I thanked her for letting me know and went outside to the meditation gazebo, my favourite place to be still and quiet. At a stroke, the peace, serenity and protection of the Crossroads Centre had changed and I didn't feel so safe any more. I looked over at the bay and in the distance saw a small boat. Was it a fisherman or was there a *News of the World* photographer in there with a powerful lens on his camera? It's one thing for a newspaper to claim that it has a public duty to expose an illegal activity like drug taking. It's quite another for a newspaper to attempt to undermine a person's efforts to get better. I felt deeply sad that the *News of the World* wanted to destroy my struggle to become a better person.

I suppose from the tabloid perspective I was on some kind of luxurious Caribbean holiday, but the reality of rehab is very different. It is hard, and there are many who leave for the nearest bar or drug dealer and don't stay the course. During our short afternoon break around the pool, I told the others about Nancy's news and the suspicious fishing boat that was still moored in the same place out in the bay.

'Well, let's give 'em something to photograph,' said Bill, who promptly stood up, dropped his swimming trunks and stuck out his bare arse towards the bay.

'Jesus, Bill, they'll think it's mine.'

We all laughed and I felt a little better. A couple of days later, Nancy told me she'd heard the reporters had left as they couldn't find anyone who would talk. The local people who worked at Crossroads were very loyal to the centre, and supportive of all those who came for help, and I'm very grateful to them.

The challenge of the outside world was getting ever closer for The Fortunate Four. We had grown really close over the twenty-eight days we had spent at the centre. When off duty we usually ate our meals together and sometimes, late in the evening, we'd share the outdoor wooden jacuzzi, gaze at the stars, tell stupid jokes, talk about our counsellors and generally chew over philosophy and the meaning of life.

All month long we'd noticed two small white birds who had built their nest in a nearby tree. We could just about see into it and carefully checked for progress every day. The nest contained four eggs and there was always one bird sitting on the eggs while the other went for food. We saw the eggs hatching as the first cracks appeared, then little beaks poking through, and eventually all four chicks pecked their way free, emerging wet, bedraggled and hungry. I suppose it was inevitable that we would draw comparisons between ourselves and the birds in the nest.. We were the same in number, we had our struggles together and we all hoped to emerge from a safe haven to start a new life. But it was uncanny that the very day that Sindy prepared to leave Crossroads, the first fledgling began to leave the nest. It was wonderful to watch and all four of us could relate very much to the obvious parallels. It took great courage for the tiny fledglings to launch themselves into the unknown. For us, given all the help and support of the Crossroads staff, it wasn't that much of a challenge to stay off drinks and drugs when none were available. Our big test would come when we went back into the outside world with all its temptations.

For Sindy's farewell we all gathered in the largest room at the centre. Seated on chairs all round the walls were virtually the entire staff of Crossroads. To mark her completion of the course, Sindy would be presented with a special Crossroads medallion with the centre's motif on one side and the 'Serenity Prayer' on the other. The coin was passed to each member of staff in turn. They would hold the coin and say a few words about their experience of working with Sindy, wishing her all the best for the future. There was much joy and laughter during the ceremony. Afterwards, Bill, Pat and I said our own goodbyes. There were big hugs and quite a few tears. We had all gone through so much together and had grown very close.

Over the next two days the same farewell ceremony was held for Bill and Pat, and then it was time for me to pack my bag and be given my own send-off. I had received so much help, kindness and understanding from all the people there and, in a way, I was reluctant to leave. Some wonderful words were spoken at my leaving ceremony and I asked many of the staff to write a few words in my special book. My counsellor, Nancy, wrote:

Dear Peter,

Thanks for sharing yourself with me. It has been a privilege to work with you and watch you learn to live again.

Be patient and gentle with yourself – the magic is in you.

Love,

Nancy

Somehow I had to hold on to that magic and keep my strength for the trials that lay ahead.

Now I had to go back to England, fight to prove my innocence in court, and decide what kind of future I should build for myself.

Chapter Forty-Three

My first big test came in the departure hall of Antigua Airport.

At Crossroads I had struggled with accepting the fact I was an alcoholic, rather than just addicted to cocaine. Halfway through the treatment, it seemed much the wisest thing to accept I had a problem with all drugs. As I was always tempted to buy cocaine after a boozing session, alcohol was obviously a 'gateway' drug to the harder stuff and, by the time I left, I was off everything including tobacco.

I knew one of the other counsellors, Paul Sunderland, was going back to the UK on the same flight as me. Although I didn't see him, I felt sure he was watching me as I approached the huge bar. I had a weird attraction to the row of beer pumps and optics lining the back of the bar. Alcohol suddenly seemed more tempting and powerful than ever. I put my hand in my pocket and felt my Cross-roads medallion; it reminded me that I had been through far too much to throw it all away now. It was a clean and sober JW who landed back at Heathrow and that's the way I wanted it to stay. I had to have all my wits about me for the legal battles that lay ahead.

The next few weeks were spent in interminable meetings with my lawyers, Keith and Simon from Schillings. Expensive meetings with a barrister took place to get expert advice and plan our strategy. The Crown Prosecution Service seemed hell-bent on proceeding with the more serious charge of intent to supply. In line with the due process of legal proceedings, we had sight of the evidence they would submit to the court and they made a great deal out of my intention to supply cocaine in order to gain favour with the so-called Arab princes and secure the job of providing radio programmes for their chain of hotels. The fact that I had already been given the job long before my meeting at Claridge's didn't seem to make any difference.

There were more appearances at Horseferry Road Magistrates Court and, again, more adjournments. I kept Jim Moir in touch with the legal developments and he told me that, maybe, the BBC could accept a conviction for possession but there was no way back if I was found guilty on the dealing charge. I understood this and accepted it. I wasn't sure I even wanted to go back on Radio Two.

The four of us at Crossroads had all talked about our history and how we had ended up in a rehab clinic. Sindy's reaction to my story was blunt and to the point.

'Knowing what your job has got you into and all this press intrusion, you might just want to give up all this DJ shit and find a quieter, less public way to live.' Her words really struck a chord and I thought about an alternative way of life a lot but I put off any decisions about my future until after the court case.

On Monday, 11th October 1999, three days before the case was due to be heard, Keith Schilling called.

'Johnnie, some good news. We've just heard from the CPS that if you're willing to plead guilty on possession, they'll drop the dealing charge.'

'Keith, I've said all along I would plead guilty to possession. Why are they asking me now?'

'Who knows? The important thing is the dealing charge is to be dropped. This is a really good development.'

And, of course, it was. But it was still bloody frustrating. All these weeks of worry, legal bills building up all the while and then, at the last minute, they decide not to proceed with the dealing charge. All this fuss, publicity and expense for just two small lines of cocaine! Although I thought the way I was enticed into the trap was unfair, I had been in possession of an illegal drug and I had owned up to that from the very beginning, hoping that a totally honest approach all the way through would see justice done in the end.

Wednesday was the big day of the all-important court case. The previous evening, my daughter Beth had called and asked me if I wanted some support. Both she and Sam had been such comforts to me during the terrible time of the exposé and my spell in rehab, even though Sam was miles away, working for a merchant bank in Sydney.

Beth said, 'I'll come with you, Dad, if you'd like me to be there.'

'Beth, that's really good of you. Yes, I would love you to come. But I must warn you, there'll probably be lots of press and photographers there.'

'That's okay, Dad. I can cope with that.'

That morning, I put my best suit on and Beth and I took a taxi that dropped us off at the top of Horseferry Road. She took my arm and I did my best to hide my nerves. We walked through the media scrum and into the courthouse. Keith Schilling was waiting for me along with Carl (Charly) Wayne. It had been too many years since I'd introduced him and The Vikings onstage at the Carlton Club in Birmingham. He'd called me out of the blue and kindly volunteered to come along and give his support.

I said, 'Keith, this is my daughter, Beth, and this is my friend, Charly.'

'Better not mention his name in court,' said Keith with a grin.

I was so nervous that the joke was completely lost on me, but the others got it and their laughter made me feel a little better.

We made our way into the crowded courtroom, Beth and Charly heading to the public gallery while I went to the dock. I took the Bible in my left hand and gave the usual oath to 'tell the truth, the whole truth and nothing but the truth'. I confirmed my name and address and then the lawyers for the CPS put their case for the prosecution. I pleaded guilty to the charge of possession and my barrister, Anthony Chinn, said a few words in mitigation.

'He found himself alone and working hard and he turned to the occasional use of cocaine. But what started off as a crutch and a friend soon turned into an enemy. It is a very addictive drug.'

In summing up, the presiding magistrate, Rosamond Keating, criticized the *News of the World* for their methods and the 'filth' they had written about me. As for me, she said I had a duty to maintain higher standards of life than other people because of my position as a celebrity. She noted that I had sought help for my addiction and added, 'I hope something good will come out of this appalling incident.'

I was fined £2,000 plus costs and was free to go. And that was it – six long months of worry finally over. We walked out of the court to be faced by the media scrum. I made a statement thanking my friends, family and the listeners for their support and we headed off up Horseferry Road. I hadn't gone more than fifty yards when my mobile rang. It was Jim Moir from Radio Two.

'Johnnie, just heard the news on the squawk box in the office. I'm very pleased it's all over and I want to read you the press statement I'd like to release about you coming back on the show.'

'But, Jim . . . I don't even know at this stage if I want to come back. It's too soon, I need more time.'

But Jim wasn't listening, or didn't want to hear, and proceeded to read out the statement.

'"The BBC is adamant that it does not tolerate the use of illegal drugs. However, the BBC Radio management is impressed with the way Johnnie has handled this crisis in his life and that he has sought professional treatment. Radio Two has listened to Johnnie's audience, who registered an overwhelming amount of support for him."'

It went on to say that they would be giving me back the *Drivetime* show. I was all a bit stressed out by the events of the day and now Jim was pressuring me to make a decision I didn't want to make right there and then. I thanked him for his support and the offer of the show back, but again said I wasn't quite ready to make a decision. No use.

'Johnnie, I'll be releasing this at two o'clock, don't you worry about a thing.'

Crafty old Jim; he always gets his way, and his announcement stopped any other offers.

The court case and conviction made the radio and TV news that evening and it was in most of the following day's newspapers, especially the tabloids. That prompted loads of calls to my mobile. Ronan O'Rahilly called and told me I should get on all the talk shows to tell my side of the story. Producers from the Jeremy Clarkson chat show called to say Jeremy wanted me on as a guest. I said no to everything. It didn't seem right to me to capitalize on a drug conviction. I just wanted all the fuss to die down, and to try and remain calm, clean and sober.

Sobriety was the number one priority for me then and I went to regular AA meetings where being with others with similar problems gave me great help and support. I also went back to my caravan on Angela's farm in Wiltshire to get a little peace and quiet and to reflect on all that had happened. Months had passed since the original articles, and the court case was the right place for it all to end. I'd been mug enough to fall for the fake sheikh scam and, in a funny sort of a way, I was grateful to the *News of the World*. I knew I was in a bad place with my cocaine use and that I had to seek some help. But how and from where? I can just imagine the reaction if I'd gone into Jim's office and said, 'Hey, Jim, I'm doing lots of coke and I want to take a month off to go into rehab.' That would probably have been the end of my job at Radio Two right there and then. I had smelt a rat when I was first approached by the fake radio producer, and at Claridge's I had known that there was something very weird going on. Maybe deep in my subconscious mind I had wanted something to happen to break the cycle of addiction I was in.

Well, happen it did and it was the biggest test and challenge to my character that I'd ever faced. I had come through to the other side and now I had the chance to make a new start. I still wasn't sure about returning to Radio Two although, given Jim Moir's press announcement, people were expecting me to come back. It was the pressure of daily radio and the temptations of the easy availability of cocaine that had got me into the whole mess in the first place. Why would I want to put myself back in the spotlight and risk something similar happening again?

But, and it was a big but, if I could hang on to this new, cleaner way of life and do the radio show, there'd be no lurid story for the *News of the World* to publicize. There's no question that if it hadn't been for the tremendous support the listeners had shown me, I probably wouldn't have been invited back to the BBC. I started to realize that if I didn't return, in a way the *News of the World* would have won and all that listener support would have been in vain.

Jude Howells, who had produced my programmes on Radio Five, was now at Radio Two and she called me up to suss out my mood and plans for the future. I told her I wasn't sure which way to go and she suggested a lunch meeting with herself and Brian Stephens, the editor of Radio Two programmes. We had lunch in Langan's Bistro on Devonshire Street, a cosy, old-fashioned restaurant that was a quiet and discreet place for a chat. I was grateful that neither of them had ordered any wine. We did the usual bit of small talk and then Brian steered the conversation towards the future. He told me that Richard Allinson would continue doing the Saturday-afternoon programme, Des Lynham had given up the Friday show to concentrate on TV work, and so my working week would be a more normal Monday to Friday with a two-day weekend off.

'Now all your troubles are over,' he finished, 'we'd really like you to take up your *Drivetime* slot again – and so would all the listeners.'

I grinned. 'I bet you're all wondering whether I could still do the show as well without the help of the rocket fuel.'

Brian smiled as he and Jude exchanged glances.

'Well, um, er . . . the point was raised as to whether the new organic Johnnie Walker would have quite the same energy and pizzazz as the old version.'

'I bloody knew it, I just knew someone would mention that.'

We all laughed and in that instant my mind was made up. I'd go back and I'd bloody show 'em that I didn't need cocaine to do a good show.

'Not only can I do a show as good minus the charlie, I can do one even better. Tell Jim I'll give him a call.'

Smiles all round, lunch over. Jude and Brian went back to the Beeb and I headed back to Wiltshire. On the journey home, my head was spinning with a million and one thoughts. Would I really be able to go back and pick up from where I had left off? Did I still have the confidence to face an audience of millions, some of whom no doubt thought I should have been fired and never heard of again? And on the practical side, where was I going to live?

I was on my way to meet up with Jim Moir to talk about coming back to Radio Two and, as I turned the car left into Weymouth Street, I felt an incredibly strong psychic signal. It urged me to look to my right. So I did. I was looking at an estate agent's window. The feeling was so strong that I stopped, parked the car and checked out the properties in the window. £1 million, £1.2 million, £750,000 – they were all way out of my reach. I wondered why on earth I'd been led to look in here and was about to give up when I noticed the figure of £300. It was the weekly rental of a third-floor flat in Marylebone. That's more my level, I thought. I went inside and arranged to have a look at the flat later.

The meeting with Jim went well and I agreed to come back to *Drivetime* in a couple of weeks. I then went back to the estate agent and was taken round to check out the flat. It was perfect: a two-bedroom place, ten minutes' walk from the BBC, and available straightaway. I said a mental thank you for the guidance. And it wasn't just for the roof over my head. Soon after moving in, I discovered there was a daily lunchtime AA meeting five minutes' walk away and a weekly early-morning meeting almost next door.

Six months before, I had been addicted to cocaine, publicly disgraced, suspended from the BBC and homeless. I had really thought back then I was done for, that there would be no way back. Now here I was with my old job, a place to live and steering clear of all coke, alcohol and tobacco. Dealing with it had taxed my reserves of strength and fortitude but I couldn't have done it alone. I was so lucky to have such great support, and I had so many people to thank for my survival. There were my children and my friends, who had stuck by me, Jim Moir at the BBC, the Radio Two listeners and, of course, all the good people at Crossroads. They had all believed in me and helped so much.

Frances called and suggested I offer Beth the second bedroom in my flat as she was having a hard time in Brighton. Maybe a move to London would be just what she needed? Sam had lived with me in Maida Vale and now Beth's arrival completed the cycle of getting back some of the time I'd lost after Frances and I broke up in 1987. Beth was great company for me during the important lead-up to going back on air after a six-month break. I played her a favourite track of mine by Todd Snider called 'Alright Guy'. I loved the whole irreverent vibe of the song. The character in the song sings about smoking a little dope, getting a bit wild and drunk but, despite all that, he's 'an alright guy'.

'Hey, Beth. I reckon this would make a great opening record for my first day back. What do you think?'

'Go for it, Dad. I reckon it's perfect. Do it.'

Good old Beth. She gave just the right encouragement at the right time.

At 5.05 p.m. on my first day back, the sound of a rebellious Todd Snider signalled that I was back on the radio. I don't really know what the listeners' reaction was to the song, but it seems to have become a favourite for many and, from then on, I'd get regular emails and texts requesting it. It set the tone for the show. For my first words, I borrowed Brian Stephens' phrase and welcomed listeners to the 'new organic Johnnie Walker' show.

Once I was up and running, the nerves lessened and, with the usual banter going on between Sally Boazman and Martin Shankleman, I soon felt I was back home. The most important thing was to try and express my enormous gratitude to the listeners for the way in which they had supported me. I really do believe that without their cards, letters and emails my BBC career would have ended. So, to all those who took the trouble to write and email the BBC to offer support during my difficult times, I'd like to use the opportunity this book presents to say again: thank you very much for your help, kindness and understanding.

I was enjoying my new life as the clean, organic JW. I kept up the routine of at least two or three AA meetings a week. There were temptations, of course. I tried to reduce these by staying away from pubs. If I did go to a do where there was drink, I would stick to water and leave around the time people started repeating themselves – it's amazing, when you're sober, to observe the gradual effect of alcohol on people's behaviour, something you never notice when you're drinking with them.

Lunches with my old mate Adrian Williams were different now. We'd had a reputation in the music business for living it a bit too large at times. In our bad old charlie days, people would say, 'Watch out, here come the chemical brothers.' But now things were different and our lunches were a mineral water affair. Not quite as much fun as a bottle of Rioja and a couple of large Amarettos but the no-booze rule was the right way for me to go in those early days after rehab.

All seemed to be going well on *Drivetime* between five and seven p.m. I gave it my absolute all, as I was determined to prove that I had plenty enough energy to do a good programme without the supplements. After all, I'd done virtually all my thirty-plus years on the radio straight; it was only those stressful six months combined with a sad and lonely personal life that had sent me off the rails. Of all the drugs, I think cocaine is an evil, nasty, sneaky drug. Users think they can handle it, and they don't realize how nasty it makes them. Too much cocaine, and paranoia and irritability become a way of life. Relationships can be destroyed and bank accounts emptied.

I never, ever miss it and am so glad that's all in the past now.

Chapter Forty-Four

Who on earth was this big scruffy guy marching into the *Drivetime* office at Radio Two? He looked like a farmer and completely out of place. He came straight up to my desk and plonked down a CD and some blurb.

''Ere, Walker. I was told to make sure I put this on your desk. You are now the proud owner of the latest album by Gordon Haskell.'

Gordon Haskell. My mind went racing back to the late sixties and Polydor Records when Gordon was in the band Les Fleur de Lys. Over the years he had sent me some records and the odd flyer for a gig, but I never really did catch up with him. Now, forty years later, his music was being given to me by this unlikely character, whose name was Ian Brown and who indeed used to be a farmer – a pig farmer, no less – and was now dabbling in the music business. He was a character, and I always warm to characters.

'So, how's Gordon, then?' I asked. 'I haven't seen him for years, so it's good to know he's still making music.'

'He's doing all right,' said Ian. 'Doing regular gigs down along the South Coast and living in a nice little cottage in the country. Not making a fortune, but he's comfortable and has got himself a new lady friend. Yeah, life's pretty sweet. I'm sort of looking after him and promised him I'd make sure you got his new CD.'

The moment Ian mentioned Gordon's new lady friend, I started to get a tingling sensation in my spine, which meant my psychic radar was tuning into something. I just had to ask him about this woman.

'So what's she like, then, Ian?'

'Fantastic, very attractive, brilliant personality, does something in advertising and has done very well for herself.'

Again, as Ian talked about her, I had the strongest feeling that she was somehow going to be very important in my life. I couldn't stop the psychic impressions but I felt very guilty about them. Here I was, keen to renew contact with someone I hadn't seen for nearly forty years and I seemed to be getting obsessed with his new girlfriend, whom I hadn't even met. Hardly the way to renew a friendship by coming on to his lady – not how gentlemen should behave at all.

I genuinely did want to see Gordon again and asked Ian for his mobile number. That evening I listened to Gordon's new album and the next day gave him a call. We caught up a bit on our mutual news and arranged to have a drink after my show the following Monday. Ian mentioned that Gordon spent a couple of days in London every now and then at his lady's flat so I innocently asked for his London landline number: 'Just in case something comes up and I can't get you on the moby.' Now I cheekily had his girlfriend's home number, even if I didn't intend to use it.

Monday came and Gordon was waiting in Radio Two reception. We went to the BBC club next door, had a couple of drinks, played pool and did a big catch-up on our many adventures since the sixties.

'You hungry?' asked Gordon.

'Yeah, wouldn't mind something to eat. Any thoughts where you'd like to go?'

'Well, we could go to Tiggy's club, the Union, in Soho. She might join us for dinner,' said Gordon, oh so casually.

Oh my God. I hadn't expected this.

The Union is a small, intimate, members-only club in Greek Street, Soho. Gordon rang the bell and then we were ushered into a cosy room with a bar in the corner and tables round the walls. I followed him down a corridor towards the back, where there were sofas and comfortable chairs. He ordered a drink, water for me, and we continued filling in the years since we'd last met.

'Tiggy's gone to yoga tonight. She might come down later, so we'll wait a while before we order.'

I wasn't sure whether I wanted her to come or not. I felt very nervous, but excited at the same time. On the one hand, I was fascinated to meet this person whose very name had caused such a strong intuitive reaction in me. But then again, it might be a big anticlimax and leave me wondering what all the fuss was about. Maybe I had been reading far too much into my feelings. Perhaps all that rehab and self-examination had left me slightly out of touch with reality.

All these thoughts were rushing around my head as the evening wore on with still no sign of her. Watching others enjoying their wine and spirits, I was getting more and more bored with water and was desperate for something to eat. She obviously wasn't coming and I was about to ask Gordon if we could order some food. Then suddenly she was there. It was as though a ball of energy, light and laughter had materialized directly in the room. We stood, Gordon did the formal introduction and I just took her hand and kissed her on both cheeks. It was like greeting a long-lost friend. We sat in a triangle with Gordon and Tiggy in opposite chairs and myself on the small sofa between them. And we started talking. We talked and talked and talked.

There was so much we didn't need to talk about and so much we did. I felt I had known her for hundreds of years and now we were just catching up. I mentioned I had read a book called *Eat Right For Your Type*, which recommended a diet according to your blood group, and I was blood group A. Tiggy had also read the book and was type A. Punctuating this flow of words was a lot of laughter. Tiggy laughed a lot – and I immediately loved her for that alone. We talked about spirituality: how so many people in the West seemed to be lost without any sort of compass or something unseen to believe in; how materialism, selfishness and a lack of care or thought for others seemed to be the norm; how some cataclysmic event had to take place to make the West really wake up to examining their lives and discovering the real values of love, friendship, caring, tolerance and understanding.

Tiggy and I connected the instant we came into each other's space. Something very magical was happening and there was nothing we could do to prevent the flow.

It must have been after midnight when this incredible evening came to an end. Catching up again with Gordon after so many years had passed was great, and as for Tiggy . . . well, she was simply an amazing person. But she was with Gordon. Much as I would have loved to arrange to meet up again, I knew I shouldn't. I would just have to wait and let things take their course.

The next day was 11th September 2001, the day the world changed. Along with millions around the planet, I watched the events unfold on the TV news channels. It is the kind of time when you want so much to talk to like-minded people, to share the shock and try and make sense of it all. My mind went back to the previous night and our conversation about the West needing something to shock people into re-evaluating the meaning of life. We hadn't anticipated anything like this, let alone it happening the very next day. I wanted to call Tiggy but knew I shouldn't. I liked and respected Gordon and didn't want to do anything to cause him pain.

On Thursday Tiggy forwarded an email to my Radio Two address. I read it the next day. It was from an artist friend of hers in Chicago and Tiggy thought it might give me an insight into how an ordinary American citizen was reacting to the events of that week. I wanted an excuse to see her again so we could share our thoughts and feelings, so I emailed her back to thank her for her message, and I mentioned that I'd done some yoga in Antigua and was interested in finding out more. We arranged that I would meet her at a yoga centre in Primrose Hill the following Monday.

I was so nervous and was pacing up and down the hall when she arrived, all smiles and warm welcomes. I gave her a sheepish smile.

'This is a beginner's class, I hope. I haven't really done proper yoga before.'

'Oh yes, don't worry, nothing too difficult, you'll be fine.'

Tiggy went right up to the front of the class and I hid in the back corner as far away from the teacher as possible.

The class was most definitely not for beginners. Christ almighty, I couldn't do any of it. I thought yoga was all relaxed and gentle, this was bloody hard work. Everyone around me, mostly women, seemed to be having no problems at all getting into all the various positions but I was really struggling. I realized just how unfit and unsupple I really was. I was pretending to join in, all the while doing my best to be out of sight while managing to keep Tiggy in view.

After what seemed like hours, the lesson finally came to an end with some relaxing music and chanting as everyone lay on their mats. That bit I could do. I was sweating and exhausted, thinking what a big price I'd paid just to be able to see Tiggy again. She came over looking all apologetic.

'I'm so sorry, it was an advanced class and must have been a struggle for you.'

'Yeah, it was. But it wasn't all bad. I spent the last ninety minutes admiring your beautiful bum.'

Thankfully, she laughed and asked if I'd like to come for something to eat. We went to a small vegetarian restaurant across the road and were getting along fine – and then Simon, the instructor, came in and joined us. He was a very nice guy but I was hoping to have Tiggy all to myself.

At last, supper was over and I offered Tiggy a lift home. Then, for the first time, we were alone. I wanted to play her some of my favourite songs from the CDs I kept in the car. Funny how I only seemed to select the romantic love songs. We parked up outside her flat and I put in the John Prine CD *Lost Dogs And Mixed Blessings*. I'd played it a lot at Crossroads and I loved all the songs, but most especially 'All The Way With You'. It was very soon to play a song like that, but I wanted to share the beauty of it with her. It was a very different 'all the way' to the phrase used in my teenage years. This song spoke of being together for always and that was exactly what I wanted. From the first moments of our meeting at the Union, I had felt lifted into some magical, spiritual place in Tiggy's presence, and I never wanted that feeling to end. But she had Gordon in her life, and I didn't want to lose the friendship so recently rekindled.

And so I was ready to just say goodnight and didn't expect to be invited in for coffee. But I was, and I couldn't refuse. Tiggy made herbal tea and played me some of her music as we sat perched on opposite ends of the sofa. It all seemed so strange, trying to be physically distant when I think we were both yearning to hold each other. I asked if this platonic friendship could allow a hug. She said yes. We moved closer together, I put my arm round her and she snuggled into my shoulder. I looked down at her face and her beautiful mouth and, unable to resist, we kissed. And what an amazing kiss: now I knew nothing would be quite the same again. There was no need for words apart from a polite thank you for a lovely evening. We wished each other goodnight and I went home.

Gordon had no idea about my yoga evening, or that I'd been in contact with Tiggy at all. But in an amazing piece of good fortune for me, he called Tiggy the day after our first kiss to say that he didn't feel their relationship was working any more. And so, their summer dalliance came to an end. Tiggy and I were now free to be together, and we still had Gordon's mutual friendship. He had always told Tiggy that he felt his role in her life would be as a stepping stone to something or someone else.

I managed to return his goodwill when Tiggy encouraged me to listen properly to Gordon's album *Harry's Bar*. In the weeks after 9/11, people were taking a long hard look at their lives and evaluating the things that were truly important. The song 'How Wonderful You Are' just seemed to jump out from the album as a good song for the times. It didn't have a big production but was a simple, pure song about the importance of love. I felt it had a healing power, so I took it in to the studio one evening and played it on the air.

The response was immediate and dramatic. Hundreds of emails and texts came flooding in from people who were moved by the record, keen to know more about the singer and to hear it again. So the following day, I gave it another play and, again, we had the same massive response. Michael Parkinson heard it in his car and immediately contacted his producer to get him a copy of the record for his Sunday-morning programme.

Head of music at Radio Two, Colin Martin, also heard it on the way home and the next day came to ask me about it and to tell me he wanted to put it on the playlist. Gordon's manager went into overdrive on the press and promotion and, as we got nearer and nearer to the end of the year, 'How Wonderful You Are' looked a strong contender for the all-important Christmas Number One. Gordon signed a big record and publishing deal and, almost overnight, his life changed dramatically. From having a loyal but very small following in the south of the country, he was rapidly becoming a household name. The whole thing was a lovely karmic reward for Gordon's grace and dignity in accepting Tiggy and me falling in love. He so nearly had the Number One but was up against the heavyweight duo of Robbie Williams and Nicole Kidman's version of 'Something Stupid'. They had the last *Top of the Pops* slot before Christmas; maybe if Gordon had been on the show as well, things might have been different.

But we all had a great time. Gordon and his management team didn't take too seriously all that was happening. They had fun and enjoyed it. When Tiggy came back from making a commercial in Australia, we decided to give her a special welcome. She came into the arrivals lounge to be met by a pantomime horse and a gorilla playing and singing 'How Wonderful You Are'.

I don't know who suffered the most – me in the back of the horse or Gordy, who was sweating buckets inside the gorilla suit.

Chapter Forty-Five

2002

Tiggy and I just clicked from the start. We didn't move in together but spent as much time together as we could. Sam and Beth got on with her immediately, which made me very happy.

I wanted to introduce Tiggy to the joys of motorcycling and one weekend, on the spur of the moment, we decided to ride to Cornwall. I thought Tiggy was very brave in agreeing to ride pillion, having never been on a bike before. My mate Snapper, a wild Somerset farmer who was as mad about Harleys as I was and often accompanied me on biking trips, joined us and we set off on two yellow Harley Fat Boys. There was an autumn chill in the air as we headed west and, as usual with Snapper, there were all sorts of unplanned stops and detours along the way. It was getting cold and dark as we neared our planned destination of Tintagel. My admiration for Tiggy soared. She had no proper biking clothes, and it was much colder riding pillion than she'd expected, but she courageously carried on without complaint.

How wonderfully welcoming, then, were the big log fires and hot baths at the Camelot Hotel, a huge imposing castle-like building standing atop the cliffs with the wild Atlantic crashing on the rocks far below. It was all very Arthurian as we ate at an enormous round table, lit by candles in the massive wrought-iron chandelier overhead. Thanks to the warmth of the hotel, some good food and wine, we enjoyed a deep restful sleep.

It was sunny and warm the next day as we cruised along the coast road, a reward for having endured the hardship of the journey down. We stopped at a small bay and Snapper stayed with the bikes as Tiggy and I walked along the shore and then sat on the rocks gazing out to sea. It was a scene of great beauty, peace and calm. We were so in love and anything seemed possible. It was a place to reflect on our lives, our hopes, our dreams. I asked Tiggy what her dream was, and after some thought she told me about *Antonia*, a novel she'd been given by her father when she was sixteen. He had planted a seed by saying that it might make a good film one day. Tiggy's big ambition in life was to make a wonderful film based on Antonia's amazing life.

'What's yours?' she asked.

'To spend the rest of my life with you.'

It's what I genuinely felt and wanted. Yes, we were right in those heady moments of a new love, and perhaps after a while it would all change and I'd come back down to reality but, right there and then, a connection was made that would prove to be strong enough to survive anything. Reluctantly we had to head back home and leave behind that magical place, and soon we were back on the busy M5, returning to all the hustle and bustle of normal life. We stopped at a service station and Tiggy bought me a coffee and muffin and I joked with Snapper that here was a woman I should marry.

Some weeks later, we went for dinner at a friend's house and, as the evening wore on, they suggested we stay the night as long as we didn't mind having to sleep in a single bed. We fell asleep in each other's arms and awoke with our arms still wrapped round each other. I looked into Tiggy's eyes. They say eyes are the windows to the soul and, at that moment, I really felt I was seeing hers. It was then that I wanted to propose but, knowing that a week later we'd be in Florence for my birthday weekend, I decided that the Ponte Vecchio Bridge would be a much more romantic location.

So, when we had arrived in Florence and enjoyed a lovely dinner together, we walked to the bridge and stopped in a small coffee place at one end where I had an espresso and a brandy – I had started drinking moderately again and this was definitely a time when I needed to steady my nerves. There were young Italians laughing and joking as I rehearsed the words. We strolled to the centre of the bridge. Now was the time.

'Tiggy, as I'm going to spend the rest of my life with you, I wonder if you would do me the honour of being my wife.'

There was a stunned silence before she asked me several times, 'Are you sure, Johnnie, are you sure?'

I told her I had never been more sure of anything and she finally said yes.

The next day I had to leave her and fly back to London as the weekend was the beginning of a month-long language course for Tiggy. It was hard being without her for a month but at last she returned to me, now my fiancée. We planned for a summer wedding in the beautiful Larmer Tree Gardens in Dorset. It was to be a big do with Tiggy's friends and relations flying in from Italy, Germany and even Australia. Then, to my eternal shame and regret, I chickened out with just five weeks to go.

Instead of accepting the wondrous gift life had given me, I began to let fears and doubts take over. Was I allowing myself to get carried away with the whole romantic notion of living happily ever after? Would being married spoil what we had? What if I was making a terrible mistake and was heading into another failure? I had wanted my marriage to Frances to last for ever, and the pain of our separation and leaving Sam and Beth were memories that still hurt deep inside. I had told a wise and knowing massage therapist at Crossroads about throwing away my past when I hurled the battered old rock into the ocean. She told me that was something you can't really do. Those events happened and cannot be undone; it's better to acknowledge, learn from and accept the past, and then do one's best to move on. That's the part I find so hard: the letting go and moving on. Perhaps it is a lack of self-esteem. I somehow don't feel I deserve good things. Here I was again, destroying something potentially so good.

I'd had a weekend apart from Tiggy worrying about all this. Then, on the Monday, I phoned her and told her of my fears and that I didn't feel sure enough to go through with the wedding. I think most women's reaction would be one of enormous anger and betrayal, and the relationship would have been over there and then. Tiggy, of course, was different.

'Well if you're not ready, you're not ready,' she said.

I was amazed at her calm reaction.

'What shall we do about the honeymoon?' I asked. We'd booked the Residencia in Majorca. 'I don't suppose you still fancy going?'

She thought about it for what seemed like an age and then stunned me with her reply.

'Yes, I'll come with you. And if you want, we could try and extend the stay so we're not in the country on what would have been our wedding day.'

I was very humbled by her acceptance of my behaviour. I'd been expecting a terrible scene and perhaps the end of our relationship. Instead, I got a calm, measured, forgiving response. Later, when I asked her why she had been like this, she said simply, 'I knew I might have to wait but I also knew without a doubt that we were always going to be together.'

When we arrived at the Residencia, neither of us had the heart to inform the hotel that we hadn't actually got married and we were shown into the honeymoon suite with its fabulous four-poster bed covered in red rose petals formed into the shape of a heart, and a bottle of champagne cooling in an ice bucket on the table. It didn't feel right to drink it and so we left it behind for the chambermaid. But what we did have was the most blissfully happy holiday either of us had ever known.

It was there, far away from pressure, from outside expectations and reminders of the past that we truly fell in love. Days were spent lazing around the small pool high up on a beautiful terrace, playing backgammon for a thousand pretend pounds a point, enjoying grilled fish and salad at Deya beach and late at night, high above the hotel, we'd sit in the jacuzzi gazing at the stars.

We discussed marriage again, with thoughts of a Christmas wedding in the little village church in Ashmore, Dorset. Perhaps having the honeymoon first was the best way for us. It reminded me of the Native American way of preparing for marriage. In their tradition, two people in love would leave the village or camp and go off on a walkabout together for weeks or months, however long it took to really get to know each other and have the space and time to plan their future without any pressure. If they came back separately, there was no inquisition about what went wrong, just an acceptance back into the tribe as single people. If they came back together, they would be considered man and wife, and celebrations would be planned to honour and bless their union. But before then, there was another marriage to celebrate. While he was out in Sydney, Sam had fallen in love with a wonderful girl called Julianne and they got married there in the autumn of 2002. Beth, Frances and I flew out to be there and it was a beautiful family occasion. We were warmly welcomed by Julianne's family and it was a delight to have her as part of ours.

When I got back, Tiggy and I had several meetings with Ashmore's vicar. A quiet wedding with just our respective families and a handful of friends was planned for 21st December 2002. Sam agreed to be my best man with support from Gordon and Snapper. This time there was no wavering, but that didn't stop the nerves. The night before the wedding, Sam and I stayed at Gordy's place in Shaftesbury and we had a quiet boys' night in. I was starting to feel nervous but also very excited about the coming big day.

The wedding day was a damp, misty, Sherlock Holmes sort of a day, very different to the beautiful sunshine that had shone down on Larmer Tree Gardens on what would have been our wedding day in June. But somehow the wintry weather suited this time of year and that pre-Christmas magic was already in the air. As I arrived at the church, I could imagine all the last-minute fuss going on in Tiggy's cottage across the road. They'd had a girls' night there: her best friend, Jacquie; Sam's wife, Julianne; and Dennie, a stylist from London who had come down to do Tiggy's hair and make-up. For the umpteenth time, I made sure Sam had the ring, and we checked each other for smartness, greeted those outside the church and headed into the front pew. I could hear the little church filling up with people and looked behind to see my brother Michael and sisters Maureen and Christine take their places behind me and Sam. Tiggy's folks were on the other side. The time was five to one, with the bride due to arrive at one o'clock. Phew, it was all going according to schedule.

I got more and more nervous as the minutes ticked slowly away: five past one, ten past one . . . still no sign of the bridal party.

It got to a quarter past and the whispers and rustling behind me were getting louder. I sneaked a look and Maureen caught my gaze. She mouthed the words, 'I think she's changed her mind.' Which maybe she found funny, but I didn't. Simon Everett, the vicar, came through from the vestry and he nervously checked his watch and walked down the aisle to the church entrance to see if there was any sign of the bride.

And then, suddenly, I picked up a change in the atmosphere. The church went noticeably quieter and there was a strong feeling of anticipation. At last, they must be here. The organist began playing. Sam and I were almost at attention, standing shoulder to shoulder, trying to look tall and impressive. I wanted to sneak a look behind. Should I? For some reason I felt tradition thought it unlucky, so I kept my gaze to the front. I felt her come near and looked sideways and there, on her father's arm, was my precious Tiggy.

Her normal curly hair was long and straight and she was wearing a deep-purple full-length velvet dress. Around her neck was a narrow purple ribbon with a small silver cross encrusted with purple stones and she carried a lovely bouquet of antique white roses. She looked radiantly beautiful and completely took my breath away.

The church felt so full of love and Simon conducted a wonderful service. I will never forget the moment when, after having exchanged rings, Tiggy and I held hands and then Simon took the long, embroidered silk stole vicars wear round their necks and wrapped it round our hands several times. He cupped our hands in his and then spoke with such strength and conviction.

'What God has joined together, let no man put asunder.'

Tiggy smiled and we went forward to sign the register. Then it was time for us to walk down the aisle, this time as husband and

wife, to the music of The Doors song 'Light My Fire'. Just as we
began our walk, my friend Snapper stood up on his pew and,
with an almighty holler, yelled out, 'YEEEEEE HAWWWWW!
They've finally done it!'

Everybody erupted into applause, cheers and laughter. The
formality of atmosphere and behaviour in a place of worship was
instantly transformed – another piece of magic from the unique
Snapper. As we stepped through the porch into the grounds outside, there was a very special visitor. Standing proudly on the
church path was Wicked Willy, Tiggy's horse. He was groomed
magnificently and looked immaculate. From his bearing he obviously thought he was the most important guest of all.

Gordon's wedding gift was to arrange for a gorgeous little vin-
tage car to take us off to our wedding lunch. The usual confetti
was thrown and we set off for the short journey to the nearby
village of Farnham and the Museum Inn. Sitting at two long tables
with Tiggy heading up one and myself at the other, we all enjoyed
an excellent lunch – and then came the speeches. Best man Sam's
was very good, embarrassing me by touching on some lurid tales
from my past. All the guests enjoyed it, with the possible exception
of Diana, my new mother-in-law, who seemed rather shocked.
After my speech, I announced we would 'open the floor' and
anyone who would like to say a few words was very welcome to
do so.

My sister Christine stood up and began her speech by announcing that, as Tiggy's family might not know that much about our
family history, she would like to tell the assembled throng all about
her brother Peter. Without any notes, Christine then gave the
most magnificent speech, touching on the various milestones in
my life and the bold decisions I had made to realize my ambition
to be a DJ. It was brilliantly delivered and I was enormously proud
of her. It was also well received by Diana, whose faith in her
daughter's choice of husband was now somewhat restored.

Gordon gave us the benefit of his slightly off-the-wall Reginald
Perrin humour and then Snapper decided this was his moment to
entertain the room. He talked and talked, and then he talked some

more. I thought he was never going to stop. There was lots of good-natured heckling and banter and our wedding lunch drew to a close.

Tiggy and I went off to her cottage in Ashmore to change and rest up before part two of the celebrations. I had come up with the idea of going off to a favourite little pub on the South Coast for our first night together. The Anchor Inn was a well-kept secret in a tiny little place called Seatown. Perched on the side of a small bay virtually on the beach, it was run by David and Sadie, who believed in serving good, wholesome, home-cooked food and David, who loved music, would arrange special nights when groups or singer-songwriters would come and play. There were a couple of rooms on the first floor and, although it was normally closed in the winter, I asked Sadie if we could possibly come and stay there on our wedding night.

It was terrible weather that night, but we arrived safely and found that we had the pub to ourselves as no one else wanted to venture out. We were joined by a group of close friends and, at the end of an amazing, memorable day and a wonderful, jolly evening, the new Mr and Mrs Walker climbed the stairs. In our room there was a card waiting for us with the words: *December 21st – Shortest Day – Longest Night!*

It hadn't even crossed our minds that it was the winter solstice but we were entirely happy with the 'longest night' bit. The card was from David and Sadie, who'd also scattered paper petals on our bed. Such thoughtful touches made our little room overlooking the sea all the more special. We had been blessed with a most wonderful wedding day and now we had Christmas and the rest of our lives together to look forward to.

I was booked to do the Radio Two breakfast show for Christmas week, apart from Terry Wogan's Christmas Day show. It didn't matter that I was working because it didn't feel like work. Tiggy and I were both on such a high, it was a very special time. We had a wonderful, traditional Christmas in Ashmore and then returned to London so I could carry on doing the breakfast show the following week.

When the breakfast show was over, we packed ready for our trip to India. We'd debated about whether to have another 'honeymoon' or not – after all, we'd already had one the previous June in Majorca. But the idea of getting away to somewhere warm and sunny in January was too good to resist, so we went to the Kerala region on the south-west coast.

Landing at the airport, I was unprepared for the total assault on all the senses. The heat, the noise, the crowds, the chaos were incredible. But I loved everything about the place: the people, the fantastic vegetarian food, the madness of the roads and the spirituality of life there. Such poverty, so many people with nothing in Western terms, and yet they had so much. They were content, happy, with a deep connection between each person as if they were one huge family. Anyone they didn't know was just a friend waiting to be met.

The holiday was made up of short stays in different places. Fascinating as it all was, some days were a real effort as I just didn't seem to have my normal amount of energy, but I put it down to the intense heat. The energy problem carried on, though, even after we got back to London. It always takes a while to get over a long flight and time-zone change but it seemed like I never recovered. And there were other problems too.

What happened next should be told by my wife, Tiggy.

Chapter Forty-Six
Tiggy's Chapter

When I married Johnnie, I knew life was never going to be dull again. But I don't think anyone could have predicted just how dramatic the first year would be.

Over two months after our return from India, Johnnie still had 'Delhi belly'. He had to get up at least three times a night and it was exhausting him. Thinking that he may have picked up a tropical disease, he agreed to go to see his doctor, who promptly told him to have a colonoscopy. It took place on Friday, 25th April 2003 at the Princess Grace Hospital near Baker Street in London.

I was standing at the fish counter in Waitrose when he called me. I was surprised to be hearing from him so soon – I thought they knocked you out for some time. But all had not gone according to plan.

'Darling,' he said, 'it's not good. I think you'd better come and join me.'

There was only one thing he could mean. I ran up Marylebone High Street in panic. He met me in the reception, took my hand and led me outside to the grey London afternoon.

'I'm so sorry, darling, it seems I've got cancer. I'm so sorry. I'm so sorry.'

It was typical of Johnnie. He was not thinking about himself, but someone else – in this case, me. He explained that they could not get the camera inside him because there was a huge obstruction, almost certainly a tumour. He had waited for me to join him before getting the full low-down from Mr Darudi, the specialist (or 'bum bandit' as we affectionately refer to him). We sat in his small consulting room, clinging on to each other as we waited to hear his sentence. He told us that Johnnie would need a serious operation to remove the tumour. It was a massive shock and we were stunned as he took us through the issues of risk, timing, side effects and likelihood of survival. Mr Darudi told us that Johnnie's attitude was of paramount importance in getting through this. It was going to be a rollercoaster of a ride.

Hours later, we were driving down to our Dorset cottage. We talked about who should know, whether he'd lose his job, how we would survive financially, whether he would ever lay a proper turd again . . . I am usually the 'together' one, but that evening, I fell apart, and Johnnie was the one who stayed strong – he even drove us down to the cottage. I think I was in a greater state of shock than he was.

Telling his family was difficult. Johnnie called them from the cottage and told them the news as gently as he could but, of course, Sam and Beth were dreadfully upset. The week that followed was also hard, as he had a CT scan and waited for results. On the Tuesday he called me fifteen minutes before going on air. He was in a real state and asked that I come in to the studio. It is the only time I have ever sat by his side throughout a show. His team wondered what on earth I was doing there but, as usual, he was a complete professional and managed to make it through with no one any the wiser.

We were due to see Mr Darudi on Wednesday. It was cancelled. So was Thursday's appointment. Johnnie was beside himself, spending the nights on the Internet and coming back to bed with statistics laden with doom. He worked out he had a twenty per cent chance of survival. After several agonizingly long days, we finally saw Mr Darudi on Friday to hear the results of the biopsy. As we waited in his consulting room, Johnnie picked up his file to have a quick peep at the scans.

'If it's on my lungs, I'm giving up,' he said bleakly.

His father had died from lung cancer, and his brother John of bowel cancer just five years earlier.

Darudi joined us. His mood was positive and, to our huge relief, he told us that it was a non-Hodgkin's lymphoma, not a tumour. The way to attack it was with chemotherapy, not an operation. His relief, too, was palpable. Only then did we learn just how dangerous an operation could have been – not least, the risk to the erectile function. We were handed over to the care of Professor Lister at St Bartholomew's. As one of his young doctors said, 'They broke the mould after Lister.' They certainly did. He was brusque and supremely confident. I started to cry in the initial consultation and he looked at me incredulously before barking at the nurse, 'Sister! Tissues!', which he thumped down on the desk before me. But he knew his stuff and we learnt that under that hard exterior was a man of the driest wit, who genuinely cared.

He wanted to start chemo as soon as possible. However, quite by chance, we had recently been invited by Vodafone to attend the Monaco Grand Prix at the end of May. Going there was one of Johnnie's long-held dreams, but if he started the chemo now, it would not be safe to travel. He bravely explained to Lister that he really had to go.

'Why?' retorted the Prof. 'Are you driving?'

He did agree to the delay, and we did go to Monaco. It was possibly the best weekend of our lives together. We were treated to a weekend of unparalleled hospitality. We dined on a boat in the harbour, we saw qualifying and the race from a fantastic balcony just near the start/finish line, and just to finish it off nicely, we were flown back to Nice airport in a chopper. The weekend gave us both an incredible lift. We actually forgot about cancer for a while.

Fate is a strange thing. Having won a stay of execution so that we could go to the race, Johnnie had not started the chemo when Dr Francisco Contreras, author of *The Coming Cancer Cure*, flew in from Mexico to give a lecture in London about an alternative form of treatment. We learnt how, at his Hospital of Hope in Mexico, he was having incredible results healing cancer patients and prolonging their lives with vitamin B17, which is found in apricot kernels. This lecture spoke volumes to Johnnie, who all his life had resisted any use of chemicals in his body (especially the legal ones). As chance would have it, the one place in the UK where you could receive this treatment was in Verwood, Dorset – not far from our cottage. Within a few days, Johnnie was booked on to the next available course, which was to start on 23rd June.

In the meantime he had to tell Professor Lister his decision. Lister's response was as expected.

'It will not work. Unless you have chemotherapy, you will die.'

But Johnnie stuck to his guns. While he psyched himself up to become a detoxed vegan, I got it in the neck from his then-agent, Michael Cohen, whose wife had once had cancer, and from the professor. They both cared deeply, but I was starting to find the pressure tough; the phone calls telling me he would not survive were hard to take. But when Johnnie has decided on a course of action, it is hard to persuade him otherwise. Besides, I really respected him for going down the alternative route and I embraced it with the same fervour he did. I was going to do all I could to help and be there on every step of whichever path Johnnie chose.

Before he could start treatment, Johnnie had to let his listeners know that he was not going to be around. The Radio Two bosses, Jim Moir and Lesley Douglas, had been wonderfully supportive, and also extremely discreet. But now, six weeks after diagnosis, it was time to go public. On Thursday, 5th June he made an announcement at the end of his show. It was not at all self-pitying, but he explained that having such a public job and needing time off for treatment, it was best that he was open. When he had finished, he played Simon and Garfunkel's 'Bridge Over Troubled Water' for everyone who is affected by cancer. I can't hear that track today without thinking of Johnnie's braveness that evening. It was the most moving piece of radio I have ever heard. There was an immediate outpouring of love and sympathy from the listeners: an avalanche of emails, text messages and cards arrived, all expressing shock and upset at the news, and offering all their support. It was a great boost for Johnnie.

The treatment at the Brackendene Clinic in Verwood consisted of six patients and five spouses sitting in Dr Paul Layman's front room each weekday morning for three weeks. As the patients sat there, receiving three-hour infusions of vitamin B17, we took part in discussions about weird and wonderful forms of healing and we all followed an extremely strict vegan detoxing regime. This suited some more than others. One patient, George, fantasized about roast beef, Yorkshire pud and apple crumble on an almost daily basis. I just hope he had a good helping of it before he passed away five months later.

It was a fascinating time and cleansing on all levels – emotional, spiritual and physical. We went through some extremely heavy counselling, as a couple and individually. Emotions were released and tears flowed; it was cathartic and also very supportive. As the weeks passed, the patients really set up a bond because only they could understand what the others were going through. For the partners and spouses, it was a great help to have others in the same position to share with.

While it was a fascinating time, in Johnnie's case, the treatment did not help and his condition deteriorated. His lymphoma grew, and extra lumps appeared in his neck. These proved to be new lymphomas. Damn it – we had lived this pure, stress-free life but to no avail.

We returned to Professor Lister, cap in hand, and honestly quite afraid. As well as the disease spreading, Johnnie had lost heaps of weight, was passing much blood and had become chronically anaemic. The professor didn't say, 'I told you so.' He was just extremely glad to have Johnnie back in his care and a chance to make him better. He told us to go straight to a restaurant in Smithfield Market and eat a steak. Having been committed vegans for three weeks as a part of the healing, this was hard to hear. Johnnie had to have an additional biopsy on the lumps in his neck, and then, because of the passage of time, go through all the tests again including the CT scan and dreaded bone-marrow test.

The tension between us rose as soon as we were back in this environment. In the taxi on the way to St Bart's for the bone-marrow test, we started to bicker. By the time we got to Smithfield Square, Johnnie was explosive. And explode he did. In full view of everyone in the square he screamed at me, 'It's my fucking cancer. Leave me alone with it. Just fuck off!'

He turned on his heels and stormed in to the hospital. I had walked about half a mile in a state of shock when his text came begging forgiveness and asking me to join him. When I did, I could see why he was so on edge. Taking the bone-marrow is an awful procedure. So, for Johnnie, is giving blood. He has very wispy, weak veins, which meant every time he gave a blood sample or had a canula inserted, he was in real pain. I will always remember seeing his agonized screwed-up face, teeth fully exposed like a braying horse and eyes tight shut, as they inserted the needle into various parts of his body to try and find a receptive site.

His anaemia was so bad that the first chemo session had to be delayed. He needed to have two bags of blood transfused into him before he could start the treatment.

Johnnie had been afraid of chemo since his diagnosis, and, as it happens, he had every reason to be. To say that he and chemo did not get on is an understatement. At the end of it all, they had to admit that they had never known anyone have such a hard time of it. It was as though he was allergic to it.

There is a dangerous phase during each chemo cycle when your immune system is not strong enough to fight any infection. Without fail, Johnnie would get ill each time and have to be admitted to the dreaded Bodley Scott ward at St Bart's. It was always such a sinking moment for us both when his temperature would rise up above the safe level and the hospital staff would tell me to bring him straight in.

One night I woke to find him crawling on the bathroom floor throwing up bile. He was in such a state. Like a critically wounded animal, he just cried, 'Please let me die. Please let me die.' I have never seen anyone in such a sorry state. I almost felt guilty as I collected him up, grabbed a bucket and dressing gown and took him back to St Bart's. It was four a.m. so at least getting there was quick.

The summer of 2003 was incredibly hot in London. Needless to say, Bodley Scott had no air conditioning, and the windows could only be opened a small amount – 'So we don't jump out,' Johnnie would say. As he was usually in there with a blazing temperature, he truly suffered.

He hated the food, felt dreadful, had every conceivable side effect, including mouth ulcers, constipation and nausea, and so spent his day thinking about what might cheer him up. He would send out numerous text messages asking for anything from a home-made egg and cress sandwich to a particular item of clothing from a specific shop. I would run around all day trying to fulfil his desires and, in the late afternoon, come by with the requests and a picnic, which we ate in the ward kitchen. In truth, he really lost his appetite, so finding anything he would eat was challenging.

I was not always obliging. When his request was for a portable DVD player I put my foot down. Why did he need one of these when he could watch films on his laptop? Well, he'd seen someone else on the ward with one and he was *not* going to be held back by me just because he lay in a hospital bed. How smug he was when I next went in, and there sitting on his lap was a brand-new Panasonic DVD player. He had called a dealer he knows in Tottenham Court Road and got it biked over. Putting one over on me made it all the more satisfying.

Another time he requested a white linen shirt with long sleeves, which would hide his canula so he could sneak out of hospital. We called it his 'Freedom Shirt'. One 'Freedom' evening, his son, Sam, joined us. We had dinner in a local Indian restaurant. A couple of bottles and many hours later, we were the last to leave the restaurant. Johnnie's mobile went. It was the night nurse looking for him as his next drugs were due. Having told her he was just outside and coming back to the ward, Johnnie felt like a naughty boy, delighted to be breaking the rules and getting away with it. It made him feel alive again.

We mostly had to stay in London so that we were close to the hospital, but during Johnnie's few safe days, we could get down to Dorset. One day down there he realized that his hair was starting to come out in clumps when he washed it. I think this was one of his greatest fears. Not only was it a profound milestone that proved the chemotherapy was affecting all of his body, but the change in his physical appearance turned sadness to anger. He stormed off to Shaftesbury, returning two hours later – bald. He'd had it all shaved off. It was a shocking moment, but one that had to happen. It was part self-torture and part self-preservation.

Another bad day was when we heard that Noel Edmonds would be taking over his show for a couple of months. Poor Johnnie was so scared. Not only was he fighting for his health, but now his job was under threat. Stuart Maconie had been doing so well replacing him: he kept the same format, and had a great loyalty to Johnnie. But Noel was a different story. It seemed he was desperate to re-establish himself with the BBC after a lengthy absence and press stories about him taking over the show were everywhere. It was the only time I was upset with his bosses. How could they have been so insensitive? Johnnie was lying in Bodley Scott ward when Noel's first show was on. He listened to the start of the show and was decidedly depressed by what he heard. Noel was not only doing the show, but it sounded as if he was making it his own. Texts came in from friends, begging Johnnie to get better soon. These, and emails from the listeners, certainly bolstered him up, and his paranoia gradually subsided.

Throughout the time, his listeners were absolutely wonderful, sending cards, messages, presents and prayers. The response was overwhelming. Great box-loads of mail would be delivered, and when Johnnie felt energetic enough we would have hour-long sessions opening envelopes and reading messages of love and support. I don't think he could understand why so many people cared. I certainly hadn't realized how loved he was.

But despite huge amounts of love being sent his way, he sank further and further into depression. As the chemo progressed, he simply descended into a darker and more lonely place with each day that passed. In my diary I described him as a zombie spending his entire time shuffling between the television and his computer. He was exhausted. He usually slept in the spare room and at times the communication between us almost broke down completely. While I would try to guess his every need, he rejected everything. He would hardly eat, and became quite cruel. I now realize that the poison that was being pumped into him was coming back out with almost as much venom. But, at the time, we were still only eight months into our marriage, and I feared that the beautiful, kind, spiritual soulmate that I thought I had wed was, in fact, an utter bastard.

One day he gave me a verbal savaging that almost broke me. I felt more lost than I have ever been. I couldn't speak to him, so I wrote instead – a very long and angry letter – and then went out, leaving it for him. When I returned later, the letter had been read and he realized just how unrecognizable and self-absorbed he had become. It wasn't a fairytale ending – we didn't kiss and make up and go back to our old selves – because Johnnie was still hurting so very much. But he thawed towards me and I knew then I would have to sit it out. It is shocking to read that letter again now. It is full of hurt and anger and is my own cry for help. But at least it cleared the air for a while.

Then, something good happened. After some more tests, we were given an amazing surprise. The lymphoma had gone. All the pain and suffering had been worthwhile. But when Professor Lister said he wanted to give Johnnie three more sessions of chemo, just to be sure, I retorted, 'But it will kill him.' In the most uncharacteristic act of compliance, Johnnie agreed that he should have the treatments. I couldn't believe my ears; he had suffered so much.

Shortly before chemo was due to begin, we watched a programme about the up-coming demise of Concorde. Johnnie sorrowfully told me that it had always been one of his dreams to fly on it. I looked up his schedule of treatment and calculated that there were about four 'safe' days in the next chemo cycle. Next morning I called BA, raided my rainy-day savings account and booked us two Concorde flights to New York for the final Thursday it was due to fly – 16th October 2003. Johnnie just could not believe it. For the first time in months, he was not just happy, he was incredibly excited. Professor Lister and his team really came up trumps, making sure that the dates would work.

But nine days before we were due to go, I woke in the early morning to Johnnie screaming in pain. The treatment often caused painful constipation – this time it seemed even worse. St Bart's told me to bring him straight in.

'I can't – we're in Dorset!'

They told me to get him to the nearest hospital.

Crawling round the bathroom floor, Johnnie screamed at me, 'Call a fucking ambulance!'

It was a nightmare day. I followed the 'fucking' ambulance to Salisbury District Hospital, where I found Johnnie in a side room in A&E. I don't think anyone knew what to do with him. He was given some morphine and then left alone. After an hour or so in this room, Johnnie started to panic. He was beside himself. He knew this was serious and had read about people being left on trolleys for up to eight hours.

He yelled at me, 'If they don't come and see me and give me some more morphine, I'm going to smash this room up.'

As he was flat out on a stretcher, immobilized by pain, I doubted he would be able to. I pleaded with every nurse and doctor I saw. Six hours later he was moved to the oncology ward. He was going rapidly downhill. Finally, consultant surgeon Nick Carty (or 'Superhero', as we know him now) arrived to take a look at him. He was convinced something was very wrong, as vast quantities of morphine had not quelled the pain at all. While everyone else wanted him moved to intensive care, Carty insisted he go for a scan. Thank heavens he did, for only then did they realize that Johnnie's intestines had burst open and he was suffering from acute peritonitis. The chemo had weakened the bowel wall where the tumour had been, and the constipation caused the burst. Without an operation that night, Johnnie would certainly die.

I was asked to break the news to him. It was one of the most difficult moments of my life. As I did, I remembered that Martha Thompson, a clairvoyant he had visited, had once told him that he would have an operation and would be taken right to the edge, but that he would survive. Reminding him of that was a huge comfort to us both. The last I saw of him was at 10.30 p.m. He was laid out on the trolley outside the theatre.

My final words were to Mr Carty: 'Take great care of him. He's very precious.'

Johnnie waved weakly and smiled. I drove home, numb and exhausted.

I got the call from Mr Carty at 3.30 a.m. Johnnie had survived – just. He was now in the ICU but in a very grave condition. The next four hours were critical. I sat in bed, fighting off thoughts of a funeral. Several times I called his dedicated nurse. I was told each time he was 'critical but stable'. Once he had survived the initial four hours, I called Sam and Beth and they were both with me at the hospital by early afternoon. For all of us, it was a huge shock to see Johnnie unconscious on a life-support machine with bleeping monitors and tubes everywhere.

Nick Carty and the head nurse took Sam, Beth and me into a small room for a briefing. Nick was sweating profusely. I knew he'd been up till about four a.m. with Johnnie, and then working again a few hours later, but even so, it was a worrying sign. He must have seen the look on my face, as he excused his soaking appearance – he was in training and had just run a half marathon. He then warned us that the situation was critical: anything could happen in the next four days; Johnnie was far from safe.

Sam asked questions about survival rates, and grappled with statistics. I, however, felt confident. I simply could not believe that my husband had gone through the past few months of suffering just to pop his clogs now. I felt all along that he was going through this whole drama for a spiritual reason that none of us could understand. This was a lesson, and from this lesson he would be able to help others in the future. So I said that Johnnie had always proved himself to have an incredibly strong spirit and that he would certainly survive. The rest of the room looked at me utterly unconvinced.

My worst fright was the next morning when I was woken at 5.30 a.m. by a call from the hospital.

'Yes?' I shouted in fear down the receiver. 'What's happened?'

His nurse was calling.

'I told your husband it was too early to call but he insisted that I phone you to tell you he loves you so much and he's doing okay. Also, could you bring in his glasses.'

Huh! Not only had he come to, but the requests had already started. This was indeed a good sign.

That morning I went into hospital as usual. Seeing Johnnie conscious was wonderful and extremely emotional. I wanted to lie on the bed and give him a hug. It seemed impossible without accidentally pulling out some vital tube or wire, but the nurse read my mind, reassured me it was okay, rearranged some tubes and, with great sensitivity, said she had to leave for a few moments to get some supplies from the storeroom. We were on our own at last. Johnnie edged himself to the side of the bed and I carefully climbed up next to him. We lay there and, despite all his attachments, managed to hold on to each other.

'I love you,' he whispered and tears flowed.

If ever there was a moment to truly understand what love is, this was it.

In ICU, Johnnie had one gorgeous blonde nurse after another. He couldn't believe his luck. He was still able to flirt, so I knew his spirit was strong. (He invited one nurse to a desert island with him while I was sat beside him!)

Day by day he got stronger; he started to breathe unaided, began taking food normally and had one tube after another removed. Because he was neutropenic – his immune system was completely inactive and he had no resistance at all – he was filled to the gills with antibiotics. It was after about five days that he asked me if there was a strange sound in the room.

The antibiotic he was put on was Gentamicin. He was on incredibly large doses and it was only weeks later that he realized he had tinnitus and his hearing had become impaired, which in turn affected his balance. These are known side effects of Gentamicin. Sadly these effects have been permanent and have truly reduced the quality of his subsequent life. He will never hear music again in quite the same way; he has to wear hearing aids; at night he cannot sleep properly because of dreadful tinnitus; and, because of the balance problems it causes, he can't ride his bike with the same confidence or skill he used to have.

The other traumatic side effect of the operation was that Johnnie was left with a colostomy bag. It was the one thing he had always prayed would not happen. He lay in his intensive care room with tears pouring down his face as he told me. I already knew he would have one – Nick Carty had told me before the operation. To him, his whole body had been mutilated and ruined. He felt it was so cruel.

As his wife, all I could think and express was: 'But, darling, you're alive!'

He was in denial for many days. When Sandra, the stoma care nurse, came to visit him for the first time, I was there. We learnt how it worked, what the side effects would be, what foods he had to avoid. We discussed the effects on our sex life. He managed one joke – what if it should fart when he was doing a sensitive interview on air? But his distress could not be joked away.

One day I saw the anaesthetist who had done Johnnie's operation, and I thanked him for getting Johnnie through. I felt quite sick when he told me that it was down to Johnnie's strength, not his skill.

'Three times I thought I'd lost him, but he just fought back,' he said.

I hadn't realized Johnnie had taken it quite so close to the edge.

When Johnnie was well enough, he was moved from ICU to the cancer ward. He was given his own little room, which became decorated with autumn leaves. This period was so happy compared with the chemo days. He was recovering from an operation, he had great medical care, and I could almost feel him getting stronger.

Now he had more visitors. Close friends like Snapper, Gordon Haskell and Adrian Williams came by, bringing gifts of magic wands, musical interludes and Jack Daniels respectively. Even Sally Boazman drove down for an afternoon. She was very supportive and understanding, but I know she was shocked. When she spoke on air the next day about seeing him, her voice cracked and I thought she was going to lose it. Let's face it – he looked like a man who would never walk again, let alone work. He was eight and a half stone, bald, sickeningly white and quite unrecognizable as the colleague she was used to sparring with.

Most days saw a little improvement. After a couple of weeks Johnnie took his first few faltering steps. He had to learn to walk all over again, and knew he wouldn't be allowed home until he was more mobile. Every day the walking improved – he would shuffle up and down the ward, and exchange smiles and little quips with the other patients. To our great joy, Johnnie's cancer seemed to be cured and he was just getting back up to strength, waiting for the huge open wound in his gut to heal. By 4th November, when he had passed the final test of negotiating the stairs, and the wound was sufficiently closed up to be safe, he was told he could go home the following day. What a day that was. Getting into the car was a huge effort and extremely painful, but the bigger surprise was to come.

While he was in hospital, I had moved house. We had decided months ago that we should get a new cottage as a fresh start for our married life, the old one having been mine before we married. Timing is a strange thing, and everything to do with the move had happened as he lay in the ward. I had busted my arse at nights to get the new cottage into a fit state for a patient. I had a wood-burning stove installed, chimneys swept, curtains and pictures hung, and had turned it into as cosy a love nest as I could.

When Johnnie walked in, he burst into tears. He could not believe how beautiful it was. He sat by the stove, and hardly moved for several months. We bought a working cocker spaniel, Fergus, who sat with him, giving him doggy healing and love. As exercise, each lunchtime we would walk very gingerly across the road to the Museum Inn for his prescribed half of Guinness and a bit of lunch. The new village welcomed him with open arms and kindness. Nurses popped in daily, doctors occasionally. We had a wonderfully simple existence. We had never been so happy.

The healing process was greatly aided by a holiday in Jamaica at a fantastic place called Tensing Pen in Negril. Johnnie swam, socialized and laughed more than he had in months. The great people we met, the sun, the sea, the delicious local food and the warmth of the Jamaicans made this holiday a turning point. Johnnie's health, hair and happiness grew. It was magical.

Returning on a high in February, Johnnie decided he was ready to go back to his show. But as the day drew nearer, the nerves increased. By the weekend before, he had broken out in shingles and could only open one eye. I couldn't bear it. I knew he was going back too early. Johnnie had more hair by now, and had put some weight back on, but he was still far from his former self. But the 'show must go on' attitude prevailed in him and, on 1st March 2004, in he went. Fergus and I joined Johnnie for the show. It was such a nervous moment.

His first words were, 'I'm not sure I can remember how to do this.' He was a bit shaky, but he survived. At the end he fell into my arms and Fergus's paws and we had a huge, relieved, family hug. He'd done it. Despite this huge, life-challenging ordeal, Johnnie was still the great radio man. The public response was, once again, overwhelming. I felt as if I had handed the most incredibly valuable package back to Radio Two.

In retrospect, Johnnie went back too soon. It took every ounce of his energy to do the show each day, and it wiped him out. And he will never have the same energy again. The worst culprit is his constant tinnitus, which will always affect him. The most galling thing is that it was caused by an antibiotic known to have this side effect. Other antibiotics can be used but, apparently, Gentamicin is cheap. If only the doctor who had decided to use it had thought about Johnnie's ears being his most precious tools.

But, as I used to say when he complained, 'Darling, at least you are alive.'

Sometimes, though, it got so bad, he wished he wasn't – but that was only on really bad days.

Chapter Forty-Seven

'There is someone very special who will come into your life. This woman is quite unlike those you've been close to in the past. She's brunette, quite small but with great energy. She has so many qualities: intelligence, wisdom, great sense of humour. She is like a ray of sunshine and she will help you a great deal in your life and your work. But you are not ready to meet her yet. She is a gift that will come to you at the right time.'

My friend, clairvoyant Angela Donovan, had spoken those words way back in 1998. In the months and years that followed, I decided she'd been wrong and I was never going to meet this person. How wrong *I* was – and how incredibly accurate Angela had been.

Tiggy never ceases to amaze me. She had the most extraordinary introduction to married life with me but never wavered in the face of everything we had to endure. I am ashamed of the way I sometimes behaved towards her during the cancer treatment. I think I tried hard to be a good patient in hospital, but I must have saved up my fears and frustrations to take them out on her. I'm truly sorry for giving her such a hard time, for she certainly saved my life. I don't think I could have made it through without her, and I often wonder quite what I have done to deserve her. I know I need to do my best to make it up to her in the years ahead.

Now the worst part of my journey was over: I had survived. I was so very lucky to have had so much love and support from so many quarters. Friends and family, of course, but in particular I will never forget the doctors, nurses and hospital volunteers for all they did. It was a huge lesson in humility to be on the receiving end of such dedication, skill and help from those who are rarely in our thoughts when our health is good, but who are there for us when we need them. And then there are the listeners, people who, even though we haven't met, I regard as friends, some of whom have known me via the radio for over forty years. Their emails, cards and letters and, in many cases, their prayers, were a huge source of comfort and strength to me. I am so very grateful to them and wish that all people facing life-threatening illness could have such support.

If I could go back in time with the knowledge I have now and be given the choice of going through cancer or not, I truly believe I would choose the same path. I learnt so much about myself and now have an empathy and understanding that I couldn't have gained any other way. It was a very big life lesson but one I am convinced I elected to learn.

I went back to *Drivetime* on Monday, 1st March 2004. I was scared. Would I still be able to do it? Would I have enough energy? It was going to be such a big day that I was quivering with nerves when I arrived, but all my friends at Radio Two gave me an incredibly warm welcome back. Phil Hughes, Moneypenny, Helen Thomas, Sally Boazman, Bob Ballard, Martin Shankleman and others had all helped so much getting listeners' messages and emails to me while I'd been away, and it was lovely to see them all again. I really wanted Tiggy to be with me, and together we also managed to smuggle in our dog, Fergus. He had been such a loyal and happy friend to have around in Dorset and it was great to have him in the studio for that first show.

It's always hard to choose the first record at a time like that. If I remember rightly, it was Eric Clapton's 'Hello Old Friend (It's Really Good To See You Again)'. It was a very emotional moment. There had been many times when I thought I would never be back in this studio again, but here I was, joking with Sally, chatting with Bob and with Martin on the business news, doing the mystery voice competition – and it all felt so natural. I am sure there was an extra bit of love in the airwaves that day and it was going both ways.

A special thank you goes to Stuart Maconie, who sat in for me during my illness. He did a wonderful job. It's not easy when you're covering to find the right balance of doing things your way while staying true to the style of the show. Stuart had it just right and managed to be himself but keep the spirit of the Johnnie Walker *Drivetime* alive and well. I am very grateful for all he did.

In May came the annual Sony Radio Awards. They are a good opportunity for people's skill and hard work to be recognized but I have never been a huge fan of award evenings. They seem to go on and on and I wasn't keen to go. Lesley kept on at me to agree to attend.

'Come on, Johnnie, you haven't been nominated for anything. So why not just come along, get pissed and have a laugh?'

Eventually I agreed, if only to shut her up. I went along and, with no worries or nerves at having to make a public appearance, I relaxed and had a good time. I had started drinking red wine again a few months after meeting Tiggy – after two and a half years of being completely clean and sober. I love a good red wine and felt sure I could be a moderate drinker, and the last few years have proved that to be the case.

I was drinking in moderation at the awards evening, when Lesley said, 'Johnnie, I don't think you should have any more wine.'

I began to wonder if something might be up.

Host Paul Gambacinni was announcing the final award of the evening, the Gold Award. He gave a glowing introduction to the person who was to present the award, ending with the words, 'Ladies and gentlemen, please welcome Elton John!' The place erupted. Everyone stood and all eyes swung to the grand staircase as Elton descended from the balcony into the main hall, looking every inch the superstar that he is. He joined Paul onstage to view a video montage of the award winner's career.

Oh my God! They were going to give the Gold Award to me!

As the realization dawned, the video came to an end and Paul called me up on to the stage. It was a great honour to receive such an award, but especially to receive it from Elton John. He had been so kind and generous to me over the years and had arranged for a beautiful orchid to be delivered when he heard I was ill. He made a very nice speech, thanking me for the help and support I'd given him in the early years when he was just getting started. Then it was my turn to say a few words.

'Lesley Douglas conned me into coming here tonight. Said how I wasn't nominated, so I should just come along, have a good time and get pissed. So I did, and I am.

'You know how people tend to knock the NHS, but the NHS has been very good to me. You wouldn't believe the amount of drugs I took last year – and they were all free.'

I got a good laugh for that one, then thanked all those who'd helped me over the years. Holding my award and aware of the generous applause all around me, I returned to my table. I hugged and kissed Tiggy, Lesley was in tears, and all the team from the show came up and gave me a hug. It was just the most fantastic night. I'm incredibly proud to have a Sony Gold. I'm so thankful I was still around to receive it.

Another wonderful life-enhancing event happened in May the following year, 2005. I became a grandfather when Sam's wife, Jules, gave birth to James – 'Sweet Baby James', as he became known. He is a gorgeous little chap. Tiggy and I were delighted and I loved becoming a granddad; holding a grandchild in one's arms gives such a good feeling of the cycle of life continuing on.

As the year progressed, I was finding it quite a strain doing five shows a week. A two-hour show may seem a complete doddle but when you factor in hours spent researching, reading up on guests, listening to and sorting out all the music, it does become a full-time job. The whole day's focus was on the performance at five o'clock and I would get home exhausted, go to bed early and lie in a bit in the morning. My whole life seemed to be built around the show and I only just had enough energy each day to pull it off. I talked with Lesley about a possible job share with Stuart – he could do two days and I'd do the other three. Or perhaps a move from *Drivetime* to a weekend show might be an idea.

In November, Lesley invited me out for dinner to discuss the following year. She told me she really didn't want me to come off *Drivetime* in April and urged me to agree to do another year. I was feeling stronger now and was really enjoying doing the show and didn't want to give it up. I told her that I would love to do another year and Lesley was delighted.

My eventful year continued apace when I received a double whammy in the post. The first was a letter from the Radio Academy, who invited me to their annual lunch on 1st December where, if I accepted, I was to be inducted into the Radio Academy Hall of Fame. Another great honour. The other letter was marked '10 Downing Street' on the front of the envelope. I didn't want to open it.

'I don't like the look of it, Tigs. It must be bad news. And if it's some kind of invite to a reception to meet Tony Blair, I'm definitely not going.'

'There's only one way to find out,' said Tiggy. 'Go on, open it.'

It was quite a bulky envelope with forms inside and a letter from the prime minister's office. I couldn't believe what I read. My name had been put forward to receive an MBE in the New Year's honours list. Enclosed was a form on which I could ask not to be considered or to accept the award.

I was delighted – it was wonderful to have my work recognized in this way, and it also rather amused me. After all, I'd started my career on an illegal radio station and gone on to defy the government and the establishment and here they were, all these years later, asking me to accept an honour. From pirate DJ to MBE – who would have thought it? It didn't take long to decide. For one, my mother and father would have been so proud. I remembered reading John Peel's book, in which he wrote of his children's advice to accept his honour, otherwise he'd spend the rest of his life explaining how he was offered one but turned it down.

I filled in the form, ticking the 'delighted to accept' box and signed an acceptance of complete confidentiality until the public announcement in the New Year. Tiggy's parents, Peter and Diana, joined us for Christmas lunch and it was very hard keeping a lid on our news. It was a lovely Christmas with Tiggy's birthday on

Boxing Day and then came the public announcement of the New Year's honours.

I rang Sam and Beth to tell them the news. Sam was very nonchalant about the whole thing, and Beth said, 'An MBE, what's that?' I think Diana was the most excited and, in the absence of my parents, it was nice to share it with her and Peter, who have both made me feel such a welcome part of their extended family. I also got a lot of calls from friends, whose reaction was mostly one of astonishment: 'Walker, you old bugger, you've been a rebel all these years, and now it would seem you're part of the establishment.'

With all this going on, and with my sitting in for Terry Wogan for two weeks, it was a wonderful and auspicious start to a new year. On a real high, Tiggy and I flew off to Australia for a three-week holiday, where we spent time in Byron Bay with her brother and his family, then went on to Sydney and Melbourne. My phone was off most of the time but one morning I got a call from my agent, Alex Armitage, who had just received a letter from Radio Two with a formal contract offer for another year on *Drivetime*.

Now we could really relax, safe in the knowledge that I had work and security for another year.

Chapter Forty-Eight

2006

I came back to *Drivetime* on the last Monday in January, and towards the end of the first week I got a call to meet up with Lesley after the show on Friday. Strange time for a meeting, I thought, seven o'clock on a Friday evening. Lesley seemed very nervous. There were just the two of us in her office in a deserted building; it all felt a bit odd. Lesley started talking and referred back to the conversation we'd had at the end of the previous summer when I'd suggested coming off the high-pressure weekday schedule and opting for a gentler workload at weekends. She said she'd come up with a plan whereby I could carry on sitting in for Terry Wogan on the breakfast show, present some high-profile interviews with the big names in music, and also take over Ed Stewart's show on Sundays at five o'clock. She suggested I go off for the weekend and talk it over with Tiggy. I was stunned, to put it mildly.

I asked, 'And if I come back on Monday and turn down this offer? What would happen then with *Drivetime*?'

The answer was that *Drivetime* was not an option.

I left the building in a complete state of shock. I just couldn't figure it out. What had changed during the couple of weeks since my agent received a *Drivetime* offer in writing? Yes, I had planted the seed by mentioning coming off the show for an easier workload, but I had been begged to stay on for another year and so I had geared myself up for it. So why the sudden about-turn? That was the strange part. I could only think that the chance to sign a major name to do the show had come along. It's always very suspicious when you receive ringing endorsements and congratulations. When the plaudits come, that's the time to watch your back.

Tiggy was as shocked as I had been when I told her the news. We talked in the car on the way down to Dorset, and about little else over the weekend. We tried to figure out the reason. Was there a big name waiting in the wings or had my show been getting tired and stale? If it had, then why the formal offer on 6th January? I remembered a song I'd heard with the words 'it's the not knowing what's going on that I can't stand'. I think I had done a few below-par shows in December. I was having more problems with my hearing and one ear was worse than usual. I really couldn't hear properly, which made me feel very disconnected. There were also times when I wondered whether my joshing with Sally Boazman had run its course and if we were now repeating ourselves.

As the shock began to subside, I started to look on the other side of the situation. Maybe it was time for a change. I had been on the show for seven years, minus the rehab gardening leave and nine-month cancer journey. I'd wanted a change – this one was just coming a year earlier than I thought. And on the plus side, my new life would give me more free time and be less demanding on my energy, which would be a good thing healthwise.

After some time and thought, I wondered if it was best to accept the situation and look forward to a quieter life, enjoy my time with Tiggy and realize some of my other dreams. I'd seen other broadcasters leave the BBC angry and bitter, unable to accept the reality of their situation. BBC executives don't have a good track record in imparting bad news; usually the victim is the last to know. In my case, Lesley Douglas did have the guts to tell me to my face and I admire her for that.

As the days passed, Tiggy and I tried our best to get used to the idea of our lives without my being on *Drivetime* every night. The hardest thing for me was the idea of not being connected to all those listeners every day: they had been so good to me through two traumatic episodes in my life, and I felt such a strong bond with my listeners. Terry Wogan's role was to get people up ready for a new day and off to work in the best possible frame of mind, and I felt mine was to help them forget the workday stresses and strains and arrive home smiling and hopeful. I knew I would miss my audience and that connection very much. But I was determined to leave with as much style as I could muster.

I went in to tell Lesley that I accepted the new situation, and, given the option, I decided to say that the departure from *Drivetime* was my decision. We agreed that I would do my last show at the end of March. That day was a few weeks away yet. Before that, I had an appointment at Buckingham Palace.

We set off on the morning of 24th February. I'd hired a morning suit and top hat, and Tiggy, Sam and Beth were all dressed for the occasion. We had a car pass and felt very grand as we were checked at the gate and waved through into the inner courtyard of the palace. We were welcomed by the palace staff, then I was directed towards the waiting area, while the others were shown to their seats in the Throne Room.

There were about fifty of us in the waiting room, admiring the great works of art on the walls and sipping orange juice and mineral water while doing our best to control our nerves. They were a complete cross-section of people from all walks of life, many of whom did very much more valuable work than I did, and many as surprised as I was to be there and honoured in this way. I met and briefly got to know some really lovely people and my faith in the honours system was very much strengthened. We were coached in what we had to do by an equerry before filing into another holding area, just off the Throne Room where the cere-mony was to take place. We watched on monitors as Prince Charles and his party made their entrance exactly at the appointed time, and it all began. It was a long ceremony and I hoped that Tigs and Sam and Beth were doing okay.

When my turn came, I walked in and paused to await the announcement: 'Mr Johnnie Walker, for services to broadcasting.'

I walked forwards, turned, bowed to HRH and stepped up to receive my medal. As he had with all the others, Prince Charles made me feel as if I was the only person in the room for the few minutes we chatted. When he asked me what my plans for the rest of the day were, I'm sure he expected to hear about a grand lunch. But I seem to remember offering him my congratulations for his excellent work as a political subversive, which had been very much in the news that day. He attached the medal to my lapel, congratulated me and warmly shook my hand. Then, as I'd been instructed, I walked backwards, bowed, turned and went through to the anteroom, where my medal was put into a velvet-lined box and presented to me with some documentation.

Phew! It was all over. I was now Johnnie Walker, MBE. My nerves calmed down and I could enjoy the rest of the day. I met up with Tiggy, Sam and Beth outside where we posed for photographs. It had been a memorable and very enjoyable experience. Every member of the palace staff went out of their way to make all of us feel so very welcome. In great spirits, we all set off to enjoy an excellent lunch at Elena's L'Etoile in Charlotte Street.

At the beginning of February, I announced on the show that I'd be leaving *Drivetime* at the end of March. Almost at once, there was a huge response from the listeners, asking why I was leaving and telling me how much they would miss me. I was heartened by the enormous number of cards, letters, emails and texts I received. Between now and the end of March, I was determined to make every show the very best I could, and I think that I possibly did the best shows of my career in those last few weeks on *Drivetime*. It was a point of pride: I wanted to show them what they'd be missing.

A few weeks before I was due to leave, I heard the news that Chris Evans would be taking over from me, and everything became a lot clearer. His style is completely different from mine; it was obvious that a new approach was wanted, and this was the way the BBC had decided to go.

The final *Drivetime* was on 31st March 2006, the day after my sixty-first birthday. My guest for that last show was Neil Diamond and his appearance would end a week of surprise phone calls from people like Nancy Griffith, Todd Snider, Jackson Browne and

Bonnie Raitt. Unknown to me, Tiggy had got in touch with Paul Rodgers,the show's producer, to suggest he arrange for Sir Alan Sugar to phone in at the very end of the show and utter the immortal words: 'Walker, you're past it. You're fired!' She thought that would be funny, as we were both big fans of *The Apprentice*. What a shame it didn't happen.

Going in for the last show provoked an extraordinary mixture of emotions in me: it was one thing knowing I was going to leave and another actually going in for the last time. I was, on the one hand, desperately sad and still finding it hard to grasp that, after this, there would be no more *Drivetime*. But there was also a sense of celebration in the air as we looked back at the good times, and I was very touched by all the affectionate and supportive messages from friends and listeners alike.

The hour with Neil Diamond was great fun. He was there to talk about his new album, *Twelve Songs*, but instead talked mostly about his horses, one of whom he had named 'Shag' as it got very excited whenever Neil's girlfriend was nearby. Neil has a wonderful dry sense of humour and much of the hour was spent falling about with laughter, especially when he danced with Sally Boazman. So many of the listeners had requested Sally and I have one final dance together but with Neil as our very special guest, it seemed fitting that he should have the honour. Rather than stay seated and pretend, as Sally and I used to, Neil took her hand and waltzed her round the studio. Sally was both surprised and, I suspect, delighted when his hand playfully slipped down on to her bum.

The last two hours of *Drivetime* simply flew by. The studio was full of almost all of those who had worked on the show in the past. It was one big happy party. I'd wanted to go out with style and I think together we managed that. As the studio emptied and Tiggy and I gathered up the huge pile of farewell emails, texts, cards and flowers, the reality hit me that this was the end of a show that had been such a huge part of my life for the past seven years. It was a very strange feeling leaving the studio, knowing I wouldn't be there the following Monday; someone else would be sitting in that seat. It's an odd coincidence that, for the second time in my BBC career, I was making way for the arrival of Chris Evans.

Drivetime might be over, and a chapter of my life closed, but there were new challenges to face: now I had to plan the new show on Sundays at five p.m. I felt great sympathy for Ed Stewart and for his listeners who, like mine, were very loyal, and really didn't like change. I wanted to take the programme in a spiritual direction, both in terms of guests and the music I played, but perhaps there was too much about dealing with death and life-threatening illnesses. The idea was to give hope, but many found it depressing and, for the millions who were driving home, it was the wrong sort of radio at the wrong time. I gradually steered the show back to a more mainstream style to give it broader appeal. My Sunday show has now naturally developed into one more suited to a Sunday-evening audience, many of whom are driving home at that time.

I would still love to do a specialist show that is listed and presented as a spiritual programme, and given a suitable time slot, so that people know what to expect. It seems to me there are a huge number of people in Great Britain who are not at ease with organized religion, but do believe in the existence of a higher power and are interested in matters of a spiritual nature.

The loss of daily contact with listeners following the end of *Drivetime* is, in part, remedied by filling in for Terry Wogan whenever he goes off on holiday – which, luckily for me, is quite often. I really enjoy doing the breakfast show as my energy seems to be much stronger first thing in the morning than at the end of the day. As luck would have it, I was doing the breakfast show on 3rd May 2006, the fortieth anniversary of my first-ever broadcast on Radio England. I wanted to mark it in some way, so asked the listeners to send me their memories of May 1966. The response was incredible: hundreds of people sent in emails and texts that were touching, amusing and a fascinating insight into a moment in history when life was much more carefree and optimistic. The production team pulled out all the stops. Alan Dedicoat had sourced some old embarrassing radio clips, which he delighted in playing at the end of the news; Moneypenny had arranged for a cake; and Fiona Day had put some champagne on ice. From out of nowhere the show spontaneously became one of those special radio programmes that stay in the memory forever.

Tiggy had managed to get a table at The Ivy, and a small group of us including ex-controller Jim Moir, Mark Goodyer, Jeff Griffin and my old mucker Adrian Williams, met for lunch at one o'clock. In true inimitable Jim Moir style, he arrived declaring that this was to be a lunch to remember and there was a good chance we'd all get thrown out. Mark read out a speech from Johnny Beerling, who couldn't make it, and Jim gave me the gift of a small photo of Winston Churchill, saying that of all the portraits he'd seen at the National Portrait Gallery that morning, this was the person he most likened me to.

'Johnnie, far be it from me to compare you to such a great man, but you both had the love of a good woman, had black-dog depressions, and you both had the grit and determination to get through some very difficult times. Johnnie, I tip my hat to you, my son. I think you're a diamond geezer and I salute you on the magnificent achievement of presenting great radio programmes over forty years.'

They were very touching words from a man for whom I have a great deal of love and admiration.

It's unlikely there will be another fortieth anniversary, but I'm not finished yet.

Epilogue

I do believe in seven-year cycles and I had done five days a week on *Drivetime* for seven years. It took a lot of energy and, although I found it hard to make the break with the regular listeners after all we'd been through together, my life has changed a great deal, in many ways for the better.

Tiggy and I sold our cottage in Dorset and our lovely flat in Marylebone and with the proceeds we've bought an old farmhouse on the Dorset-Somerset border. There are beautiful views over the Blackmore Vale, and there's an old barn attached to the house, part of which was used as an artist's studio. My dream is to convert it to a radio studio and broadcast live programmes from there, much as John Peel used to do from his home in Suffolk.

Not doing *Drivetime* has given me the chance to have an operation to reverse the effects of my emergency operation at Salisbury. Two brilliant surgeons, Professor Bill Heald and Mr Brendan Moran, used their great skills to restore me to the way I was before cancer got a hold. They've given me a new lease of life. I can be naked with Tiggy now without feeling shame and can swim and sunbathe with a new freedom.

Sam jokingly refers to me in emails as OM – old man. So he has become YM, young man, and now there is LM, little man, in the form of my grandson, James. Sam, Jules and James recently started a new life in Singapore. Jules's family are in Sydney, so they're now equidistant between grandparents. At the time of writing, LM is soon to be joined by someone presently known as Twinkle.

Beth, who admits she wasted her time at school (much like her dad), has now discovered her great creative gifts and has surprised herself with her achievements on a degree course in advertising and photography.

When I met Tiggy, she was a dynamic and successful freelance producer of commercials, whose job took her all over the world. Just a few short weeks after our wedding, I was diagnosed with cancer and she put her career on hold to support and care for me. Now she can devote her time to realizing her lifelong dream of producing the film *Antonia*, which she told me about on the rocks in that little bay in Cornwall on our weekend together. There are uncanny parallels in that Antonia's husband develops a serious illness early in the marriage. Tiggy has written an amazing screenplay for the film, something she said was only possible because of what we went through together. All being well, the film will be in full production next year and her life and career will really open up again.

I'm crazy enough to believe that not only do we get a review of our lives during the process of passing back into spirit, but that we are also given a preview of the new life we're about to incarnate into. So my soul chose this life, and to experience all that has happened to me.

I feel sure there's so much more to do.

Johnnie Walker
February 2007